D0773273

CRITICAL KEYWORDS IN
LITERARY AND CULTURAL THEORY

CRITICAL KEYWORDS IN LITERARY AND CULTURAL THEORY

Julian Wolfreys

First published 2004 by
PALGRAVE MACMILLAN
Houndmills, Basingstoke, Hampshire RG21 6XS and
175 Fifth Avenue, New York, N.Y. 10010
Companies and representatives throughout the world

PALGRAVE MACMILLAN is the global academic imprint of the Palgrave
Macmillan division of St. Martin's Press, LLC and of Palgrave Macmillan Ltd.
Macmillan® is a registered trademark in the United States, United Kingdom
and other countries. Palgrave is a registered trademark in the European
Union and other countries.

ISBN 0–333–96058–0 hardback
ISBN 0–333–96059–9 paperback

This book is printed on paper suitable for recycling and made from fully
managed and sustained forest sources.

A catalogue record for this book is available from the British Library.

Library of Congress Cataloging-in-Publication Data

Wolfreys, Julian, 1958–
  Critical keywords in literary and cultural theory / Julian Wolfreys.
     p. cm.
  Includes bibliographical references and index.
  ISBN 0–333–96058–0 – ISBN 0–333–96059–9 (pbk.)
  1. Literature—Terminology. 2. Criticism—Terminology. 3. Literature, Modern—History
and criticism. 4. Criticism—History—20th century. I. Title.

PN44.5 W64 2003
803—dc21
                                                              2003053643

10   9   8   7   6   5   4   3   2   1
13 12 11 10 09 08 07 06 05 04

Typeset by Cambrian Typesetters, Frimley, Camberley, Surrey

Printed and bound in China

For Jean-Michel Rabaté

CONTENTS

PREFACE

Critical Keywords in Literary and Cultural Theory offers the reader explorations of more than forty terms, concepts and motifs that are employed to greater or lesser degrees in what is called, generally, literary and cultural theory. More specifically, the keywords explored here acknowledge, whether directly or indirectly, a range of interests and investigations into areas of knowledge that have informed literary and cultural study: psychoanalysis, philosophy, linguistics, feminism, Marxism, postcolonialism, gay studies and queer theory, and what is referred to as 'identity politics'. Admittedly, there are many more such terms and figures, and it is certainly not the purpose of the present volume to be exhaustive. One intention of this book is to introduce the reader to the complexity of particular words through the presentation, under each keyword's heading, of a series of citations from different critics. What the reader will see, it is hoped, is that, far from being simply or easily defined, the various terms in question here share a certain semantic and conceptual slipperiness. Words change their meanings in varying contexts, and contexts themselves are neither finite nor exhaustible.

Another objective of this volume, therefore, is not to resolve instances of paradox, contradiction or ambiguity but rather to emphasise and even affirm such qualities. Indeed, implicit to the organization and purpose of *Critical Keywords* is the understanding that language is never stable; it is not simply that the 'language of theory' – to suppose, naively, that such a thing exists, separate or separable from language in general – is difficult because resistant to semantic determination; rather, one arrives at an understanding that the 'language of theory' merely highlights an aspect of all language. The irony of most, if not all, literary study is that, while one is asked to focus on the operations of language in particular forms, the address is based on a refusal to read the undecidable condition that haunts all production of meaning. The most appropriate response, I would argue, in the face of this comprehension is to be open to, rather than suspicious of, such instability, and to respond in an affirmative manner to the fluxes and intensities at work in what is referred to as 'theoretical' language, inasmuch as such a 'language' (supposing once again that it exists as a separable form or identity) is comprehensible not as jargon but, instead, as *just* the most transparent example of the way words work.

Each keyword is provided with a minimal running commentary, inter-woven with various citations. It will be seen from the commentaries that, far from offering potted definitions, I point frequently to the fact that the terms and concepts in question resist definition, and furthermore, that there is often little real consensus – except through certain vague accommoda-tions – over the meaning of even the most seemingly straightforward words, such as *gender, identity, postmodernism, sexuality*, or *writing*. We all have the habit of treating words as though they were names, as though they created simple, complete identities for us, and as though such names or identities can do the work of thinking. It is very much a point that, with regard to critical thinking – or let's just call it thinking at all – glossaries conventionally understood, with their apparatus of headnotes and neatly packaged semantic determinations, no longer work, precisely because such volumes, conventionally understood, operate through simplification, reduc-tion, and the misplaced notion that ideas can be summed up in a nutshell, as the phrase goes. With regard to certain ideas or constellations of notions, the glossary or dictionary-like definition does not function, it ceases to function and falls into ruins in the face of the ongoing tensions, the contest of flow and intensification, of language itself.

Another point to consider is that, while the significance of a word given in isolation (but this can never really happen; if you see only a single word written on a page or screen, you still attempt to provide context and defi-nition, you still bring to bear on that single word the complex linguistic, semantic and conceptual network you have already learnt) can appear unproblematic, the ideas being expressed around and through such a term are resistant to immediate comprehension, if for no other reason than that, often, they are expecting the reader to examine values and beliefs from radically different perspectives. While this might occasion what could be considered obfuscating or turgid prose – and this is an accusation that has frequently been levelled against so-called literary theory, though often without either justification or any signs of reading attentively – it is more often the case that ideas which reorient the reader's perspective and under-standing are irreducibly complex; a true comprehension could only arrive, if it arrives at all, through a resistance to transparency. Few, if any, writ-ers or critics write so as *not* to be understood. But what is called under-standing often involves patience and attentiveness – rereading as reorientation – on the part of the reader rather than a passive consump-tion. The reader has to be open to textual complications. She or he must be willing to return to a text, bringing with this a recognition that language and the ideas being conveyed, if they are to have any lasting worth, are not necessarily transparent or self-evident. What kind of a text would it be, about which everything could be comprehended at a glance, in the blink of an eye? Could such a text exist even? Nothing can be read instantaneously

– not even advertising posters comprising a single image, the barest minimum of words or a logo – without highly sophisticated processes of deciphering taking place.

What is termed accessibility by some, equally runs the risk of simplification and reductiveness. The writer who aims at such accessibility can do great violence to ideas, while assuming, condescendingly, that he or she can know his or her audience. How can I know who will read this book? Even if I am told by the publisher that the volume is marketed with specific readers in mind, how can I ever begin to have the presumption of believing I can know or assume each and every member of my audience or the knowledge which he or she possesses? (It is impossible even to assume a single entity called an 'audience'.) This is impossible, and the various manufactured crises which have been aired and which still persist around critical language, the 'language of literary theory', have often proliferated around this very issue of accessibility, while pretending to speak for 'the greatest number'. *Critical Keywords in Literary and Cultural Theory* resists appeals to the mystifications of 'plain speaking' and in doing so refuses to believe in the myth of a lowest common denominator. Instead, it trusts to the openness and willingness to engage, in whatever manner, however it may be received, on the part of whatever readers it may come to have. If this book is marketed within a specific context such as higher education, then there has to be a question of trust: a trust which is also a belief that whatever recipient this may reach will work with this text, in the spirit in which this text is constituted. Whatever goes by the name of education, in this name there never can be, nor should there be, the illusion of immediacy, transparency or accessibility in a kind of programmed rush equivalent to journalistic haste, by which or to which thinking comes to be sacrificed. *Critical Keywords* risks everything on a certain belief in thinking and an openness to thinking, which, it is believed, is always the difference of thinking; not only the difference between thinking and not-thinking (habits of assumption or prejudice), but also a different thinking, a thinking of difference.

ABOUT THIS VOLUME

The terms, concepts or motifs discussed in the present volume are used throughout the book, both in my commentaries and in the citations; these references are too numerous, and have too many other tangential associations, to make it practical to highlight their appearances, but the reader is advised to pay close attention to the use of the various keywords and to refer back to the entries on those terms.

In a small number of cases, a quotation will have found its way into other sections, in order to stress that terms cannot be isolated for particular uses or contexts; in a number of places a quotation will be repeated because it employs several of the keywords that are considered here.

After each collection of quotations three questions are provided to direct the reader towards further consideration. The questions do not assume a single addressee; some may be found to be more appropriate for individual research and consideration, while others might function more actively in seminar and other group discussions. It is not necessarily the case, nor is it assumed, that such questions have precise answers; they are merely intended to open other avenues of thought. In some cases, the questions will ask the reader to consider the work of a particular term in relation to another which is also to be found in the volume.

Following each entry, explanatory and bibliographical notes are provided for foreign, archaic, and obscure or rarely used words. In addition, notes are provided which amplify on matters related to theoretical discourse, while also offering sketched definitions of philosophical and other terms. Of course, selection of words for inclusion in notes is a risky business, but I have sought to highlight those which stick in the mind because students have asked for a definition during lectures and discussion. Notes have also been given where a proper name occurs, for the most part. Such notes give biographical dates for critics, philosophers, and other writers, and brief bibliographies are also offered. These are, admittedly, by no means exhaustive and should not be taken as such. Only publications not listed in Works Cited at the end of this book have full bibliographical details in the notes.

Short bibliographies follow each entry, offering the reader possible 'first ports of call' of significance in relation to the keyword under consideration. Bibliographical details are given in full, regardless of whether they have been cited or not.

ACKNOWLEDGEMENTS

To borrow an image from Edmund Spenser, there may be no cantos to be found in the present volume but, in the course of writing and editing, it has shown all the hallmarks of mutability, becoming on occasion the baggiest of monsters. I would therefore like to thank Emily Garcia for her invaluable editorial assistance in the initial stages of this project, which served to keep some of the more Spenserian excesses at bay. Ruth Robbins and Ken Womack inadvertently caused this volume to come about, as have students in various criticism and theory courses in England, Scotland, and the United States. Speaking of students, the following are exemplary in their sense of inquiry, intellectual endeavour and commitment to study and research, and I would like to thank Alissa Fessell, Jonathan Hall, Lessley Kynes and Christina Leon, for reading through various drafts, and commenting on, as well as questioning, obscurity and obfuscation (my own and that in some of what follows).

CRITICAL KEYWORDS

CRITICAL KEYWORDS

ABJECTION

Abjection is employed by Julia Kristeva[1] in an effort to destabilize the binary[2] logic of much psychoanalytic thought, where the notions of (desiring) subject and object (of desire) often represent a co-dependent oppositional pairing. In order to understand Kristeva's point it is necessary that we recognize 'subject' and 'object' not only as opposed locations or two halves of a logical model, but also as supposedly discrete and complete identities in and of themselves. Each figure in the pair is accorded its own self-sufficient meaning with definable boundaries. Such boundaries are the psychic limits by which the self separates itself from its *other* within the psychoanalytic framework of Kristeva's text. Indeed, another way of positing the subject/object dyad would be to comprehend it, as already implied, in terms of 'self/other'. The abject, says Kristeva, is 'neither subject nor object'; instead it opposes the ego by 'draw[ing] me to the place where meaning collapses'. While the subject/object structure makes logical meaning possible, the abject produces, or is otherwise comprehensible as, an uncanny effect of horror, threatening the logical certainty of either the subject/object or self/not-self binarism. Abjection is thus the process or psychic experience of a slippage across the boundaries of the self, and with that a partial erasure of the borders of the psyche which define the ego. The abject is, amongst other things, the fluid locus of forbidden desires and ideas whose radical exclusion is the basis of the subject's cultural determination; in comprehending the process of abjection thus, we come to see, as Kristeva makes apparent, that that which threatens the self is not simply, necessarily locatable outside the self but rather emerges or erupts within subjectivity.

Beginning, then, with abjection, it is clear from this term that there is, in one sense, an intimate relationship between the psychic construction of the human body and that which both revolts and yet in some manner belongs to that body. In literary or filmic forms, such revulsion and rejection need not be figured literally. While it can be the case that the image of a corpse, a character vomiting or the metaphor of vomit may be employed, it is often the case that the abject is symbolized, given a determinate form outside the self and other than the self and yet causing a visceral, often violent response.

Seeing the monstrous and the repulsive in any narrative representation is, in effect, to witness an exteriorized manifestation of that which is already incorporated in my psyche and yet which is irrecuperable as belonging to my 'self'. As the discussion of the break-down of binary oppositions and the concomitant evacuation of stable semantic value makes plain, there is therefore a mobile structural relationship to be understood here, whether that which makes me abject is actually external to me or is incorporated with me, whether within my body or in my psyche. The relationship is structural because I am reacting to something which, though not me, none the less brings about a response, described in the following manner by Julia Kristeva, in her definition of the term *abjection*:

> repelling, rejecting; repelling itself, rejecting itself. Ab-jecting.
> Julia Kristeva (1982: 13)

As Kristeva's brief comment and, in particular, her hyphenated gerund, *ab-jecting*, should make clear, I am speaking here not simply of a subject–object relationship, nor yet a static structural model but, instead, a process or movement that defines the structurality of the structure. This is expressed through both the particular gerund and also the function of the gerund throughout the citation. For abjection to be felt it has to get under-way. It is thus less important, perhaps, that we understand the concept as a moment, than as a motion, if we are to register the fundamentally destabilizing aspect of abjection. This will help to explain how what makes one person feel abject will not do the same for others.

> The abject threatens life ... Although the subject must exclude the abject, the abject must, nevertheless be tolerated for that which threatens to destroy life also helps to define life ... The abject can be experienced in various ways – one which relates to biological bodily functions, the other of which has been inscribed in a symbolic (religious) economy.
> Barbara Creed (1993: 9)

That the abject threatens and creates a violent sensation of disorientation is very clear. Moreover, as Barbara Creed explains, the abject is irreducible to any particular type of experience. Abjection can take place anywhere, in any context, and its nature is such that, while it is so intimately connected to our own sense of identity, whether individual or communal, social or private, personal or national, its unnerving force comes from the fact that, however much a part of us the abject might be, it is radically, irreducibly other than any element of our identities which we take to be normal or healthy. What we therefore reject, or whatever it is we are repulsed by, belongs to being.

There looms, within abjection, one of those violent, dark revolts of being, directed against a threat that seems to emanate from an exorbitant outside or inside, ejected beyond the scope of the possible, the tolerable, the thinkable. It lies there, quite close, but it cannot be assimilated ... Unflaggingly, like an inescapable boomerang, a vortex of summons and repulsion places the one haunted by it literally beside himself.

Julia Kristeva (1982: 1)

The abject is unequivocally excessive; psychic in its condition, it is a response either to something material or to something psychic, and it can produce physical or material effects. Such is its excessiveness, following from previous comments, we might wish to suggest that the abject cannot be defined except through its effects. We see this problem here, when Julia Kristeva describes her response to the skin on milk. You or I may have no such response to this particular phenomenon, and yet, through the physiological and psychic response described by Kristeva, we comprehend the feeling of abjection. What is also significant here is the fact that Kristeva makes explicit the relation between abjection and the self, signalled in her passage through the suspension of the first person pronoun in quotation marks. It is not so much the fact that she is recounting a particular experience, though this is the point from which she begins, but rather that the 'I', the subject, is disturbed in the assumed security of its identity by the involuntary response to the milk.

Loathing an item of food, a piece of filth, waste or dung. The spasms and vomiting that protect me. The repugnance, the retching that thrusts me to the side and turns me away from defilement, sewage, and muck ... Food loathing is perhaps the most elementary and most archaic form of abjection. When the eyes see or the lips touch that skin on the surface of milk ... I experience a gagging sensation and, still farther down, spasms in the stomach, the belly ... Along with sight-clouding dizziness, *nausea* makes me balk at that milk cream ... 'I' want none of that element ... 'I' do not assimilate it, 'I' expel it. But since food is not an 'other' for 'me' ... I expel *myself*, I spit *myself* out, I abject *myself* within the same motion through which 'I' claim to establish myself.

Julia Kristeva (1982: 2–3)

However, what has to be acknowledged and repeatedly stressed, between Kristeva's and McAfee's comments, is that the object is neither the milk, nor indeed any particular object as such. The subject rids itself of something that is other than itself and yet part of itself, thereby seeking in the process of 'ab-jecting' to re-establish the boundaries of the self.

Abjection is the state in which one's foothold in the world of self and other disintegrates. The abject is the symptom of being on the border, pushing toward psychosis where the I blurs and is *not yet* . . . In anxiety or abjection – through this overwhelming ill-ease – there can be no differentiating between beings.

Noëlle McAfee (1993: 120)

So, to reiterate: abjection or, as Kristeva has it above, *ab-jecting* names the work of a psychic traversal resulting in a corporeal, physiological and psychological response which, due to the extremity and violence of subjective experience, breaks up the subject's sense of identity in the very process by which 'I' strive to maintain myself, my identity, my life. Abjection effects a violent revelation to me about my selfhood: that identity, comprehended as a fixed meaning, is only an illusion promoted by the psyche; rather, the self is nothing but a fiction, a series of narratives precariously assembled and always susceptible to the erasure of its boundaries and the dissolution of its assumed sovereignty or autonomy.

The abject is that which, although intimately a part of early experience, must be rejected so that the self can establish the borders of its unified subjectivity: the familiar foreign(er) who is suddenly recognized as a threat to (national) identity. This rejection (abjection) of certain aspects of physical immediacy, whether of the personal body or the body politic, is the act which establishes subjective identity, but this act also establishes that identity as a prohibition, and as lacking an earlier bodily continuity. The subjective self, therefore, is always haunted by the possible return of the abject that was part of the presubjective experience . . . Abjection contradicts the self's (national or individual) claim to unity and knowledge, but this contradiction is so profound precisely because it emerges from the gestures with which the self attempts to assert such a claim . . . Abjection blurs the usually clearly marked space between the self and the other . . . the abject is that which seems to confound the possibility of meaning . . . The self abjects that which is most necessarily inescapable and rejected: the bodily reminders of physical dependence and necessity.

Norma Claire Moruzzi (1993: 144–5)

Questions for further consideration

1. In what ways might the abject be thought of in relation to the uncanny?
2. Is the abject purely a negative determination or negation of self, or can it be read as a configuration, a provisional difference or non-identity within identity, of otherness or alterity?

3. In light of the emphasis on corporeality in discussions of the abject, is there discernible an articulation of abjection in relation to the carnivalesque body?

Explanatory and bibliographical notes

1. Julia Kristeva (*b*.1941): *Desire in Language: A Semiotic Approach to Literature and Art* (1980); *Powers of Horror: An Essay on Abjection* (1982); *Revolution in Poetic Language* (1984).
2. Throughout, the reader will find the occasional reference to binaries, binarisms, binary oppositions. While binary oppositions operate in the history of Western thought at least since the Aristotelian text, the phrase *binary opposition* is given significant emphasis in the work of a Swiss linguist, Ferdinand de Saussure (*b*.1857–*d*.1913): *Course in General Linguistics*, rev. edn, Introduction by Jonathan Culler, ed. Charles Bally and Albert Sechehaye, with Albert Reidlinger, trans. Wade Baskin (London: Fontana/Collins, 1981). Saussure's work in linguistics (which became the principal influence on structuralist critics) stressed the structural nature of signs. The sign consists of two components, the signifier (the word) and the signified (the object, thing or idea represented or signified). Signifiers are not representative of the things they indicate; language is arbitrary, and we arrive at meaning through common agreement rather than by creating words which in some manner resemble that which we wish to signify. Therefore, no word bears meaning intrinsically: we know 'cat', not because the word has any similarity to the creature it names, but rather, because it is neither a 'bat' nor a 'hat', much less a 'cut'. Moreover, signifiers only have a particular meaning or range of meanings relationally; that is to say, we only know the meaning of a word by the structural–semantic context in which we find it. Significantly, then, many meanings are comprehended through comparison with what they are not: we know what day means because it is not night, absence and presence are not absolute values or concepts but are only determined and determinable by being comprehended in relation to one another; we know what good is, because it is not bad, and so on. Such pairs are referred to as binary oppositions, which structural pairing not simply operates at a semantic level but also governs much human conceptualization (see, for example, entries under *alterity*, *culture*, *deconstruction*, *difference/différance*, *gender*, *materialism/materiality*, *other*, *race*, *sexuality*, *subjectivity*, *uncanny*).

Further reading

Creed, Barbara (1993), *The Monstrous-Feminine: Film, Feminism, Psychoanalysis* (London: Routledge).

Geyer-Ryan, Helga (1994), *Fables of Desire: Studies in the Ethics of Art and Gender* (Cambridge: Polity Press).

Kristeva, Julia (1982), *Powers of Horror: An Essay in Abjection*, trans. Margaret Waller, Introduction by Leon S. Roudiez (New York: Columbia Press).

AESTHETICS

Aesthetics is derived from the Greek *aistetikos*, meaning perceptible to the senses; aesthetic approaches to literature are ones which concern themselves primarily with the work's beauty and form, rather than with extra-textual issues such as politics or context. Aesthetics, which involves the exploration of beauty and nature in literature and the fine arts, involves two theoretical approaches: (a) the philosophical study of the nature and definition of beauty; and (b) the psychological examination of the perceptions, origins, and subjective effects of beauty. In the wake of much politically oriented criticism, the critical interest in identity politics, and the assumption that aesthetic discourse is necessarily formalist or hermeneutic[1] and therefore depoliticized, the very notion of the aesthetic has, in some areas, acquired a somewhat pejorative value, while in others, the aesthetic has assumed a much more contested value.

However, one should not assume that the question of aesthetics is free from a history, that its theoretical interests are unchanging, or that the development of aesthetics is separate from other forms of thought, even though in numerous instances art is treated as though it were autonomous. On the historical transformation and the contexts of aesthetic discourse, Helga Geyer-Ryan remarks:

> it is no accident that the emergence of a discourse about art takes place during the Enlightenment,[2] the era of rationality and science. The aesthetic attitude and the discourse associated with it are consequences of the rational–scientific emancipation of man from nature and thus of the emergence of the capacity for distancing ourselves from given particular contexts . . . The transition from poetics to aesthetics . . . testifies to the historical break with the immediate relationship to the world accomplished through art . . . By virtue of this abstraction from the immediate, subjective and idiosyncratic relationship to the world . . . the subject is able to experience the dimension of universality which belongs . . . to the field of sense perception.
>
> Helga Geyer-Ryan (1994: 186–7)

So, we might say, the historical and cultural context of the emergence of aesthetics as a determinable discourse arises as a result of an epistemological[3] rupturing of context. Or, to put this another way, the context of aesthetic discourse's arrival and that which marks it as modern is registered in and as its sundering from, and occlusion of, the forms of thought that have made it possible. The other aspect of aesthetics to be taken account of here is its being rooted in 'sense perception' or, as Michèle Barrett has it, a 'mode of perception' from which pleasure arises.

The questions raised by the term 'aesthetic' may be summarized as follows: (1) Can we say that there is a distinctive faculty or mode of perception called 'aesthetic' and what would be the nature of the pleasure afforded? (2) Can we identify objects or works to which universal aesthetic value adheres? These questions are difficult to formulate in a non-circular way and the history of attempts to get to grips with them is, perhaps surprisingly, very sparse. Aesthetics constitutes a minor subfield of philosophy in which the questions are considered in the abstract (what is beauty? and so on) rather than in respect to the claims of particular instances.

Michèle Barrett (1992: 34)

The problematic of the aesthetic and of inquiry into aesthetics to which Barrett alerts us is evaded by a circularity of argument, a certain self-closing of the language concerning the subject, which tends towards the autonomy premised in the rupture already spoken of, above. The following remark acknowledges the autonomous condition of the discourse:

aesthetics, the category of the aesthetic, is a rigorous philosophical discourse's way of attempting to ground its own discourse on principles internal to its system and thereby to close it off *as* a system: that is, as a logic.

Andrzej Warminski (1996: 21)

So, aesthetics determines its own logic. This has two implications at least. On the one hand, aesthetic discourse, in situating its own parameters, appears to police what is appropriate to its range of interests, modes of inquiry, methods of proceeding. On the other hand, it appears to attempt to make itself impervious to any mode of questioning which does not conform to the rules, the rhetoric or grammar, by which aesthetics addresses its subjects and mediates its conclusions. It is perhaps for these, as well as other reasons, that aesthetics is available as an assumed universal language. Such is the power of aesthetic categorization that its uses and foci have historically encroached on other philosophical areas of inquiry:

traditionally the aesthetic mode of being had been conceived of as a particular and secondary one, which was firstly relevant only for objects of human origin and secondly to be subordinated to the foundational mode of being of the real. In modern conditions, however, a principalization and universalization of the aesthetic occurs. The notion that aesthetic categories could be suited to the understanding of even the elementary and general constitution of reality is suggesting itself more and more forcefully. The place of the classical ontological[4] categories of being, reality, constancy, actuality, and so on, is now being taken by aesthetic categories of state such as appearance, mobility, baselessness and suspension. In previous centuries a second set of categories had been developed in the shadow, so to speak, of the primary categories of reality (and only with regard to the secondary realities of human fabrication) which then suddenly, once reality itself had idealistically, romantically, historically, and so on, revealed itself to be a fabrication generally proved itself to be suitable for the understanding of the primary and universal reality too.

Wolfgang Welsch (1997: 37)

Such pervasive interrogation and the expansion of analytical inquiry suggested by Welsch is allied closely to the understanding of the role of subjective reflection and interpretation.

Initially, as regards the question of the conditions of knowledge in general, 'aesthetic' means to grasp the givens of sensible intuition in the *a priori*[5] forms of space and time. In the third *Critique*,[6] the term designates reflective judgment, only insofar as it excites the interest of the 'faculty of the soul' that is the feeling of pleasure and of displeasure.

Jean-François Lyotard (1994: 9)

As Lyotard has us understand, human analytical ability, where intellectual perception considers the values of objects in the real world in relation to matters of emotional response, is closely tied to the determination of aesthetic qualities. However, this is at odds with the notion of universal aesthetic values, precisely because the processes of judgement and reflection are always subjective. This returns us to the problematic of aesthetics once again, a problematic which might be read as historically governed, as Terry Eagleton argues.

The aesthetic is at once . . . the very secret prototype of human subjectivity in early capitalist society, and a vision of human energies as radical ends in themselves which is the implacable enemy of all dominative or instrumentalist thought. It signifies a creative turn to the sensuous body, as well as an inscribing of that body with a subtly oppressive law; it represents on the one hand a liberatory concern with concrete particularity, and on the other hand a specious form of universalism.

Terry Eagleton (1990: 9)

Eagleton's commentary ties the subjective analytic to broader historical transformations. In grounding the development of aesthetic discourse in this way, he makes it possible for us to begin to comprehend the ways in which the paradoxes of aesthetics and its autonomous severing from other forms of inquiry can serve particular interests in society. If the aesthetic is an autonomous discourse, it need not have to consider, according to its own rules, the economic contexts or material bases from which the objects of its inquiry are produced. Furthermore, if aesthetic discourse aspires to a universalism, it can automatically rule out any social or historical inquiry as irrelevant to its interests. In addition to this, in granting primacy to subjective perception, it can also make implicit claims about humanity and about matters of taste and pleasure as though these also are universal or intrinsic and not matters of education, privilege, leisure, and so on. Karol Berger argues the principal aspects of such assumptions.

> We may take the aesthetic pleasure in a real object or an imaginary representation. What demarcates this sort of pleasure from other kinds of delight is that it is independent of the dictates of our appetites or reasons and thus remains unconnected with our desires ('disinterested' and 'free'). The delight in the agreeable or good necessarily generates a desire that the object of our delight be real and be ours, and it, potentially at least, also generates an action designed to satisfy desire. The aesthetic pleasure ends in itself, not in a desire or an action.
>
> Karol Berger (2000: 100–1)

Yet, such aesthetic pleasure is not innate. It is learnt, it does change, and it does have a history, a history tied closely to the advent of modernity:

> The aesthetic, then, does not cover the whole scope of truth; rationality is also indispensable. But the aesthetic is concerned with the base level, whereas rationality is first concerned with the subsequent structures. It is precisely this primary character of the aesthetic that one traditionally hasn't grasped or wanted to admit to. The modern development, however, has allowed us to recognize it enduringly.
>
> And this was decreed not by some aesthetician or other, but was a recognition forced upon us by science, the guiding authority of modernity. It prescribed an *epistemological aestheticization* – an on-principle aestheticization of knowledge, truth and reality by which no issue remains unaffected. This epistemological aestheticization is the legacy of modernity.
>
> Wolfgang Welsch (1997: 47)

So, far from being neutral, universal, and autonomous, aesthetics is, we might argue, irredeemably political in its functions, if not directly in its modes of interpretation. The work of what is termed literary theory, in numerous guises, has been to unveil the occluded politics of aesthetic discourse, summarized here by Marc Redfield; Redfield's argument explicitly

draws out the location of aesthetic judgement in a materially and linguisti-
cally constituted human subjectivity. In doing so his text enacts an irreversible shift from the supposed autonomy of aesthetics to the always
historical and material conditions of ideology.

> Aesthetics is ... the model of all ideology, since aesthetics builds its
> system out of linguistic functions that it treats as attributes of conscious-
> ness or spirit. In theory's aesthetic allegory, the disruptive free play of
> Kant's *pulchritude vaga*[7] becomes the figure for a potential randomness
> of the signifier, a randomness which can never appear without undergo-
> ing a 'subreptive'[8] ascription of meaning but which remains incoherently
> necessary if language is to occur. The subject of language, 'man', becomes
> the subject of judgment and the 'ideal of beauty', thanks to a play of the
> signifier which remains lodged at the heart of 'man's' possibility – the
> kernel of trauma, rendered in Kant as the threatening, basilisk gaze of a
> pure judgment of taste. And since 'man', in this narrative, reads his possi-
> bility – or has it read for him – in the signifier, the catachresis[9] that estab-
> lishes the signifier's legibility thereby also establishes the subject's
> interpellation by language, and insertion into the symbolic order. The
> catachresis is prosopopoeiea:[10] a 'giving face', as Cynthia Chase says, to
> something that may or may not be a sign, but which is taken as one in
> being *perceived*. This illegible, radically external insistence making up the
> possibility of the sign's production is what theory calls materiality. We
> may recall that the term 'ideology' originally signalled the attempt to
> derive ideas from the senses, and that in the wake of Marx[11] and
> Engels's[12] displacement of Destutt de Tracy's[13] term, the critique of ideol-
> ogy became a troubled inquiry into the materiality of phenomenal form.
> If the notion of 'ideology' preserves in its history an aesthetic ascent from
> the sensuous to the ideal, the critique of ideology becomes a critique of
> aesthetics in seeking to explain the effectivity of fiction, or, conversely, the
> fictionality of the real, since any materiality at the origin of ideology must
> be able to generate ideological illusion. In a rigorous Marxism, material-
> ity resists itself, and thereby generates history. Theory pursues this
> thought to its limit in locating the materiality and interpellative force of
> ideology in language's self-resistance.
>
> Marc Redfield (1996: 33–4)

Questions for further consideration

1. Why should it be the case that the questions asked of aesthetic value are gener-
    ally posed in the abstract, rather than with regard to singular objects, instances
    or works of art?

2. Is the aesthetic a category free of or distinct from ideological considerations?
3. In what ways is aesthetic pleasure distinct from other forms of pleasure? How might such distinctions be articulated?

Explanatory and bibliographical notes

1. *Hermeneutics*: the science of interpretation.
2. *Enlightenment*: commonly understood as an eighteenth-century European intellectual movement, it would be more accurate to define the 'Enlightenment' as particular currents in thought and culture, many of the ideas of which persist today. The Enlightenment did not produce a unified body of thought, but its principal thinkers did seek to call into question the various ideological structures, especially those relating to political absolutism, feudal social organization, and religious dogmatism, thereby articulating more liberal philosophical positions. The ideas of the Enlightenment permeated art, literature, and music as well as philosophy and social theory. Principal figures in the history of Enlightenment thought are Denis Diderot (*b*.1713–*d*.1784): *Rameau's Nephew/D'Alembert's Dream*, ed. and trans. Leonard William Tancock (London: Penguin, 1966); *The Nun*, trans. Leonard William Tancock (London: Penguin, 1974); *Jacques the Fatalist*, trans. and ed. David Coward (Oxford: Oxford University Press, 1999); Jean-Jacques Rousseau (*b*.1712–*d*.1778): *The Confessions*, trans. and Introduction by J. M. Cohen (London: Penguin, 1953); *A Discourse on Inequality*, trans. Maurice Cranston (London: Penguin, 1984); *The Social Contract and Other Late Political Writings*, ed. Victor Gourevitch (Cambridge: Cambridge University Press, 1997); and Voltaire (François-Marie Arouet) (*b*.1694–*d*.1778): *Philosophical Dictionary*, trans. Theodore Besterman (London: Penguin, 1972); *Letters Concerning the English Nation*, ed. and Introduction by Nicholas Cronk (Oxford: Oxford University Press, 1994); *Candide*, trans. Norman Cameron (London: Penguin, 1997).
3. *Epistemology*: branch of philosophy dealing with the grounds of knowledge.
4. *Ontology*: branch of philosophy, especially metaphysics, concerned with the study of being as an abstract concept, or the being or essence of things.
5. *A priori*: deductive logic or reasoning, proceeding from causes to effects.
6. Immanuel Kant (*b*.1724–*d*.1804): *The Critique of Judgement* (1952), p. 45; *Critique of Practical Reason*, trans. and ed. by Mary Gregor, Introduction by Andrew Reath (Cambridge: Cambridge University Press, 1997); *The Critique of Pure Reason*, ed. and trans. by Paul Guyer and Allen W. Wood (Cambridge: Cambridge University Press, 1998).
7. *Pulchritude vaga*: random, shifting or inconsistent beauty.
8. *Subreptive*: obtaining something by misrepresentation or suppression of the truth, or otherwise a deceptive argument or misrepresentation.
9. *Catachresis*: an incorrect use, or misapplication, of words.
10. *Prosopopoeia*: representation in human form; a figure of speech in which either (a) an imaginary or absent person is represented as speaking, or (b) an abstract or inanimate figure is personified or anthropomorphized.

11. Karl Marx (*b*.1818–*d*.1883): *Capital*, trans. S. Moore and E. Aveling (New York: International Publishers, 1967); *The Communist Manifesto*, Introduction by Eric Hobsbawm (London: Verso, 1998); *The German Ideology* (1970).
12. Friedrich Engels (*b*.1820–*d*.1895): *The Origin of the Family, Private Property, and the State*, Introduction by Evelyn Reed (New York: Pathfinder Press, 1972); *The Condition of the Working Class in England*, trans. and ed. W. O. Henderson and W. H. Chaloner (Stanford, CA: Stanford University Press, 1968).
13. Antoine Louis Claude Destutt de Tracy (*b*.1754–*d*.1836): *A Treatise on Political Economy*, trans. Thomas Jefferson, Foreword by John M. Dorsey (Detroit: Center for Health Education, 1973).

Further reading

Barilli, Renato (1993), *A Course in Aesthetics,* trans. Karen E. Pinkus (Minneapolis, MN: University of Minnesota Press).
Bronfen, Elisabeth (1992), *Over Her Dead Body: Death, Femininity, and the Aesthetic* (Manchester: Manchester University Press).
De Man, Paul (1996), *Aesthetic Ideology*, ed. and Introduction by Andrzej Warminski (Minneapolis, MN: University of Minnesota Press).
Eagleton, Terry (1990), *The Ideology of the Aesthetic* (Oxford: Blackwell).
Redfield, Marc (1996), *Phantom Formations: Aesthetic Ideology and the Bildungsroman* (Ithaca, NY: Cornell University Press).
Regan, Stephen (ed.) (1992), *The Politics of Pleasure: Aesthetics and Cultural Theory* (Buckingham: Open University Press).
Welsch, Wolfgang (1997), *Undoing Aesthetics*, trans. Andrew Inkpin (London: Sage).

ALTERITY

Alterity names a condition of absolute, radical otherness in critical and philosophical discourse. While the notions of otherness and alterity are, to some extent, interchangeable in critical discourse, in *Time and the Other*[1] and other texts Emmanuel Levinas addresses the absolute exteriority of alterity, as opposed to the binary, dialectic or reciprocal structure implied in the idea of the other. For Levinas, the face of the other is the concrete figure for alterity. My sense of self is interrupted in my encounter with the face of the other, and thus the self, the I as Levinas puts it, knows itself no longer in its self-sameness but in its own alterity, in coming face to face with the face of the other. It is important to register the fact that the other is not simply a 'location' or 'identity' distinct and separate, outside one's own, but that alterity names the other, the non-same, within any attempt to think the self, or identity. Several of the extracts below will substitute otherness or the other for alterity and vice versa, and, similarly, this will also be seen in the entries under 'Other'.

Beginning with this commentary on Levinas, we encounter the difficulty of thinking the other in any authentic manner.

> According to Lévinas, it is impossible to arrive at an authentic thought of the Other (and thus an ethics of the relation to the Other) from the despotism of the Same, which is incapable of recognizing this Other. The dialectic of the Same and the Other, conceived . . . under the dominance of self-identity . . . ensures the absence of the Other in effective thought, suppresses all genuine experience of the Other, and bars the way to an ethical understanding of alterity.
>
> Alain Badiou (2001: 18–19)

As Badiou avers, one always thinks the Other from the location referred to as the Same, or otherwise, in any given, singular instance, my subjectivity or selfhood. This has the consequence, a consequence always already in place in the very act of thinking, of situating a dialectical and uneven structure.

Radicalizing this notion further, opening the structure beyond any simple binary or dialectic structure, Levinas comments that 'There is an abyss between . . . the ego and the alterity of mystery' (1987: 81). Alterity is so absolutely or wholly other, that structure gives way to an abyssal breach. Any relationship is always nonreciprocal therefore:

> in the very heart of the relationship with the other that characterizes our social life, alterity appears as a nonreciprocal relationship.
>
> Emmanuel Levinas (1987: 83)

As Levinas's language clarifies, the disorganization of the structural relationship is fundamental to its very possibility.

More locally, this disjunction is identified by Simon Critchley as that which makes any deconstructive reading possible:

> what takes place in deconstruction is double reading – that is, a form of double reading that obeys the double injunction for both repetition and the alterity that arises within that repetition. Deconstruction opens a reading by locating a moment of alterity within a text . . . What takes place in deconstruction is a highly determinate form of double reading which pursues alterities within texts . . .
>
> Simon Critchley (1999: 28)

We might take Critchley's assertions further, by suggesting that decon-struction is not the method of reading that locates alterity, so much as it is another name for that alterity, for the structural difference that opens any sign through the possibility of its iterability outside of its original inscrip-tion or context. Such alterity is the condition by which any sign is legible and transmissible. However, if we recall the abyssal nature of alterity – that 'it' is not, simply, an identifiable meaning, location or identity in relation to some selfsame identity or ego-position – then the comprehension of the alterity at the heart of any sign as that which makes the sign available to reading also implies that the sign, forever disinterred within itself as its own condition, can never be closed by any act of reading, and no act of reading therefore can ever come to a close.

The question is not merely one of reading, though. If we return to the earlier remarks by Badiou and Levinas, it can be seen that the concern is with structural identities having to do with being. My being, your being, all experience and articulation of the condition of being is not self-contained or essential to any self, or separable from an understanding of being as shared and therefore structural. It might be said that being is structured like a language, it is comprehended through differential relationships, by which meaning and identity are only available through an understanding of that which does not belong to the selfsame, that which is, as Samuel Weber puts it, the trace of difference or the other:

> the Heideggerian,[2] and even more the Derridean,[3] notion of 'difference' implies a structure of language and a process of articulation that includes a practical, performative moment which, I am convinced, is where one has to start – and probably end – if one is to respond to the trace of the other, to that dimension of alterity to which thinking is so profoundly indebted.
>
> Samuel Weber (1996: 171)

While Weber speaks of 'a structure of language and a process of articula-tion' he indicates that the concern with structure and trace is not merely formal but is bound up with the understanding of being and thinking through the references to Martin Heidegger and Jacques Derrida, two philosophers who, arguably, have done more than any other thinkers to explore the differential structures of being.

There is in the thinking of the radical grammar of being a dissymmetry that disables any merely dialectical thought, and which opens up finite ontologies from within themselves onto an infinitude of difference:

> the phenomenon of the other (his face) must . . . attest to a radical alter-ity which he nevertheless does not contain by himself. The Other, as he

appears to me in the order of the finite, must be the epiphany of a properly infinite distance to the other, the traversal of which is the originary ethical experience.

This means that in order to be intelligible, ethics requires that the Other be in some sense *carried by a principle of alterity* which transcends mere finite experience. Lévinas calls this principle the 'Altogether-Other' . . . There can be no Other if he is not the immediate phenomenon of the Altogether-Other. There can be no finite devotion to the non-identical if it is not sustained by the infinite devotion of the principle to that which subsists outside it.

Alain Badiou (2001: 22)

Of course, it is impossible, strictly speaking, to think this infinitude:

the very activity of thinking, which lies at the basis of epistemological, ontological, and veridical comprehension, is the reduction of plurality to unity, alterity to sameness. The very task of philosophy, the very task of thinking is the reduction of otherness. In seeking to think the other, its otherness is reduced or appropriated to our understanding. To think philosophically is to comprehend . . . and master the other, thereby reducing its alterity.

Simon Critchley (1999: 29)

One cannot think without constituting unity and identity, without imposing delimitable and exclusionary meaning. Alterity is so radically other that it is irreducible to any determination. Thus anything said in these citations and in my commentary is always reductive, as Simon Critchley makes plain, and always acknowledges how alterity exceeds any attempt to address its undecidability.

This does not mean that we should give up speaking, however. There is a highly tentative, always provisional, and always limited possibility of indicating through indirection the very possibility of radical alterity (what is referred to by Jacques Derrida as the *tout autre*, the wholly other, the completely or absolutely other) by addressing a finite and localized instance of the other.

In 'The Meridian' [by Paul Celan[4]] . . . [t]he poem as 'conversation' will always involve otherness. The identification of the other brings its alterity into play, the alterity already determined by the 'self' of the poem. (It will be a self that inscribes within it itself that which is already other; the other within the same.) . . . In 'The Meridian', this complex reflection continues by working away from the possibility of a founding singularity. The question will be the place of otherness.

. . .
This other is in its being within. It is not an either/or. The poem incor-
porates alterity.

Andrew Benjamin (1997: 126, 136)

As Andrew Benjamin's commentary on a poem by Paul Celan makes clear,
the experience of a specific other intimates the wholly other. Moreover, this
alterity is not, to stress the point once more, a dialectical position but is
always already within the same, it is the radical difference – what is termed
by Derrida différance – that makes possible any comprehension of the
same. Because of this 'I' can never see myself authentically as absolutely
singular or unique. 'I' is always traced, haunted, by the marks of alterity.
This haunting is articulated by Joan Brandt in the final citation in this
section:

> when Derrida speaks of 'radical alterity', he does not assume a pure exte-
> riority whereby heterogeneity as a hypostasised[5] 'Other' would ulti-
> mately be subsumed under a notion of the Same; he points to an
> otherness that inhabits the self-identical, not as the result of some
> subversive or transgressive act but as an alterity that has always been
> internal to any closed structure, be it linguistic or otherwise . . . By bring-
> ing the temporal deferral of presence and the spatial distinction that
> places it in relation to an other, *différance* marks the impossibility for an
> identity to close in on itself. In this sense, spacing becomes indissociable
> from the concept of alterity.
>
> Joan Brandt (1997: 120)

Questions for further consideration

1. How does alterity differ from otherness?
2. Consider the ways in which you might begin an analysis of non-identity *within*
    any given identity.
3. How might we comprehend alterity as a figure of the other at once both
    distanced *and* having an intimate proximity?

Explanatory and bibliographical notes

1. Emmanuel Levinas (*b*.1906–*d*.1995): *Time and the Other* (1987); *Totality and
    Infinity: An Essay on Exteriority*, trans. Alphonso Lingis (Pittsburgh, PA:
    Duquesne University Press, 1969); *Otherwise Than Being: or Beyond Essence*,
    trans. Alphonso Lingis (Pittsburgh, PA: Duquesne University Press, 1998).

2. Martin Heidegger (*b*.1889–*d*.1976): *Being and Time* (1962); *On the Way to Language*, trans. Peter D. Hertz (New York: Harper and Row, 1971); *Poetry, Language, Thought*, trans. and Introduction by Albert Hofstadter (New York: Harper and Row, 1971).
3. Jacques Derrida (*b*.1930–): *Dissemination* (1981); *Margins of Philosophy* (1982); *On the Name* (1995).
4. Paul Celan (*b*.1920–*d*.1970): *Breathturn*, trans. Pierre Joris (Los Angeles, CA: Sun and Moon, 1995); *Threadsuns*, trans. Pierre Joris (Los Angeles, CA: Sun and Moon, 1997); *Poems of Paul Celan*, trans. and Introduction by Michael Hamburger (London: Anvil, 1988).
5. *Hypostasise*: to embody, personify, or represent as substantial or real.

Further reading

Critchley, Simon (1999), *The Ethics of Deconstruction: Derrida and Levinas* (1992), 2nd edn (Edinburgh: Edinburgh University Press).

Levinas, Emmanuel (1987), *Time and the Other* (1947), trans. Richard A. Cohen (Pittsburgh, PA: Duquesne University Press).

Levinas, Emmanuel (1999), *Alterity and Transcendence* (1995), trans. Michael B. Smith (New York: Columbia University Press).

Robbins, Jill (1999), *Altered Reading: Levinas and Literature* (Chicago: University of Chicago Press).

Taussig, Michael (1993), *Mimesis and Alterity: A Particular History of the Senses* (London: Routledge).

APORIA

Deriving from the Greek for 'unpassable path' or 'impasse' or, otherwise, 'without passage', 'without issue', *aporia* has been used by Jacques Derrida to describe the effects of différance: the aporetic and the experience of its impassable, unbridgeable excess is figured in the recognition of the undecidable in meaning; irreducible to a limited semantic horizon, language and the concepts it puts to work announce a radical undecidability at the heart of meaning or value, whereby contrary to the limits of logic, a concept is shown to be identifiable as being disturbed internally: on the one hand, as neither this nor that, while, on the other hand, as both this and that. A particularly striking example of the experience of the aporetic appears in Karl Marx's consideration of the commodity fetish, where he finds it logically impossible to explain, within the limits of his discourse, what transforms material into its mystified form as desired commodity, and what invests the commodity object with its commodified mystique. Derrida first explores the aporetic in the concept of time as articulated by Aristotle,[1] in the essay 'Ousia and Gramme: Note on a Note from Being and Time', published in Margins of Philosophy,[2] extensive extracts of which are presented below, in order to demonstrate how Derrida, in elucidating the movements of Aristotelian thinking, effects a radical, transformative critique of the Aristotelian model in order to determine the aporia otherwise.

> Aristotle begins by proposing . . . an aporia . . . how is it to be thought that time is what it is not? By giving in to the obvious, that time is, that time has as its essence, the nun . . . which functions in Greek like our word 'now'. . . . If one thinks of time on the basis of the now, one must conclude that it is not. The now is given simultaneously as that which is no longer and as that which is not yet. . . . Now, that which bears within it a certain no-thing, that which accommodates nonbeingness, cannot participate in presence, in substance, in beingness itself (ousia[3]).
>
> This first phase of the aporia involves thinking time in its divisibility. Time is divisible into parts, and yet none of its parts, no now, is in the present . . . The nun, the element of time, in this sense is not in itself temporal. It is temporal only in becoming temporal, that is, in ceasing to be, in passing over to no-thingness in the form of being-past or being-future.
> . . .
> The first phase . . . supposed that time was composed of . . . nows (nun). It is this presupposition that the second phase . . . contests: the now is not a part, time is not composed of nows, the unity and identity of the now are problematical . . . Aristotle affirms that the now, in a certain sense, is the same, and in another sense, is the nonsame . . . that time is continuous according to the now and divided according to the now. . . . And all these contradictory affirmations are reassembled in dialectical manipulation of the concept of gramme[4] . . . It seems at first that Aristotle rejects the representation of time by the gramme, that is . . . by a linear inscription in space, just as he rejects the identification of the now with the point . . . Time is distinguished from space in that . . . the relationship of points [along a line, or within a given space] cannot be the same as that of the nows between themselves. Points do not destroy each other reciprocally. But if the present now were not annulled by the following now, it would coexist with it, which is impossible. Even if it were annulled only by a now very distant from it, it would have to coexist with all the intermediate nows, which are infinite (indeterminate[5]: apeiros) in number; and this too is impossible . . . this impossibility, when barely formulated, contradicts itself, is experienced as the possibility of the impossible. . . . The impossibility of coexistence can be posited

as such only on the basis of a certain coexistence, of a certain *simultaneity* of the nonsimultaneous, in which the alterity and identity of the now are maintained together in the differentiated element of a certain same . . . The impossible . . . appears . . . in a certain complicity . . . *maintaining* together several current nows [*maintenants*] which are said to be the one past and the other future. The impossible comaintenance of several present nows [*maintenants*] is possible as the maintenance of several present nows [*maintenants*]. Time is the name for this impossible possibility.

Jacques Derrida (1982: 39–40, 53–7)

Derrida's commentary is both lucidly self-explanatory and rigorously thorough in its working-through of the temporal and spatial implications of the figure of the aporetic, and it is not necessary here to comment at length on what is already carefully and patiently laid out for us. It is worth drawing the reader's attention to the maintenance in French of the word *maintenant* by the translator, for its performative power. The French has been left in by the translator to indicate that Derrida is playing on the temporal slippage within the word, which, though present in the English *maintain*, is not as immediately accessible as in French. While *maintenant* signifies 'now', every utterance displaces the 'now' that is signified even as it 'maintains' a certain 'now', though never the same 'now' as any other, nor, indeed, the now or *nun* as such. Thus the maintenance of the *maintenant*, the *now* or *nun* simultaneously articulates *and* disarticulates in a performative manner the work of the aporia as it is traced in Aristotle. Derrida's insistence on the graphic movement in (and as) writing of the *now* emphasizes the spatial as well as temporal disruption within the signifier which supposedly acts as guarantor of any present moment.

As is clear, the figure of *maintenant* does not only foreground structural issues of displacement and reiteration. It also names a temporal dimension, as the following citation acknowledges.

An aporia is something which is impracticable. A route which is impracticable is one that cannot be traversed, it is an uncrossable path. Without passage, not treadable. For . . . Zeno[6] . . . aporia implied the suspension (*epokhe*) of judgement. At the point where the path of thinking stopped, judgement was suspended. This definition of aporia was inherited by the presocratic sophists who called an aporia two contradictory sayings of equal value. The suspension of judgement was a mode of perplexity before the inability to ground either saying . . . For Aristotle . . . time both is and is not. If time is thought in terms of its divisibility, it is to be thought in terms of *now*. And yet, the very *now* of time which gives it its being also robs it of any being, since *now* is always already past or future.

The thinking of time is, therefore, . . . an 'aporetic'. Time provokes a thinking which ends up as the aporia (without passage) of thinking.

Richard Beardsworth (1996: 32)

The thinking of time in Aristotle brings thinking up against a limit, an impassable place whereby the aporetic is encountered. Thinking thus succumbs to an experience of that which had supposedly been the object of its inquiry. Thinking reaches a border and, as Derrida puts it, 'paralyzes us'.

[Of the aporia and the experience of the aporetic] It had to be a matter of . . . the nonpassage, or rather from the experience of the nonpassage, the experience of what happens [se passe] and is fascinating . . . in this nonpassage, paralyzing us in this separation in a way that is not necessarily negative: before a door, a threshold, a border, a line, or simply the edge or the approach of the other as such.

Jacques Derrida (1993: 12)

Again, a French phrase is retained by the translator, which articulates in a radical fashion that which the phrase 'what happens' does not make available to us. The French reflexive verb se passer indicates a passage or movement, a 'happening' for want of a better phrase, which takes place, which places itself in motion as it were, without and before a determining consciousness or subjectivity. 'I' do not make some experience happen. This question of 'what happens' is alluded to by Derrida on a couple of occasions elsewhere (see the entries under 'Deconstruction') as a provisional definition for deconstruction, where he employs the expression ce qui arrive: that which arrives, that which happens. Another possible way of translating this might be to use a phrase familiar from certain English-language editions of the Bible, which is 'it came to pass'. This phrase is apposite in the context of the discussion of temporality because, as with the French maintenant apropos of the Aristotelian consideration of a series of 'nows', the English implies a constant motion, an unstoppable traversal of instances arriving from the future, moving into a past, without ever coming to rest in a present. Something, which is not a thing, takes place, traversing space and time ineluctably, and transforming itself in the traversal, exceeding its own condition, determination or identity, as a motion of differential translation, so to speak. It is this unceasing overflow that is identified by Richard Beardsworth, in his summary of Derrida's comprehension of the aporia:

aporia, for Derrida, is not, as it was for the presocratics, an oscillation between two contradictory sayings . . . 'contradiction' [for Derrida] applies to one and the same entity, not to two different entities.

Richard Beardsworth (1996: 32)

This constant condition, perhaps provisionally nameable as the event-ness of the aporetic, is signalled here by Derrida:

> in *The Other Heading*[7] . . . at a precise moment, without giving in to any dialectic, I used the term 'aporia' . . . for a *single duty* that recurrently duplicates itself interminably, fissures itself, and contradicts itself without remaining the same . . . I suggested that a sort of nonpassive endurance of the aporia was the condition of responsibility and decision.
>
> Jacques Derrida (1993: 16)

Importantly, in this passage, there is the acknowledgement of both a constant, 'interminable' fissuring, and reduplication, whereby reduplication *and* fissure are identified as the contradictory traces of the transformation of the same by the other within, which, taking place before and outside any subject, imposes on the subject both the endurance of the aporia and the responsibility arising in the subject in response to this encounter. The question of responsibility is recast by Drucilla Cornell in the example of the necessity of true judgement in the face of the aporia of the law.

> [Of justice as aporia] If law is just calculation, then it would not be self-legitimating, because the process of legitimation implies an appeal to a norm. The judge is called to judge, which means that she not only states what the law is, she confirms its value as what ought to be . . . But at the same time, the judge is called to judge according to the law. That is part of the responsibility of a judge: he must judge what is right, which means he appeals to law, to rules and not only to his opinion. So the judge is caught in a paradox. He must appeal to law and yet judge it through confirmation or rejection. But this act of judgement would not be a 'true' judgement, fresh, if it were simply calculation of law . . . To be just, is to be in the throes of this paradox.
>
> Drucilla Cornell (1992: 133–4)

Cornell's specific example is recast in broader terms by Gayatri Spivak, who considers the question of ethical decisions and, in doing so, lays stress on the aporetic as an experience and not merely some logical problem.

> When one decides to speak of aporias, one is haunted by the ghost of the undecidable in every decision. One cannot be mindful of a haunting, even if it fills the mind. When we find ourselves in the subject position of two determinate decisions, both right – or both wrong of course – one of which cancels the other, we are in an aporia which by definition cannot be crossed. Yet, it is not possible to remain in an aporia. It is not a logical or philosophical problem like a contradiction, a dilemma, a

paradox, an antinomy. It can only be described as an experience. It discloses itself in being crossed. For, as we know every day, even by supposedly not deciding, one of those two right or wrong decisions gets taken, and the aporia remains. Again, it must be insisted that this *is* the condition of possibility of deciding. In the aporia, to decide is the burden of responsibility . . . In the aporia, *to decide* is the burden of responsibility.

> Gayatri Chakravorty Spivak (2001: 221–2)

Questions for further consideration

1. Derrida's discussion of the aporia in Aristotle reveals an irreducible structurality having to do with both space and time; compare this with the articulation of the expanded concept of writing in the final part of the present volume.
2. Given the consideration of aporia above, is it reasonable to suggest that, far from being merely formal, any analysis of the aporia does, in some measure, involve a political dimension?
3. Why does the experience of the aporetic impose a sense of duty, rather than alleviating responsibility?

Explanatory and bibliographical notes

1. Aristotle (*b*.384BC–*d*.322BC); *Poetics*, trans. and Introduction by Malcolm Heath (London: Penguin, 1996); *Metaphysics*, trans. and Introduction by Hugh Lawson-Tancred (London: Penguin Books, 1998); *Physics*, ed. David Bostock, trans. Robin Waterfield (Oxford: Oxford University Press, 1999).
2. Jacques Derrida, '*Ousia* and *Gramme*: Note on a Note from *Being and Time*', in *Margins of Philosophy* (1982), pp. 31–67.
3. *Ousia* signifies the foundational principle of being, which governs and orders all manifestations of being.
4. *Gramme*: Written character or inscription.
5. Perhaps, in the context of the discussion of aporia, the figure here might, more appropriately, be 'undecidable' rather than 'indeterminate'. Nicholas Royle sums up the difference between the two terms succinctly: 'To classify a text, or a moment in a text, as indeterminate is to put an end to the question of judging: it is, in a sense, the opposite of undecidability. To talk about undecidability is not to suggest that making decisions or judgements is impossible but rather that any and every judgement is haunted by an *experience* of the undecidable, the effects of which remain to be read. To refer to the meaning of a text, or a moment in a text, as indeterminate is in fact to determine a reading, to stop the process of reading' (1995: 161).
6. Zeno, otherwise Zenon (*b. circa* 490–*d. circa* 425): *Zeno of Elea*, ed. and trans. Henry Desmond Prichard Lee (Cambridge: The University Press, 1936).

7. Jacques Derrida, *The Other Heading: Reflections on Today's Europe*, trans. Pascale-Anne Brault and Michael B. Naas (Bloomington, IN: Indiana University Press, 1992).

Further reading

Derrida, Jacques (1982), '*Ousia* and *Gramme*': Note on a Note from *Being and Time*', in *Margins of Philosophy* (1972), trans., with notes, by Alan Bass (Chicago, IL: University of Chicago Press), pp. 31–67.
Derrida, Jacques (1993), *Aporias*, trans. Thomas Dutoit (Stanford, CA: Stanford University Press).
Keenan, Thomas (1997), *Fables of Responsibility: Aberrations and Predicaments in Ethics and Politics* (Stanford, CA: Stanford University Press).

CARNIVAL/CARNIVALESQUE

Forms of *carnival* and other related communal celebratory practices are found throughout the world. Throughout Christian Europe, carnival has existed for several hundred years and is traditionally expressed through feasting, music, dance, and other forms of entertainment. From the Latin, *carnelevarium*, meaning 'removal of meat', carnival was traditionally staged as a licensed or authorized activity taking place in town centres and other civic spaces prior to Lent, the 40-day preparation for Easter. With respect to cultural studies and critical discourse, carnival and *carnivalesque* are drawn from the work of Mikhail Bakhtin[1] on the novel, particularly his study of Rabelais's *Gargantua and Pantagruel*[2] and its exemplary exploration of 'low' or popular cultural practices in relation to the ecclesiastical and feudal political culture of the Middle Ages. Bakhtin identifies the particular features of what he terms folk culture in the following manner.

A boundless world of humorous forms and manifestations opposed to the official and serious tone of medieval ecclesiastical and feudal culture . . . folk festivals of the carnival type, the comic rites and cults, the clowns and fools, giants, dwarfs, and jugglers, the vast and manifold literature of parody . . . belong to one culture of folk carnival humor.

The manifestations of this folk culture can be divided into three distinct forms.

1. *Ritual spectacles*: carnival pageants, comic shows of the marketplace.

2. *Comic verbal compositions*: parodies both oral and written, in Latin and in the vernacular.
3. *Various genres of billingsgate*:[3] curses, oaths, popular blazons.

These three forms of folk humor, reflecting in spite of their variety a single humorous aspect of the world, are closely linked and interwoven in many ways.

Mikhail Bakhtin (1984: 4–5)

Amplifying on Bakhtin's work, Pam Morris provides a cogent and lucid summary of Bakhtin, stressing the carnivalesque as a structural, rather than a merely anthropological form:

> Bakhtin gives an impressively detailed and scholarly account of carnival as a complex system of meaning. As such it is derived from two bases. Carnival . . . [is] a symbolic network of concretely sensuous forms accumulating over a centuries-long tradition of popular festivals, carnivals, celebratory and seasonal rituals, market-place spectacles. The other basis . . . is associated with verbal form. Bakhtin links it with the tradition of comic vernacular literature which existed in the ancient world alongside high forms, frequently travestying and mocking them. In particular, he picks out the important influence of three ancient forms: the Socratic dialogue, the Menippean satire[4] and the symposium as banquet dialogue. These forms are themselves carnivalized and dialogic[5] and are important mediating vehicles by means of which carnival meaning can be transposed into literature . . . Bakhtin stresses the sensuous concrete forms of carnival gesture and ritual because its whole meaning derives from the physical materiality of the human body . . . The grotesque exaggeration of the body in carnivalesque forms, and especially the persistent emphasis upon the body and genitals mocks Medieval religious repudiation of the flesh . . . This grotesque body [is] at the heart of all carnival meaning . . . it is the body of all the people and as such cannot die.

Pam Morris (1994: 21)

Peter Stallybrass and Allon White also develop Bakhtin's thinking:

> carnival in its widest, most general sense embraced ritual spectacles such as fairs, popular feasts, and wakes, processions and competitions . . . comic shows, mummery and dancing, open-air amusement with costumes and masks, giants, dwarfs, monsters, trained animals and so forth; it included comic verbal compositions (oral and written) such as parodies, travesties and vulgar farce; and it included various genres of 'Billingsgate', by which Bakhtin designated curses, oaths, slang, humour, popular tricks

and jokes, scatological forms . . . Carnival is presented by Bakhtin as a world of topsy-turvy, of heteroglot exuberance, of ceaseless overrunning and excess where all is mixed, hybrid, ritually degraded and defiled.

Peter Stallybrass and Allon White (1986: 8)

The carnivalesque is in part, therefore, that in both society and narrative forms where social hierarchies and power structures oriented around positions of 'high' and 'low' are temporarily inverted, often through forms of parody, in order to destabilize in order to make comic that which is taken seriously within social order. As well as the emphasis on the possibility of subversion through bodily functions and bodily parts, attention is also drawn to the subversive and transgressive potential of language.

Language is capable of producing laughter, as are corporeal acts and excesses, but laughter is also responsible, quite literally, for shaking the body out of its 'proper' form and propriety; laughter thus causes an eruption, we might suggest of the other within the self, and it is perhaps for such a reason – the transgression of bodily propriety, that Bakhtin places particular emphasis on laughter.

[C]arnivalesque laughter . . . is, first of all, a festive laughter. Therefore it is not an individual reaction to some isolated 'comic' event. Carnival laughter is the laughter of all the people. Second, it is universal in scope; it is directed at all and everyone, including the carnival's participants. The entire world is seen in its droll aspect, in its gay relativity. Third, this laughter is ambivalent: it is gay, triumphant, and at the same time mocking, deriding. It asserts and denies, it buries and revives.

Mikhail Bakhtin (1984: 8)

Laughter is also transgressive, according to Bakhtin, because it traverses the limits of all social forms, and is, in addition, ambiguous.

It is not only laughter which is ambiguous, however. As Terry Eagleton shows, carnival is both transgressive *and* authorized, it is both critical of social order and complicit with it:

carnival is so vivaciously celebrated that the necessary political criticism is almost too obvious to make. Carnival, after all, is a *licensed* affair in every sense, a permissible rupture of hegemony, a contained popular blow-off as disturbing and relatively ineffectual as a revolutionary work of art.

Terry Eagleton (1981: 148)

From Eagleton's politically suspicious perspective, the idea of carnival is problematized from within, and by, its very premises; the social activity of carnival cannot take place without some form of institutional authorization. However, this is to read the work of carnival solely from an externalized, sociological perspective, there is still a dimension to the carnivalesque that Eagleton does not take into account as fully as he might. The ambiguity of the carnivalesque renders a single reading of it undecidable. This being the case, when Bakhtin writes that

> in the world of carnival the awareness of the people's immortality is combined with the realization that established authority and truth are relative
>
> Mikhail Bakhtin (1984: 10)

and – in a gesture that resists the facile acceptance of purely externalized reading –

> Carnival is not a spectacle seen by the people; they live in it, and everyone participates because its very idea embraces all the people. While carnival lasts, there is no other life outside it. During carnival time life is subject only to its laws, that is, the laws of its own freedom. It has a universal spirit; it is a special condition of the entire world, of the world's revival and renewal, in which all take part
>
> Mikhail Bakhtin (1984: 7)

it should be noted that the very complicity noted by Bakhtin at the level of celebratory participation, while, in principle, a 'democratizing' feature of the carnivalesque, is also, to recall Eagleton once more, that very aspect of social involvement that may occlude the political containment which carnival is licensed to effect. However, even though there is an ambivalence about carnival's cultural and ideological function which no one can doubt, the very real radical potential for critique and subversion in carnival and the carnivalesque should not be underestimated. The ambivalence emerges historically from the fact that carnival itself has never had a simple, unified determination, as Stallybrass and White make clear:

> on the one hand carnival was a specific calendrical ritual: carnival proper, for instance, occurred around February each year, ineluctably followed by Lenten fasting and abstinence bound tightly to laws, structures and institutions which had briefly been denied during its reign. On the other hand carnival also refers to a mobile set of symbolic practices, images and discourses which were employed throughout social revolts and conflicts before the nineteenth century.
>
> Peter Stallybrass and Allon White (1986: 15)

It is in the reading of constellated mobile practices and textual forms that the Utopian, affirmative condition of the carnivalesque resides, and, with that, the impossibility of a completely carnivalesque social transformation.

Carnival and laughter are described as utopian in the sense that they challenge all social norms that have ever been or *ever will be*; they incorporate a spirit of joyful negation of everything completed or to be completed. Because there are always some norms in force, this negation can never ultimately succeed . . . in replacing the world as we know it with another world.

Gary Saul Morson and Caryl Emerson (1990: 94)

From this, we must comprehend carnival not as a form of universal political response to conditions of political oppression and containment, but instead as an ongoing strategic interruption in social norms, in ideological containment, and in corporeal order and propriety. Not an effective revolution in itself, carnival none the less stages, however ritually, the possibility of limited revolt and, with that, the articulation of critique through the praxis of the carnivalesque. One aspect of this is the transformative comprehension of the human body in collective rather than in individualistic terms.

Taking sheer delight in Heraclitian[6] flux, carnival understands the human body not as the mortal husk of an individual . . . but as the collective great body of the people.

Gary Saul Morson and Caryl Emerson (1990: 92–3)

Julia Kristeva's critical work has in part been a response to, and influenced by, the work of Bakhtin, especially in her earliest publications. Here, Kristeva emphasizes the manifestation of protest through carnivalesque language, as a form of polyglot textuality that refuses to be contained by the boundaries of particular forms.

History and morality are written and read within the infrastructure of texts. The poetic word, polyvalent[7] and multi-determined, adheres to a logic exceeding that of codified discourse and fully comes into being only in the margins of recognized culture . . . Carnivalesque discourse breaks through the laws of a language censored by grammar and semantics and, at the same time, is a social and political protest.

Julia Kristeva (1980: 65)

For Kristeva, as for other critics, the carnivalesque is patently a structural form, capable of moving across and thereby dissolving or dismantling, at least in part, the discrete parameters of particular social and cultural identities and concepts on which society relies for its calm maintenance. In taking part in carnival, the participant slips between assigned social roles, and thus momentarily escapes delimiting determination.

> Carnivalesque structure is like the residue of a cosmogony[8] that ignored substance, causality, or identity outside of its link to the whole, *which exists only in or through relationship*. This carnivalesque cosmogony has persisted in the form of an antitheological (but not antimystical) and deeply popular movement. It remains present as an often misunderstood and persecuted substratum of official Western culture throughout its entire history . . . It is a spectacle, but without a stage . . . A carnival participant is both actor and spectator; he loses his sense of individuality . . .
>
> Julia Kristeva (1980: 78)

Questions for further consideration

1. If carnival is always licensed or authorized, to what extent can it be truly subversive?
2. In what ways do carnivalesque effects and images dismantle distinctions between high and low culture?
3. Why is the excessive or grotesque body crucial in the articulation or representation of the carnivalesque?

Explanatory and bibliographical notes

1. Mikhail Bakhtin (*b*.1895–*d*.1975): *Rabelais and His World* (1984); (and P. N. Medvedev): *The Formal Method in Literary Scholarship: A Critical Introduction to Sociological Poetics* (1978); *The Dialogic Imagination: Four Essays*, ed. Michael Holquist, trans. Caryl Emerson and Michael Holquist (Austin, TX: University of Texas Press, 1981).

   Bakhtin employs terms other than 'carnival' and 'carnivalesque' which have entered critical discourse, though not, arguably, to the extent which this keyword has. Dialogism and monologism are explained in note 5, below. Another significant keyword in Bakhtin's critical language is *heteroglossia*. Heteroglossia signifies an incompatible multiplicity of discourses occurring within a given language on a microlinguistic scale. Translated from the Russian, *raznorechie*, heteroglossia means 'different-speech-ness'. Bakhtin employed the word in order to explain the hybrid condition of narrative and its competing utterances in the modern novel.

2. François Rabelais (*b*.1483?–*d*.1553): *The Histories of Gargantua and Pantagruel*, trans. J. M. Cohen (London: Penguin, 1955).

3. Bakhtin takes the name *Billingsgate* from the London fishmarket, which, as far as official records reveal, is one of the city's oldest markets, dating at least back to the eleventh century. While the origins of the name are obscure, London historians from John Stow to Peter Ackroyd have speculated on its etymology.
4. *Menippean satire*: style of satire associated with or deriving from the Greek philosopher Menippus (third century BC).
5. *Dialogic*: in the form of a dialogue. Bakhtin opposes the figure of dialogism to monologism in his account of narrative forms. *Dialogism* indicates the poly-phonic or multivoiced play in a text where there is no clear, dominant or mono-lithic authorial position or voice. *Monologism* is employed to describe characters or narratives clearly dominated by a single position or ideology.
6. Heraclitus (fifth century BC); in the fragments of his writings which sur-vive, Heraclitus proposes a concept of eternal mutability, hence the notion of Heraclitean 'flux'; *Fragments: the Collected Wisdom of Heraclitus*, trans. Brooks Haxton, Foreword by James Hillman (New York: Viking, 2001).
7. *Polyvalent*: having multiple meanings, signifying in multiple ways, often simul-taneously.
8. Cosmogony: theory explaining the origins of the universe.

Further reading

Bakhtin, Mikhail (1984), *Rabelais and His World* (1965), trans. Hélène Iswolsky (Bloomington, IN: Indiana University Press).

Booker, M. Keith (1991), *Techniques of Subversion in Modern Literature: Transgression, Abjection and the Carnivalesque* (Gainesville, FL: University Press of Florida).

Castle, Terry (1986), *Masquerade and Civilization: The Carnivalesque in Eighteenth-Century Culture and Fiction* (Stanford, CA: Stanford University Press).

Stallybrass, Peter, and Allon White (1986), *The Politics and Poetics of Transgression* (Ithaca, NY: Cornell University Press).

White, Allon (1993), *Carnival, Hysteria, and Writing: Collected Essays and Autobiography* (Oxford: Clarendon Press).

CLASS

The notion of *class*, commonly understood as indicating the various hierar-chical gradations or ranks within society and by which society is composed, has been employed in this manner at least since the seventeenth century. However, this apparently more or less neutral definition has been irreversibly transformed by Karl Marx in his critique of social and economic relations. In critical language subsequently then, class has been transformed into a keyword in Marxist and other left-wing political discourses, belonging to a larger project concerned with the political transformation of society, which transformation is grounded in the belief in the possibility of the emergence of a classless society through the overthrow of forms of economically determined exploitation:

> The constitutive form of class relationships is always that between a dominant and a labouring class: and it is only in terms of this axis that class fractions (for example, the petty bourgeoisie) or ec-centric or dependent classes (such as the peasantry) are positioned. To define class in this way is sharply to differentiate the Marxian model of classes from the conventional sociological analysis of society into strata, subgroups, professional elites and the like, each of which can presumably be studied in isolation from one another in such a way that the analysis of their 'values' or their 'cultural space' folds back into separate and independent *Weltanschauungen*,[1] each of which inertly reflects its particular 'stratum.' For Marxism, however, the very content of a class ideology is relational, in the sense that its 'values' are always actively in situation with respect to the opposing class, and defined against the latter.
>
> Fredric Jameson (1981: 83–4)

Comprehension of the ways in which ideas of class are mobilized in the maintenance of hierarchical manifestations of social power, economic relations, modes of production, and social inequality, is crucial to politicized critical accounts of society and culture. In the act of demystifying the social and ideological processes by which class, class-location, and class-relations become occluded in capitalist societies, critical analysis addresses, amongst other things, the mystification of class-positions as autonomous or 'natural', and the realities of their economic–structural interdependence. Analyses of class relations also serve as a corrective to generalizations concerning humanity and human identity in humanist, conservative or right-wing determinations.

In making these remarks, and in suggesting a certain structurality to, and as a necessary component of, class relations, it is none the less important that we do not ignore the historicity of class and class relationships:

> the notion of class entails the notion of historical relationship. Like any other relationship, it is a fluency which evades analysis if we attempt to stop it dead at any given moment and anatomise its structure . . . Class happens when some men, as a result of common experiences (inherited or shared), feel and articulate the identity of their interests as between themselves, and as against other men whose interests are different from (and usually opposed to) theirs. The class experience is largely determined by productive relations into which men are born – or enter involuntarily.

Class consciousness is the way in which the experiences are handled in cultural terms: embodied in traditions, value-systems, ideas and institutional forms.

E. P. Thompson (1968: 8–9)

That class relations are fluid, that they develop and transform over time, and that they carry in them the residue of earlier social, cultural and class relations, cannot be stressed too strongly. In order to keep this in mind, it is perhaps polemically and strategically appropriate if we adopt as a slogan Thompson's phrase *Class happens*. Such a phrase acknowledges both the fluidity of class positions and the historical transformations which class mediates and by which it is determined.

Ellen Meiksins Wood provides a careful consideration of the intersection between Marxist and socialist conceptualizations of class within broader theories of historical and social development, aiming eventually to bring about the possibility of a classless society.

The Marxist conception of [the socialist project] . . . as the abolition of class carried out by means of class struggle and the self-emancipation of the working class . . . provided a systematic and coherent account in which socialist objectives were grounded in a theory of historical movement and social process . . . the objectives of socialism were seen as real historical possibilities, growing out of existing social forces, interests, and struggles. If the social relations of production and class struggle were the basic principles of historical movement to date, socialism was now on the historical agenda because there existed . . . a class which contained the real possibility of a classless society: a class without property or exploitative powers of its own to protect, which could not fully serve its own class interests without abolishing class altogether; an exploited class whose specific interest required the abolition of class exploitation; a class whose own specific conditions gave it a collective force and capacity for collective action which made that project practicable. Through the medium of this specific class interest and this specific capacity, the universal emancipation of humanity from class exploitation . . . could be translated into a concrete and immediate political programme.

Ellen Meiksins Wood (1986: 90)

As Wood avers, within the Marxist paradigm it is the working class or proletariat which provides the possibility of a classless society. As the passage demonstrates forcefully, the working class is, in effect, the hope of both Marxism and socialism, it is the class through the mobilization of which, theory is transformed into social reality via revolutionary praxis. Thus,

The working class is revolutionary, Marxists have maintained, because of its historically constituted nature as the exploited collective producer within the capitalist mode of production. As the *exploited* class, it is caught in a systematic clash with capital, which cannot generally and permanently satisfy its needs. As the main *producing* class, it has the power to halt – and within limits redirect – the economic apparatus of capitalism, in pursuit of its goals. And as the *collective* producer it has the objective capacity to found a new, non-exploitative mode of production. This combination of interest, power and creative capacity distinguishes the working class from every other social or political force in capitalist society, and qualifies it as the indispensable agency of socialism.

                                        Ellen Meiksins Wood (1986: 91)

Of course, any class is always comprised of individual subjects, and so E. P. Thompson again raises the historical question of how social organization came to assume its various hierarchical forms.

The question, of course, is how the individual got to be in this 'social role', and how the particular social organization (with its property rights and structure of authority) got to be there. And these are historical questions. If we stop history at a given point, then there are no classes, but simply a multitude of individuals with a multitude of experiences. But if we watch these men over an adequate period of social change, we observe patterns in their relationships, their ideas, and their institutions. Class is defined by men as they live their own history, and, in the end, this is its only definition.

                                        E. P. Thompson (1968: 10)

Importantly, in stressing relationships and patterns, Thompson admits to the structural condition of class while also clarifying the understanding of structure as a historical phenomenon capable of transformation.

Understanding how class is also a product of ideology as well as of lived social relations is important. People think and act in the ways they do, not only because of external factors, but also because of received ideas and structures of belief.

The ruling ideology is . . . the ideology of the ruling *class*. But the ruling class does not maintain with the ruling ideology, which is its own ideology, an external and lucid relation of pure utility and cunning. When during the eighteenth century, the 'rising class', the bourgeoisie, developed a humanist ideology of equality, freedom and reason, it gave its own demands the form of a universality, since it hoped thereby to enrol at its side, by their education to this end, the very men it would liberate only for their exploitation. This is the Rousseauan[2] myth of the origins of inequality: the rich holding forth to the poor in 'the most deliberate discourse' ever conceived, so as to persuade them to live their slavery as their freedom. In reality, the bourgeoisie has to believe in its own myth before it can convince others . . . so as to take up, occupy and maintain its historical role as a ruling class. Thus, in a very exact sense, the bourgeoisie *lives* in the ideology of *freedom* the relation between it and its conditions of existence: that is, *its* real relation (the law of a liberal capitalist economy) *but invested in an imaginary relation* (all men are free, including the free labourers). Its ideology consists in this play on the word *freedom*, which betrays the bourgeois wish to mystify those . . . it exploits, as much as the bourgeoisie's need to *live* its own class rule as the freedom of those it is exploiting.

Louis Althusser (1977: 234–5)

Coming to terms with the function of ideology and imaginary relations leads one to an understanding of the ways in which members of one class may well identify not with their class but with other classes which serve in their oppression.

A member of one class may well feel no antagonism towards members of other classes; and there may be mobility between classes. But classes nevertheless remain irreconcilably divided, whether conflict occurs or not, and independently of the forms it may or may not assume.

Ralph Miliband (1986: 18)

The imaginary structures by which classes persist will, therefore, frequently embody contradictions and paradoxes expressed as the lived relations of real men and women. The complexity of structure, both lived and imaginary, cannot be overstressed:

ideology, like social class itself, is an inherently *relational* phenomenon: it expresses less the way a class lives its conditions of existence, than the way it lives them *in relation to the lived experience of other classes*. Just as there can be no bourgeois class without a proletariat, or vice versa, so the typical ideology of each of these classes is constituted to the root by the ideology of its antagonist. . . . There are social classes such as the petty bourgeoisie . . . whose ideology is typically compounded of elements drawn from the classes both above and below them; and there are vital ideological themes such as nationalism which do not 'belong' to any particular social class, but which rather provide a bone of contention between them.

Terry Eagleton (1991: 101)

As Eagleton demonstrates, there are ideas, such as nationalism, capable of uniting members of all classes and thereby serving to militate against particular class interests.

But in the final analysis, if class relations are always structural and historical, and if they are also fraught by contradictory elements and cross-class interests and ideologies, it is also therefore the case that class relations and class domination (where we began with the commentary of Fredric Jameson) are, as Ralph Miliband asserts, never purely economic.

> Class domination is economic, political, and cultural. . . . Class domination can never be purely 'economic', or purely 'cultural': it must always have a strong and pervasive 'political' content, not least because the law is the crystallized form which politics assumes in providing the necessary sanction and legitimation of all forms of domination.
>
> Ralph Miliband (1986: 20)

Questions for further consideration

1. Why is it considered necessary for the working class to assume a revolutionary function, doing away with capitalism as a necessary precursor to emancipation? Why is social reform inadequate?
2. In what ways do class identifications extend beyond or between particular classes? What are the mechanisms by which a member of the working classes might identify with the interests of the ruling classes, against the interests of his or her own class?
3. In what ways might matters of culture and aesthetics be read so as to comprehend how they both mystify and reproduce existing class relations in any given social situation?

Explanatory notes

1. *Weltanschauungen*: plural of German *Weltanschauung*, meaning philosophy of life, or world view.
2. *Rousseauan*: referring to philosophical concepts originating in the work of Jean-Jacques Rousseau. See note 2 in the entry on 'Aesthetics'.

Further reading

Miliband, Ralph (1986), *Marxism and Politics* (Oxford: Oxford University Press).
Thompson, E. P. (1986), *The Making of the English Working Class* (London: Penguin).

Wood, Ellen Meiksins (1986), *The Retreat from Class: A New 'True' Socialism* (London: Verso).

CULTURE

A term or figure employed aesthetically, ideologically and anthropologically, *culture* is employed, most fundamentally, as an oppositional term, implicitly or explicitly, to the idea of nature. The notion of culture identifies broadly those patterns of human knowledge that refer to the customary beliefs, social formations, and traits of racial, religious, or social groups. Furthermore, the notion of culture signifies an acquaintance with the humanities, fine arts, and other intellectual or scientific pursuits and is often synonymous with a sense of 'good breeding' with regard to particular individuals. However, it is important that we start by acknowledging that 'culture' is not a universal term. Nor has its meaning remained the same over its long history.

> 'Civilization' and 'culture' . . . were in effect, in the late eighteenth century, interchangeable terms. Each carried the problematic double sense of an achieved state and of an achieved state of development . . . 'culture' as a general process of 'inner' development was extended to include a descriptive sense of the means and works of such development: that is, 'culture' as a general classification of 'the arts', religion, and the institutions and practices of meanings and values . . . The religious emphasis weakened, and was replaced by what was in effect a metaphysics[1] of subjectivity and the imaginative process. 'Culture' . . . [was] seen as the deepest record, the deepest impulse, and the deepest resource of the 'human spirit'. 'Culture' was then at once the secularization and the liberalization of earlier metaphysical forms. Its agencies and processes were distinctly human, and were generalized as subjective, but certain quasi-metaphysical forms – 'the imagination', 'creativity', 'inspiration', 'the aesthetic' . . . were in effect composed into a new pantheon.
>
> Raymond Williams (1977: 15–17)

Raymond Williams[2] points to specific histories and the semantic and ideological transformations that the notion of culture has undergone. What is immediately apparent from the extract above is that there is a process of secularization concerning the understanding of culture. In addition to Raymond Williams's reading, the notion of culture is also applied to assemblages of social practices defined periodically and in terms of race, belief, and class.

Antonio Gramsci,[3] while never articulating a coherent Marxist theory of culture, none the less provides in his *Notebooks* a fruitful means of orienting cultural analysis according to history, culture and society.

> [While] the concept of culture is never theoretically defined by Gramsci ... [c]ulture functions loosely – and very productively – as a sort of middle term between the world of art and study on the one hand and society and politics on the other ... For socialists of his generation, culture largely meant literature and education – which the working class were to make their own, wresting them from the hands of the bourgeoisie ... [Gramsci's] concept of culture ... retained uncriticized residues of its original bias towards the written word as the core of cultural formation in individuals and society ... Nevertheless there is ... at least an implicit theoretical concept of culture which can be seen to inform his scattered observations over a wide field. What this underlying concept is can be deduced from his procedure in approaching not just literature and art but other topics as well ... In all cases his interest is not so much in the object in itself as in the place it occupies within a range of social practices ... what interests him in relation to literature and art is again their culture, the place they hold generally within what he calls the 'complex superstructures' of a social formation ... The fundamental concepts in play in Gramsci's observations on cultural themes are ... state and civil society, intellectuals, hegemony and so forth. Just as culture has only a limited autonomy from other social practices, so within Gramsci's theoretical schema its meaning is dependent on the meaning of other concepts.
>
> David Forgacs and Geoffrey Nowell-Smith (1985: 13–14)

This citation, taken from Gramsci's editors, does not provide a succinct definition of Gramsci's theory of culture because, as they make plain, he did not propose one as such. Rather, it is included because of the way in which it highlights how Gramsci's understanding of culture emerges as a result of what might be described provisionally as a 'structural' analysis of society, if by this we can indicate not some formalism so much as a recognition of the ways in which the various strata of the social are neither autonomous nor distinct from one another. This is already implied by both Williams and Gramsci's editors. It is also exemplified in the following commentary:

> it could then be understood that culture, while impossible to grasp theoretically as the 'object' of a description or scientific definition, is impossible to bypass practically as the semantic 'horizon' of all the discourses that try to signify identity in a world of nations (dominant and dominated, recognized or denied, in search of their unity or already showing

signs of being integrated into larger ensembles). It could also be understood that *the very word* 'culture' after a long prehistory and period of crystallization at the turn of the eighteenth and nineteenth centuries, acquired the strategic function that it has today (including in philosophy) at the precise moment that the nation form definitively won out over other forms of state in Europe, and began to become generalized in the world. Thenceforth any collective appropriation of knowledge, rights or traditions has had to be thought of as 'culture': either as the institution of a *cultural order*, or as the contestation of the existing order *by culture*. And all identity has had to be founded in a past cultural origin, or projected into a future of culture that is ceaselessly interrogated in the light of origins.

Étienne Balibar (1995a: 179–80)

Like Williams, Balibar acknowledges the transformation of the meaning of the term culture in specific historical contexts. He also points to the hegemonic function termed 'cultural order'.

Despite the fact, presented by Balibar, that culture is 'impossible to grasp theoretically as the "object" of a description or scientific definition', there has taken place, none the less and perhaps inevitably, the rise of the academic discourse of cultural studies:

the very definition of culture current in 'cultural studies' tends to be exclusively concerned with meaning. It is illustrative of this that signification theory – analysis of the meanings constructed in systems of signs – is now a consensual position in the debate on the definition of the term 'culture'.

Michèle Barrett (1999: 92)

Such a discourse, Michèle Barrett argues warily, has itself been marked by the hegemonic ascendance of structural–semantic analysis of culture, an approach typified in the later work of Jean Baudrillard.[4]

Commodities obviously are produced, whereas women are not, and they are produced differently to words. Nevertheless, at the level of distribution, commodities and objects, like words and once like women, constitute a global, arbitrary, and coherent system of signs, a *cultural* system which substitutes a social order of values and classifications for a contingent world of needs and pleasures, the natural and biological order.

This is not to claim that there are no needs, or natural utilities, etc. The point is to see that consumption, as a concept specific to contemporary society, is not organized along these lines. For this is true of all societies. What is sociologically significant for us, and what marks our era under the sign of consumption, is precisely the generalized reorganization of this primary level in a system of signs which appears to be a particular mode of transition from nature to culture, perhaps *the* specific mode of our era.

Jean Baudrillard (1988: 47–8)

Complicating such a focus on signifying functions within cultural analysis, Barrett signals other determinations of culture.

There is culture in the classical anthropological sense of a way of life, the fabric and texture of a people's distinctive manner of going about things. Of course, in the contemporary world, where migration and diasporization have produced more complex 'hybrid' cultural identities, these generic descriptions of culture as a 'way of life' have become far more complex. This points to issues of 'cultural difference' and the question of whether and how we could, or should, 'translate' experience.
. . .
[T]he term 'culture' bears an irreducible trace of the distinction between the arts and popular culture; popular if you like it, or 'mass culture' if you don't . . . 'Cultural studies' has made a valiant effort to break down the binary opposition between high and low culture, developing new theories and methods to show us what is common across this value-laden divide, and to challenge the hierarchy itself as well as the value attributed to the products of 'high culture'.

Michèle Barrett (1999: 1–2)

Barrett's attention to material manifestations, to questions of ethnicity and difference, and to social hierarchies of culture, seeks to ground the complexity of the notion of culture through attention to various social practices. In addition, there are a number of other critical approaches concerning the question of the cultural as the manifestation of material practices. For example, Pierre Bourdieu[5] employs the expression 'cultural capital' in his sociological critiques to describe the hidden value attached to learning and education in Western capitalist societies and, most importantly, the ways in which knowledge assumes a function akin to capital inasmuch as the acquisition of forms of socially approved and disseminated bodies of knowledge operates according to matters of cultural value.

There is an economy of cultural goods, but it has a specific logic. Sociology endeavours to establish the conditions in which consumers of cultural goods, and their taste for them, are produced . . . But one cannot fully understand cultural practices unless 'culture', in the restricted, normative sense of ordinary usage, is brought back into 'culture' in the anthropological sense, and the elaborated taste for the most refined objects is reconnected with the elementary taste for the flavours of food.

Whereas the ideology of charisma regards taste in legitimate culture as a gift of nature, scientific observation shows that cultural needs are the product of upbringing and education: surveys establish that all cultural practices ... and preferences ... are closely linked to educational level ... The manner in which culture has been acquired lives on in the manner of using it ... A work of art has meaning and interest only for someone who possesses the cultural competence, that is, the code, into which it is encoded. The conscious or unconscious implementation of explicit or implicit schemes of perception and appreciation which constitutes pictorial or musical culture is the hidden condition for recognizing styles characteristic of a period, a school or an author, and, more generally, for the familiarity with the internal logic of works that aesthetic enjoyment presupposes ... Thus the encounter with a work of art is not 'love at first sight' ... the act of empathy ... which is the art-lover's pleasure, presupposes an act of cognition, a decoding operation, which implies the implementation of a cognitive acquirement, a cultural code.

Pierre Bourdieu (1984: 1–3)

Bourdieu's argument seeks to make connections between varying definitions and understandings of culture, from the sociological and the anthropological, to those developed in relation to questions of ideology and the culturally encoded perception of the subject. There is perhaps to be discerned in this passage a traversal from external to internal relations, from the discourses of economy and commodity, to those of subjectivity and signification. But, as Geoffrey Hartman reminds us,

not all uses of 'culture' converge. But whatever the word touches receives at present a sort of credibility. One hears of a smokers' culture, of [Australia's] beach culture: do such things really exist? The point is that the term bestows, like rights language run amok, a certain dignity, one that is based not so much on numbers as on a sense that *a meaningful nucleus of life, a form of social existence, has emerged or is emerging.* And we pay attention to it, I suggest, because social fragmentation means two things that together amount to a disabling paradox: the general culture seems too distant or alien, while the hope for some unity of being – which I call embodiment – can migrate to groupings often held together by parochial, sectarian, self-serving, and even antisocial interests.

These interests range from the folklore of indigenous or immigrant cultures, or the practices of a religious cult that has broken with a mainstream denomination, to the lifestyle of gay people or the agenda of political, commercial, and even criminal organizations (a TV report on the Bank of Credit and Commerce International talked as easily of 'BCCI's criminal culture' as of a 'Washington culture'). So abusive is the extension of the word, so strong and vulgar its pathos, that I begin to understand an Africanist claim about the West. It is alleged that an ingrained Cartesianism has *ghosted* the colonizers, abstracted them from life, so that 'culture' becomes a dream for what is missing, a phantom or proxy comforting the 'white-man-who-has-problems-believing-in-his-own-existence'.

Geoffrey H. Hartman (1997: 33–4)

Hartman's cautionary narrative suggests that 'culture' has been so widely employed and deployed, to so many ends, and for so many purposes, that any sense it might have had is all but unavailable.

Questions for further consideration

1. Consider the ways in which that which we name 'culture' is always, in a certain manner, the articulation of class, gender, or ethnic divisions, distinctions and differences.
2. Has the notion of culture become so diffuse that it is no longer operable?
3. What problems arise in treating the works of 'mass' or 'popular' culture as merely so many instances of commercialization and commodifications, rather than attempting to comprehend them as different manifestations of 'art'?

Explanatory and bibliographical notes

1. *Metaphysics*: signifying that which is beyond the physical, material world, metaphysics is that branch of philosophy addressing first or founding conceptual principles, including such concepts as being, substance, essence, time, space, identity.
2. Raymond Williams (*b*.1921–*d*.1988): *Culture and Society, 1780–1950* (1961); *Marxism and Literature* (1977); *Politics and Letters: Interviews with the New Left Review* (London: New Left Books, 1979).
3. Antonio Gramsci (*b*.1891–*d*.1947): *Selections from Prison Notebooks*, ed. and trans. Quentin Hoare and Geoffrey Nowell-Smith (London: Lawrence and Wishart, 1971); *Selections from Political Writings, 1921–1926*, trans. and ed. Quentin Hoare (London: Lawrence and Wishart, 1978); *Selections from Cultural Writings*, ed. David Forgacs and Geoffrey Nowell-Smith (Cambridge, MA: Harvard University Press, 1991).
4. Jean Baudrillard (*b*.1929–): *For a Critique of the Political Economy of the Sign* (1981); *Simulations* (1983); *Selected Writings* (1988).

5. Pierre Bourdieu (*b*.1930–): *Distinction* (1984); *The Field of Cultural Production*, ed. and Introduction by Randal Johnson (New York: Columbia University Press, 1993); *The Rules of Art* (1996).

Further reading

Bhabha, Homi K. (1994), *The Location of Culture* (London: Routledge).
During, Simon (ed.) (1999), *The Cultural Studies Reader*, expanded edn. (London: Routledge).
Nelson, Cary and Lawrence Grossberg (eds) (1988), *Marxism and the Interpretation of Culture* (Urbana, IL: University of Illinois Press).
Sinfield, Alan (1989), *Literature, Politics, and Culture in Postwar Britain* (Berkeley, CA: University of California Press).
Williams, Raymond (1961), *Culture and Society, 1780–1950* (1959) (Harmondsworth: Penguin).

DECONSTRUCTION

Deconstruction is conventionally recognized as a school or method of criticism. Equally conventionally, when thought of as a school, method or critical 'programme', deconstruction is understood to have been developed by Jacques Derrida. This is, however, a misunderstanding that is all the more appallingly and hilariously inaccurate because it is so widespread and so eagerly accepted, accepted we might suggest without ever having been thought about or considered carefully. Take, for example, this following definition, which the dictionary component of the software package 'Worldbook' provides: 'a method of literary criticism, applied especially to poetry, in which the text is reduced to its basic linguistic and semantic elements'. *Chambers Dictionary* is equally inaccurate, as are many other dictionaries, encyclopaedia, guides to critical theory and even books the principle subject of which is, allegedly, deconstruction. According to such conventional narratives, Derrida's 'method' of reading, which apparently sought to unearth contradictions and paradoxes in the logical structures of philosophical and literary texts, became adopted in North American universities from the late 1960s and in British universities from the early 1980s.

> From the beginning . . . there existed a certain Americanization of a certain deconstruction . . . by Americanization I mean a certain appropriation: a domestication, an institutionalization, chiefly academic, that took place elsewhere in other forms as well, but here in a massively visible fashion . . . And among the examples of these procedural and formalizing

formulae that I had proposed, and which were circulating precisely as possibilities, new possibilities offered by deconstruction, there was the reversal of a hierarchy. After having reversed a binary opposition . . . and after having liberated the subjugated and submissive term, one then proceeded to the generalization of this latter in new traits, producing a different concept . . . Or to take another example: the privilege granted to the self-contradictions or the performative contradictions of a discourse, contradictions that could furnish a strategic lever in the consideration of marginalia, a minor text, a brief essay, a bizarre foot-note, a symptomatic phrase or word, in order to dislocate and destabi-lize the autointerpretive authority of a major canonical text . . . this slightly instrumentalizing implementation tended to reduce the impetus or the languages, the desire, the arrival so to speak, the future, of decon-structions, and might well arrest [deconstructions] . . . at a body of possi-bilities, of faculties, indeed of facilities, in a word, a body of easily reproducible means, methods, and technical procedures, hence useful, utilizable; a body of rules and knowledge; a body of powerful know how . . . offered for didactic transmission, susceptible of acquiring the aca-demic status and dignity of a quasi-interdisciplinary discipline.

Jacques Derrida (2001: 18–19)

The process of appropriation and domestication herein described is commented on further by Peggy Kamuf.

Concerning the institution that is the university put in question by the PC debate, the term 'deconstruction' is most often presumed to refer to a theory, a method, a school, perhaps even a doctrine, in any case some identifiable or localizable 'thing' that can be positioned – posed and opposed – within that institution, but also that can be excluded from within this defined enclosure.

Peggy Kamuf (1997: 141)

Kamuf's commentary identifies a specific tendency or problem in the recep-tion of deconstruction, which is that all institutional discourses and other efforts to systematize so-called deconstruction presume for the term an ontology, a discernible and delimitable identity the contours and compo-nent elements of which are consistent within the identification of 'decon-struction' and which, furthermore, are repeatable from one instant or act to another. Yet, as J. Hillis Miller[1] remarks,

sentences of the form 'Deconstruction is so and so' are a contradiction in terms. Deconstruction cannot by definition be defined, since it presupposes the indefinability or, more properly 'undecidability' of all conceptual or generalizing terms. Deconstruction, like any method of interpretation, can only be exemplified, and the examples will of course all differ.

J. Hillis Miller (1991a: 231)

As Miller, Kamuf, and Derrida assert, therefore, all narratives pertaining to the determination of deconstruction are wide of the mark in their efforts at definition and containment on several counts. More generally still, Derrida has never presented a coherent theory of reading or analysis which functions in the same manner from one text to another.

All of Derrida's texts are already applications, so there is no separate 'Derrida' in the form of a theory who might *then* be applied to something else. Insofar as 'Deconstruction' tends to become a method or a school, we might say that it has forgotten this, and has begun at least to make Derrida into a theory which it wants to put into practice.

Geoffrey Bennington (1996: 17)

As can be seen from Geoffrey Bennington's comment, the reception of deconstruction involves an act of forgetting, a kind of institutional amnesia, in order that the university can proceed with its work. There is thus an institutional politics at work, which typically maintains its own institutional identity or ontology through making thought conform to certain repeatable patterns and procedures. Yet Derrida has remarked on numerous occasions that deconstruction is unavailable as a method of reading or analytical mode.

Deconstruction doesn't consist in a set of theorems, axioms, tools, rules, techniques, methods . . .

Jacques Derrida (1996: 218)

This seems straightforward enough, but in case the point is not yet clear enough, here is Derrida again, making the same assertion but in more detail, in relation to acts of reading.

I am not sure that deconstruction can function as a literary *method* as such. I am wary of the idea of methods of reading. The laws of reading are determined by that particular text that is being read. This does not mean that we should simply abandon ourselves to the text, or represent or repeat it in a purely passive manner. It means that we must remain faithful, even if it implies a certain violence, to the injunctions of the text. These injunctions will differ from one text to the next so that one cannot prescribe one general method or reading. In this sense deconstruction is not a method.

Jacques Derrida (1984: 124)

And if you remain unconvinced, another commentary, which returns us to the double question of reception and ontologization.

> All the same, and in spite of appearances, deconstruction is neither an *analysis* nor a *critique* . . . It is not an analysis in particular because the dismantling of a structure is not a regression toward a *simple element*, toward an *indissoluble origin*. These values, like that of analysis, are themselves philosophemes[2] subject to deconstruction. No more is it a critique, in a general sense . . .
>
> I would say the same about *method*. Deconstruction is not a method and cannot be transformed into one . . . It is true that in certain circles (university or cultural, especially in the United States) the technical and methodological 'metaphor' that seems necessarily attached to the very word 'deconstruction' has been able to seduce or lead astray. Hence the debate that has developed in these circles: Can deconstruction become a methodology for reading and for interpretation? Can it thus let itself be reappropriated and domesticated by academic institutions? . . . It must also be made clear that deconstruction is not even an *act* or an *operation*. Not only because there would be something 'passive' about it . . . Not only because it does not return to an individual or collective subject who would take the initiative and apply it to an object, a text, a theme, etc. Deconstruction takes place, it is an event that does not await the deliberation, consciousness, or organization of a subject.
>
> Jacques Derrida (1985: 273–5)

The notion of an event without or before the subject is commented on elsewhere, as a strategic possibility, the very possibility of which it is impossible to predict.

> Necessarily, since it [deconstruction] is neither a philosophy, nor a doctrine, nor a knowledge, nor a method, nor a discipline, not even a determinate concept, only what happens if it happens [*ce qui arrive si ça arrive*].
>
> Jacques Derrida (2000b: 288)

As an event which takes place, which happens or comes to pass, if it takes place or happens at all (and nothing could be less certain), deconstruction therefore calls into question any possibility of a programme of reading and also any ontological process:

> for deconstruction, or what is called by that name, begins by calling into question the question 'what is it?', the question that sets itself up under the authority of the 'is', i.e., of a determination of Being, and of a Being

thus nominalized on the basis of the indicative or the present participle of the verb 'be'. From the being . . . of this 'is' (or of being as an object in general) is organized a fundamental ontology or a transcendental phenomenology[3] which, in principle and de jure,[4] dominates vertically the pyramid of ontologies, of phenomenologies or the so-called regional disciplines.

Jacques Derrida (2000b: 297)

So, we might suggest, if a deconstruction arrives or comes to pass, 'I' can only ever register its effects after the event. 'I' am always late, with regard to this event, and my recognition, my response must therefore always be governed not by any determinate interpretive act on my part but by the contours, rhythms, interruptions and suspensions that make any text possible and transmissible.

So, let us both recap certain points and move forward: as Jacques Derrida has pointed out, 'deconstruction' is a very old French word. Despite this, it has been assumed that Derrida coined the word and the concept of 'deconstruction', and that it is therefore a neologism. However, as the *Oxford English Dictionary* (*OED*) shows, the word exists not only in French but also in English, and pre-exists Derrida and other critics' use of the word. Derrida used the word in an effort to 'translate' German philosopher Martin Heidegger's use of the words *destruktion* and *abbau*, in order to demonstrate that which exists within or inhabits, in a certain fashion, any structure or the idea of any structure by which the articulation of that structure is made possible, and yet which is heterogeneous to the self-identity of the structure, whether one is talking of a conceptual, logical, discursive, institutional, or philosophical formation. Because that which is deconstructive – supposing that there 'is' deconstruction – is thus internal to the very idea of structure, and yet not definable within the logic of the self-same by which ideas, concepts and beliefs maintain their 'truth' or significance, it is therefore not generalizable as a 'theory' of structure, or structure's internal contradictions. It also therefore follows, as Miller has put it, that because every example of deconstruction differs from every other example, it cannot be transformed or translated into a method of reading or a programme for critical analysis, much less into a set of rules available for use by a so-called 'school' of deconstructive criticism. For these and other reasons, it is problematic, to say the least, to define deconstruction, except by a negative process which moves cautiously by speaking, at least provisionally and in the first instance, of what deconstruction is not.

It does have to be said, however, as a cautionary caveat, that even this is fraught, for as Derrida points out, to recall the remarks above concerning the impossibility of constructing an ontology for deconstruction, to define deconstruction in terms of either 'deconstruction is' or 'deconstruction is not', is to rely on an ontological procedure which ascribes to 'deconstruction' a 'thingness', an objectivity and identity available to definition and awaiting patiently the ontological delimitation of the word. As Derrida seeks to explain, deconstruction always already takes place in structures, makes their existence and their transformation possible, prior to any consciousness or subjectivity and is thus patently neither that which is applied in the name of reading nor some formalist exercise in determining how something is put together but is, instead, of political and philosophical import, if not directly political *per se*, because that which is deconstructive is precisely that in any formation, whether discursive or institutional, which we overlook, which we pass over in silence and which, in Nicholas Royle's words, remains to be read.

> Deconstruction – which is never single or homogeneous, but which can here, at least provisionally, be identified with 'the work of Derrida' – is concerned with the lucid, patient attempt to trace what has not been read, what remains unread or unreadable within the elaboration of concepts and workings of institutions.
>
> Nicholas Royle (1995: 160)

Here is Derrida making a similar point about irreducible plurality or, more properly, a certain excess beyond any simply defined consensual plurality as a contest between languages to which one must attend.

> Deconstruction ... if it is anything [is] an attention paid to the irreducible plurality of signatures and an ethico-juridical vigilance, a political one too, to the effects of hegemony of one language over another, between one language and the other.
>
> Jacques Derrida (2000b: 290)

In Derrida's words, deconstruction, if it is anything, is an 'economic concept designating the production of differing/deferring'. This provisional definition opens rather than closes any reading going by this strange name over which so many have had such trouble.

> As a transformative strategy without finality, as the destabilizing differential effects always already at work everywhere, deconstruction is never single but necessarily multiple and incomplete.
>
> Nicholas Royle (1995: 128)

However, such multiplicity and incompletion, strategic in its multiple responses, does not mean that deconstruction or deconstructions are either nihilistic or evidence of a formalist retreat from history, politics or ideology.

We may always begin with the question of language but reading which takes seriously the responsibility of and for its act must acknowledge the presuppositions, as Derrida says here, by which institutionalized reading acts proceed.

> In short, deconstruction not only teaches us to read literature more thoroughly by attending to it *as language*, as the production of meaning through *différance* and dissemination, through a complex play of signifying traces; it also enables us to interrogate the covert philosophical and political presuppositions of institutionalized critical methods which generally govern our reading of a text . . . It is not a question of calling for the destruction of such institutions, but rather of making us aware of what we are in fact doing when we are subscribing to this or that institutional way of reading.
>
> Jacques Derrida (1984: 125)

And here is a similar point, developed at greater length, where Derrida spells out both the inappropriateness of transforming deconstruction into an institutional method of analysis, and simultaneously, the necessity for reading deconstructions at work within those very same institutional locations:

> [The premises of a discourse] are not absolute and ahistorical . . . They depend upon socio-historical conditions, hence upon nonnatural relations of power that by essence are mobile and founded upon complex conventional power structures that in principle may be analyzed . . . and in fact, these structures are in the process of transforming themselves profoundly and, above all, very rapidly (this is the true source of anxiety in certain circles, which is merely revealed by 'deconstruction': for before becoming a discourse, an organized practice that *resembles* a philosophy, a theory, a method, which it is *not*, in regard to those unstable stabilities or this destabilization that it makes its principal theme, 'deconstruction' is firstly this destabilization on the move in, if one could speak thus, 'the things themselves'; but it is not negative. Destabilization is required for progress as well. And the 'de-' of *de*construction signifies not the demolition of what is constructing itself, but rather what remains to be thought beyond the constructivist or deconstructionist scheme). What is at stake here is the entire debate, for instance, on the curriculum, literacy, etc.
>
> Jacques Derrida (1988b: 147)

Questions for further consideration

1. In the light of the various commentaries on 'deconstruction' and the understanding of the word articulated here, consider to what extent the uses of the word elsewhere in the present volume are appropriate or otherwise.

2.   What might be said to generate the desire to transform or translate 'decon-struction' into a concept available for application in an act of reading?
3.   Why is it necessary and more accurate to signify deconstruction*s* in the plural, rather than assuming a single, homogeneous meaning or identity for this word?

Explanatory and bibliographical notes

1.   J. Hillis Miller (*b*.1928–): *The Ethics of Reading: Kant, de Man, Eliot, Trollope, James, and Benjamin* (1987); *Topographies* (1994); *Speech Acts in Literature* (2000).
2.   The term *philosopheme* defines 'units', if you will, of conceptual meaning which operate within greater semantic and signifying structures in a manner akin to the operation of a phoneme in spoken language, being a common and recurring signifying structural feature. However, while the phoneme is commonly held to be the smallest unit of language, 'philosopheme', at least in Derrida's sense, defines a unit which is not, as he puts it, a *simple element*, but is, rather, constructed itself; it has a structural nature and can itself be read as a structural form composed of differing elements (which themselves are, also, not simple elements).
3.   *Phenomenology*: a branch of philosophy, associated with Edmund Husserl (*b*.1859–*d*.1938). Phenomenology addresses the subjective or conscious apprehension of the nature and meaning of phenomena, contending that their significance is only available to consciousness through subjective mediation. Husserl's publications hold a great significance for a number of critics and philosophers associated with the term 'poststructuralism'; amongst these are: *The Crisis of European Sciences and Transcendental Phenomenology: An Introduction to Phenomenological Philosophy*, trans. and Introduction by David Carr (Evanston, IL: Northwestern University Press, 1970); *Experience and Judgement: Investigations in a Genealogy of Logic*, rev. and ed. Ludwig Landgrebe, trans. James S. Churchill and Karl Ameriks, Introduction by James S. Churchill, Afterword by Lothar Eley (Evanston, IL: Northwestern University Press, 1973); *Cartesian Meditations: An Introduction to Phenomenology*, trans. Dorion Cairns (Dordrecht: Kluwer Academic Publishers, 1995).
4.   *De jure*: by right, according to law.

Further reading

Bloom, Harold, Paul de Man, Jacques Derrida, Geoffrey H. Hartman, J. Hillis Miller (1979), *Deconstruction and Criticism* (New York: Continuum Books).

Caputo, John (1997), *Deconstruction in a Nutshell: A Conversation with Jacques Derrida* (New York: Fordham University Press).

Critchley, Simon (1999), *The Ethics of Deconstruction: Derrida and Levinas* (1992), 2nd edn (Edinburgh: Edinburgh University Press).

Derrida, Jacques (1985), 'Letter to a Japanese Friend', trans. David Wood and Andrew Benjamin. In David Wood and Robert Bernasconi (eds), *Derrida and Différance* (Coventry: Parousia Press), pp. 1–6.

McQuillan, Martin (ed.) (2000), *Deconstruction: A Reader* (Edinburgh: Edinburgh University Press).

Royle, Nicholas (ed.) (2000), *Deconstructions: A User's Guide* (London: Palgrave).

DESIRE

Desire is an ineluctable force in, or perhaps more accurately, process of the human psyche, to be distinguished from need. Its prevalence in contemporary critical discourse is seemingly so all-pervasive that it defies any absolute determination, and thereby makes manifest a certain aspect of its process, even as it slips away from any determination within discourse, only to resurface as the simultaneous exposure of a lack within language and at the limit of articulation, and yet also being a product of the motions and rhythms of academic language incapable of pinning down the object of its inquiry. Desire holds a crucially central position in Lacanian[1] psychoanalysis and, subsequently, in psychoanalytically inflected critical discourses. Desire, for Lacan, is always an unconscious drive, conscious articulations of desire being merely symptomatic of this unstoppable force. Need is seen as a purely biological instinct, while desire, a purely psychic phenomenon, is a surplus or excess beyond all articulation of demand. Desire, writes Lacan, comes always from the unconscious, and is thus unlocatable as such, while being, equally, 'desire for something else' (as it is expressed in *Écrits*), by which formula Lacan indicates that one cannot desire what one has, while what is desired is always displaced, deferred. Rethinking the processes of desire as these have been defined within psychoanalytic discourse as a function of the human subject, Deleuze and Guattari[2] describe desire as machinic. In doing so, they are not seeking to supply an estranging metaphor. Instead, they see the flow of desire as simply an endless and unstoppable 'flight'. It has no organizing or generative organic centre or origin. Nor does desire arise as some function of the self. Desire is subject to no law and the comprehension of the desiring machine serves to deterritorialize those forms of thinking which apply to some law or identity. The subject does not produce desire but the flow of desire plays a role in the constitution of the subject.

Lacan lays out the particular 'qualities' of desire: its structurality, its relation to a psychic lack in the human subject, and its manifestation through the contours of language:

Let us articulate that which structures desire.

Desire is that which is manifested in the interval that demand hollows within itself, in as much as the subject, in articulating the signifying chain, brings to light the want-to-be, together with the appeal to receive the complement from the Other, if the Other, the locus of speech, is also the locus of this lack or this want.

. . .

Desire is produced in the beyond of the demand, in that, in articulating the life of the subject according to its conditions, demand cuts off the need from that life. But desire is also hollowed out within the demand, in that, as an unconditional demand of presence and absence, demand evokes the want-to-be . . . desire is . . . a pure action of the signifier that stops at the moment when the living being becomes sign . . .

Jacques Lacan (1977: 263, 265)

Lacan's definition of the structures of desire are given further exploration here.

'Desire' is founded on loss and is consequently the source of significa-tion. It seems apt as a mythology for a period in which deep-rooted belief in the inevitability of social and economic progress begins to waver and, at the same time, bourgeois ideology, with its dependence on the credi-bility and seriousness of the signified gives way to an explosion of repre-sentation – images of proliferation of style.

Laura Mulvey (1984: 28)

Lack, or loss, is not merely an empirical absence. It is to be understood as linguistic in nature, expressed indirectly and only through forms of signifi-cation. Speech is thus always haunted by what it cannot say even as it speaks its inability to give name to desire as such. For this reason,

desire is not something that is simply found; it must be created. But it can be created only on the basis of the sheer contingency of experience, whether that of an individual person or of a culture. As the attempt to refind the traumatic but individuating object of the first satisfaction, desire is always historical. It involves a retrospective reading of the past that rearranges the past, simultaneously giving it a new meaning and cordoning off within it a zone of senselessness, of sheer otherness, in short, of the real.

Gilbert D. Chaitin (1996: 10)

As we see here, the lack or loss is not merely structural but also historical; furthermore, one only knows what one does not have access to after the loss, which in turn constitutes an unsuturable gap, as the next citation asserts.

> In psychoanalytic theory . . . desire is generated by loss, loss of the mother as first love object and then the threat of another loss, castration, which she epitomizes.
>
> Laura Mulvey (1984: 29)

In drawing on French, specifically Lacanian psychoanalytic discourse, we should not, however, take desire to be simply translatable between languages; there is already a loss marked between one language and another, which in turn is further haunted by another translation, from Freud's German:

> the term [desire] comes to us . . . from the French, *désir*, which in turn translates Freud's[3] *Wunsch* (also, we might add, *Lust*). *Whose* desire? And for *what*? . . . it is the *unconscious* subject that desires . . . But the conscious object of desire is always a red herring. The object is only the representative, in the real, of a psychical representative, in the unconscious . . . In fact, desire *is* the instinct . . . the *trace* of a primal, *lost*, satisfaction. The real object . . . is 'chosen' . . . because something about it allows it to represent the lost object, which is *irretrievably* absent . . . The lost object is something which – it is believed – will repair the rent which has opened up between the subject and the maternal body.
>
> Victor Burgin (1984: 32)

As we see here, what we think we desire is not the desired object at all. This is a fundamental misrecognition on the part of the subject, because that which is desired is inaccessible to comprehension, lodged in the unconscious. However, before going any further it has to be said that

> the unconscious exists, not because there is unconscious desire, in the sense of something impenetrable . . . which emerges from the depths of all its primitiveness, in order then to raise itself to the higher level of consciousness. Quite the contrary, if there is desire, it is only because there is the unconscious, i.e., a language, whose structure and effects escape the subject: because at the level of language, there is always something that is beyond consciousness, which allows the function of desire to be situated.
>
> Jacques Lacan (1967: 45)

Any object of desire, any articulation of desire only gives the most indirect access to the unconscious locus of desire through the primordial traces that, returning from the unconscious, mark our language. As both this and the previous citation suggest, for psychoanalytic theory, the originary object of desire from which the subject is irretrievably separated is the mother:

> desire . . . is created by language transforming need into desire in answer to the unsatisfiable demands of the (m)other for love. Desire . . . is never fulfilled, always there, continually displaced and transformed.
>
> John Forrester (1990: 110–11)

However, this is not to suggest that, because the figure of the mother is understood as this originary object or imaginary locus of desire, desire can be fulfilled. For the mother is precisely one more signifier, one more figure in an endless chain of signification at the level of articulation. Hence the Lacanian injunction that desire must be taken literally.

> Psychoanalysis, via Lacan, maintains that the exclusivity of the surface or of appearance must be interpreted to mean that appearance always routs or supplants being, that appearance and being never coincide. It is this syncopated relation that is the condition of being. . . . Lacan insists that we must take desire literally . . . To say that desire must be taken literally is to say simultaneously that desire *must be articulated*, that we must refrain from imagining something that would not be registered on the single surface of speech, and that desire *is inarticulable*. For if it is desire rather than words that we are to take literally, this must mean that desire may register itself *negatively* in speech, that the relation between speech and desire, or social surface and desire, may be a negative one.
>
> Joan Copjec (1994: 13–14)

Here, taking something literally means for Lacan not that we invest in the empirical object, but that we recognize there is no 'beyond' language, no beyond 'the single surface of speech'. Because we can never get beyond or outside signification we can never get to what we desire. As human subjects we are always 'in' signification, 'we', 'I', is in fact constituted as a subject by the fact that we inhabit signification. And because of this, we cannot get outside it. There is no outside signification.

> In one sense need is what can be satisfied, as for example hunger by food; but in another, more complex sense, it is the bearer of unsatisfiable desire in its archaic, inchoate form. The emergence of desire is a question of *Aufhebung*[4] in the strict sense, as the realization of the *truth of need* in its cancellation. Desire is 'already there' in need in a complex meta-physical modality, no doubt, and we have to make all the necessary concessions to the negativity of it in Lacan's discourse. The 'before' of

the particularity of the subject is projected retrospectively, *nachtraglich*,[5] and as nothingness.

Henry Staten (1995: 169)

Because there is no outside signification, and because as subjects we enter into signification as an irreversible historical or temporal process of our being, we are always in a sense both inside and after signification. Having learned language we have no access to being prelinguistic or presignificatory. Desire is thus inaccessible because it is inscribed within our psyches before we can reflect on it after the fact. Desire is therefore a sign of a negativity.

This is difficult to grasp, however. (How could it be otherwise?) So, perhaps inevitably, we ontologize desire and remain steadfastly within an equation that premises desire as desire *for* some thing. And it is for this reason that it is argued below that desire is not truly a lack at all, it is its own 'thing'.

> To a certain degree, the traditional logic of desire is all wrong from the very outset . . . From the moment we place desire on the side of acquisition, we make desire an idealistic (dialectical, nihilistic) conception, which causes us to look upon it as primarily a lack: a lack of an object, a lack of the real object . . . In point of fact, if desire is the lack of the real object, its very nature as a real entity depends upon an 'essence of lack' that produces the fantasized object . . . If desire produces, its product is real. If desire is productive, it can be productive only in the real world and can produce only reality . . . Desire does not lack anything; it does not lack its object . . . Desire and its object are one and the same thing: a machine . . . Desire is not bolstered by needs, but rather the contrary, needs are derived from desire: they are counterproducts within the real that desire produces . . . Desire . . . becomes this abject fear of lacking something.
>
> Gilles Deleuze and Félix Guattari (1983: 25–7)

How do we move beyond the problem of limiting the consideration of desire to the ever-open ended and repetitive formula ('desire is desire for something which can never be attained'). Perhaps in the following manner:

> each time the demand of the child is answered by the satisfaction of its needs, so this 'something other' is relegated to the place of its original impossibility. Lacan terms this 'desire'. It can be defined as the 'remainder' of the subject, something which is always left over, but which has no content as such. Desire functions much as the zero unit in the numerical chain – its place is both constitutive *and* empty.
>
> Jacqueline Rose (1986: 55)

Desire as the remainder of the subject: as that which remains and haunts our being and simultaneously that which, as the vestigial remains of the inaccessible, remains to come and remains always in excess, always already as more than any possible significatory process or acquisition. While being empty, desire is not simply the sign of lack in a binary structure, such as presence/absence; it is, rather, the mark of no thing as such *and* more than – in Lacan's words, above, 'something more than' – any definable thing.

And if we never have access it is, once again, because we do not control the articulation of desire. Instead this articulation arises from the some other place:

- if desire functions in the subject by virtue of the conditions imposed upon him by the existence of discourse, namely that his need must go by way of the processions . . . of the signifier;
- if, on the other hand . . . we must establish the notion of the Other . . . as being the locus of the deployment of speech (the other scene, *ein andere Schauplatz*,[6] of which Freud speaks in 'The Interpretation of Dreams');
- it must be posited that, produced as it is by an animal at the mercy of language, man's desire is the desire of the Other.

Jacques Lacan (1977: 264)

Finally, it is also important to understand that, in speaking of desire, we are not speaking of a psychic phenomenon or attribute of the subject separable from the subject's immersion in the world. Desire, though nothing as such, strictly speaking, in always already being in excess of any determination, flows everywhere and informs all modes of productivity.

There is no such thing as the social production of reality on the one hand and a desiring-production that is mere fantasy on the other . . . The truth of the matter is that *social production is purely and simply desiring production itself under determinate conditions.* We maintain that the social field is immediately invested by desire, that it is the historically determined product of desire . . . *There is only desire and the social and nothing else.*

Gilles Deleuze and Félix Guattari (1983: 28–9)

Questions for further consideration

1. Why is it impossible to fulfil desire?
2. Compare the structure of desire with that of difference.
3. Given Joan Copjec's paradoxical determination of desire, how might we think desire as an aporetic figure?

Explanatory and bibliographical notes

1. Jacques Lacan (*b*.1901–*d*.1981): *Écrits: A Selection* (1977); *The Four Fundamental Concepts of Psycho-Analysis* (1994); *The Seminar: On Feminine Sexuality. The Limits of Love and Knowledge. Book XX. Encore 1972–73* (1998).
2. Gilles Deleuze (*b*.1925–*d*.1995); Félix Guattari (*b*.1930–*d*.1992): *Anti-Oedipus: Capitalism and Schizophrenia*, Preface by Michel Foucault, trans. Robert Hurley, Mark Seem and Helen R. Lane (Minneapolis, MN: University of Minnesota Press, 1983); *Kafka: Toward a Minor Literature*, trans. Dana Polan, Foreword by Réda Bensmaïa (Minneapolis, MN: University of Minnesota Press, 1986); *What is Philosophy?*, trans. Graham Burchell and Hugh Tomlinson (London: Verso, 1994).
3. Sigmund Freud (*b*.1856–*d*.1939): *Introductory Lectures on Psychoanalysis* (1982); *On Sexuality: Three Essays on the Theory of Sexuality and Other Works* (1991); *Writings on Literature and Art* (1997).
4. *Aufhebung*: not easily translatable, though usually or conventionally given as 'sublation'. The concept is associated primarily with the work of Georg Wilhelm Friedrich Hegel (*b*.1770–*d*.1831): *Phenomenology of Spirit*, trans. A. V. Miller, Foreword by J. N. Findlay (Oxford: Oxford University Press, 1977); *Elements of the Philosophy of Right*, ed. Allen W. Wood, trans. H. B. Nisbet (Cambridge: Cambridge University Press, 1991); *Introductory Lectures on Aesthetics*, trans. Bernard Bosanquet, Introduction by Michael Inwood (London: Penguin, 1993). Hegel, playing on the word's multiple meanings in order to indicate the general characteristics of dialectical transformation from one modality of historical consciousness to another (the dialectical movement is commonly indicated by the formula: *thesis–antithesis–synthesis*), employs the term to signify paradoxical 'processes' whereby there occurs an elevation, a raising up, a preservation, and also negation, abolition, or overcoming. Thus there is the connotation of simultaneous annulling, preserving and elevation.
5. *Nachtraglich*: additional, later, belated, posthumous.
6. *Ein andere Schauplatz*: another scene.

Further reading

Boothby, Richard (1999), *Death and Desire: Psychoanalytic Theory in Lacan's Return to Freud* (New York: Routledge).

Freud, Sigmund (1982), *Introductory Lectures on Psychoanalysis*, Penguin Freud Library, volume 1, trans. James Strachey, ed. Angela Richards (Harmondsworth: Penguin).

Kristeva, Julia (1980), *Desire in Language: A Semiotic Approach to Literature and Art* (1969, 1977), ed. Leon S. Roudiez, trans. Thomas Gora, Alice Jardine and Leon S. Roudiez (New York: Columbia University Press).

Lacan, Jacques (1977), *Écrits: A Selection* (1966), trans. Alan Sheridan (New York: W. W. Norton).

Lacan, Jacques (1994), *The Four Fundamental Concepts of Psycho-Analysis* (1973), ed. Jacques-Alain Miller, trans. Alan Sheridan, Introduction by David Macey (London: Penguin).

Williams, Linda Ruth (1995), *Critical Desire: Psychoanalysis and the Literary Subject* (London: Edward Arnold).

DIFFERENCE/DIFFÉRANCE

The 'concept' of *difference* – if it can in fact be said to be a concept and not something which, though strictly speaking it is nothing, none the less is a 'motion' or 'process of gradation' (as the citation from Kant insists) – being that which makes possible any meaning or identity, might be said to derive from the political and ontological necessity of recognizing that different groupings (for example female people, Black people, gay and lesbian people) not only differ from the white heterosexual norm favoured by Enlightenment thought, but also differ amongst themselves: women, for example, may be middle-class or working-class, Black or Chicana, straight or gay or bi, and/or any combination of any set of attributes. Given that the question of difference is simultaneously political and ontological, it can also be suggested that the matter is, in a certain way, fundamentally semantic: that is to say, we only recognize the meaning or identity of one entity according to its manifest difference from another entity, while also comprehending resemblance, partial similarity, or shared characteristics, so that meaning is understood as relational rather than absolute or intrinsic. Such is the comprehension of the ways in which language operates in Saussurean linguistics and structuralist criticism: meaning is neither intrinsic to a word nor produced solely through reference to a signified or object, but in and through the differential relation to other signifiers.

Beginning with conceptual thought, the notion of difference is not available as a concept, even though the work of difference, of differences, makes possible conceptualization.

> Specific difference . . . in no way represents a universal concept (that is to say, an Idea) encompassing all the singularities and turnings of difference, but rather refers to a particular moment in which difference is merely reconciled with the concept in general . . . Difference then can be no more than a predicate in the comprehension of a concept.
>
> Gilles Deleuze (1994: 31–2)

Deleuze's statement posits difference as a necessary 'moment', one amongst many differences, which serve in the constitution of any conceptual identity.

However, it is necessary to attend to the work of difference precisely because, in any conceptualization, in any use of concepts, the function of difference becomes occluded. Derrida examines the effacement of difference with regard to the notion of self-presence, the sense I have of myself as being uniquely 'here', my identity an undifferentiated, autonomous phenomenon.

> All the concepts of metaphysics . . . *cover up* the strange 'movement' of this difference.
> But this pure difference, which constitutes the self-presence of the living present, introduces into self-presence from the beginning all the impurity putatively excluded from it. The living present springs forth out of its nonidentity with itself and from the possibility of a retentional trace. It is always already a trace. This trace cannot be thought out on the basis of a simple present whose life would be within itself; the self of the living present is primordially a trace. The trace is not an attribute; we cannot say that the self of the living present 'primordially is' it. Originary being must be thought on the basis of the trace, and not the reverse. This protowriting is at work at the origin of sense. Sense, being temporal in nature . . . is never simply present; it is always already engaged in the 'movement' of the trace, that is, in the order of 'signification'. It has always already issued forth from itself . . . *the temporalization of sense is, from the outset, a 'spacing'.*

> Jacques Derrida (1973: 85–6)

Because of the spacing and temporality of difference that makes up any 'living present', any moment of supposedly pure presence is always marked or traced by the movement of an infinitely divisible instance. (See the discussion of moments of 'now' in Derrida's analysis of Aristotle's reading of the aporia, in the section on 'Aporia' above.) As a result of thinking such spacing and temporal motion, one cannot conceive of an identity or being, an absolutely discrete, full or simple concept, as the source or origin of all subsequent copies or representations. Instead, it is the trace, it is difference that makes available the very idea of a concept or 'originary being'; it is this spacing–temporalizing signifying process which gives access to a meaning or a sense. And how does Derrida show this? Through the example of sense: meaning does not arrive or exist immediately, without mediation, but comes into being over time, even in the swiftest moment of the subject's apperception. Any identity, concept, or meaning is therefore written, it is structured by a writing and is an effect of writing, if by writing we think the concept beyond the narrow conceptualization as a series of graphic marks on a page or screen. (See the section on 'writing', below.)

The understanding of difference as constitutive of identity is further explored here:

the subject's identity is related to difference in three ways. It is *opposed* to difference in general, insofar as difference creates the disparity or exteriority of being-outside-the-self, or insofar as it posits that otherness with respect to which the identical pulls itself together from itself and upon itself. But identity, while pulling itself together, *assumes* and reabsorbs within itself the differences that constitute it: both its difference from the other, whom it posits as such, and its difference from itself, simultaneously implied and abolished in the movement of 'grasping itself'. In this way, finally, identity *makes difference*: it presents itself as preeminently different from all other identity and from all nonidentity; relating itself to itself, it relegates the other to a self (or to an absence of self) that is different. Being the very movement proper to self-consciousness, identity – or the Self that identifies itself – therefore makes difference itself, difference *proper*, and this property designates or denotes itself as 'man'.

Jean-Luc Nancy (1993a: 9–10)

In this citation, difference is not only constitutive of identity but is produced by it. Furthermore, the passage traces the way in which there is both that difference within and productive of identity, as well as that 'externalized' difference between an identity and its other. Identity knows and determines its selfhood by identifying what it is not, what is other than itself. Such a fundamental difference is most basically expressed in the following manner.

Axiom 1: People are different from each other

It is astonishing how few respectable conceptual tools we have for dealing with this self-evident fact. A tiny number of inconceivably coarse axes of categorization have been painstakingly inscribed in current critical and political thought: gender, race, class, nationality, sexual orientation are pretty much the available distinctions. They, with the associated demonstrations of the mechanisms by which they are constructed and reproduced, are indispensable, and they may indeed override all or some other forms of difference and similarity. But the sister or brother, the best friend, the classmate, the parent, the child, the lover, the ex-: our families, loves, and enmities alike, not to mention the strange relations of our work, play and activism, prove that even people who share all or most of our own positionings along these crude axes may still be different enough from us, and from each other, to seem like all but different species.

Eve Kosofsky Sedgwick (1999: 247)

Of course, the axiom, while fundamental, none the less addresses complex social relations and hierarchies, the very existence of which points to the necessity for comprehending difference in all its ramifications. As the following citation makes explicit, in the context of colonial discourse, difference is hierarchical and is wielded in oppressive ways.

An important feature of colonial discourse is its dependence on the concept of 'fixity' in the ideological construction of otherness. Fixity, as the sign of cultural/historical/racial difference in the discourse of colonialism, is a paradoxical mode of representation: it connotes rigidity and an unchanging order as well as disorder, degeneracy and daemonic repetition. Likewise the stereotype, which is its major discursive strategy, is a form of knowledge and identification that vacillates between what is always 'in place', already known, and something that must be anxiously repeated . . . as if the essential duplicity of the Asiatic or the bestial sexual license of the African that needs no proof, can never really, in discourse, be proved.

Homi K. Bhabha (1994: 66)

Within colonial discourse, difference is projected as a difference from a fixed or 'true' identity. Such thinking typifies the metaphysical assumption – an assumption that is also political and ideological – of what Derrida, above, terms originary being. The 'truth' of my identity, if it can be fixed in place, can control a range of meanings by designating as different all those not like myself, which 'self' is assumed absolute and therefore unavailable to any interrogation. According to this logic all colonized others are imperfect copies of, different from, the colonial 'I'.

It is this logic which also determines racial and sexual difference – concrete examples of the strategic hierarchization between the self and its other, where the self assumes the role of a conceptual absolutism. Yet, despite the attempted hierarchization, the figure of difference reveals that the self is only capable of constructing its identity through a registration of difference as so many negative traces.

Racial difference, like sexual difference, provides one of the instituting conditions of subjectivity. It helps to set limits between self and other, precariously identifying where the 'I' ends and unknowable other begins. Whiteness, for example, defines itself in opposition to blackness; the 'I' knows itself by what it is not. Thus, an hypostatized blackness is actually part of the meaning of whiteness. The race of the Other, his or her own 'immutable' difference (and this is a difference that conventionally assumes also a moral form, of superiority/inferiority), announces and confirms the self-identity of whiteness. But it is a self-identity that must always look anxiously outside for its confirmation, disavowing any relation between inside and outside, self and mirroring image.

Ann Pellegrini (1997: 7)

It would be all too easy at this stage to read the matter of difference as one of obviously marked differences between self and other, between whiteness and blackness, for example. The reader should avoid such crudely drawn and facile divisions. As is suggested here, the divisions are infinite:

> but there nonetheless is, between reality (sensory representation) and nothing i.e., the complete emptiness of intuition in time, a difference that has a magnitude, for indeed between every given degree of light and darkness, every degree of warmth and the completely cold, every degree of heaviness and absolute lightness, every degree of the filling of space and completely empty space, yet smaller degrees can be thought, just as between consciousness and the fully unconscious . . . yet smaller degrees occur; therefore no perception is possible that shows a complete absence . . .
>
> Immanuel Kant (1997: 60)

Kant's delineation of ever smaller degrees of difference cannot be overstated, because such minute traces inform every identity, every meaning, in all their complexity, and the work of reading must necessarily attend with patience and rigour to both the broad and the fine distinctions, realizing all the while that every broadly defined difference is, itself, constituted through countless smaller gradations.

Turning from difference, we move to différance. The difference is not great, apparently. However, difference is not différance, even though the two have a structural relationship:

> we will designate as *différance* the movement according to which language, or any code, any system of referral in general, is constituted 'historically' as a weave of differences.
>
> Jacques Derrida (1982: 12)

The difference between the two is minimal and yet crucial. Différance is a neologism coined by Jacques Derrida. Derrida makes this differ from the more conventional 'difference' by spelling it with an 'a'. (It is common to find that critics speaking of différance maintain the 'a' but abandon the accent over the 'e'; I have retained the accent here merely to draw your attention more graphically to the difference between the two words.) He does so in order to acknowledge simultaneously that which differs (spacing) and that which defers (temporalization) as the condition of signification, meaning, ontology, or identity.

> An interval must separate the present from what it is not in order for the present to be itself, but this interval that constitutes it as present must,

by the same token, divide the present in and of itself, thereby also dividing, along with the present, everything that is thought on the basis of the
present, that is, in our metaphysical language, every being, and singularly
substance or the subject. In constituting itself, in dividing itself dynami-
cally, this interval is what might be called *spacing*, the becoming-space
of time or the becoming-time of space (*temporization*). And it is this
constitution of the present, as an 'originary' and irreducibly nonsimple
(and therefore, *stricto sensu*[1] nonoriginary) synthesis of marks, or traces
of retentions and protensions . . . that I propose to call . . . *différance*,
which (is) (simultaneously) spacing (and) temporization . . . Differences,
thus, are 'produced' – deferred – by *différance*.

Jacques Derrida (1982: 13)

The purpose immediately in Derrida's graphic emphasis is to point out that
there is that in writing, that, in the legible mark or trace, which escapes
aural comprehension ('a' in the French pronunciation of 'difference' sounding the same as 'e' in 'différence'). Any difference, Derrida asserts, is always
and only ever available as the result of the spatio-temporal structuring, as
a form of writing beyond the narrow sense of the term whereby meaning or
identity comes into being.

The difference between difference and 'différance' is graphic, thereby
marking or re-marking a certain inscribed iterable pulsation that displaces,
differs and defers any sense of originary or otherwise stable, fixable location.

You have noticed that this *a* is written or read, but cannot be heard. And
first off I insist upon the fact that any discourse – for example, ours, at
this moment – on this alteration, this graphic and grammatical aggression, implies an irreducible reference to the mute intervention of a written sign. The present participle of the verb *différer*, on which this noun
is modeled, ties together a configuration of concepts I hold to be systematic and irreducible, each one of which intervenes, or rather is accentu-
ated, at a decisive moment of the work. *First, différance* refers to the
(active *and* passive) movement that consists in deferring by means of
delay, delegation, reprieve, referral, detour, postponement, reserving. In
this sense, *différance* is not preceded by the originary and indivisible
unity of a present possibility that I could reserve, like an expenditure that
I would put off calculatedly or for reasons of economy. What defers
presence, on the contrary, is the very basis on which presence is
announced or desired in what represents it, its sign, its trace.

Jacques Derrida (1981a: 8)

The writing effect silently inscribes the spacing, the deferral and differenti-
ation. Moreover, it is not simply the case that writing is opposed to orality

in any simple sense, for Derrida employs this quasi-concept in order to expand in radical fashion any notion of textuality, writing and related notions beyond immediate notions of 'books', 'literature', and so on. Différance is the written weaving, the text-ile if we can put it like this, by which being is traced and produced, and which disrupts any access to the notion of a full or simple presence which the spoken word supposedly guarantees.

Différance is not an object, not some 'thing'; it is irreducible to any onto-logical determination. It is, rather, a process or motion by which one comes to comprehend being or consciousness as unique, self-present:

> one comes to posit presence – and specifically consciousness, the being beside itself of consciousness – no longer as the absolutely central form of Being but as a 'determination' and as an 'effect'. A determination or an effect within a system which is no longer that of presence but of *différance*, a system that no longer tolerates the opposition of activity and passivity, nor that of cause and effect, or of indetermination and determination, etc.
>
> Jacques Derrida (1982: 16)

Derrida extends the logic of différance to a radicalization of the compre-hension of being, drawing implicitly from the text of Martin Heidegger. Noting the specificity, the historicity or facticity, of beings as constituent in the thinking of the concept of Being, he then posits the notion of différance as that which makes possible any thinking of Being.

> Since Being has never had a 'meaning,' has never been thought or said as such, except by dissimulating itself in beings, then *différance*, in a certain and very strange way, (is) 'older' than the ontological difference or than the truth of Being. When it has this age it can be called the play of the trace. The play of the trace which no longer belongs to the horizon of Being, but whose play transports and encloses the meaning of Being: the play of the trace, or the *différance*, which has no meaning and is not. Which does not belong. There is no maintaining, and no depth to, this bottomless chessboard on which Being is put into play.
>
> Jacques Derrida (1982: 22)

Questions for further consideration

1. Is it possible to conceive an identity or meaning which is not determined by difference?
2. While Derrida's notion of *différance* might be assumed initially to be restricted to questions concerning phonetic and graphic manifestations of language – or,

perhaps more precisely, the immanence[2] of any graphic trace always already within and as the possibility of any phonetic communication – consider whether and in what ways the notion radically exceeds, and is therefore irreducible to, difference thought conventionally.

3. Is the notion of difference irreducible to the conventional logic of conceptualization?

Explanatory notes

1. *Sricto sensu*: strictly speaking, in the strictest sense.
2. *Immanence*: inherent, indwelling, within; that which pervades or dwells within as opposed to being transcendent.

Further reading

Attridge, Derek (1988), *Peculiar Language: Literature as Difference, from the Renaissance to James Joyce* (Ithaca, NY: Cornell University Press).

Deleuze, Gilles (1994), *Difference and Repetition*, trans. Paul Patton (London: Athlone Press).

Derrida, Jacques (1978), *Writing and Difference*, trans. Alan Bass (London: Routledge and Kegan Paul).

Derrida, Jacques (1982), 'Différance'. In *Margins of Philosophy*, trans. Alan Bass (Chicago, IL: University of Chicago Press), pp. 1–28.

Felman, Shoshana (1993), *What Does a Woman Want? Reading and Sexual Difference* (Baltimore, MD: Johns Hopkins University Press).

Irigaray, Luce (1993), *An Ethics of Sexual Difference*, trans. Carolyn Burke and Gillian C. Gill (Ithaca, NY: Cornell University Press).

DISCOURSE

A brief definition of *discourse* might be the work of specific language practice: that is, language as it is used by and within various constituencies (the law, medicine, the church, for example) for purposes to do with power relationships between people. However, while this definition comes some way towards delineating the work of discourse, discursive formations and discursive events, it does not adequately register the structural network – or 'sets of statements' – of language particular either to specific institutions or within historical epochs. The work of Michel Foucault[1] has drawn out the structural and historical processes of discursive activity. Foucault has taken the idea of discourse further than the identification of a language practice arising as a result of organizational or institutional forms in society, in his analysis of the ways in which discursive formations are active in the production, replication and dissemination of the power intrinsic to the various 'ideological state apparatuses', to borrow Louis Althusser's[2] phrase. More than merely an adjunct to forms of power embodied in institutions, language manifested in particular discourses is the articulation of that power, those politics, as so many imaginary and symbolic expressions. Foucault takes this further: for, rather than suggesting that there are specific discourses and then merely language (described below by Foucault as 'the broad types of discourse') as employed by individuals outside various institutional practices and discursive formations, human subjectivity and identity itself is produced out of various discursive formations as a result of the subject's entry into language always already shot through and informed by figurations and encryptions of power, politics, historical, cultural and ideological remainders organized through particular relationships and networks.

In this first citation, Michel Foucault argues that the possibility of a discourse on a particular subject does not depend on the attempted definition of a particular object or identity. Rather, a discursive structure arises at any particular historical moment as a result of the interaction between a constellation of codes and forms of address from different disciplines and fields of thought.

> The unity of discourses on madness would not be based upon the existence of the object 'madness', or the constitution of a single horizon of objectivity; it would be the interplay of rules that make possible the appearance of objects during a given period of time: objects that are shaped by measures of discrimination and repression, objects that are differentiated in daily practice, in law, in religious casuistry, in medical diagnosis, objects that are manifested in pathological descriptions, objects that are circumscribed by medical codes, practices, treatment, and care.
>
> Michel Foucault (1972: 33)

It is this interaction or interplay which gives the reader of Foucault an understanding of the ways in which bodies of knowledge are produced and developed in particular historical eras. Moreover, Foucault's analysis of discursive networks draws attention to the contexts which make such articulations possible.

> In direct contrast to the concerns associated with 'textuality', Foucault's use of the concept of discourse . . . is very much related to *context* . . . Foucault's concept of a discourse . . . enables us to understand how *what*

is said fits into a network that has its own history and conditions of existence.

Michèle Barrett (1991: 126)

For Foucault, discursive networks serve to articulate social and cultural relations between power and knowledge. Here, the efficacy of discourse or, as Foucault has it elsewhere, a discursive network, is presented through a recognition of its strategic mobility.

Indeed, it is in discourse that power and knowledge are joined together. And for this very reason, we must conceive discourse as a series of discontinuous segments whose tactical function is neither uniform nor stable. To be more precise, we must not imagine a world of discourse divided between accepted discourse and excluded discourse, or between the dominant discourse and the dominated one; but as a multiplicity of discursive elements that can come into play in various strategies. It is this distribution that we must reconstruct, with the things said and those concealed, the enunciations required and those forbidden, that it comprises; with the variants and different effects – according to who is speaking, his position of power, the institutional context in which he happens to be situated – that it implies, and with the shifts and re-utilizations of identical formulas for contrary objectives that it also includes.

Michel Foucault (1990: 100)

From this understanding of the ways in which discourse operates it is all too easy to see how,

far from being a type of conversation between equals, the discursive situation is more usually like the unequal relation between colonizer and colonized, oppressor and oppressed . . . discourse often puts one interlocutor above another . . .

Edward Said (1983: 48–9)

This power of discourse articulated from a specific location, such as a university or medical institution, asserts itself not only through its access to specialized forms of knowledge (which, in turn, reassert discursive power; for Foucault, the relationship between power and knowledge is reciprocally and mutually re-enforcing and generative), but also through the rhetorical capability of proving one's own point and disproving others'.

Rhetoric started from and ended with the running together of the forms and the subjects in a continuous utterance – in, exactly, a discourse. It is within this perspective that we can consider discourse as indicating the articulation of language over units greater than the sentence. The major divisions of rhetoric accomplish just such suprasentential[3] division: *exordium, narratio, argumentatio, refutatio, peroratio* [4] (Curtius 1953, 70). A particular set of articulations will produce a field of discursivity – the site of the possibility of proof and disproof . . .

Colin MacCabe (1985: 82–3)

The rhetorical work of discourse is also emphasized by Foucault:

> in the most general, and vaguest way, [discourse] denoted a group of verbal performances; and by discourse, then, I meant that which was produced (perhaps all that was produced) by the groups of signs. But I also meant a group of acts of formulation, a series of sentences or propositions. Lastly . . . discourse is constituted by a group of sequences of signs, in so far as they are statements, that is, in so far as they can be assigned particular modalities of existence. And if I succeed in showing . . . that the law of such a series is precisely what I have so far called a *discursive formation*, if I succeed in showing that this discursive formation really is the principle of dispersion and redistribution, not of formulations, not of sentences, not of propositions, but of statements[5] . . . the term discourse can be defined as the group of statements that belong to a single system of formation . . .

Michel Foucault (1972: 107)

However, it is important to speak not merely of 'discourse' but, following Foucault, of discursive formations, in order to see, as accurately as possible, the ways in which forms of articulation concerning specific subjects (Foucault has addressed, amongst other topics, sexuality, madness, imprisonment, knowledge) operate within a culture at given historical instances.

> Rather than being identified by their reference to essential objects (such as madness), by a style of descriptive statements (such as clinical discourse), by the permanence of concepts used (as in grammar), by the persistence of themes (as in political economy), a discursive formation can be said to exist when there are regular relations between its objects, style of description, concepts and thematic choices.
>
> Foucault identifies the systematicity of relations between different elements of discourse . . . Rules of formation are conditions of existence for a particular discourse . . . They constitute a system that enables statements to become intelligible or significant . . . Yet the rules of regulation of discourse are not only limits that enable the truth to be told, but are also constraints. They govern what may be said, in what mode . . . what

is considered valid, what is considered appropriate to be circulated in an educational system or another public setting, and who may say what.

Jon Simons (1995: 24)

Discourse must be understood then not merely as a neutral tool concerned with the assertion of objective veracity, but as a structurally interactive flow serving, inescapably, a political or ideological function, even though it makes truth claims in order to mystify its ideological functions:

> the will to exercise dominant control in society and history has discovered a way to clothe, disguise, rarefy, and wrap itself systematically in the language of truth, discipline, rationality, utilitarian value, and knowledge. And this language, in its naturalness, authority, professionalism, assertiveness, and antitheoretical directness, Foucault has called *discourse* . . . The power of discourse is that it is at once the object of struggle and the tool by which the struggle is conducted. In penology, for example, the juridical language identifying the delinquent and the intellectual schema embodied in the prison's physical structure are instruments controlling felons as well as powers . . . to keep for oneself and deny it to others. The goal of discourse is to maintain itself and, more important, to manufacture its material continually . . .

Edward Said (1983: 216)

Questions for further consideration

1. Is a 'pure' discourse possible, or are discourses always contaminated by other languages, forms of knowledge, modalities of articulation?
2. To what extent is the human subject constituted by various discursive formations?
3. In what ways might the novel as a genre be considered as a field or network of discursive activity? How do novels serve in the reinforcement of discursive norms?

Explanatory and bibliographical notes

1. Michel Foucault (*b*.1926–*d*.1984): *The Archaeology of Knowledge and the Discourse on Language* (1972); *The Order of Things: An Archaeology of the Human Sciences* (1973); *The History of Sexuality, Volume I: An Introduction* (1990).
2. Louis Althusser (*b*.1918–*d*.1990): *Reading Capital* (1970); *Lenin and Philosophy and Other Essays* (1971); *For Marx* (1977).
3. *Suprasentential*: above or beyond the order of sentences or propositions.

4. *Exordium, narratio, argumentatio, refutatio, peroratio*: beginning, introduction or preface; narrative or story; argumentation or proof; refutation; conclusion or final part of speech. See Ernst Curtius, *European Literature and the Latin Middle Ages* (New York: Pantheon Books, 1953).

5. Shortly before this passage, Foucault has occasion to define 'statement' in the following fashion: 'We will call *statement* the modality of existence proper to [a] group of signs: a modality that allows it to be something more than a series of traces, something more than a succession of marks on a substance, something more than a mere object made by a human being; a modality that allows it to be in relation with a domain of objects, to prescribe a definite position to any possible subject, to be situated among other verbal performances, and to be endowed with a repeatable materiality' (1972: 107).

Further reading

Foucault, Michel (1972), *The Archaeology of Knowledge and the Discourse on Language*, trans. A. M. Sheridan Smith (New York: Pantheon Books).

Genette, Gérard (1980), *Narrative Discourse: An Essay on Method*, trans. Jane E. Lewin, Foreword by Jonathan Culler (Ithaca, NY: Cornell University Press).

Hennessy, Rosemary (1993), *Materialist Feminism and the Politics of Discourse* (New York: Routledge).

Simons, Jon (1995), *Foucault and the Political* (London: Routledge).

Smith, Anna Marie (1994), *New Right Discourse on Race and Sexuality: Britain 1968–1990* (Cambridge: Cambridge University Press).

EVENT

To rethink the *event* is to call into question commonsense notions of that which happens, and, in addition, notions of structure, space, articulation, temporality and all manner of architectonic[1] arrangement generally. Such consideration in a number of fields directs us away from the restrictive logic of epistemological models reliant on, for example, semantic and ontological assumptions governed by, and generative of, seamless, finite, complete meanings and identities, the elements of which are assumed to be organically commensurate within their objects or conceptualizations as though there were some possibility of undifferentiated entirety, whether at a given moment or across time.

The radical thinking of events in critical discourse is then best perceived perhaps, at least initially, as involving processes of transformation or translation which cannot be anticipated or described by any programme or method, whether the discursive context is literary or architectural, philosophical or political, as can be seen from the citations. On the one hand, one can expect the possibility that an event might occur without being able to define or account for the singularity of the event's manifestation; on the other hand, one can narrate the event after the fact, but it is as much the case that narration determines both the specificity of the event, its uniqueness, and also its linguistic iterability.

What is implied in each of the remarks and extracts is the idea that the event is more a 'quasi-concept' than a concept as such. That is to say, while the notion of the event appears to nominate or ontologize that which takes place, thereby providing an identity for forms or manifestations of interaction, it has to be admitted that the event of reading and the event of representing a political or historical moment are both singular even though, arguably, they share aspects in common. What this 'in common' names is, again, that act of translation drawing our attention towards the work of language and narrativization, rather than any intrinsic, discernible quality separable from any perception or recounting. It is thus the singularity and the unpredictability that disturbs any possible purity in the identity of the event *qua* concept. Events will always necessarily differ from each other and, in saying this, there can be seen in operation a certain performativity – an unpredictable or singular event if you will – in the conceptual or general structure of 'the event'; the attempt objectively to define an 'event' is ruined by what might be called the event-process itself.

Derek Attridge addresses reading as the possibility of an event. The dimension of reading as event is situated by Attridge in its response to the singularity and otherness of the text, which is also, in its uniqueness, understood as an event.

> The way remains open . . . for the reading of *any* literary text . . . in an attempt to track down, or at least make evident the tracks of, the 'literary' moment or movement. These encounters with texts would not be 'readings' in any conventional sense of the term . . . [They would, instead, be] events of responding as responsibly as possible to the event of the text, answerable to the uniqueness of the text and thus producing their own uniqueness . . . The responsibility involved in such an event of response is a responsibility to the other . . . and at the same time a responsibility to the future, since it involves the struggle to create openings within which the other can appear beyond the scope of any of our programs and predictions, can come to transform what we know or think we know. But responsibility . . . is not something we simply take: we find ourselves summoned, confronted by an undecidability which is also always an opportunity and a demand, a chance and a risk.
>
> Derek Attridge (1995: 118)

An aspect of the event to emerge here is its absolute unpredictability, an aspect already discussed above. Such an unpredictability involves the possibility of transformation which no method or programme of reading can control or determine.

The process of transformation is spoken of in the following citation:

> events are incorporeal transformations which are expressed in language but attributed to bodies and states of affairs. In so far as language serves to express such incorporeal transformations, it does not simply represent the world but intervenes in it . . . Event attributions do not simply describe or report pre-existing events, they help to actualize particular events in the social field. The manner in which a given occurrence is described determines it as a particular kind of event. That is why politics frequently takes the form of struggle over the appropriate description of events.
>
> Paul Patton (2000: 27–8)

Here we are given to understand how an event is not simply something that takes place 'in the real world' and is subsequently reported. Language, for Paul Patton, partakes in the determination of an event, and thus, in responding to an event, opens the possibility for other transformations and responses to take place, in a manner akin to that described in the structural dimension of reading spoken of by Attridge, above.

An event is therefore active, a process; it takes time. To address the example of architecture as event, the event is read also as not so much a place as what takes place.

> Architecture is as much about the events that take place in spaces as about the spaces themselves . . . the static notions of form and function long favored by architectural discourse need to be replaced by attention to the actions that occur inside and around buildings – to the movement of bodies, to activities, to aspirations; in short, to the properly social and political dimension of architecture. Moreover, the cause-and-effect relationship sanctified by modernism, by which form follows function (or vice versa) needs to be abandoned in favor of promiscuous collisions of programs and spaces, in which the terms intermingle, combine and implicate one another in the production of a new architectural reality.
>
> Bernard Tschumi (1994b: 13)

Raising the question of the event therefore involves one in a comprehension of certain structural dimensions involving space and temporality. The example of the architectural event is particularly forceful because it forces us to abandon the reading of architectural space in purely static or monumental terms. The event-structure, if this phrase is appropriate, serves to undo the notions of order and presence, or propriety, and of architectonics that inform conventional thinking on architectural form.

That an event takes time means that there is no pure present moment. Here Deleuze marks this traversal between the 'what-is-going-to-happen' and the 'what-has-just-happened' as an endless disorganization of any presence or present.

> Just as the present measures the temporal realization of the event – the event in turn . . . has no present. It rather retreats and advances in two directions at once, being the perpetual object of a double question: What is going to happen? What has just happened? The agonizing aspect of the pure event is that it is always and at the same time something which has just happened and something about to happen . . . the living present happens and brings about the event. But the event nonetheless retains an eternal truth . . . The event is that no one ever dies, but has always just died or is always going to die . . . Each event is the smallest time . . . because it is divided into proximate past and imminent future . . . But it is also the longest time . . . because it is endlessly subdivided . . .
>
> Gilles Deleuze (1990: 63)

The endless subdivision, the doubling and division of an infinitude of differences without presence that constitute an event suggest that '*Events "take place." And Again. And Again*' (Bernard Tschumi 1994a: 160). The apparent transparency of this statement belies the radical complexity of the provisional definition of the operation of events. For, if we accept Deleuze's analysis of an event as an endless seriality of instances always about to happen or always having just happened but never happening as such, then the last citation enacts this seriality through an event-ness of iterability caught in the process of writing, while implicitly resisting an ontology of the event. Thus writing affirms as it performs its subject without fixing that subject into a finite object or meaning.

To go back to the beginning, though: speaking of an event does not amount to an event.

> That which occurs, and thereby occurs only once, for the first and last time, is always something more or less than its possibility. One can talk endlessly about its possibility without ever coming close to the thing itself in its coming. It may be, then, that the order is other . . . and that only the coming of the event allows, after the event [*après coup*], *perhaps*, what it will previously have made possible to be thought. . . . Among the immense consequences of this strong logical necessity, we

must reckon with those concerning nothing less than revelation, truth and the event.

Jacques Derrida (1997: 18)

Questions for further consideration

1. How might Bernard Tschumi's consideration of architecture as event be rethought so as to address narrative?
2. Consider the possible relationship between Gilles Deleuze's discussion of the event's temporality in relation to the matters of responsibility and undecidability informing any act of reading described by Derek Attridge.
3. Consider the relationship between spatial and temporal concerns addressed in the understanding of the event.

Explanatory note

1. *Architectonic*: the systematic organization of knowledge.

Further reading

Deleuze, Gilles (1990), *The Logic of Sense*, trans. Mark Lester, with Charles Stivale, ed. Constantin V. Boundas (New York: Columbia University Press).
Tschumi, Bernard (1994), *Architecture and Disjunction* (Cambridge, MA: MIT Press).
Patton, Paul (2000), *Deleuze and the Political* (London: Routledge).

GENDER

Gender denotes the cultural constitution of femininity or masculinity, the notions concerning what is 'appropriate' to either gender, and the ways in which these serve ideologically to maintain gendered identities. In much sociological and feminist thought, gender is defined against biological sex. It represents the socially acceptable, and socially acquired, forms of being either male or female. Gender might then include everything a person does, from the clothes s/he wears, to choices of leisure activity, and from career and education to tone of voice. The notion of gender argues that a person may have male sex, but may have feminine attributes in relation to the cultural norms of his society, and vice versa, a female person may exhibit masculine traits. It provides grounds for arguing against essentialist[1] articulations of selfhood and sex. Gender therefore describes the ways in which masculinity and femininity (the performance of gender, as opposed to the biology of sex) serve ideologically to maintain a particular status quo in society at large. More recently, the binary opposition underlying this kind of definition (the opposition between biology and performance) has been attacked and dismantled by critics working in queer theory, and particularly by Judith Butler,[2] who argues against the priority given to biology as essence under-pinning the very idea that gender is performative. The phrase *gender parody*, referred to below, has been deployed by Judith Butler and refers to the manner in which transvestism or 'drag' can expose the inevitably artifi-cial and restrictive nature of gender identity.

Having said all of this, the only thing we can say for sure, at least to begin, is that

> *gender* is a much contested concept, as slippery as it is indispensable, but a site of unease rather than agreement.
>
> David Glover and Cora Kaplan (2000: ix)

In this contested condition, gender, an apparently straightforward term, comes to appear as problematic as any of the other terms and figures explored in the present volume. The slipperiness is doubtless registered in the fact that, while gender is irreducible to one's corporeal existence, confu-sion exists precisely over precisely what is identifiable by the name 'gender', and that this confusion is amplified, furthermore, by a further semantic confusion: of that between sex and gender.

> [O]ne can speak of the male sex or the female sex, but one can also talk about masculinity and femininity and not necessarily be implying anything about anatomy or physiology. Thus, while sex and gender seem to common sense to be practically synonymous, and in everyday life to be inextricably bound together . . . the two realms (sex and gender) are not at all inevitably bound in anything like a one-to-one relationship, but each may go in its quite independent way.
>
> Robert Stoller (1968: xiii)

Thinking gender distinct from sex makes possible the reading of gender in other ways, according to particular politics of representation and definition:

> the notion of gender as sexual difference . . . [has] become a limitation, something of a liability to feminist thought . . . [gender is better under-stood as] a symbolic system or system of meanings, that correlates sex to cultural contents according to social values and hierarchies.
>
> Teresa de Lauretis (1987: 1, 5)

The reading of gender as socially constructed has been of great importance within feminist critique, though it has not gone uncontested.

> Central to . . . debates [on gender and race] is a reworking of the classic nature/nurture distinction. Recent work in feminist theory and race theory has exposed the need for a thorough confrontation with the concept of history that is often invoked by those who argue against the view that gender or race is grounded in some unchanging, ahistorical, determinist category (such as innate characteristics, or a feminine or racial essence). The suggestion that race or gender is in some sense socially constructed, culturally mediated, or historically constituted, has served to combat racist or sexist assumptions that traditionally have been used to constrain the behavior and potential of certain groups of individuals. Presupposing some timeless or eternal essence has advanced and substantiated the privileges of other groups.
>
> Tina Chanter (2001: 11)

One of the 'other groups' to have benefited historically and materially through the assumption and construction of gender as 'timeless', 'eternal', or 'natural' is patriarchy:

> patriarchy is a material practice through which gender is naturalized in order to bring down the cost of labor power of women and in so doing increase the rate of profit for capitalists – as is so aptly demonstrated by the overwhelming numbers of women now employed in wage labor globally.
>
> Teresa Ebert (1996: 90)

It is important to note here that patriarchy is not merely a cultural or ideological category but a power structure implicated closely – albeit perhaps in more or less occluded ways – with the manifestations of economic oppression and inequality. The material conditions maintained through the promotion and maintenance of gender codings extends, through repressive patriarchal practices, to the containment of sexuality as heteronormative, with the family as its ideal economic expression.

> Heterosexuality depends upon the assumption that sex differences are binary opposites and the simultaneous equation of this binary sex difference with gender. The naturalizing function of this equation contributes to the expressive model of the individual in that the opposition of the sexes is taken to be substantive, preceding social and historical bodies as an essence which the core of the self manifests. In disguising itself as a law of nature, this 'fiction' regulates the sexual field it purports to

describe ... The fiction of heterosexual coherence is one of the most firmly entrenched and invisible anchors for the ideology of individualism ... The heterosexual and patriarchal 'family cell' ... provides sexuality with permanent support. It is the site where systems of sexuality, gender, and alliance are articulated ... The four specific mechanisms of knowledge and power centering on sex which Foucault targets – the hysteriazation of women's bodies, the pedagogization of children's sex, the socialization of the couple as a reproductive unit, and the psychiatrization of 'perverse' pleasure – all reinforce a naturalized equation of sexuality and reproduction which assumes a heterosexual patriarchal gender system.

Rosemary Hennessy (1993: 88)

Gender, we might say, is 'produced' in various imaginary ways for material purposes and resulting, in turn, in both material and imaginary effects. At the same time, though, it can be said as well that:

Gender ought not be conceived merely as the cultural inscription of meaning on a pregiven sex ... gender must also designate the very apparatus of production whereby the sexes themselves are established.

Judith Butler (1990: 7)

Clearly, then, if something which is constructed and which constructs can be put to work for oppressive or marginalizing purposes, then that which functions in this constructed and constructing fashion (which perhaps, we might suggest, is textual) rather than being merely natural, essential or given, can equally be a source of cultural contestation, resistance and even affirmation.

In this sense, *gender* is not a noun, but neither is it a set of free-floating attributes, for we have seen that the substantive effect of gender is performatively produced and compelled by the regulatory practices of gender coherence. Hence, within the inherited discourse of the metaphysics of substance, gender proves to be performative – that is, constituting the identity it is purported to be. In this sense, gender is always a doing, though not a doing by a subject who might be said to preexist the deed.

Judith Butler (1990: 24–5)

Gender as a site of ideological contest is recognized in the next quotation not only as an abstract principle but as an historically grounded series of material effects and practices:

representations of gender [in mid-Victorian Britain] were part of the system of interdependent images in which various ideologies became accessible to individual men and women. In another sense, however . . . representations of gender constituted one of the sites on which ideological systems were simultaneously constructed and contested; as such, the representations of gender . . . were themselves contested images, the sites at which struggles for authority occurred, as well as the locus of assumptions used to underwrite the very authority that authorized these struggles . . .
. . . the unevenness within the construction and deployment of mid-Victorian representations of gender, and representations of women in particular . . . not only characterizes the conservative ideological work of these representations, but . . . also allowed for the emergence in the 1850s of a genuinely oppositional voice.

Mary Poovey (1989: 2, 4)

The historical struggle for meaning is an indication that gender identity is irreducible to any fixed semantic or ideological horizon. That there is no one stable gender identity does not mean that there is no meaning for gender but that gender identities are open to transformation, to reading and rewriting, an openness most visibly foregrounded through the matter of trans-sexualism.

The trans-sexual represents the overcoming or blurring of gender-identities and the collapse of the classical notion of identity as a whole.

Rosi Braidotti (1991: 123)

Codes, once comprehended in their cultural–grammatical functioning, can be appropriated and effectively translated, destabilized, though the difficulty in so doing is marked by the fact that the performativity of gender is, for some, pre-subjective: what I consider 'my' gender is an effect of my interpellation as a social subject. Importantly, however, the reading of gender can take place beyond any mere binary opposition, either of male/female or sex/gender, about which Judith Butler has the following to say:

if gender is the cultural meanings that the sexed body assumes, then a gender cannot be said to follow from a sex in any one way. Taken to its logical limit, the sex/gender distinction suggests a radical discontinuity between sexed bodies and culturally constructed genders. Assuming for the moment the stability of binary sex, it does not follow that the construction of 'men' will accrue exclusively to the bodies of males or that 'women' will interpret only female bodies. Further, even if the sexes appear to be unproblematically binary in their morphology and constitution . . . there is no reason to assume that genders ought also to remain as two. The presumption of a binary gender system implicitly retains the belief in a mimetic relation of gender to sex whereby gender mirrors sex or is otherwise restricted by it. When the constructed status of gender is theorized as radically independent of sex, gender itself becomes a free-floating artifice, with the consequence that *man* and *masculine* might just as easily signify a female body as a male one, and *woman* and *feminine* a male body as easily as a female one.

This radical splitting of the gendered subject poses yet another set of problems. Can we refer to a 'given' sex or a 'given' gender without first inquiring into how sex and/or gender is given, through what means? And what is 'sex' anyway? Is it natural, anatomical, chromosomal, or hormonal, and how is a feminist critic to assess the scientific discourses which purport to establish such 'facts' for us? . . . If the immutable character of sex is contested, perhaps this construct called 'sex' was as culturally constructed as gender; indeed, perhaps it was always already gender, with the consequence that the distinction between sex and gender turns out to be no distinction at all.

Judith Butler (1990: 6–7)

Butler cleverly and, to my mind, convincingly, takes the sex/gender distinction and irreversibly transforms the reading of the former of the two terms from an understanding of the latter as complexly encoded, whereby 'sex' now comes to be comprehended as being as much a construct as gender, as that which is written on the body rather than being the truth of that body.

There are those critics, however, who are wary of problems that have arisen as a result of the privileging of gender within feminist thought:

with gender as the central concept in feminist thinking, epistemology is flattened out in such a way that we lose sight of the complex and multiple ways in which the subject and object of possible experience are constituted. The flattening effect is multiplied when one considers that gender is often solely related to white men. There's no inquiry into the knowing subject beyond the fact of being a 'woman'. But what is a 'woman' or a 'man' for that matter?

Norma Alarcón (1990: 361)

Another problem perceived in the privileging of gender is its relationship to sex, and what is described below as the 'obfuscation of bodies'. Clearly, while the significance of gender, specifically to feminist studies, and more generally, to matters of identity politics, is incontestable, the focus on gender has, in turn, drawn the critic's attention to other equally urgent lines of inquiry.

> Recent feminist theory . . . [has] gone some way toward redressing the obfuscation of bodies, realizing that . . . to focus on the constructed or symbolic meanings of self identity, is to recast the Cartesian[3] privilege of mind over body. Here, gender is construed as a psychological or mental interpretation of physical or material realities, or as an active or voluntary choice of traits that were previously seen as prescribed by our bodily nature. But if the emphasis of gender over sex alleviated the problem of determinism, by conceiving gender as malleable and changeable, rather than as resulting from our inherent and unchanging natures, it created new problems. It papered over, rather than thinking through, the relationship between sex and gender.
>
> Tina Chanter (2001: 12)

Questions for further consideration

1. What agency, might we hypothesize, does the subject acquire if gender is considered as a culturally determined 'apparatus of production', rather than being merely an inscription?
2. If Teresa Ebert's assertion that 'patriarchy is a material practice through which gender is naturalized' is correct, how do we (a) determine the modalities of that naturalization, and (b) read 'patriarchy' as, itself, a mystified because naturalized gendered position?
3. Consider the ways in which the unease generated by gender's slipperiness is a sign of the potentially affirmative or productive force of gender mobility. What other disturbances might the mutability of gender effect from within normative cultural models?

Explanatory and bibliographical notes

1. *Essentialism* generally refers to a belief that there are 'real essences', such as human nature, or that sexuality is given, is 'natural' or intrinsic, rather than learned, acquired or otherwise socially or culturally constructed behaviour. An essentialist view of culture would subscribe to the position that particular values, beliefs or habits belong to the essence of that culture: for example, the idea that freedom is an American value, or, as in the eighteenth century, that the term 'Oriental' was in some manner synonymous with sensuousness or barbarity. At once ludicrous *and* highly dangerous in its more common manifestations, essentialist thought takes seriously notions such as people of African origin being good at sports, the Chinese being good at mathematics, or Jews having heightened financial acumen.

2. Judith Butler (*b*.1956–): *Gender Trouble: Feminism and the Subversion of Identity* (1990); *Bodies that Matter: On the Discursive Limits of 'Sex'* (1993); *Excitable Speech: A Politics of the Performative* (1997).

3. 'Cartesian' refers to the work of René Descartes (*b*.1596–*d*.1650): *Meditations and Other Metaphysical Writings*, trans. and Introduction by Desmond M. Clarke (London: Penguin, 1998). Specifically, this adjective is commonly employed to refer to the mind/body dualism by which Descartes comprehends the nature of Being. In a citation on the 'subject' by Mikkel Borch-Jacobsen (below, in the entry on 'Subject/ivity'), the phrase 'Cartesian Cogito' refers to Descartes's well-known axiom, *Cogito ergo sum*: I think, therefore I am.

Further reading

Butler, Judith (1990), *Gender Trouble: Feminism and the Subversion of Identity* (London: Routledge).

Deutscher, Penelope (1997), *Yielding Gender: Feminism, Deconstruction, and the History of Philosophy* (London: Routledge).

Glover, David and Cora Kaplan (eds) (2000), *Genders* (London: Routledge).

Lauretis, Teresa de (1987), *Technologies of Gender: Essays on Theory, Film, and Fiction* (Basingstoke: Macmillan).

Stoller, Robert J. (1968), *Sex and Gender: On the Development of Masculinity and Femininity* (London: Hogarth Press).

HEGEMONY

Hegemony emerges in its now commonly accepted sense from the writings of Antonio Gramsci. It refers to the cultural, political and intellectual processes related to dominant economic practices and activity within a given society by which domination of one class is achieved over another (or others). This is effected chiefly, though by no means exclusively, through non-coercive means, such as the dissemination of forms of knowledge, which constitutes and constructs socially normative subject positions, through institutionally authorized means and discourses such as those of education, the law, journalism and the media, religion, or, in a more diffuse manner, through the very idea of a normative or dominant culture itself.

(1) The education system; (2) newspapers; (3) artistic writers and popular writers; (4) the theatre and sound films; (5) radio; (6) public meetings of all kinds, including religious ones; (7) the relations of 'conversation' between the more educated and less educated strata of the population . . . (8) the local dialects . . . Since the process of formation, spread and development of

a unified national language occurs through a whole complex of molecular processes, it helps to be aware of the entire process as a whole in order to be able to intervene actively in it with the best possible results ... if the intervention is 'rational', it will be organically tied to tradition, and this is of no small importance to the economy of culture ... Every time the question of language surfaces, in one way or another, it means that a series of other problems are coming to the fore: the formation and enlargement of the governing class, the need to establish more intimate and secure relationships between the governing groups and the national–popular mass, in other words to reorganize the cultural hegemony.

Antonio Gramsci (1988: 356–7)

Social control is achieved in part via ruling hegemonic groups or what Gramsci terms collectively 'civil society', as a result of those groups deploying knowledge, information and ideologically situated 'values' so as to convince subaltern groups of the ethical or moral truth of such views or systems of organization.

Undoubtedly the fact of hegemony presupposes that account be taken of the interests and the tendencies of the groups over which hegemony is exercised, and that a certain compromise equilibrium be formed – in other words, that the leading group should make sacrifices of an economic–corporate kind. But there is also no doubt that such sacrifices and such a compromise cannot touch the essential; for though hegemony is ethico-political, it must also be economic, must necessarily be based on the decisive function exercised by the leading group in the decisive nucleus of economic activity.

Antonio Gramsci (1988: 211–12)

Gramsci stresses hegemony as dynamic (what he calls a 'continuous process of formation and superseding of unstable equilibria'), the process and development of political social control in the domination of certain groups by others, rather than emphasizing more static social and economic relationships.

What we can do, for the moment, is to fix two major superstructural 'levels': the one that can be called 'civil society', that is the ensemble of organisms commonly called 'private', and the 'political society' or 'the State'. These two levels correspond on the one hand to the function of 'hegemony' which the dominant group exercises throughout society and on the other hand to that of 'direct domination' or command exercised through the 'State' and 'juridical' government.

Antonio Gramsci (1971: 12)

Rather than merely positing a critique of ruling-class interests, hegemonic analysis for Gramsci would stress forms of interaction between social groups and classes. The so-called 'post-Marxist' work of Ernesto Laclau and Chantal Mouffe[1] has engaged in a radical rethinking and extension of Gramsci's articulation. Here, Laclau and Mouffe trace a brief history of the notion:

> even in its humble origin in Russian Social Democracy, where it is called upon to cover a limited area of political effects, the concept of 'hegemony' already alludes to a kind of *contingent* intervention required by the crisis or collapse of what would have been a 'normal' historical development. Later, with Leninism,[2] it is a keystone in the new form of political calculation required by the contingent 'concrete situations' in which the class struggle occurs in the age of imperialism. Finally, with Gramsci, the term acquires a new type of centrality that transcends its tactical or strategic uses: 'hegemony' becomes the key concept in understanding the very unity existing in a concrete social formation. Each of these extensions of the term, however, was accompanied by an expansion of what we could provisionally call a 'logic of the contingent'.
>
> Ernesto Laclau and Chantal Mouffe (1985: 7)

Clearly, as radical political praxis and its discourse develop, so an understanding of the history of the concept is necessary as the concept becomes both more nuanced and more significant in any effective critique of social structure. This 'history' is also remarked elsewhere.

> Lenin saw imperialism as a structural stage in the evolution of the modern state. He imagined a necessary and linear historical progression from the first forms of the modern European state to the nation-state and then to the imperialist state. At each stage in this development the state had to invent new means of constructing popular consensus, and thus the imperialist state had to find a way to incorporate the multitude and its spontaneous forms of class struggle within its ideological state structures; it had to transform the multitude into a people. This analysis is the initial political articulation of the concept of hegemony that would later become central to Gramsci's thought.
>
> Michael Hardt and Antonio Negri (2000: 232–3)

At this juncture, it might be useful to state the salient features of hegemony. As a useful summary, it can be said that

> hegemony is the formulation and elaboration of a conception of the world that has been transformed into the accepted and 'normal' ensemble of

ideas and beliefs that interpret and define the world. Such a process is immediately political, for such a transformation cannot be accomplished without the people viewed as a social force. Hegemony is thus, in a very real and concrete sense, the moment of philosophy as politics and the moment of politics as philosophy . . . if hegemony is constituted by the unity of politics and philosophy, then it must also follow that hegemony implies the unity of philosophy and history, for 'concrete action' and the 'transformation of reality' (which are the object of politics) presuppose a social reality and a conception of the world that are anchored within 'time and space' . . . to Gramsci history is the history of *egemonia* [hegemony] – that is, the history of the unity of philosophy and politics, thought and action.

Benedetto Fontana (1993: 20–1)

In this sense, all history is understood as a series of successive, though not necessarily progressive, social, cultural and ideological structures determining historical reality. Furthermore,

hegemony is defined by Gramsci as intellectual and moral leadership . . . whose principal constituting elements are consent and persuasion. A social group or class can be said to assume a hegemonic role to the extent that it articulates and proliferates throughout society cultural and ideological belief systems whose teachings are accepted as universally valid by the general population. Ideology, culture, philosophy, and their 'organizers' – the intellectuals – are thus intrinsic to the notion of hegemony. Since, to Gramsci, reality is perceived, and knowledge is acquired, through moral, cultural, and ideological 'prisms' or 'filters' by means of which society acquires form and meaning, hegemony necessarily implies the creation of a particular structure of knowledge and a particular system of values . . . Hegemony is thus conceived as the vehicle whereby the dominant social groups establish a system of 'permanent consent' that legitimates a prevailing social order by encompassing a complex network of mutually reinforcing and interwoven ideas affirmed and articulated by intellectuals.

Benedetto Fontana (1993: 140–1)

Yet, it should not be thought that the notion of hegemony can be comprehended as operating in some more or less coherent or uncontested fashion.

Nonetheless, the entire construction rests upon an ultimately incoherent conception, which is unable fully to overcome the dualism of classical Marxism. For Gramsci, even though the diverse social elements have a merely relational identity – achieved through articulatory practices – there must always be a *single* unifying principle in every hegemonic formation, and this can only be a fundamental class. Thus two principles of the social order – the unicity of the unifying principle, and its necessary class character – are not the contingent result of hegemonic struggle, but the necessary structural framework within which every struggle occurs. Class hegemony is not a wholly practical result of struggle, but has an ultimate ontological foundation. The economic base may not assure the ultimate victory of the working class, since this depends upon its capacity for hegemonic leadership. However, a failure in the hegemony of the working class can only be followed by a reconstitution of bourgeois hegemony, so that in the end, political struggle is still a zero-sum game among classes. This is the inner essentialist core which continues to be present in Gramsci's thought, setting a limit to the deconstructive logic of hegemony.

Ernesto Laclau and Chantal Mouffe (1985: 69)

It might be suggested that hegemonic maintenance relies on and requires strategic incoherence and disorganization for its efficacy. Laclau and Mouffe clearly seek to engage with Gramsci in a manner that opens the latter's valuable comprehension of social formation to a more mobile conceptualization – what is termed here the 'deconstructive logic of hegemony' – one which, while not seeking to reduce the contradictions at work, none the less makes available a more widespread and therefore efficacious understanding of hegemony, at least in principle, in radical ways, connecting both to material and 'textual' or discursive praxes.

Working to extend Gramsci's elaboration of the concept of hegemony, Laclau sees hegemony not as the imposition of a pregiven set of ideas but as 'something that emerges from the political interaction of groups'; it is not simply the domination by an elite, but instead is a process of ongoing struggle that constitutes the social. Hegemonic struggle requires the identification of what Laclau calls 'floating signifiers', those signifiers that are open to continual contestation and articulation to radically different political projects. 'Democracy', in his view, is a key example of a floating signifier – its meaning essentially ambiguous as a consequence of its history and widespread circulation. To hegemonize a content for 'democracy' would require a fixing (always provisional) of its meaning. Indeed, the open nature of the social and the very possibility of hegemonic struggle stem from the impossibility of total fixity. As Laclau reminds us, it is 'urgent' that progressive intellectuals understand the logic of hegemony and the nature of hegemonic struggle (which the neoconservative right has mastered so well in recent years), and that they develop their own hegemonic strategies.

Lynn Worsham and Gary A. Olson (1999: 130)

As this citation makes apparent, the work of Laclau and Mouffe does not amount to a 'retreat' into linguistic formalism or excess, as has been claimed, but there takes place a necessary recognition of the extent to which social power is a fluid, textual phenomenon. In fact, as a result of this recognition, we can remark that

> hegemony is . . . a broader category than ideology: it *includes* ideology, but is not reducible to it. A ruling group or class may secure consent to its power by ideological means; but it may also do so by, say, altering the tax system in ways favourable to groups whose support it needs, or creating a layer of relatively affluent, and thus somewhat politically quiescent, workers. Or hegemony may take political rather than economic forms: the parliamentary system in Western democracies is a crucial aspect of such power, since it fosters the illusion of self-government on the part of the populace.
> . . .
> Hegemony, then, is not just some successful kind of ideology, but may be discriminated into its various ideological, cultural, political and economic aspects . . . hegemony is also carried in cultural, political and economic forms – in non-discursive practices as well as in rhetorical utterances.
>
> Terry Eagleton (1991: 112–13)

Hegemony is thus at work in both linguistic and textual structures and also, importantly, in and through concrete institutions and the lived relations of individuals and groups of people within societies. For the reasons outlined immediately above, it may also be stated that

> the question of hegemony is always the question of a new cultural order. Hegemony is not a state of grace which is installed forever. It's not a formation which incorporates everybody. The notion of a 'historical bloc' is precisely different from that of a pacified, homogeneous, ruling class.
>   It entails a quite different conception of how social forces and movements, in their diversity, can be articulated into a set of strategic alliances.
>
> Stuart Hall (1988: 170)

And, if irreducible to ideology, hegemony, in its far-reaching effects, is also irreducible to culture, even though its work comprehends both:

> 'hegemony' goes beyond 'culture' . . . in its insistence on relating the 'whole social process' to specific distributions of power and influence . . .

Gramsci . . . introduced the necessary recognition of dominance and subordination [in class-based society] in what has . . . to be recognized as a whole process.

It is in just this recognition of the *wholeness* of the process that the concept of 'hegemony' goes beyond 'ideology'.

Raymond Williams (1977: 108–9)

Hegemony therefore escapes any finite definition precisely because it is so comprehensive, so all-encompassing in its political processes. To recap, therefore,

Hegemony is . . . a whole body of practices and expectations, over the whole of living . . . It is a lived system of meanings and values – constitutive and constituting – which as they are experienced as practices appear as reciprocally confirming. It thus constitutes a sense of reality for most people in the society, a sense of absolute because experienced reality beyond which it is very difficult to move, in most areas of their lives . . . its forms of domination and subordination correspond . . . closely to the normal processes of social organization and control in developed societies . . .

Raymond Williams (1977: 110)

How might we think this in relation to the experience of politics? A practical expression of this is found in the following citation:

Gramsci's concept of hegemony (the securing of consent) allows us to see Thatcherism for what it was: a project to change the way in which people live out social and political conflict.

Michèle Barrett (1999: 163)

Thatcherism understood as a hegemonic force allows us to understand structural interrelation, thereby effectively initiating a demystification implicit in the privileging of any single figure such as Margaret Thatcher, Ronald Regan, George W. Bush or Tony Blair, all of whom are only privileged agents within, and supportive of, the hegemonic process. The singular example of Thatcherism is, in conclusion, developed here by Stuart Hall.

Thatcherism was a project to engage, to contest that project [of welfare social democracy], and, wherever possible, to dismantle it and to put something new in place. It entered the political field in a historic contest, not just for power, but for popular authority, for hegemony.

Stuart Hall (1988: 166)

Questions for further consideration

1. In light of the comment by Ernesto Laclau, in what ways might one understand the 'logic of hegemony' as 'deconstructive'?
2. Consider the ways in which 'New Labour' (in Great Britain) is a hegemonic project aimed at transforming society. In what ways has 'New Labour' sought to bring about a new cultural order?
3. To what extent might the success of hegemonic power (a) be said to rest on contradiction and overdetermination, and (b) be understood as involving a mystification of contradictions?

Explanatory and bibliographical notes

1. Ernesto Laclau (*b*.1935–) and Chantal Mouffe (*b*.1943–): Laclau and Mouffe, *Hegemony and Socialist Strategy: Towards a Radical Democratic Politics* (London: Verso, 1985); Laclau, *Emancipation(s)* (London: Verso, 1996); Mouffe, *The Return of the Political* (London: Verso, 1993).
2. *Leninism* is named after Vladimir Ilyich Lenin (*b*.1870–*d*.1924): *What is to be Done?* (Oxford: Clarendon Press, 1963); *Imperialism, the Highest Stage of the Revolution* (Peking: Foreign Languages Press, 1965); *The State and Revolution* (New York: International Publishers, 1932). Emerging from within Marxism and due in large part to the theoretical writings of Lenin, Leninism is concerned primarily with the active seizure of power on the part of the proletariat rather than relying on a more purely Marxist conceptualization of the inevitable coming to consciousness of the working classes.

Further reading

Fontana, Benedetto (1993), *Hegemony and Power: On the Relation between Gramsci and Machiavelli* (Minneapolis, MN: University of Minnesota Press).
Gramsci, Antonio (1971), *Selections from the Prison Notebooks*, ed. and trans. Quintin Hoare and Geoffrey Nowell Smith (London: Lawrence and Wishart).
Gramsci, Antonio (1985), *Selections from Cultural Writings*, ed. David Forgacs and Geoffrey Nowell-Smith, trans. William Boelhower (Cambridge, MA: Harvard University Press).
Gramsci, Antonio (1988), *An Antonio Gramsci Reader: Selected Writings, 1916–1935*, ed. David Forgacs (London: Lawrence and Wishart).
Laclau, Ernesto, and Chantal Mouffe (1985), *Hegemony and Socialist Strategy: Towards a Radical Democratic Politics* (London: Verso).
Larsen, Neil (1990), *Modernism and Hegemony: A Materialist Critique of Aesthetic Agencies*, Foreword by Jaime Concha (Minneapolis, MN: University of Minnesota Press).

HYPERREALITY

As its prefix suggests, the notion of *hyperreality* indicates that which is over and above, in excess of reality, something which is more real than the real. As a critical term employed extensively in the humanities, hyperreality is associated with the work of Jean Baudrillard, defined succinctly by him as 'the meticulous reduplication of the real, preferably through another, reproductive medium, such as photography'. The real disappears, vanishes from perception, through representational forms. It is not simply that a representation, such as a photographic image, is 'meticulous' or accurate but that it comes to be more real than the reality represented, assuming a power and value all its own.

> Reality itself founders in hyperrealism . . . From medium to medium, the real is volatilized, becoming an allegory of death. But it is also, in a sense, reinforced through its own destruction. It becomes *reality for its own sake*, the fetishism of the lost object: no longer the object of representation, but the ecstasy of denial and of its own ritual extermination: the hyperreal.
>
> Jean Baudrillard (1988: 145)

The representation of the real assumes a reality of its own, and thereby achieves a fetishistic condition, no longer simply being the sign of the concrete real.

> What Jean Baudrillard has dubbed the 'hyperreal' world of simulations means we have become seduced by images that are signs of nothing but themselves. Because such images now precede their referents – Baudrillard calls it 'the precession of simulacra' – they can no longer be understood in terms of the panopticon[1] or the spectacle, concepts that imply a prior intentionality using visual means for other ends, such as the maintenance of power or the perpetuation of capitalism. We are no longer even in front of a mirror, but rather stare with fascination at a screen reflecting nothing outside it.
>
> Martin Jay (1994: 544)

Indeed, to the extent that the hyperreal sign has become increasingly abstract, it is hard to see how the symbol or figure in question is, any longer, a representation of anything existing in the world.

> Hyperrealism is only beyond representation because it functions entirely within the realm of simulation . . . hyperrealism is an integral part of a coded reality, which it perpetuates without modifying.
>
> Jean Baudrillard (1988: 146)

Rather, the transcendence to the realm of hyperreality is signalled in the transformation of the image so that it implies qualities of being and concepts with which we seek to identify. From this understanding,

> Baudrillard argues [that] it is necessary to analyse the way in which the modern idea of reality . . . was connected to a phase of the evolution of western society, a phase which was reflected in the theory of political economy (itself, resting on the law of value in use and exchange[2]). Today, the system is increasingly indeterminate; reality has been displaced, in the consumer society, by the 'hyper-reality' of the code. For this system has abolished the effectivity of 'external reality'.
>
> Mike Gane (1991: 77)

Therefore signs of this kind – the Coca-cola or Nike logos, for example – are excessive in their significatory power in that they not only precede the object, they have come to supplant any value or significance that the real might have.

> Abstraction today is no longer that of the map, the double, the mirror or the concept. Simulation is no longer that of a territory, a referential being or a substance. It is the generation of models of a real without origin or reality: a hyperreal.
>
> Jean Baudrillard (1983: 2)

The sign, in having become hyperreal and in belonging to a constellation of hyperreal figures, acquires its own resonance, circulating within a network of other fetishized images, icons and symbols. Such is the excessive power of the hyperreal that it is not simply a question of the power of the sign *qua* sign. Instead, so prevalent are the images by which we accord significance to ourselves and the world in which we live that, for Baudrillard, the world itself has taken on a hyperreal condition. The extent to which this can be said to be the case can be seen if we consider how forms and media of reduplication without origin, such as computer network tele-technologies (whether called the world-wide web, the internet or hypertext), have assumed a cultural and informational significance beyond the relatively simple function of consumer signs, which in turn has led, and been a response, to what Baudrillard terms a 'crisis of representation'.

> Out of the crisis of representation the *hyperreal* has had to be connected to repetition, first in relation to a reproduction of reality, but as reproducibility is established as dominant it ceased to require this support . . . *Hyperreality* entails the end of depth, perspective, relief . . .
>
> Mike Gane (1991: 103)

Questions for further consideration

1. How appropriate is the notion of the hyperreal to commercial logos such as the Nike 'flash'? Why do such 'figures' have such power?
2. Can the work of hyperreality be thought of in terms of interpellation? Does the hyperreal 'call', and is the power of hyperreality manifested in particular images attributable in part to the paradoxical suggestion of uniqueness *and* iterability?
3. Are the signs of hyperreality more seductive because they signify nothing as such?

Explanatory and bibliographical notes

1. *Panopticon*: taken from Jeremy Bentham (*b*.1748–*d*.1832): *An Introduction to the Principles of Morals and Legislation*, in John Stuart Mill and Jeremy Bentham, *Utilitarianism and Other Essays*, ed. and Introduction by Alan Ryan (London: Penguin, 1987), pp. 65–112; Bentham first employed the term in 1791 to describe a new prison design, the main feature of which would be a central office serving as an observatory for warders, by means of which prisoners could be observed 24 hours a day. The term is to be found in Foucault's writings as an institutional structure which makes available surveillance, and therefore control, of inmates of asylums and prisons.
2. *Use value / exchange value*: derived from Marx in his analysis of the value of a commodity: 'Since the commodity is a product which is exchanged, it appears as the union of two different aspects: its usefulness to some agent, which is what permits the commodity to enter into exchange at all; and its power to command certain quantities of other commodities in exchange. The first aspect . . . [is] *use value*, the second, *exchange value* . . . while use value is a necessary condition for a product to enter into exchange . . . the use value of the commodity bears no systematic quantitative relation to its exchange value, which is a reflection of the conditions of the commodity's production . . . [Marx] argues that the proper object of study of political economy is the laws governing the production and movement of exchange value' (Bottomore, Harris, Kiernan, Miliband 1983: 504).

Further reading

Baudrillard, Jean (1983), *Simulations* (New York: Semiotext(e)).
Baudrillard, Jean (1988), *Selected Writings*, ed. and Introduction by Mark Poster (Stanford, CA: Stanford University Press).
Gane, Mike (1991), *Baudrillard's Bestiary: Baudrillard and Culture* (London: Routledge).

HYPERTEXT

Hypertext first appears in print in 1965, in the work of Ted Nelson (who, while a student at Harvard University in 1960, invented the first computer-based hyptertext model as a term project), in whose work it is defined as a practice of composition, including summaries, maps, annotations, footnotes and additions. For Nelson it defines a form of text in which are naturally assumed practices of reading and writing that are not comfortably accommodated by conventional textual forms reliant on a linear method of information assimilation and dissemination. Hypertext now refers to a database format or 'medium', as Christopher Nash calls it in the first extract below, in which highlighted links to other texts, databases and virtual locations are marked within a particular electronic document so as to offer further access, as part of a larger informational network.

> The word 'hypertext' (the medium in which, among other things the World Wide Web currently operates) . . . articulates as richly as any utterance could . . . a constellation of ideas . . . By means of HyperText Mark-up Language (the ubiquitous 'html', a universal computer-language protocol) or some augmented form of it, any utterance or graphic or audial sign, once electronically registered in digitised form, may be 'hyperlinked' with any other utterance or sign, anywhere within whatever whole hypertext 'book', 'picture' or digital video or 'soundtext' in which it's been imbedded, *or* . . . with any text in any other place that can be reached by electronic, digital communication, anywhere on the planet.
>
> Christopher Nash (2001: 182)

Items of information relating to subjects are linked electronically, often through highlighted reference to a term, phrase or concept, or otherwise an author's name, important dates or the names of particular publications. HyperText Mark-up Language (html) is the principal means by which information is encoded. In the context of literary studies and with reference to what is called literary and cultural theory, George Landow has elucidated the relationships between the assumptions concerning reading, information and communication expressed by so-called poststructuralist thinkers, and the form of hypermedia in general:

> traditional notions of reading or assimilating information – linear, logical and hierarchical – have, since the computer revolution of the 1980s, been replaced by new methods of storing and retrieving information . . . This change has been largely effected through the cyberconstruct of the

World Wide Web and the expanding possibilities of hypertext. Not only has hypertext enabled the functioning of the World Wide Web but open-ended hypertext has subverted traditional notions of master narratives and definitive readings.

Stacy Gillis (2002: 207–8)

The assumption that the hypertextual medium presents a radical challenge to conventional models of reading is related to a concomitant assumption, having to do with the greater freedom afforded the reading subject by hypertext.

Superficially this freedom to choose one's links would seem to accord with postmodern notions of how texts are determined by their readers, and encourage belief in the freedom and power of the individual, the user. How free is s/he? This has several dimensions. For one, what such notions don't take into account is the effects of the psychological constraint placed on the reading of *conventional linear* texts – which tend to invoke end-directed thinking. Invited to believe that the point of reading is to consume the *entire* text, to see 'how it all comes out', we're compelled to *work our way* page-by-page *through* the text, engaging with all the traps and ambiguities the writer may have inscribed there; complexity . . . is part of the 'signification' of the work. The fundamental difference, the 'value added', in hypertext is the opportunity to choose to seek, to avoid seeing what one doesn't want to see, and to immerse oneself in the feeling that – with or without reason – all things are connected, and in something like the way we *want* them to be.

Christopher Nash (2001: 183–4)

The question of reading differently is further extended, at least in principle, by the possibility of potentially endless augmentation and supplementation of any given hypertext.

Hypertext . . . can be read non-sequentially. Such projects as [George] Landow's *The Dickens Web* or the *Victorian Women Writers Project* (http://www.indiana.edu/~letrs/vwwp) exemplify this. The former, primarily an undergraduate study aid, puts into practice the hypertextual arguments that Landow advanced in *Hypertext*. Much like electronic footnotes, hyperlinks make connections between items. The latter is a more diffuse project, sustained by Indiana University, and a classic example of academic research, which may be difficult to publish, finding a home on the Internet. What is crucial about the *Victorian Women Writers Project* is that it is always being updated and its hyperlinks checked, so that it remains at the cutting edge of research, unlike a book which can quickly become critically moribund.

Stacy Gillis (2002: 208)

But it is not only matters of the reading subject's enhanced 'freedom' or the idea of an infinitely open condition of the text to supplementarity that are at stake in thinking through hypertext's potential. There is also to be taken into account the spatial, not to say topographical reorientation of the reading experience.

> The interplay between spatiality and text is central to electronic hypertexts . . . hypertexts are now becoming the standard way to convey information in many technical and engineering areas because they are easily updated, richly associational, and reader-directed . . . The World Wide Web is a vast hypertext, and most of the documents within it are also hypertexts . . . In literary hypertexts, spatial form and visual image become richly significant. For hypertexts written in Storyspace (a hypertext authoring program . . .), the map view shows how different lexias are linked to one another. The way they are arranged in space is used to indicate logical and narrative relationships. Some lexias may nest inside others; others may have multiple connections; still others may function as autonomous units or dead ends. Color coding also indicates various kinds of relationships from highlighted text within lexias to different-colored links and boxes . . . space in hypertext operates as much more than an empty container into which virtual objects are placed. Rather it becomes a topography that the reader navigates using multiple functionalities, including cognitive, tactile, auditory, visual, kinesthetic[1] and proprioceptive[2] faculties.
>
> N. Katherine Hayles (1997: 197–8)

Questions for further consideration

1. Do hypertextual media radicalize the act of reading?
2. What is the relationship between hypertext and freedom?
3. Consider the spatial and topographical matters of orientation that hypertext appears to raise.

Explanatory and bibliographical notes

1. *Kinaesthesis*: the sense of muscular effort that accompanies a voluntary motion of the body. Also, the sense or faculty by which such sensations are perceived.

2. *Proprioception*: the sense indicating corporeal limits, associated with nerve endings and the mechanisms of the inner ear.

Further reading

Bolter, J. David (2001), *Writing Space: Computers, Hypertext, and the Remediation of Print* (Mahwah: Lawrence Erlbaum).
DeWitt, Scott Lloyd (2001), *Writing Inventions: Identities, Technologies, Pedagogies* (Albany, NY: State University of New York Press).
Landow, George (1992), *Hypertext: The Convergence of Contemporary Critical Theory and Technology* (Baltimore, MD: Johns Hopkins University Press).
Landow, George (1993), *Hypertext in Hypertext* (Baltimore, MD: Johns Hopkins University Press).
Landow, George (ed.) (1995), *Hyper/Text/Theory* (Baltimore, MD: Johns Hopkins University Press).

I/DENTITY

What happens every time you say 'I'? Is this 'I' the same 'I' as I use to indicate myself? The slash in the spelling of *identity* above is a somewhat clumsy and obvious attempt to indicate the notion of selfhood or subjectivity that informs or is commented on by the term being considered at this point. Every time I enunciate 'I', even in my thought, an identity is assumed, and this identity is itself not simple, but a figure for a complex gathering of personal and impersonal histories, texts, discourses, beliefs, cultural assumptions, and ideological interpellations. Yet we hardly ever think about the vast 'hypertextual' reality of our identities, certainly not at those instances when 'I' is pronounced or written (as throughout this commentary). Yet, the possibility of articulation of 'I' in the world is intrinsic to the most basic enunciation of identity, which in turn,

> is central to human/social praxis . . . it is not an artifact but a process, namely its own construction . . . it only exists as the dual of alterity . . . both identity and alterity are contained and conveyed through narrative . . . the notions of identity and alterity, of 'us' and 'them,' are closely linked to the sense of place, that is, to notions of 'here' and 'there.'
>
> Irvin Cemil Schick (1999: 23)

When 'I' is spoken, a focal or suturing point within a discursive, psychic, historical, national, gendered and ideological network constituting an identity is implied in even this apparently simplest of words:

how one thinks and feels is at once lived as intensely personal, yet made up of matters that in themselves are not unique to one . . . identity politics . . . is founded on an affirmation of the needs and rights of a group defined in terms of . . . gender, class, and sexuality. Crucial to such affirmation is the construction of a sense of oneness with a social grouping.

Richard Dyer (1997: 7–8)

In the constitution of any identity, therefore, there is always an oscillation between determinants that are 'external' or which pre-exist the subject's identity:

identity . . . comes to be through enactment, through performance, that is through practices that construct it using a host of discursive instruments which might be called 'technologies of identity'

Irvin Cemil Schick (1999: 20)

and internal psychic drives such as desire:

desire not only drives the individual subject in different directions, it is also constitutive of the representational activity of subjectivity itself – to, for example, people's core sense of identity.

Anthony Elliot (1996: 40)

'Identity' is, however, problematic because as with a number, if not all, of the other terms, motifs, or concepts in the present volume, the one thing which can be said for certain is that no one definition for identity as a conceptual term will suffice:

some realistic dilemma as to how I should speak about myself will rarely get resolved for long by means of an 'identity'. So often conceived as a thing to be unearthed, my identity (if I am forced to locate such an object at all) may turn out to be not so much a matter of what it is . . . [I] take tacit issue with the conviction that it's politically imperative to hang onto an asserted category, since any time spent reading in archives or through old newspapers (or simply living long enough) demonstrates that the collisions and shattering of identities have been as decisive for progress as their consolidations – while the latter have so frequently been disastrous that one could make a counterclaim for the historical necessity of the strongest identity to the most reactionary cause.

Denise Riley (2000: 9–10)

Every identity differs from every other identity and, this being the case, identity is simply this recognition of the attempt to define a 'self' or 'presence', a community or group, against an other, against that which, while having its own identity, remains, none the less, not the identity which is in the process of determination.

> There's a world of difference between settling some context for yourself – and discovering 'an identity'. For instance, to be brought up as the child of one set of parents, then much later to stumble upon the fact that these were not one's original parents at all, might well be assumed to generate 'a crisis of identity'. Yet it can do the very opposite . . . As is often the case, this 'lack' is really a kind of plenitude – not mournful, but a positively productive lack . . . it's the felt need for information about their past which has brought people to question the laws of concealment . . . Pressure groups flourish for mutual aid in the hunt for ancestors . . . This need to unearth some history of yourself is hardly belittled by its consequence: that what you may establish, through discovering background facts and perhaps some living relatives, may not be an 'identity' so much as a short history of the impossibility of having an identity.
>
> Denise Riley (2000: 135–6)

Every identity being singular, 'identity' has no identity as such. Identity is a fluid process. There are, however, numerous traces which give the sense of stability to an identity.

> Though identity is a permanent process of construction and reconstruction, this fluid or mutable nature does not mean that it never enjoys any stability. Clearly, a person's identity does not vary significantly from day to day, so that there must be a slowly varying envelope containing (and constraining) the vicissitudes of self-enactment. This envelope is narrative.
>
> Irvin Cemil Schick (1999: 20–1)

For narratives of identity to be possible, there needs be a certain repetition possible of the marks and traces of the singular identity.

> Identity . . . depends upon repetition, which however, in turn, supposes something like an identity. . . . That is to say, in order to be apprehended or identified as such – and every signifying element must be *identifiable as such* in order for it to signify – every signifier or 'mark' must be recognizable, re-peatable. It never can present itself simply once.
>
> Samuel Weber (1996: 138)

In light of this, identity becomes a convenient, yet powerful term in the service of politics for example. For, whether one speaks of party or national politics, identity becomes a measuring stick by which to judge those who belong to a party or a nation, and those who do not. Colour of skin can serve in certain discourses as a marker of identity, as can physical attributes indicating gender identity.

> Identity is the socially constructed, socially sanctioned (or at least recognized) complex of self-significations deriving from an individual's membership in such collectivities as class, race, gender, sexuality, generation, region, ethnicity, religion, and nation. It plays a decisive role in human behaviour: one acts from a certain positionality and in accordance with a certain worldview or set of values, interpreting data with the help of certain parameters – all these deeply rooted in identity. At the same time, identity is never 'complete'; rather, it is always under construction. To put it more explicitly, identity is not an object but a *process*. Furthermore, this process is not even: times of crisis or transition are often periods of particularly intensive identity construction . . . *identity is (a) representation, and the representation of identity, whether to oneself or to others, is in fact its very construction.*
>
> Irvin Cemil Schick (1999: 19)

The values and beliefs one holds are also the markers of identity, those invisible inscriptions on the subject's psyche which determine his or her subjectivity and relation to others around him or her. Clearly, the question of identity and its cognate identification has to do with a number of variables ranging from the psychic to the social or from the individual to the group. Yet what this question also reveals is, first, the fact that an identity is never autonomous completely: it is only definable according to what it is not. Secondly, identity is always a construction, however minimal, whether one is speaking of sexual identity, national identity, cultural identity, historical identity or personal identity, and whether one believes one chooses one's identity for oneself, or whether this is constituted for one by one's family dynamic, by philosophical considerations of identity in relation to the question of being, or by a broader socio-cultural dynamic. Thus, to summarize, the matter of identity formation is, on the one hand, a matter of narration:

> identity is its own construction . . . and narrative is the medium through which that construction is realized. But the construction of identity is inseparable from that of alterity – indeed, identity itself only makes sense in juxtaposition with alterity.
>
> Irvin Cemil Schick (1999: 21)

and, on the other hand, a matter of the iterability of a constellation of particular traces:

> in order to be *cognizable*, an element must be recognizable as the *same*, which in turn presupposes a process of *com-parison* and *repetition*. It must be compared with earlier instances of itself in order to be recognizable *as a self*, as an identity.
>
> This process of repetitive comparison, out of which self-sameness emerges and which it therefore must *pass through*, introduces an element of *heterogeneity*, of *otherness*, into the constitution of the same. The question, however, now becomes: precisely what is the role of this heterogeneity in the process of repetition that is presupposed by every identification and by all identity?
>
> Samuel Weber (1996: 138–9)

Questions for further consideration

1. Consider the various discussions of selfhood and identity above in relation to the thinking of difference.
2. In what ways does the introduction of the temporal dimension to the thinking of identity destabilize or transform our conceptions of our 'selves'?
3. Can identity ever be addressed separately from the determinate coordinates of gender, class, or sexuality, or autonomously from considerations of space, place or time?

Further reading

Baucom, Ian (1999), *Out of Place: Englishness, Empire, and the Locations of Identity* (Princeton, NJ: Princeton University Press).

Butler, Judith (1990), *Gender Trouble: Feminism and the Subversion of Identity* (London: Routledge).

Dyer, Richard (1997), *White* (London: Routledge).

King, Nicola (2000), *Memory, Narrative, Identity: Remembering the Self* (Edinburgh: Edinburgh University Press).

Laclau, Ernesto (2000), 'Identity and Hegemony: The Role of Universality in the Constitution of Political Logics'. In Judith Butler, Ernesto Laclau and Slavoj Žižek, *Contingency, Hegemony, Universality: Contemporary Dialogues on the Left* (London: Verso), pp. 44–89.

Laclau, Ernesto (ed.) (1994), *The Making of Political Identities* (London: Verso).

Rajchman, John (ed.) (1995), *The Identity in Question* (New York: Routledge).

IDEOLOGY

Modern uses of the notion of ideology within literary and cultural studies have tended to have developed from and been influenced by Marxist and post-Marxist thinking, as is typified by the examples presented here (with the obvious exception of the citations from Paul de Man), even while, within Marxian discourse, there is still debate and contention over a word and idea which is notable for its absence from Marx's *Capital*. While ideas vary to greater or lesser degrees in their understanding of the definition and functioning of ideology, as well as the contexts defining its use, what can be said is that ideology always bears on material conditions of lived existence. The idea of ideology remains notoriously contested, and its very slipperiness seems to indicate its power, the facility with which the ideological positions of particular social groups can be promoted as universal.

> We can construe the dominant ideology as a kind of 'symbolic capital' of the ruling class itself, as the body of representations that expresses its *own* conditions and means of existence (for the bourgeoisie, for instance, commodity ownership, juridical equality, and political liberty), or at best as the expression of the relation of average members of the ruling class to the conditions of domination common to their class (hence the kind of universal values this domination assumes for each of them) . . .
>
> Étienne Balibar (1988: 169)

This position is succinctly described by Terry Eagleton,[1] who defines ideology as those

> ideas and beliefs which help to legitimate the interests of a ruling group or class specifically by distortion and dissimulation.
>
> Terry Eagleton (1991: 30)

Noting the tendentious nature of definitions pertaining to ideology, Raymond Williams has suggested that three principal definitions may be offered.

> The concept of 'ideology' did not originate in Marxism and is still in no way confined to it . . . The difficulty . . . is that we have to distinguish three common versions of the concept, which are all common in Marxist writing. These are, broadly:
> (i)   a system of beliefs characteristic of a particular class or group;

(ii)   a system of illusory beliefs – false ideas or false consciousness –
       which can be contrasted with true or scientific knowledge;
(iii) the general process of the production of meanings and ideas.

Raymond Williams (1977: 55)

Ideology is, then, a system of cultural assumptions, or the discursive
concatenation, the connectedness, of beliefs or values which uphold or
oppose social order, or which otherwise provide a coherent structure of
thought that hides or silences the contradictory elements in social and
economic formations. However, despite the apparent straightforwardness
of the remarks just provided, ideology is a notoriously difficult and equivocal concept to define. Consider, for example, the following commentary.

> All class consciousness – or in other words, all ideology in the strongest
> sense, including the most exclusive forms of ruling-class consciousness
> just as much as that of oppositional or oppressed classes – is in its very
> nature Utopian.
>
> Fredric Jameson (1981: 289)

If all ideology is Utopian then every ideology, at least in principle, has any
specificity erased, the apparent truth claims of an ideology being discernible
as merely so many effects serving in the maintenance of particular class
interests. On the one hand there is no escape from ideology, and on the
other, no ideological position necessarily has any greater claim than any
other, except in relative or dialectical terms. Or consider the limits to any
political efficacy implied by an acceptance of classical models of ideology.

> If our concept of ideology remains the classic one in which the illusion is
> located in knowledge, then today's society must appear post-ideological:
> the prevailing ideology is that of cynicism; people no longer believe in
> ideological truth; they do not take ideological propositions seriously.
> The fundamental level of ideology, however, is not of an illusion mask-
> ing the real state of things but that of an unconscious fantasy structuring
> our social reality itself. And at this level, we are of course far from being
> a post-ideological society. Cynical distance is just one way – one of many
> ways – to blind ourselves to the structuring power of ideological fantasy:
> even if we do not take things seriously, even if we keep an ironical
> distance, *we are still doing them*.
>
> Slavoj Žižek (1989: 33)

It would appear that we remain entrenched ideologically at the very
moment – at every moment historically – where ideology is both universal-
ized *and* read as having had its day, as being a thing of the past. Perhaps

the most elusive and Utopian ideology of all is the one expressed through the announcement that we live in a post-ideological age, as the previous citation makes plain.

Part of ideology's slipperiness comes from its own strategic ability to serve in the definition of other concepts in equivocal, if not ambivalent and even antagonistic or dialectical ways, as already implied. Moreover, it has to be stressed that while ideology is clearly immaterial in one sense, as Louis Althusser avers,

> Ideology is the system of ideas and representations which dominate the mind of a man or a social group . . . Ideology represents the imaginary relationship of individuals to their real conditions of existence.
>
> We commonly call religious ideology, ethical ideology, legal ideology, political ideology, etc., so many 'world outlooks'. Of course, assuming that we do not live one of these ideologies as the truth (e.g. 'believe' in God, Duty, Justice, etc. . . .), we admit . . . that these 'world outlooks' are largely imaginary, i.e. do not 'correspond to reality'.
>
> However, while admitting that they . . . constitute an illusion, we admit that they do make allusion to reality, and that they need to be interpreted to discover the reality of the world behind their imaginary representation of the world (ideology = *illusion/allusion*)
>
> Louis Althusser (1994: 122–3)

it none the less has material effects, as Althusser has just clarified, and as the following citation also argues.

> All the products of ideological creation – works of art, scientific works, religious symbols and rites, etc. – are material things, part of the practical reality that surrounds man. It is true that these things are of a special nature, having significance, meaning, inner value. But these meanings and values are embodied in material things and actions. They cannot be realized outside of some developed material.
>
> Nor do philosophical views, beliefs, or even shifting ideological moods exist within man, in his head or in his 'soul'. They become ideological reality only by being realized in words, actions, clothing, manners, and organizations of people and things – in a word: in some definite semiotic[2] material. Through this material they become a practical part of the reality surrounding man.
>
> Mikhail Bakhtin and P. N. Medvedev (1978: 125)

Something material, such as a work of art or a building, in being what it is, embodies and articulates values beyond its immediate functional or aesthetic purpose. As critics such as Raymond Williams or John Berger have shown, a castle or an eighteenth-century portrait may be 'beautiful', they may be 'perfect' examples of particular techniques or forms, but they are also material expressions of abstract political and cultural notions, such as power, property, or right. The material manifestation of ideology is further foregrounded here:

> ideology has a material existence . . . an ideology always exists in an apparatus,[3] and its practice, or practices. This existence is material.
>
> Of course, the material existence of the ideology in an apparatus and its practices does not have the same modality as the material existence of a paving stone or a rifle. . . .
>
> Now I observe the following.
>
> An individual believes in God, or Duty, or Justice, etc. This belief derives . . . from the ideas of the individual . . . as a subject with a consciousness which contains the ideas of his belief. . . .
>
> The individual in question behaves in such and such a way, adopts such and such a practical attitude, and what is more, participates in certain regular practices which are those of the ideological state apparatus on which depend the ideas which he has in all consciousness freely chosen as a subject.
>
> Louis Althusser (1994: 125–6)

As is cogently presented here, ideology is not just encoded within objects; it is lived and practised on what might be termed an organic, unthought level on a daily basis. It is therefore necessary to pursue a

> study of how the ideological structure of a dominant class is actually organized: namely the material organization aimed at maintaining, defending and developing the theoretical or ideological 'front' . . . The press is the most dynamic part of this ideological structure, but not the only one. Everything which influences or is able to influence public opinion, directly or indirectly, belongs to it: libraries, schools, associations and clubs of various kinds . . . It would be impossible to explain the position retained by the Church in modern society if one were unaware of the constant and patient efforts it makes to develop continuously its particular section of this material structure of ideology.
>
> Antonio Gramsci (1985: 389)

To Gramsci's identification of the press's role, we would add, today, all tele-techno-mediatic forms, which disseminate and mediate ideologically situated constructions of the world. Given the example of the media in the perpetuation of ideological constellations and the fact that mediatic dissemination functions through the projection of signifiers as props to and constituent elements in any material, political reality, it might be suggested that

> what we call ideology is precisely the confusion of linguistic with natural reality, of reference with phenomenalism.
>
> > Paul de Man (1986: 11)

Because such 'confusion' takes place, because we, as subjects, misrecognize the structures of the world in which we live, it can therefore be remarked that

> ideologies, to the extent that they necessarily contain empirical[4] moments and are directed towards what lies outside the realm of pure concepts, are on the side of metaphysics rather than critical philosophy. The conditions and modalities of their occurrence are determined by critical analyses to which they have no access. The object of these analyses, on the other hand, can only be ideologies.
>
> > Paul de Man (1996: 72)

That one can discern a phenomenal process, and that there is always an inescapable analytic engagement in any attempt to read the ideological, suggests that

> there is no ideology except for concrete subjects, and this destination for ideology is made possible only by the subject: meaning: *by the category of the* subject and its functioning . . . the category of the subject . . . is the constitutive category of all ideology, whatever its determination (regional or class) and whatever its historical date . . . *the category of the* subject *is constitutive of all ideology only in so far as all ideology has the function (which defines it) of 'constituting' concrete individuals as subjects.*
>
> > Louis Althusser (1994: 128–9)

Slavoj Žižek[5] has acknowledged the ways in which ideology appears to signify a broad spectrum of attitudes and beliefs, if not a medium by which human subjectivity is interpellated. In attesting to such slippage and resistance to definition, Žižek draws our attention to the essentially 'psychic' or imaginary nature of ideology, as though society, before and beyond the individual subject, had something akin to an 'unconscious'. Yet, in implying such a comprehension, Žižek rejects the notion of ideology as simply illusion or false consciousness. The subject's interpellation within capitalist society is ideological but has material effects and consequences.

'Ideology' can designate anything from a contemplative attitude that misrecognizes its dependence on social reality to an action-oriented set of beliefs, from the indispensable medium in which individuals live out their relations to a social structure to false ideas which legitimate a dominant political power. It seems to pop up precisely when we attempt to avoid it, while it fails to appear where one would clearly expect it to dwell.

Slavoj Žižek (1994: 3–4)

Once again, we read in Žižek's comments ideology's power to evade capture or comprehension. And perhaps such evasiveness lies, at least in part, in the structural possibility of ideological mediation as a structure maintained by an idealizing (and possibly narcissistic) reflective process, whereby the subject's individual misrecognition is maintained.

We observe that the structure of all ideology, interpellating individuals as subjects in the name of a Unique and Absolute Subject, is *specularly*, i.e. a mirror-structure, and *doubly* specular:[6] this mirror duplication is constitutive of ideology and ensures its functioning. Which means that all ideology is *centred*, that the Absolute Subject occupies the unique place of the Centre, and interpellates around it the infinity of individuals into subjects . . . such that it *subjects* the subjects to the Subject, while giving them in the Subject in which each subject can contemplate its own image . . . the *guarantee* that this really concerns them . . .

Louis Althusser (1971: 180)

If a complex form of reflective, necessarily distorted signification process does take place, then it is no longer enough to recognize (or, perhaps, misrecognize) ideology as simply a confusion between signifier and subject; instead it should be seen as a process whereby the subject, in being reflected at all, is only ever mediated within a groundless network of ideological traces and signs.

Ideology can no longer be understood as [a] relation between a material production (system and relations of production) and a production of signs (culture, etc.) which expresses and masks the contradictions at the 'base' . . . the traditional vision of ideology still proves incapable of grasping the 'ideological' function of culture and of signs – except at the level of the signified . . . ideology is actually *that very form* that traverses both the production of signs and material production . . . Ideology . . . is the one and only form that traverses all the fields of social production. Ideology seizes all production, material or symbolic, in the same process of abstraction, reduction, general equivalence and exploitation.

Jean Baudrillard (1981: 76–8)

We therefore arrive at a radical reorientation of political thinking.

From the truth of falseness, Marx in his genius invented a key word that all modernity has adopted, at times even turning it against him. He called it *ideology*. Ideology is not just a new word for simulacra or illusion. Ideology is the word that signals the completely new status of the true that metapolitics[7] forges: the true as the truth of the false. Not the clarity of an idea in the face of the obscurity of appearances; not the truth as an index of itself and of falseness but, on the contrary, the truth of which the false alone is an index, the truth that is nothing more than highlighting falseness, the truth as universal interference . . . In inventing it, Marx invents . . . an unheard of regime of truth and a completely new connection between truth and politics. Ideology is a name for the endlessly decried gap between words and things, the conceptual connector that organizes the junctions and disjunctions between the components of the modern political apparatus. It alternately allows the political appearance of the people to be reduced to the level of an illusion concealing the reality of conflict or, conversely, . . . holding up the emergence of common interests. Ideology is the term that links the production of politics to its evacuation, that designates the distance between words and things as the falseness in politics that can always be turned into the falseness of politics. But it is also the concept by means of which anything is declared to stem from politics, to arise from a 'political' demonstration of its falseness. It is, in short, the concept in which all politics is cancelled out, either through its proclaimed evanescence, or, on the contrary, through the assertion that everything is political, which comes down to saying that nothing is . . . Ideology is, finally, the term that allows the place of politics to shift endlessly.

Jacques Rancière (1999: 85–6)

Questions for further consideration

1. Taking Althusser's argument that ideology is *specular*, in what ways may we understand our identities or subjectivities as ideological reflections? In what ways does ideology manifest itself in the lives of individual subjects?

2. Is it possible for a critique of ideology to be 'outside' ideology?
3. If much of the work of ideology is maintained through signs, representations, and other forms of symbolism or imaginary ensemble, how does it achieve its material effects?

Explanatory and bibliographical notes

1. Terry Eagleton (*b.*1943–): *The Ideology of the Aesthetic* (1990); *Ideology: An Introduction* (1991); *The Illusions of Postmodernism* (1996).
2. *Semiotics*: the science of signs and symbols, and their meaningful communication.
3. By 'apparatus' or, as in the title of the essay, 'Ideological State Apparatus', Althusser is referring to systems or institutions, such as the church and religion, the school system, the law, politics, the media and communication, and culture, whether literature, the arts, or sports, the discourses these 'apparatuses' generate, and the practices which, socially, they encourage individuals to participate in and uphold.
4. *Empiricism*: branch of philosophy which holds that experience is the only valid source of knowledge.
5. Slavoj Žižek, (*b.*1949–): *The Sublime Object of Ideology* (1989); *For They Know Not What They Do: Enjoyment as a Political Factor* (1991); *Tarrying with the Negative: Kant, Hegel, and the Critique of Ideology* (1993).
6. *Specular*: pertaining to reflection and vision; that which is not seen directly but which is reflected.
7. In defining 'metapolitics' Rancière refers to what he sees as its central and exemplary figure, the concept of 'class'. Metapolitics is that which is, on the one hand, conceptualized as beyond [*meta-*] politics, while on the other, a complement to politics in the perpetuation of certain political illusions.

Further reading

Althusser, Louis (1994), 'Ideology and Ideological State Apparatuses (Notes towards an Investigation)' (1970), trans. Ben Brewster. In Slavoj Žižek (ed.), *Mapping Ideology* (London: Verso), pp. 100–40.
De Man, Paul (1996), *Aesthetic Ideology*, ed. and Introduction by Andrzej Warminski (Minneapolis, MN: University of Minnesota Press).
Eagleton, Terry (1990), *The Ideology of the Aesthetic* (Oxford: Blackwell).
Eagleton, Terry (1991), *Ideology: An Introduction* (London: Verso).
Laclau, Ernesto (1977), *Politics and Ideology in Marxist Theory: Capitalism–Fascism–Populism* (London: Verso).
Marx, Karl, and Friedrich Engels (1970), *The German Ideology* (1846), ed. and Intoduction by C. J. Arthur (London: Lawrence and Wishart).
Miliband, Ralph (1986), *Marxism and Politics* (Oxford: Oxford University Press).
Žižek, Slavoj (1989), *The Sublime Object of Ideology* (London: Verso).

IMAGINARY–SYMBOLIC–REAL

The principal difficulty even of beginning to speak of the *imaginary–symbolic–real* is that one cannot address any one term with any efficacy without speaking of the others. Jacques Lacan's version of psycho-analytic thought posits three coterminous psychic realms, orders, or 'regis-ters' as Jean-Michel Rabaté has termed them, the imaginary, the symbolic, and the real, first established as an inextricably linked triad in Lacan's texts in 1953, and continuing to be explored by Lacan with increasing complexity into the 1970s, when he attempts to address the impossibility of speaking about any of the terms in isolation from one another by comparing the *imaginary–symbolic–real* structure as a borromean knot (a figure borrowed from mathematics), which is a way of linking three rings together in such a fashion that if you remove one, the other two fall apart. While the terms and their interrelated figuration are dauntingly difficult to speak of with any confidence, we may perhaps begin, however tentatively, by addressing the significance of language in the Lacanian schema. While Freudian psychoanalytic discourse on the psyche and its formation always addresses its subject implicitly in relation to the work of language, Lacan's radical step is to see the formation of the human psyche in explicitly linguistic terms, by which he explains the 'imaginary–symbolic–real' struc-ture:

> within the phenomenon of speech we can integrate the three planes of the symbolic, represented by the signifier, the imaginary, represented by meaning, and the real, which is discourse that has actually taken place in a diachronic[1] dimension.
>
> The subject has at his disposal a whole lot of signifying material which is his language . . . and he uses it to circulate meanings in the real . . .
>
> Jacques Lacan (1993: 63)

Every time I speak, I draw on the signifier's constitution, the symbolic, and seek to convey meaning, thereby constituting the imaginary. In doing so, I draw on the 'historically' constituted discourse – the lived experience, to put it crudely – of the real that informs my subjectivity but to which I have no direct access, hence the necessary deployment of signifiers. The follow-ing citation provides the following definition of the terms in relation to one another.

> For Lacan, the 'imaginary' designates that basic and enduring dimension of experience that is oriented by images, perceived or fantasized . . . Lacan . . . characterize[s] the Freudian 'ego' as a formation of the imag-inary . . . The symbolic is the register of language and of linguistically

mediated cognitions. In the 'symbolic order', Lacan envisions a complex system of signifying elements whose meaning is determined by their relation to the other elements of the system – a grand structure, then, in which meaning is free to circulate among associated elements or signifiers without necessarily referring to a particular object or signified. In opposition to the *gestalt* principles and relations of perceptual resemblance that govern the semiotics of the imaginary, the order of the symbolic functions in accordance with the rules internal to the signifying system itself . . . the notion of the real is perhaps best introduced as being precisely that which escapes and is lacking in the other two registers. Neither figured in the imaginary nor represented by the symbolic, the real is the always-still-outstanding, the radically excluded, the wholly unrecognized . . . In Lacan's sense . . . the real has very little to do with common 'reality' . . . The real is sheer, wholly undifferentiated and unsymbolized force or impact. It is an experience of the real, therefore, that lies at the heart of trauma. However, the real is not simply a designation of something unknown *external* to the individual. It inhabits the secret interior as well. The real is therefore also to be associated with the active yet ineffable stirrings of organic need, the unconsciousness of the body.

Richard Boothby (1991: 18–19)

The aim of the 'healthy' adult is to achieve a certain mastery within the Symbolic realm:

> the symbolic order owes much to the anthropological work of Claude Lévi-Strauss[2] . . . [i]n particular . . . the idea that the social world is structured by certain laws which regulate . . . relations and the exchange of gifts . . . The concept of the gift, and that of a circuit of exchange, are thus fundamental to Lacan's concept . . . Since the most basic form of exchange is communication . . . and since the concepts of law and of structure are unthinkable without language, the symbolic is essentially a linguistic dimension . . . However . . . language involves imaginary and real dimensions in addition to its symbolic dimension. The symbolic dimension of language is that of the signifier; a dimension in which elements have no positive existence but which are constituted purely by . . . their mutual differences.
>
> The symbolic is also the realm of radical alterity which Lacan refers to as the Other. The unconscious is the discourse of this Other, and thus belongs wholly to the symbolic order. The symbolic is the realm of the Law which regulates desire in the Oedipus complex . . . Whereas the imaginary is characterized by dual relations, the symbolic is characterized by triadic structures, because the intersubjective relationship is

always 'mediated' by . . . the big Other. The symbolic order is also the realm of death, of absence and of lack . . . The totalizing, all-encompassing effect of the symbolic order leads Lacan to speak of the symbolic as a universe . . . There is therefore no question of a gradual continuous transition from the imaginary to the symbolic . . . Once the symbolic order has arisen, it creates the sense that it has always been there . . . For this reason it is strictly speaking impossible to conceive of the origin of language, let alone what came before . . .

Dylan Evans (1996: 201–2)

The Symbolic is thus the realm of ordered, structured, paraphrasable language, the realm of Law. However, the Symbolic realm is not ideal because language itself is, following Saussure, conventional, and only arbitrarily connected to the objects it describes. Through the intersubjective and differential structures of language there is always for Lacan a relationship between the symbolic and the imaginary,

> every imaginary relation comes about via a kind of *you or me* between the subject and object. That is to say – *If it's you, I'm not. If it's me, it's you who isn't.* That's where the symbolic element comes into play. On the imaginary level, the objects only ever appear to man within relations which fade. He recognizes his unity in them, but uniquely from without. And in as much [as] he recognizes his unity in an object, he feels himself to be in disarray in relation to the latter . . .
>
> This is where the symbolic relation comes in. The power of naming objects structures the perception itself . . . It is through nomination that man makes objects subsist with a certain consistence . . . If the human subject didn't name . . . if subjects do not come to an agreement over this recognition, no world, not even a perception, could be sustained for more than an instant. That is the joint, the emergence of the dimension of the symbolic in relation to the imaginary.

Jacques Lacan (1988: 169–70)

Language for Lacan describes what is not there and expresses always a fraught, because uncloseable, gap between subject and object. He argues that a child learns to speak in response to the absence of what is misperceived as the object of desire (the mother, or her breast); the child learns to say 'I want' and thus becomes initiated into a necessary if painful accommodation within the Symbolic.

> It is necessary for the symbolic system to intervene in the system conditioned by the image of the ego so that an exchange can take place, something which isn't knowledge . . . but recognition.

That shows you that the ego can in no way be anything other than an imaginary function, even if at a certain level it determines the structuration of the subject.

Jacques Lacan (1988: 52)

This process of 'joining' the Symbolic order begins with the mirror phase which initiates the child into the beginnings of language after he catches sight of himself – or rather of a reflection of himself – in a mirror, and recognizes himself for the first time as a separate and distinct being, not one with either the world or with his mother. Lacan calls the very early beginning of acculturation 'Imaginary' because the mirror image that reveals the child to himself is, in fact, merely an image – or a signifier. His recognition of himself is therefore a misrecognition of an image, not a fact. No one, Lacan argues, no matter how well adjusted, ever leaves the Imaginary realm completely; there are always Imaginary residues (misrecognitions) even in the most powerful Symbolic forms. However, it has to be remarked that the Imaginary is

> not simply synonymous with 'the illusory' . . . it has powerful effects in the real, and is not simply something that can be dispensed with or 'overcome' . . . The basis of the imaginary order . . . [is] the formation of the ego in the mirror stage.[3] Since the ego is framed by identifying with the . . . specular image, identification is an important aspect of the imaginary order. The ego and the counterpart form the prototypical dual relationship and are interchangeable. This relationship . . . means that the ego, and the imaginary order itself, are both sites of a radical alienation [which, in Lacan's words, 'is constitutive of the imaginary order'] . . . Narcissism is another characteristic of the imaginary order . . . The imaginary is the realm of image and imagination, deception and lure. The principal illusions of the imaginary are those of wholeness, synthesis, autonomy, duality and, above all, similarity. The imaginary is thus the order of surface appearances which are deceptive . . . the imaginary is always already structured by the symbolic order . . . The imaginary also involves a linguistic dimension. Whereas the signifier is the foundation of the symbolic order, the signified and signification are part of the imaginary order . . .
>
> Dylan Evans (1996: 82–3)

The Real, Lacan's third realm, is the most problematic to define, and is not to be confused with 'reality': 'the Real is not synonymous with external reality, but rather with what is real for the subject' (Anthony Wilden 1981: 161). Moreover, the Real cannot be grasped by any signification, any determination.

> From the mid-sixties [in Lacan's discourse] . . . [t]he real was now deter-
> mined as the impossible, namely that which is logically excluded from
> any set of signifiers that form a system . . . Lacan's real is . . . profoundly
> ambivalent: as that which escapes symbolization it is both the traumatic
> *par excellence*, the unassimilable kernel at the heart of human experi-
> ence, and the contingent, the only haven for human subjectivity.
>
> Gilbert D. Chaitin (1996: 8–9)

How is it possible to speak of the Real? To risk definition, it might be
suggested that it is a 'force' (and I'm not certain about this term) which,
though inaccessible and inarticulable as such, none the less operates on the
subject from the non-place of the subject's otherness. Turning to another
attempt at definition, we see that

> the real . . . is located beyond the symbolic . . . the real . . . [is] that which
> is outside language and inassimilable to symbolization . . . The real . . .
> is impossible to imagine, impossible to integrate into the symbolic order,
> and impossible to attain in any way. It is this character of impossibility
> and of resistance to symbolization which lends the real its essentially
> traumatic quality . . . The real also has connotations of matter, implying
> a material substrate underlying the imaginary and the symbolic . . . The
> connotations of matter also link the concept of the real to . . . the body
> in its brute physicality (as opposed to the imaginary and symbolic func-
> tions of the body).
>
> Dylan Evans (1996: 159–60)

Irreducible to any symbolization, there is for Lacan only ever a glimpse of
the Real as an *après-coup*, an after-blow or effect of a catastrophic event
leaving its mark on the subject:

> the function of the *tuché*,[4] of the real as encounter – the encounter in so
> far as it may be missed, in so far as it is essentially the missed encounter
> – first presented itself in the history of psycho-analysis in a form that was
> in itself already enough to arouse our attention, that of the trauma.
>
> Jacques Lacan (1994: 55)

Lacan's recognition of the Real as the belated encounter, as the sign of an
otherwise unsymbolizable trauma is developed in the final citation around
jouissance, which for Žižek embodies the paradoxical condition of seeking
to articulate the inarticulable.

> If we define the Real as such a paradoxical, chimerical entity which,
> although it does not exist, has a series of properties and can produce a

series of effects, it becomes clear that the Real *par excellence* is *jouis-sance*; *jouissance* does not exist, it is impossible, but it produces a number of traumatic effects. This paradoxical nature of *jouissance* also offers us a clue to explaining the fundamental paradox which unfailingly attests the presence of the Real: the fact of the prohibition of something which is already in itself impossible. The elementary model is, of course, the prohibition of incest; but there are many other examples – let us cite only the usual conservative attitude towards child sexuality: it does not exist, children are innocent beings, that is why we must control them strictly and fight child sexuality – not to mention the obvious fact that the most famous phrase of all analytical philosophy – the last proposition of Wittgenstein's *Tractatus*[5] – implies the same paradox: 'Whereof one cannot speak, thereof one must by silent'. Immediately the stupid question arises: If it is already stated that it is *impossible* to say anything about the unspeakable, why add that we *must not* speak about it?

Slavoj Žižek (1989: 164)

Questions for further consideration

1. Consider the various provisional determinations of the Real in the light of its elusiveness. If it cannot be signified as such, what can be said about it?
2. What is the subject's relation to the Symbolic order?
3. Consider the distinctions made between the Imaginary and the Symbolic orders at the level of the signifier.

Explanatory and bibliographical notes

1. *Diachronic*: generally meaning 'through time', modern usage originates with Saussure, who differentiates approaches to the study of linguistics between *diachronic* and *synchronic*, where the former indicates the study of language as it has developed historically, while the latter suggests the study of the development of language at a given historical moment. A synchronic approach to linguistics lends itself more readily to a structural analysis because its attention is focused not on single words but on the relation of signs in a given field.
2. Claude Lévi-Strauss (*b.*1908–): *Structural Anthropology*, trans. Claire Jacobson and Brooke Grundfest Schoepf (New York: Basic Books, 1963); *The Raw and the Cooked*, trans. John and Doreen Weightman (New York: Harper & Row, 1969); *Tristes Tropiques*, n.t. (New York: Modern Library, 1997).
3. *Mirror stage*: a structural concept crucial in Lacanian psychoanalysis, first emerging in Lacan's thought in the 1930s and subsequently developed throughout his career, the mirror stage is fundamental in the formation of subjectivity through the recognition and identification of one's own image. As Lacan puts

it, 'the mirror stage is not simply a moment in development. It also has an exemplary function, because it reveals some of the subject's relations to his image, in so far as it is the *Urbild* [primal or originary image or picture] of the ego' (Lacan 1991: 74). It marks for Lacan a fundamental turning point in the psychic development of the infant, while also typifying an essential relationship with the image of the subject's corporeal image. Importantly, Lacan suggests, when the infant recognizes her or his reflected image, there is the assumption of mastery although in reality such recognition is really a misunderstanding, the ego being constituted through an inescapable alienation.

4.   *Tuché*: chance, a catastrophic disturbance or shocking event.
5.   Ludwig Wittgenstein (*b*.1889–*d*.1951): *Tractatus Logico-Philosophicus*, trans. D. F. Pears and B. F. McGuinness, Introduction by Bertrand Russell (London: Routledge, 1974); *The Blue and Brown Books: Preliminary Studies for the Philosophical Investigations*, 2nd edn (Oxford: Basil Blackwell, 1969).

Further reading

Althusser, Louis (1996), *Writings on Psychoanalysis: Freud and Lacan* (1993), trans. Jeffrey Mehlman (New York: Columbia University Press).

Evans, Dylan (1996), *An Introductory Dictionary of Lacanian Psychoanalysis* (London: Routledge).

Felman, Shoshana (1987), *Jacques Lacan and the Adventure of Insight: Psychoanalysis in Contemporary Culture* (Cambridge, MA: Harvard University Press).

Forrester, John (1990), *The Seductions of Psychoanalysis: Freud, Lacan and Derrida* (Cambridge: Cambridge University Press).

Lacan, Jacques (1977), *Écrits: A Selection* (1966), trans. Alan Sheridan (New York: W. W. Norton).

Lacan, Jacques (1994), *The Four Fundamental Concepts of Psycho-Analysis* (1973), ed. Jacques-Alain Miller, trans. Alan Sheridan, Introduction by David Macey (London: Penguin).

Leclaire, Serge (1998a), *Psychoanalyzing: On the Order of the Unconscious and the Practice of the Letter* (1968), trans. Peggy Kamuf (Stanford, CA: Stanford University Press).

Nasio, Juan-David (1998), *Five Lessons on the Psychoanalytic Theory of Jacques Lacan* (1992), trans. David Pettigrew and François Raffoul (Albany, NY: State University of New York Press).

INTERPELLATION

Interpellation is the process by which any individual is constituted within society as a subject. It is commonly associated with certain strands of

Marxist thought, most specifically with the work of Louis Althusser, which denotes the ways in which subjects are placed in false positions of knowledge regarding themselves by the discursive networks of ideology, often, if not always, constituted in this manner by an illusory self-knowledge the premise of which is autonomy; the subject misrecognizes him- or herself as an individual whose ideological, cultural or historical positioning is minimal or, for some, non-existent:

> *all ideology hails or interpellates concrete individuals as concrete subjects*, by the functioning of the category of the subject . . .
> . . . ideology 'acts' or 'functions' in such a way that it 'recruits' subjects among the individuals . . . or 'transforms' the individuals into subjects . . . by that very precise operation which I have called *interpellation* or hailing, and which can be imagined along the lines of the most commonplace everyday police (or other) hailing: 'Hey, you there!'
> Assuming that the theoretical scene I have imagined takes place in the street, the hailed individual will turn round. By this mere . . . conversion, he becomes a subject. Why? Because he has recognized that the hail was 'really' addressed to him . . .
> Louis Althusser (1971: 173–4)

The moment of hailing is inaugural, initiating an ongoing process by which the subject is interpellated, that is, made to enter into a process of accounting for his or her social position as subject. For Althusser, ideology pre-exists individuals:

> ideology has always-already interpellated individuals as subjects, which amounts to making it clear that individuals are always-already interpellated by ideology as subjects, which necessarily leads us to one last proposition: *individuals are always-already subjects.*
> Louis Althusser (1971: 175–6)

For this reason, subjectification is inescapable. Arguably, there is no position outside of ideology. Interpellation produces us as subjects and subject to, or subjected by, laws, beliefs, and other systems and structures of values. In order for it to do its work, ideological interpellation must call to us on the basis that, in believing ourselves to be hailed by particular ideas or concepts, we respond to that which we misunderstand as an ideal figure or subject, in which we therefore seek to see our own subjectivity reflected.

> We observe that the structure of all ideology, interpellating individuals as subjects in the name of a Unique and Absolute Subject, is *speculary*, i.e. a mirror-structure and *doubly* specular: this mirror duplication is

constitutive of ideology and ensures its functioning. Which means that all ideology is *centred*, that the Absolute Subject occupies the unique place of the Centre, and interpellates around it the infinity of individuals into subjects . . . such that it *subjects* the subjects to the Subject, while giving them in the Subject in which each subject can contemplate its own image . . . the *guarantee* that this really concerns them . . .

Louis Althusser (1971: 180)

The process of interpellation necessarily limits both autonomy and agency:

in Althusser's account of the construction of the subject through the process of interpellation, the result of the linkage of the concept of the subject to the question of social reproduction is to reduce individuals to functional supports of the system.

John Frow (1986: 76)

It should not be thought, however, that interpellation is merely a process of subjectification effected from ruling social positions, and imposed merely on the working classes:

individuals are not necessarily recruited and constituted as subjects obedient to the ruling class, the same mechanism of interpellation operates when individuals are recruited by revolutionary ideologies . . . Every ideological discourse articulates several interpellations.

Jorge Larrain (1996: 49)

The important aspect of interpellation is therefore revealed in the sense we have within us, not merely that we are called but that we are chosen.

When we *recognize* ourselves as interpellated, as the addressees of an ideological call, we *misrecognize* the radical contingency of finding ourselves at the place of interpellation; we fail to notice how our 'spontaneous' perception that the Other (God, Nation, and so on) has chosen *us* as its addressee results from the retroactive inversion of contingency to necessity: we do not recognize ourselves in the ideological call because we were chosen; on the contrary, we perceive ourselves as chosen, as the addressee of a call, because we recognized ourselves in it – *the contingent act of recognition engenders retroactively its own necessity* (the same illusion as that of the reader of a horoscope who 'recognizes' himself as its addressee by taking contingent coincidences of the obscure predictions with his actual life as proof that the horoscope 'speaks about *him*').

Slavoj Žižek (1991: 109)

This is exemplified for Žižek by the novels of Franz Kafka:[1]

> the starting point in Kafka's novels is that of an interpellation: the Kafkaesque subject is interpellated by a mysterious bureaucratic entity (Law, Castle). But this interpellation has a somewhat strange look: it is, so to say, an *interpellation without identification/subjectivation*; it does not offer us a Cause with which to identify – the Kafkaesque subject is the subject desperately seeking a trait with which to identify, he does not understand the meaning of the call of the Other.
>
> This is the dimension overlooked in the Althusserian account of interpellation . . .
>
> Slavoj Žižek (1989: 44)

Chosenness as misrecognition has, for Žižek, a psychoanalytic, specifically Lacanian, aspect to it, which also provides a corrective to Althusser's understanding.

> The Althusserian 'ideological interpellation'[2] designates the retroactive illusion of 'always-already': the reverse of the ideological recognition is the misrecognition of the performative dimension. That is to say, when the subject recognizes himself in an ideological call, he automatically overlooks the fact that this very formal act of recognition creates the content one recognizes oneself in . . . What is missing from the Althusserian account . . . is that it is a move aimed at resolving the dead-lock of the subject's radical uncertainty as to its status (what am I qua object for the Other?). The first thing to do apropos of interpellation in a Lacanian approach is therefore to reverse Althusser's formula of ideology which 'interpellates individuals into subjects': it is never the individual which is interpellated as subject, *into* subject; it is on the contrary the subject itself who is interpellated as x (some specific subject-position . . .).
>
> Slavoj Žižek (1993: 73)

As what might be seen as a tangential supplement to Žižek's reformulation, we can conclude with the following remark, which overturns the Althusserian schema, by reading subject-position as a crucial and necessary central principle on which the efficacy of ideological interpellation depends.

> If . . . the basic function of all ideology is to constitute individuals as subjects, and if through interpellation individuals live their conditions of existence as if they were the autonomous principle of the latter – as if they, the determinate, constituted the determinant – it is clear that the unity of the distinct aspects of an ideological system is given by the specific interpellation which forms the axis and organizing principle of

all ideology . . . *what constitutes the unifying principle of an ideological discourse is the 'subject' interpellated and thus constituted through this discourse.*
. . .

There are different types of interpellations (political, religious, familial, etc.) which coexist whilst being articulated within an ideological discourse in a relative unity. In what way is one interpellation articulated with another . . . what is it that enables them both to form part of a relatively unified ideological discourse? By unity we must not necessarily understand logical consistency . . . but the ability of each interpellative element to fulfil a role of condensation with respect to the others. When a familial interpellation, for example, *evokes* a political interpellation, a religious interpellation, or an aesthetic interpellation, and when each of these . . . operates as a *symbol* of the others, we have a relatively unified ideological discourse.

Ernesto Laclau (1977: 101–2)

Questions for further consideration

1. Consider the interpellation of the subject in light of the Lacanian concepts of the Imaginary and Symbolic orders, drawing out the implications of possible reciprocity between aspects of Marxist and psychoanalytic discourses.
2. If interpellation involves the subject in misrecognition as an intrinsic element of 'socialization', to what extent may this process be considered as hegemonic?
3. Consider possible examples of the 'types' of interpellation offered by Laclau; how do each of these exemplary 'calls' function?

Explanatory and bibliographical notes

1. Franz Kafka (*b*.1883–*d*.1924): the novels to which Žižek refers in this sentence are *The Trial*, trans. Willa and Edwin Muir, rev. edn trans. E. M. Butler (New York: Schocken, 1974), and *The Castle*, trans. Willa and Edwin Muir, rev. edn trans. Eithne Wilkins and Ernst Kaiser (New York: Schocken, 1982).
2. Žžek draws the phrase 'ideological interpellation' from Althusser's essay 'Ideology and Ideological State Apparatuses', in *Lenin and Philosophy and Other Essays* (1971: 127–88).

Further reading

Althusser, Louis (1971), *Lenin and Philosophy and Other Essays*, trans. Ben Brewster (New York: Monthly Review Press).

Laclau, Ernesto (1977), *Politics and Ideology in Marxist Theory: Capitalism–Fascism–Populism* (London: Verso).

Žižek, Slavoj (1991), *For They Know Not What They Do: Enjoyment as a Political Factor* (London: Verso).

INTERTEXTUALITY

Intertextuality was coined originally by Julia Kristeva, and refers to the ways in which all utterances (whether written or spoken) necessarily refer to other utterances, since words and linguistic/grammatical structures pre-exist the individual speaker and the individual speech. Intertextuality can take place consciously, as when a writer sets out to quote from or allude to the works of another. But it always, in some sense, takes place in all utterance. Thus the structure of language can be said to be intertextual inasmuch as meaning is not intrinsic to any single word. To extend this, neither the Bible nor the texts of Plato can be said to be original, because they refer to and have embedded within them prior stories, narratives, ideas, concepts. In this sense, they can be said to be intertextual and therefore serve to illustrate how any text is always and only ever constituted as, and from, a weave of references. Here is a key exposition.

As we know, Freud specifies two fundamental 'processes' in the work of the unconscious: *displacement* and *condensation* . . . To these we must add a third 'process' – the *passage from one sign-system to another*. To be sure, this process comes about through a combination of displacement and condensation, but this does not account for its total operation . . . The new signifying system may be produced with the same signifying material: in language, for example, the passage may be made from narrative to text. Or it may be borrowed from different signifying materials: the transposition from a carnival scene to the written text, for instance. In this connection we examined the formation of a specific signifying system – the novel – as the result of a redistribution of several different sign-systems: carnival, courtly poetry, scholastic discourse. The term *inter-textuality* denotes this transposition of one (or several) sign-system(s) into another; but since this term has often been understood in the banal sense of 'study of sources', we prefer the term *transposition* because it specifies that the passage from one signifying practice is a field of transpositions of various signifying systems (an inter-textuality), one then understands that its 'place' of enunciation and its denoted 'object' are never single, complete and identical to themselves, but always plural, shattered, capable of being tabulated.

Julia Kristeva (1984: 59–60)

As can be seen from Kristeva's discussion, the category or, more accurately, process of intertextuality (at least in Kristeva's understanding, this comprehension is not always carried over in subsequent critical discussions of intertextuality) has a specific resonance with psychoanalytic discourse, especially those processes of condensation and displacement that, for Freud, constitute the work of the unconscious. The notion of intertextuality is succinctly summarized thus:

> texts . . . are always already inscribed by other texts; the very condition of possibility of reading and writing *is* intertextuality. In a certain sense, all reading and all writing doubles readings and writings that have gone before. That doubling is constitutive of reading and writing.
>
> Ellen T. Armour (1999: 66)

Furthermore, intertextuality is not merely a formal, literary matter, it is also historical (and therefore cultural and ideological).

> The concept of intertextuality requires that we understand the concept of text not as a self-contained structure but as differential and historical. Texts are shaped not by an immanent time but by the play of divergent temporalities . . . Texts are therefore not structures of presence but traces and tracings of otherness. They are shaped by the repetition and the transformation of other textual structures . . . These absent textual structures at once constrain the text and are represented by and within it . . . The form of representation of intertextual structures ranges from the explicit to the implicit . . . The process of intertextual reference is governed by the rules of the discursive formation within which it occurs . . . The identification of an intertext is an act of interpretation.
>
> John Frow (1990: 45–6)

Any given text's intertextual accretion and interpolation is closely bound up with questions of reading.

> The theory of intertextuality insists that a text (for the moment to be understood in the narrower sense) cannot exist as a hermetic or self-sufficient whole, and so does not function as a closed system. This is for two reasons. Firstly, the writer is a reader of texts (in the broadest sense) before s/he is a creator of texts, and therefore the work of art is inevitably shot through with references, quotations and influences of every kind . . . Secondly, a text is available only through some process of reading: what is produced at the moment of reading is due to the cross-fertilization of the packaged textual material (say, a book) by all the texts which the reader brings to it. A delicate allusion to a work unknown to the reader,

which therefore goes unnoticed, will have a dormant existence in that reading. On the other hand, the reader's experience of some practice or theory unknown to the author may lead to a fresh interpretation.

Michael Worton and Judith Still (1990: 1–2)

Questions for further consideration

1. Consider aspects of intertextuality in a novel such as *Frankenstein* or *Heart of Darkness*.
2. In what ways does the notion of intertextuality challenge the conventional separation between text and context?
3. In what ways does the notion of intertextuality question the authority of the author as an 'originary site' of textual production? Is the category of 'the author' itself intertextual?

Further reading

Kristeva, Julia (1984), *Revolution in Poetic Language* (1974), trans. Margaret Waller, Introduction by Leon S. Roudiez (New York: Columbia University Press).

Rajan, Tilottama (1991), 'Intertextuality and the Subject of Reading/Writing'. In Jay Clayton and Eric Rothstein (eds), *Influence and Intertextuality in Literary History* (Madison, WI: University of Wisconsin Press).

Worton, Michael, and Judith Still (eds) (1990), *Intertextuality: Theories and Practice* (Manchester: Manchester University Press).

ITERABILITY/ITERATION

The notion of *iterability* is first formalized in the text of Jacques Derrida, specifically in 'Signature Event Context'. As a quasi-concept, iterability or iteration challenges the very idea of the stability of concepts, identities, and conceptuality in general. Iterability does not signify repetition simply; it signifies an alterability and, indeed, an alterity within the repetition of the same: a novel is a novel, generically, but every novel will inevitably differ from every other; therefore, the novel cannot, by definition, be defined even though there is that which amounts to the traces of an identity which are available for recognition, and by which the 'novel' as such is understood. Thus a generalized notion of the novel is destabilized by our experience of every novel we read, and we have to deal with the paradox of the simultaneity of sameness and difference.

The principle of iterability or repetition-with-a-difference is necessary for any writing. Indeed, a written sign that is not iterable is arguably unthinkable. Thus, iterability is of the very condition of writing. Here, Derrida argues that for a writing to function properly it must, in principle, be iterable in the absence of any subject or addressee.

> My 'written communication' must . . . remain legible despite the absolute disappearance of every determined addressee for it to function as writing, that is, for it to be legible. It must be repeatable – iterable – in the absolute absence of the addressee or of the empirically determinable set of addressees. This iterability . . . structures the mark of writing itself, and does so moreover no matter what type of writing . . . A writing that was not structurally legible – iterable – beyond the death of the addressee would not be writing . . . Let us imagine a writing . . . idiomatic enough to have been founded and known . . . only by two 'subjects'. Can it still be said that upon the death . . . of the two partners, the mark left by one of them is still a writing? Yes, to the extent to which, governed by a code . . . it is constituted, in its identity as a mark, by its iterability in the absence of whoever, and therefore ultimately in the absence of every empirically determinable 'subject'. This implies that there is no code . . . that is structurally secret. The possibility of repeating, and therefore of identifying, marks is implied in every code, making of it a communicable, transmittable, decipherable grid that is iterable for a third party, and thus for any possible user in general. All writing, therefore, in order to be what it is, must be able to function in the radical absence of every empirically determined addressee in general.
>
> Jacques Derrida (1982: 315–16)

Here the relationship between self and non-self, identity and alterity, is explored in light of the structural principle of iterability.

> Identity . . . depends on repetition, which, however, in turn presupposes something like identity . . . this irreducibility of repetition . . . [is taken by Derrida] to be the underlying characteristic of writing, of language and of articulation in general: 'the structure of iterability' . . . in order to be apprehended or identified as such – and every signifying element must be *identifiable as such* in order for it to signify – every signifier or 'mark' must be re-cognizable, re-peatable. It never can present itself simply once. Taking this argumentation one step further: in order to be *cognizable*, an element must be recognizable as the *same*, which in turn presupposes a process of *com-parison* and *repetition*. It must be compared with earlier instances of itself in order to be recognizable *as a self*, as an identity.

This process of repetitive comparison, out of which self-sameness emerges and which it therefore must *pass through*, introduces an element of *heterogeneity*, of *otherness*, into the constitution of the same. The question, however, now becomes: precisely what is the role of this heterogeneity in the process of repetition that is presupposed by every identification and by all identity? ... the alterity presupposed by all repetition can never be absorbed into the identification of the same. There will always ... be something left over, a remainder ...

Samuel Weber (1996: 138–9)

Within any identity therefore, as an element of that identity and yet irreducible to the order of the self-same, some remainder, some sign of difference, makes possible both the identity in question and the iterability of an identity beyond any simple presence.

> Iterability supposes a minimal remainder ... in order that the identity of the *selfsame* be repeatable and identifiable *in*, *through*, and even *in view of* its alteration. For the structure of iteration – and this is another of its decisive traits – implies both identity *and* difference. Iteration in its 'purest' form – and it is always impure – contains *in itself* the discrepancy of a difference that constitutes it as iteration. The iterability of an element divides its own identity a priori, even without taking into account the fact that this identity can only *determine* or delimit itself through differential relations to other elements and that it hence bears the mark of this difference. It is because this iterability is differential, within each individual 'element' as well as between the 'elements', because it splits each element while constituting it, because it marks it with an articulatory break, that the remainder, although indispensable, is never that of a full or fulfilling presence: it is a differential structure escaping the logic of presence or the (simple or dialectical) opposition of presence and absence ...

Jacques Derrida (1988a: 53)

Identity is thus never pure, because it is constituted only through a differentiating repetition.

> One of the corollaries of the structure of alterity, which is the revised version of the structure of identity, is that every repetition is an alteration. This would put into question both a transcendental idealism that claims that the idea is infinitely repeatable as the same and a speech act theory that bases its conclusions on intentions and contexts that can be defined and transferred within firm outlines. Iterability is the name of this corollary: every repetition is an alteration (iteration).

But repetition is the basis of identification. Thus, if repetition alters, it has to be faced that alteration identifies and identity is always impure. Thus iterability . . . is the positive condition of possibility of identification, the very thing whose absolute rigor it renders impossible. It is in terms of iterable (rather than repeatable) identities that communication and consensus are established.

Gayatri Chakravorty Spivak (1996: 86–7)

The principle of iterability applies not only to identity and communication, to notions of the self or writing in general, but also to the singularity of texts and the possibility of their transmission.

For the work to be singular, iterability demands that the work repeat itself singularly, to alter itself in order to preserve or conserve itself as singular . . . In all rigor, iterability precludes the possibility of a pure founding . . . To love [a work] . . . as mortal is to love it through its birth/death because iterability makes of the thing or text a ghost, something that begins by returning (which is what is meant by beginning as iterability).

Joseph Kronick (1999: 67)

The notion of iterability holds profound and radical implications for thinking any supposedly originary or unique moment or, more accurately, the impossibility of any such instance's purity.

What happens when the unique death is taken up into all the codes and rituals of mourning, when the singular event comes to be marked by the designated spaces and times of mourning, when all talk of death comes to be inflected by a prescribed rhetoric? Can there be other words in which to mourn?

Because of the possibility, indeed, the ineluctability of iteration, we should perhaps not assume that we can ever identify with absolute certainty the object of our mourning . . . perhaps all our mournings are but iterations of the one death that can never be identified.

Pascale-Anne Brault and Michael Naas (2001: 17)

Iterability also disrupts the possibility of a single or authoritative meaning produced by an act of reading, disrupting as well the temporality of reading.

Since the eventhood of an event of 'writing' is riven by iterability, there is never just one 'proper reading' of a 'text'; another reading is *always possible*. 'Writing' is such that it always offers itself to new readings, new responses – and, hence, new *responsibilities*. This rhythm of reading, and the ineluctable responsibility which it implies, is inescapable. It is a rhythm that does not end. Or barely, for example, ~~now~~.

Simon Glendinning (1998: 152)

Questions for further consideration

1. Compare the discussions of iterability with those concerning difference; in doing so, consider the possibility of making connections between textual and material conditions.
2. What are the implications of the concept of iterability for any notion of uniqueness or originality? Can we ever call something 'unique' without the possibility of transmission or communication implied by iteration?
3. Consider the notion of subjectivity in the light of Samuel Weber's comments.

Further reading

Derrida, Jacques (1982), *Margins of Philosophy* (1972), trans., with notes, by Alan Bass (Chicago, IL: University of Chicago Press).
Derrida, Jacques (1988a), 'Limited Inc a b c . . .', trans. Samuel Weber, *Glyph* 2 (1977). Reprinted in *Limited Inc.,* trans. Samuel Weber and Jeffrey Mehlman (Evanston, IL: Northwestern University Press), pp. 29–110.
Kronick, Joseph G. (1999), *Derrida and the Future of Literature* (Albany, NY: State University of New York Press).
Weber, Samuel (1996), *Mass Mediauras: Form Technics Media* (Stanford, CA: Stanford University Press).

JOUISSANCE

As we will see in some of the following citations, *jouissance* is an impossible term to translate. Used extensively in psychoanalytic discourse, after the work of Jacques Lacan on human sexuality, jouissance is retained in the French in psychoanalytic literary criticism published in English, signalling the difficulty of rendering the word otherwise. *Jouissance* may be translated neutrally, though not without problems, as 'pleasure' or 'enjoyment'; at the same time however, in French there are legal connotations relating to property and rights, lost in translation, referring to the right to enjoy. Concerning the matter of enjoyment, the term in French can mean the surplus value of goods and is deployed by revolutionaries, who adopted the cause of *jouissance* over the property-owning classes. Thus it might be asked, what is the connection between property rights, enjoyment and sexuality? One answer, undoubtedly crude and reductive, is excess or excess-value, that which is produced but which is of no particular use; there is, therefore, a sense of transgression implied by the term, as the first citation shows.

> There is no adequate translation in English of this word [*jouissance*]. 'Enjoyment' conveys the sense, contained in *jouissance*, of enjoyment of rights, of property, etc. Unfortunately, in modern English, the word has lost the sexual connotations it still retains in French. (*Jouir* is slang for 'to come'.) . . . 'Pleasure' obeys the law of homeostasis[1] that Freud evokes in 'Beyond the Pleasure Principle',[2] whereby, through discharge, the psyche seeks the lowest possible level of tension. '*Jouissance*' transgresses this law and, in that respect, it is *beyond* the pleasure principle.
>
> Alan Sheridan (1977: x)

This resistance to translation does however serve us usefully, albeit perhaps by accident. What remains untranslatable, the excess that resonates from within, if you will, may be read analogically at least as a sign or remainder of the excess itself of *jouissance* beyond the idea of pleasure as a form of controlled psychic release.

The word has come to be used in psychoanalytic and feminist theories to mean more than such neutral translations, coming to signify especially pleasures associated with sensuous and sexual gratification, or orgasm. As such, it refers to a fulfilment that is necessarily merely temporary, and that must therefore always be sought anew. It figures an excess beyond any economy of exchange, as is implied by mere pleasure.

> It is the use, the enjoyment, the *jouissance*, which exceeds exchange. The opposition of *jouissance* and pleasure can refer to a legal meaning of *jouissance*, as having the use of something. Notice the example of usufruct,[3] given in the dictionary under *jouissance*. 'Usufruct' is the right to the *jouissance* but *not the ownership* of something; in other words, you can use and enjoy it, but you cannot exchange it.
>
> Jane Gallop (1984: 49–50)

Furthermore, it is for Lacan the economy of pleasure which implies limits.

> For it is pleasure that sets the limits on *jouissance*, pleasure as that which binds incoherent life together, until another unchallengeable prohibition arises from the regulation that Freud discovered as the primary process and appropriate law of pleasure.
>
> Jacques Lacan (1977: 319)

Luce Irigaray moves beyond the Lacanian model, distinguishing between gendered modes.

> For women, there are at least two modes of *jouissance*. One is programmed in a male libidinal economy in accordance with a certain phallic order. Another is much more in harmony with what they are, with their sexual identity . . . if we are to discover our female identity, I do think it is important to know that, for us, there is a relationship with *jouissance* other than that which functions in accordance with the phallic model.
>
> Luce Irigaray (1991a: 45)

The political aspect of one's sexual enjoyment, of the right one has to one's *jouissance* free of governing economies, is explicitly attested to by Irigaray, who argues that women are divided and identified by two articulations of *jouissance*: that which is subordinate to patriarchal governance, and that which is a woman's own. Irigaray extends her discussion of a specifically female *jouissance*, which

> would be of the order of the constant and gradual creation of a dimension ranging from the most corporeal to the most spiritual, a dimension which is never complete and never reversible . . . woman generates through her *jouissance* . . . a bridge between what is most earthly and most celestial . . . Women's dissatisfaction . . . no doubt stems from this perpetual deferment of a *jouissance* which is theirs, where they might find themselves, or find themselves anew.
>
> Luce Irigaray (1991c: 190)

It is necessary at this juncture to return to the problem of translation and meaning, in order to grasp the structure and deferral of *jouissance* more fully.

> The French word *jouissance* means basically 'enjoyment', but it has a sexual connotation (i.e. 'orgasm') lacking in the English word 'enjoyment' . . . The pleasure principle[4] functions as a limit to enjoyment; it is a law which commands the subject to 'enjoy as little as possible'. At the same time, the subject constantly attempts to transgress the prohibitions imposed on his enjoyment, to go 'beyond the pleasure principle'. However, the result of transgressing . . . is . . . pain . . . The prohibition of *jouissance* (the pleasure principle) is inherent in the symbolic structure of language . . . The subject's entry into the symbolic is conditional upon a certain initial renunciation of *jouissance* . . . The very prohibition creates the desire to transgress it, and *jouissance* is therefore fundamentally transgressive.
>
> Dylan Evans (1996: 91–2)

As this remark suggests, there is therefore a structural resemblance between the linguistic and psychic operation of *jouissance*, which is all the more pointed when one considers, as Evans directs us to do, that the symbolic condition of language prohibits direct access to *jouissance*: language structures, signifying beyond themselves and yet maintaining signification as the possibility of the production of meaning, resist and forbid any fall or overflow into an excess perceivable as meaninglessness. It is for this reason that one has to address matters of economy. Meaning and the control or limits it implies is the product of, and functions as part of, on the one hand, a restricted, or on the other, a patriarchal economy, wherein both economies put to work and keep in order the various elements or materials (including psychic 'materials' such as pleasure), for the production of stable meanings (such as the idea of the mentally healthy subject or the hierarchical mapping of society according to the assumed primacy of the male). *Jouissance*, however, speaks of that beyond the restrictions of economy and moreover reconfigures the sexual/personal and the political, in bearing in it the question of the matter of enjoyment of rights and property.

It is impossible to overstress the significance of *jouissance* to Lacanian psychoanalytic theory, and yet also the impossibility which it signals (as with the impossibility of a full translation, there is always that in *jouissance* which remains absolutely other, inexpressible as such). It is a sign of its importance that Juan-David Nasio, a practising psychoanalyst and former member of Lacan's *École Freudienne*, begins his study of Lacan's psychoanalytic theory with a lengthy consideration of *jouissance*.

> The three states of *jouissance*: *phallic jouissance*, *surplus-of-jouissance*, and *jouissance of the Other*. Phallic *jouissance* corresponds to the dissipated energy at the time of the partial discharge and has the effect of . . . an incomplete relief of unconscious tension. This category of *jouissance* is called phallic because the limit that opens and closes access to the discharge is the phallus (Freud would have said: repression). Basically, the phallus functions as a barrier which regulates the part of *jouissance* that leaves (discharges) and that which remains in the unconscious system (residual excess) . . . surplus-of-*jouissance* corresponds to the *jouissance* that on the contrary remains confined within the psychical system and whose exit is prevented by the phallus. The term '*surplus*' . . . indicates that part of the energy is not discharged, the residual *jouissance*, a surplus that constantly increases the intensity of the internal tension . . . the *jouissance* of the Other, [is] a fundamentally hypothetical state which corresponds to the ideal case in which the tension would have been totally discharged without the impediment of any limit . . . This ideal state . . . of an absolute and impossible happiness, takes different forms according to the perspective from which one sees it . . . But

whether ideally desire is accomplished by a total cessation of tension, as in the case of death . . . it nevertheless remains that all these excessive and absolute forms are fictions, bewitching and deceptive mirages that fan the flames of desire.

Juan-David Nasio (1998: 27–8)

Nasio makes a significant point about the 'fictional' nature of an absolute experience of *jouissance*, an experience which is fictional because we, as subjects who desire, and yet who can never fulfil desire, are always frustrated.

Perhaps the experience of this frustration is caught in the following remark, that 'Jouissance is what serves no purpose' (Jacques Lacan, 1998: 3). This might appear, initially, to suggest the futility of even attempting to address *jouissance*. However, though perhaps the most straightforward, if frustrating, of remarks in the present section, Lacan's seemingly off-the-cuff assertion is arguably the most accurate and most radical assessment of this motif. Its radicality is announced in the statement's resistance to any economy. Being useless, strictly speaking, being marked and remarking moreover by this excessive inutility – this is, we might suggest, the only possible definition of *jouissance* – *jouissance* cannot be put to work within any structure, semantic or reproductive, or assigned a finite determination.

Questions for further consideration

1. Consider the ways in which *jouissance* promises (or threatens) the erasure of any stable boundaries by which the subject conceives him/herself? Does such erasure make it possible to think a relationship between *jouissance* and *abjection*? What are the implications of such a connection for consideration of the subject?
2. What is the difference between pleasure and *jouissance*?
3. In the light of various commentaries, why does the idea of *jouissance* appear to threaten economic structures and other structures which delimit meaning or value?

Explanatory and bibliographical notes

1. *Homeostasis*: the maintenance of a stable state through internal processes which regulate the system in question, thereby sustaining equilibrium. The internal process identified in this quotation is that of psychic discharge.
2. Sigmund Freud, *Beyond the Pleasure Principle*, Penguin Freud Library vol. 11, trans. James Strachey, ed. James Strachey and Angela Richards (Harmondsworth: Penguin, 1961).

3. *Usufruct*: a legal term meaning 'the right of enjoying the use of and income from another's property without destroying, damaging, or diminishing the property' (*OED*). Given the legal and sexual implications in *jouissance*, the sense is that, in theory at least, one may enjoy the body of the other without harming or possessing the other. *Jouissance* also appears in the *OED*, where, as in much that is translated from French to English, all sexual association is erased. The definition given is of 'the possession and use *of* something advantageous or pleasing'.
4. Freud names the *pleasure principle* that desire in humans to find pleasure and avoid pain, as a means of maintaining homeostasis. However, this is countered, suggests Freud, by the 'reality principle': needing to eat and clothe ourselves and find shelter, we have to work, so the pleasure principle becomes repressed, which, Freud argues, can lead to neuroses.

Further reading

Gallop, Jane (1984), *The Daughter's Seduction: Feminism and Psychoanalysis* (Ithaca, NY: Cornell University Press).

Irigaray, Luce (1985), ' "Woman's" *Jouissance*'. In *Speculum of the Other Woman* (1974), trans. Gillian C. Gill (Ithaca, NY: Cornell University Press), pp. 353–64.

Lacan, Jacques (1977), *Écrits: A Selection* (1966), trans. Alan Sheridan (New York: W. W. Norton).

Leclaire, Serge (1998a), *Psychoanalyzing: On the Order of the Unconscious and the Practice of the Letter* (1968), trans. Peggy Kamuf (Stanford, CA: Stanford University Press).

Nasio, Juan-David (1998), *Five Lessons on the Psychoanalytic Theory of Jacques Lacan* (1992), trans. David Pettigrew and François Raffoul (Albany, NY: State University of New York Press).

KHŌRA/*CHORA*

Given its principal exposition in Plato's *Timaeus*,[1] *khōra* or *chora* is a figure of multiple ambiguity, one possible translation of which would be 'the receptacle of meaning, invisible and formless, which contains intelligibility but cannot itself be understood'. Jacques Derrida, spelling it *khôra*, provides a telling analysis of Plato's text, in which he aims to demonstrate how khōra can be defined only in ways pertaining to neither the sensible (having to do with feeling and emotion) nor the intelligible (having to do with rationality and intellect), and thus names that which is resistant to naming, which cannot be gathered by any name, and yet which is neither negative nor positive. Julia Kristeva has adapted 'chora' to describe a prelinguistic realm that underpins language and meaning, but which cannot itself be pinned down according to a semantic horizon. In the process of language development the chora is split to enable words (defined by limitation – by what they leave out) to come into meaning. The chora represents endless possibility but no single significance – single significance being what defines the delimiting semantic and patriarchal economy of language itself.

Here, Kristeva defines khōra provisionally as a signifying network.

> The distortion of words, the repetition of words and syntagms, and hyperkinesia or stereotypy[2] reveal that a *semiotic network* – the *chora* – has been established, one that simultaneously defies both verbal symbolization and the formation of a superego patterned after paternal law and sealed by language acquisition.
>
> Julia Kristeva (1984: 152)

This network, without architectonic order or arrangement, is not a static arrangement but, rather, a fluid process.

> Discrete quantities of energy move through the body of the subject who is not yet constituted as such and, in the course of his development, they are arranged according to the various constraints imposed on this body – always already involved in a semiotic process – by family and social structures. In this way the drives, which are 'energy' charges as well as 'physical' marks, articulate what we call a *chora*: a nonexpressive totality formed by the drives and their stases in a motility that is as full of movement as it is regulated.
>
> Julia Kristeva (1984: 25)

As Kristeva's figure makes apparent, one must speak of khōra by analogy, if one is to speak of khōra at all, and the analogy is always structural.

> Once again, a homology or analogy that is at least formal: in order to think *khôra*, it is necessary to go back to a beginning that is older than the beginning, namely, the birth of the cosmos. . . . In that which is formal about it, precisely, the analogy is declared: a concern for architectural, textual (histological[3]) and even organic composition is presented . . .
>
> Jacques Derrida (1995: 126–7)

Structural analogy is at best approximate, indirect because, preceding and exceeding all mimesis and ontology, khōra cannot by definition be defined. No one figure for khōra will suffice, and no figure is any more justifiable than any other.

Although our theoretical description of the *chora* is itself part of the discourse of representation that offers it as evidence, the *chora*, as rupture and articulations (rhythm), precedes evidence, verisimilitude, spatiality, and temporality. Our discourse – all discourse – moves with and against the *chora* in the sense that it simultaneously depends upon and refuses it. Although the *chora* can be designated and regulated, it can never be definitively posited: as a result, one can situate the *chora* and, if necessary, lend it a topology, but one can never give it axiomatic form.

The *chora* is not yet a position that represents something for someone (i.e. it is not a sign); nor is it a *position* that represents someone for another position (i.e., it is not yet a signifier either); it is, however, generated in order to attain this signifying position. Neither model nor copy, the *chora* precedes and underlies figuration and thus specularization, and is analogous only to vocal or kinetic rhythm. We must restore this motility's gestural and vocal play (to mention only the aspect relevant to language) on the level of the socialized body in order to remove motility from ontology and amorphousness where Plato confines it in an apparent attempt to conceal it from Democritean[4] rhythm.

Julia Kristeva (1984: 26)

This being the case, being neither a position nor an identity, being unrepresentable as such and irreducible to any representational modality,

> *Khôra* is not, is above all not, anything but a support or a subject which would *give* place by receiving or by conceiving, or indeed by letting itself be conceived.
>
> Jacques Derrida (1995: 95)

However, Kristeva wishes to aver that khōra is neither simply anarchic nor formlessly chaotic either.

> Though deprived of unity, identity, or deity, the *chora* is nevertheless subject to a regulating process [*réglementation*[5]], which is different from that of symbolic law but nevertheless effectuates discontinuities by temporarily articulating them and then starting over, again and again.
>
> Julia Kristeva (1984: 26)

Derrida highlights the problem as one residing in taxonomical and definitional genres.

> The *khôra*, which is neither 'sensible' not 'intelligible', belongs to a 'third genus' . . . at times the *khôra* appears to be neither this nor that, at times

both this and that, but this alternation between the logic of exclusion and that of participation ... stems perhaps only from a provisional appearance and from the constraints of rhetoric, even from some incapacity for naming.

Jacques Derrida (1995: 89)

Khōra makes possible identity, and is here accorded the status of a place:

the semiotic *chora* is no more than the place where the subject is both generated and negated, the place where his unity succumbs before the process of charges and stases that produce him.

Julia Kristeva (1984: 28)

Derrida displaces the static location of place by identifying khōra as that which gives place.

The consequence which we envisage would be the following: with these two polarities, the thought of the *khôra* would trouble the very order of polarity, of polarity in general, whether dialectical or not. Giving place to oppositions, it would itself not submit to any reversal.

Jacques Derrida (1995: 92)

The disruptive nature of khōra is that it makes possible that very kind of thinking which it exceeds and into which it cannot be recuperated. Enabling the very possibility of ontological or other forms of determination, it is none the less irrecuperable by any such definitional process. This remark is developed further, here.

Khôra receives, so as to give place to them, all the determinations, but she/it does not possess any of them as her/its own.

Jacques Derrida (1995: 99)

Certain translations of the Greek render khōra as 'receptacle' but even this is problematic to a certain extent, and thus we are left with what might be described as a secret in plain view.

But if *khôra* is a receptacle, if it/she gives place to all the stories, ontological or mythic, that can be recounted on the subject of what she receives and even of what she resembles but which in fact takes place in her, *khôra* herself, so to speak, does not become the object of any *tale*, whether true or fabled. A secret without secret remains forever impenetrable on the subject of it/her . . .

Jacques Derrida (1995: 117)

Questions for further consideration

1. Compare and contrast Derrida's and Kristeva's comments: what are the similarities and differences between them?
2. Is it more accurate to speak of *khōra/chora* as 'process' rather than as identity or object, and, if so, why?
3. In what ways does *khōra/chora* resist representation?

Explanatory and bibliographical notes

1. Plato (*b*.469BC–*d*.399BC): *Timaeus and Critias*, trans. and ed. Desmond Lee (London: Penguin, 1977); *The Last Days of Socrates*, trans. Hugh Tredennick and Harold Tarrant, Introduction by Harold Tarrant (London: Penguin, 1993); *The Symposium*, trans. Walter Hamilton, Introduction by Christopher John Gill (London: Penguin, 1999).
2. *Hyperkinesia*: hyperactivity; *stereotypy*: frequent repetition of motion or movement with no discernible purpose or meaning.
3. *Histological*: of the science of organic tissues, dealing with the minute structure of animal and plant tissue.
4. Kristeva is referring here, in passing, to Democritus (*b*. circa 470BC–*d*.360BC), who was popularly known amongst his contemporaries as 'the mocker', and who, apparently, would laugh while expressing contempt for human weakness.
5. *Réglementation*: rules or regulation; control.

Further reading

Derrida, Jacques (1984), *Khōra* (1993). In Jacques Derrida, *On the Name*, ed. Thomas Dutoit, trans. David Wood, John P. Leavey, Jr, and Ian McLeod (Stanford, CA: Stanford University Press), pp. 89–130.

Kristeva, Julia (1984), *Revolution in Poetic Language* (1974), trans. Margaret Waller, Introduction by Leon S. Roudiez (New York: Columbia University Press).

LITERATURE

At first glance, nothing might appear more self-evident than the meaning of *literature* (the literary is far more tricky); whether by this, one refers, perhaps somewhat mystifyingly, to prose writing of a certain 'quality', to rely on the obfuscation of aesthetic assumption, or, more generally (but no less obliquely), one signals a vast amorphous corpus of published writing in general. However, any sustained consideration of literature will have to arrive at the conclusion that, on the one hand, whatever is meant by literature, whenever the notion is employed, an implicit, normative narrative with all the hegemonic effects of a certain institutionalization comes into play; on the other hand, what goes by the name of literature cannot be defined with any confidence. Critics of various political and philosophical positions and persuasions have raised the question of the cultural, historical, social, political or ideological identity or purpose of literature, while others have positioned questions in terms of ontology (the very question 'what is literature?' is fundamentally institutional, premised on a supposedly discernible entity, the very delineation of which is assumed) or epistemology. Regardless of differences between critical articulations concerning literature and the ways in which it is put to work, at work in the rethinking of any notion of literature, there is to be seen a rigorous exposure of both the limits of definition and 'our' assumptions concerning what 'we' think literature is or might be.

Perhaps an initial thing to note is that

> at different periods in its history, this term [literature] could embrace a greater or lesser amount of nonfictional writing, and has always excluded some fictional writing, such as jokes and tall stories.
>
> Derek Attridge (2000a: 106)

This would suggest that the term 'literature' is somewhat empty of specific meaning, so mobile is its applicability and use according to various historical, cultural, aesthetic and ideological contexts. (Although, of course, it must also be stressed that 'literature' is irreducible to these concerns alone.) In light of this, one would have to agree, therefore, with the following statement.

> It is relatively difficult to see 'literature' as a concept. In ordinary usage it appears to be no more than a specific description, and what is described is then, as a rule, so highly valued that there is a virtually immediate and unnoticed transfer of the specific values of particular works and kinds of work to what operates as a concept but is still firmly believed to be actual and practical.
>
> Raymond Williams (1977: 45)

Indeed, anything that can be said of literary language with regard to its resistance to being pinned down, is also true of language in general.

> The properties of literary language that prevent exhaustive and objective analysis, making it overflow boundaries or resist classifications, can be

shown to be not peculiar to literature; they are at work in all uses of
language . . .

Derek Attridge (1988: 91)

However, if what we call literature is not simply reducible either to an
object or to a specific type of language or language use, it must also be
borne in mind that

> literature is not simply a matter of novels and poems, not a given body
> of work, but a question of reading, its strategies, difficulties and condi-
> tions.

Thomas Keenan (1997: 1)

So, we cannot say for certain what literature is, even though 'literature' is
taught and general principles are assumed.

> All reading and teaching of literature is theoretical in the sense that it
> presupposes assumptions about what literature is and how it should be
> read.

J. Hillis Miller (1991b: 47)

One of the theoretical principles is the very problem of definition or, as it
is put here, and which has been implicit in the way that this section has thus
far proceeded, the 'whatness, the ontology of literature'.

> The main theoretical difficulty inherent in the teaching of literature is the
> delimitation of borderlines that circumscribe the literary field by setting
> it apart from other modes of discourse. Hence the nervousness which
> any tampering with the canonical definition of a literary corpus is bound
> to provoke. In a manner that is more acute for theoreticians of literature
> than for theoreticians of the natural or the social world, it can be said
> that they do not quite know what it is they are talking about, not only
> in the metaphysical sense that the whatness, the ontology of literature is
> hard to fathom, but also in the more elusive sense that, whenever one is
> supposed to speak of literature, one speaks of anything under the sun
> (including, of course, oneself) except literature. The need for determina-
> tion thus becomes all the stronger as a way to safeguard a discipline
> which constantly threatens to degenerate into gossip, trivia or self-obses-
> sion. The most traditional term to designate these borderlines is 'form';
> in literature, the concept of form is, before anything else, a definitional
> necessity. No literary metadiscourse[1] would ever be conceivable in its
> absence. Before berating a critic or a theoretician for his formalism,[2] one
> should realize that it is the necessary precondition of any theory. This

does not mean, however, that the concept of form is itself susceptible to definition.

Paul de Man (1986: 29–30)

Once again, we find a difficulty having to do with the definition of form that itself is not restricted to the question of literature. What we might therefore propose for literature is not so much a definition of an object or its form, as though such definitions were either universal or absolute, so much as offering a provisional determination of function.

Literature has a vital importance because it is at once a formal record of experience, and also, in every work, a point of intersection with the common language that is, in its major bearings, differently perpetuated.

Raymond Williams (1961: 248)

This gets us no closer to responding to the matter of literature's 'whatness'. Functional definitions implicitly assume that they know what it is they are talking about. Of course, such commentaries are themselves shaped by a certain cultural consensus concerning the ontology of literature, even though, once investigated, the boundaries of such an ontology are found to be necessarily vague, ill-defined. One consensus concerning literature has developed around an aesthetic definition, whereby literature is placed in, and determined by, a strictly non-utilitarian realm.

The multiple responses that philosophers, linguists, semiologists and art historians have given to the question of the specificity of literature ('literariness'), poetry ('poeticity') or the work of art in general, and to the question of the properly aesthetic perception they call for, all concur in stressing the properties of gratuity, the absence of function, the primacy of form over function, disinterestedness and so on.

Pierre Bourdieu (1996: 285)

At this juncture we might be led to offer a 'suspicious' definition of literature's function:

literature is that ensemble of objects and rules, techniques and works, whose function in the general economy of our society is precisely to *institutionalise subjectivity*.

Roland Barthes (1983: 172)

Such a commentary would appear to require further tangential amplification, which, even though it might not tell us what literature *is*, none the less indicates how the category of literature has been put to work, as a unified and domesticated concept.

It is important to insist on literature as a cultural apparatus because its institutional arrangements are often effaced, for instance in literary criticism, to the point where authors and texts seem to communicate with readers without such mediation . . .

Even the concept [of literature] has been culturally produced: it emerged in the eighteenth century and was not fully developed until the nineteenth century. Eventually it came to mean 'printed works of a certain quality'[3] . . . and suitable texts were assimilated, retrospectively, to it . . . A profession of critical and scholarly experts grew up to support it, and its use in education followed . . .

Usually, in our culture, literature is envisaged as 'rising above' its conditions of production and reception; as transcending social and political concerns and other such mundane matters. The argument most often presented for this is that great art has endured the test of time. That is an idealist position . . .

Literature is an institutional arrangement we have made to dignify some writing (at the expense of others). This is not surprising or sinister: any culture will value some texts more highly than others. But . . . we are talking about *authority claims*. To have your work accepted as art or literature, or to be judged by an expert, is to gain a voice in a discourse with certain claims to significance.

Alan Sinfield (1989: 27–8)

That literature is an institutional form, institutionally legislated, is undoubtedly true. Yet this should not be taken as simply repressive, exclusive, or elitist. There is another side to this.

What we call literature . . . implies that license is given to the writer to say everything he wants to or everything he can, while remaining shielded, safe from all censorship, be it religious or political.

Jacques Derrida (1992a: 37)

This remark is extended, in a response to the question concerning the ontology of literature.

'What is literature?'; literature as historical institution with its conventions, rules, etc., but also this institution of fiction which gives *in principle* the power to say everything, to break free of the rules, to displace them, and thereby to institute, to invent and even to suspect the traditional difference between nature and institution, nature and conventional law, nature and history. Here we should ask juridical and political questions. The institution of literature in the West, in its relatively modern form, is linked to an authorization to say everything, and doubtless too to the coming about of the modern idea of democracy. Not that it depends on a democracy in place, but it seems inseparable to me from what calls forth a democracy, in the most open . . . sense of democracy.

Jacques Derrida (1992a: 37)

The notion of 'literature' is, then, related to a certain understanding of modernity, its appearance in the West being somewhat concomitant with the advent of democracy.

> Literature is a modern invention, inscribed in conventions and institutions, which, to hold on to just this trait, secures in principle its *right to say everything*. Literature thus ties its destiny to a certain non-censure, to the space of democratic freedom . . . No democracy without literature; no literature without democracy . . . The possibility of literature, the legitimation that a society gives it, the allaying of suspicion or terror with regard to it, all that goes together – politically – with the unlimited right to ask any question, to suspect all dogmatism, to analyse every presupposition, even those of the ethics or the politics of responsibility.
>
> Jacques Derrida (1992b: 23)

The very idea of 'literature' arrives from some other place, then, defined by criteria extrinsic to the 'qualities' of any so-called literary object or literary language *per se*. Moreover,

> literarity is not an intrinsic property of this or that discursive event. Even where it seems to *reside* . . . literature remains an unstable function, and it depends on a precarious juridical status . . . it receives its determination from something other than itself. Even when it harbors the unconditional right to say anything . . . its *status* is never assured or guaranteed permanently . . . at home . . . This contradiction is its very existence . . . Before coming to writing, literature depends on reading and the right conferred on it by an experience of reading. One can read the same text – which thus never exists 'in itself' – as a testimony that is said to be serious and authentic, or as an archive, or as a document, or as a symptom – or as a work of literary fiction, indeed, the work of a literary fiction that simulates all of the positions that we have just enumerated. For literature can say anything, accept anything, receive anything, suffer anything, and simulate everything . . .
>
> Jacques Derrida (2000a: 28–9)

One thing which can be said with any certainty about literature therefore is that:

there is no essence or substance of literature: literature is not. It does not exist. It does not remain at home, *abidingly* . . . in the identity of a nature or even of a historical being identical with itself. It does not maintain itself abidingly . . . at least if 'abode' . . . designates the essential stability of a place; it only remains [*demeure*] *where* and *if* 'to be abidingly' . . . in some 'abiding order' . . . means something else. The historicity of its experience – for there is one – rests on the very thing no ontology could essentialize. No exposition, no discursive form is intrinsically or essentially *literary* before or outside of the function it is assigned or recognized by a right, that is, a specific intentionality inscribed directly on the social body.

Jacques Derrida (2000a: 28)

Given that literature as such does not exist, one can always suggest that while, from one perspective,

literature may be an artefact, a product of social consciousness, a world vision . . . it is also an industry. Books are not just structures of meaning, they are also commodities produced by publishers and sold on the market at a profit . . . Critics are not just analysts of texts; they are also (usually) academics hired by the state to prepare students ideologically for their functions within capitalist society. Writers are not just transposers of trans-individual mental structures, they are also workers hired by publishing houses to produce commodities which will sell.

Terry Eagleton (1976: 59)

Such a perspective, while doubtless valid, has limits none the less. As already averred, literature is irreducible to modes of production, to history, to contexts of its dissemination or institutionalization. There is no one adequate definition.

If history is not its own ground but rests on something else that has to do with fiction, then the historical study of literature can only ever give a partial picture of a work's historicality. More specifically, it will not account for the sense in which the work opens the possibility of a history, an opening that has its scene or its stage not in a finished and duly recorded past but always in a future. A literary work has a historical context, as we call it, but no more nor less than any document or artifact produced in the past; but the work, if it is still read and studied when this 'context' will have subsided into archival compost, has a relation as well to a future, by which it remains always to some extent incomprehensible by any given present. This is the dimension of the work's *historicality*, which is therefore not to be simply confused or conflated with historical 'context'. It is likewise the historicality of what we call literature that the institutionalization of literary studies has largely and necessarily misrecognized, for it withholds from the putative object of that discipline the stability required of an object of knowledge. What we still call literature . . . would be one means of this withheld stability of meaning, or to put it differently, it would be the *reserve* of every present, instituted meaning and thus the possibility of its transformation, that is, the possibility of a future. Furthermore, such reserve possibilities extend to the instituted meaning of literature and literary studies themselves. Despite the fact, therefore, that academic literary study has largely misrecognized this dimension of a, by definition, unknowable future 'literature', the latter will nevertheless have been working to transform its own institution.

Peggy Kamuf (1997: 164–5)

We are therefore left, finally, at the point of departure, with the instituting ontological question:

What is literature? It does not necessarily have anything whatsoever to do with 'great books', aesthetic beauty, fiction, poetry, or other constitutive genres of what is called 'literature' but has something to do with performativity and the irruptive force of all founding origins . . . When we speak of examples, as when we speak of the example of literature, we think of it as it is without making it an object, as when we offer an example of the novel in order to think the novel as such rather than this particular novel. The example of the example can go on and on; there are only examples, but the example, as such, is impossible . . . Whenever we ask what something is: what is literature? What is the law? What is . . . ? We are speaking of exemplariness, which is to say, of singularity and generality. When we hold up something to be an example, we imply it is its own commentary, it reveals in itself what it is (an example of). If you want an example of the novel, take *Tristram Shandy*.[4] The example, then, is at once singular and general. There is nothing like the example, and the example stands in place of everything it would exemplify. The more a novel, such as *Tristram Shandy*, is said to be unique, the more it exemplifies the novel. What then is so exemplary about literature? It re-marks the impossibility of the example to be an example of itself, which is to say it re-marks the impossibility of singularity to be absolutely singular . . .

Literature witnesses the undecidability between the singular and the general . . . It re-marks the non-coincidence, the non-identity, of judgement and the law that makes judgement necessary and a failure . . . Literature, more than other disciplines, bears witness to this undecidable relation between singularity and generality . . . This is not, however, an exclusive property of literature, but literature exemplifies the status of any discipline to be present to itself in its founding act . . . Literature bears witness to this secret: there are no examples and there are only examples.

Joseph Kronick (1997: 10–11)

Questions for further consideration

1. In what ways and to what extent do the 'sociological', 'materialist', and 'Marxist' commentaries above 'assume' rather than define 'literature'?
2. To what extent do definitions of 'literature' rely upon the assumption of 'intrinsic' aesthetic value?
3. Why is it impossible to provide a determinate definition of 'literature'?

Explanatory and bibliographical notes

1. *Metadiscourse*: a discourse which addresses itself specifically to the features, assumptions and methods of a particular discourse. What we call 'literary theory' might be said, at least in a number of cases, to be a metadiscourse, inasmuch as it concerns itself with questions having to do with the practice, role and function of criticism, its very ontology and the epistemological assumptions underlying institutionally organized and authorized procedures to do with the interpretation of literature.
2. *Formalism*: the formalist approach to literature is one which, allegedly, retreats from any consideration of history, ideology or context, concerning itself only with the formal aspects of the text.
3. Raymond Williams, *Marxism and Literature* (Oxford: Oxford University Press, 1977), pp. 46–54.
4. Lawrence Sterne, *The Life and Opinions of Tristram Shandy, Gentleman* (1759–63), ed. Ian Campbell Ross (Oxford: Oxford University Press, 1983).

Further reading

Attridge, Derek (1988), *Peculiar Language: Literature as Difference from the Renaissance to James Joyce* (Ithaca, NY: Cornell University Press).

Blanchot, Maurice (1982), *The Space of Literature* (1955), trans. and with an Introduction by Ann Smock (Lincoln, NE: University of Nebraska Press).

Derrida, Jacques (1992a), ' "This Strange Institution Called Literature": An Interview with Jacques Derrida' (1989), trans. Geoffrey Bennington and Rachel Bowlby. In Jacques Derrida, *Acts of Literature*, ed. Derek Attridge (London: Routledge), pp. 33–75.

Kamuf, Peggy (1997), *The Division | of Literature or the University in Deconstruction* (Chicago, IL: University of Chicago Press).

Kristeva, Julia (1980), *Desire in Language: A Semiotic Approach to Literature and Art* (1969, 1977), ed. Leon S. Roudiez, trans. Thomas Gora, Alice Jardine and Leon S. Roudiez (New York: Columbia University Press).

Miller, J. Hillis (2001), *Speech Acts in Literature* (Stanford, CA: Stanford University Press).

Sinfield, Alan (1989), *Literature, Politics, and Culture in Postwar Britain* (Berkeley, CA: University of California Press).

Williams, Raymond (1977), *Marxism and Literature* (Oxford: Oxford University Press).

MATERIALISM/MATERIALITY

Broadly speaking, *materialism*, in its various forms and articulations, proposes to treat of and analyse social and historical reality and the lived condition of human relations therein as always material. Within Marxist discourse, the notion of materialism addresses – though not without internal contention amongst different Marxisms – economically determined modes of production and human agency or subjectivity within the economic and social relations produced and reproduced by the historical and material conditions of production. It is perhaps not going too far to say that the multivalent notion of materialism is what mobilizes many if not all Marxist critique. However, it is necessary that we start by determining the different strands of materialism if we are to proceed. The various facets of Marx's conception are succinctly summarized here.

> The principal philosophically-significant connotations of Marx's '*materialist* conception of history' are: (a) the denial of the autonomy, and then of the primacy, of ideas in social life; (b) a methodological commitment to concrete historiographical research, as opposed to abstract philosophical reflection; (c) a conception of the centrality of human praxis in the production and reproduction of social life and, flowing from this, (d) a stress on the significance of labour, as involving the transformation of nature and the mediation of social relations, in human history; (e) an emphasis on the significance of nature for man . . . [where in Marx's] middle and later works . . . he conceives man as essentially opposed to and dominating nature; (f) a continuing commitment to scientific realism, throughout which Marx views the man–nature relationship as asymmetrically internal – with man as essentially dependent on nature, but nature as essentially independent of man.
>
> Roy Bhaskar (1989: 126)

Bhaskar's multivalent definition acknowledges the necessity of bearing in mind the complexity of conceptual language, if it is to be deployed rigorously and in the most politically efficacious manner. From this premise, it is important to stress that

> Marxism is . . . not a mechanical but a historical materialism: it does not assert the primacy of matter so much as it insists on an ultimate determination by the mode of production . . . the grounding of materialism in one or another conception of matter is rather the hallmark of bourgeois ideology from the eighteenth-century materialisms all the way to nineteenth-century positivism and determinism[1] . . .
>
> Fredric Jameson (1981: 45–6)

The consideration of materialism has been subsequently broadened in critical and cultural theory as part of a politicized comprehension of the materiality of human experience in general, particularly in relation to the body as matter and, therefore, that to and by which the body is socially subjected. While materialist literary and cultural critique assumes different forms with different objects of focus and there are, necessarily, areas of disagreement (even the notion of historical materialism is not agreed upon by those who advocate its centrality to Marxist praxis[2]), what is shared in such critique is an attention to, and engagement with, questions of historicity and historiographical critique, so as to demystify notions of autonomy in the question of textual or aesthetic production. It is thus the case that materialism is, at the very least, a highly fraught, if not, perhaps more accurately, a highly overdetermined concept, with a long and complex history, but having undergone a significant and irreversible transformation in the text of Marx and with the advent of Marxism. It therefore has to be recognized that

> the basic concept allows for enormous flexibility when it comes to generating theories of literature . . . Historical materialism, the type of materialism most pertinent to literary forms, posits . . . a radical break with Western philosophical idealism from Plato to Hegel. Materialist thought rejects notions of both the autonomy and the primacy of *ideas* in social life. Secondly, the materialist economist is concerned with ways in which human praxis or, more specifically, human labour and its organization transform physical nature into products and mediate social relations. The materialist literary critic adheres to these same principles but emphasizes the relation between human praxis and socio-economic formations and their joint production of various literary forms (and/or genres) and meanings . . . critics espousing a materialist conception of history and literature share a methodological commitment to rigorous and concrete historical research.
>
> Ivo Kamps (1995: 2)

The passage continues by addressing the relationship between materialist criticism and the demystification of ideology.

> An indispensable feature enveloping these aspects of materialist practice is of course ideological critique. Materialist analysis . . . remains ideological in nature, and relentlessly critiques the network of ideologies that obscures people's real relation to the relations of production.
>
> Ivo Kamps (1995: 3)

In such a critical practice emphasis is given to the fact that

> 'materialism' is opposed to 'idealism': it insists that culture does not (cannot) transcend the material forces and relations of production.
>
> Jonathan Dollimore and Alan Sinfield (1985: viii)

Such 'material forces and relations of production' are explained in the following citation, which also develops, thereby making explicit, the manifestation of ideological structures in material conditions of existence.

> The fact is . . . that definite individuals who are productively active in a definite way enter into these definite social and political relations . . . The social structure and the State are continually evolving out of the life-process of definite individuals, but of individuals, not as they may appear in their own or other people's imagination, but as they *really* are; i.e. as they operate, produce materially, and hence as they work under definite material limits, presuppositions and conditions independent of their will.
>
> The production of ideas, of conceptions, of consciousness, is at first directly interwoven with the material activity and the material intercourse of men, the language of real life. Conceiving, thinking, the mental intercourse of men, appear at this stage as the direct efflux of their material behaviour. The same applies to mental production as expressed in the language of politics, laws, morality, religion, metaphysics, etc. of a people. Men are the producers of their concepts, ideas, etc. – real active men, as they are conditioned by a definite development of their productive forces and of the intercourse corresponding to these, up to its furthest forms.
>
> Karl Marx and Friedrich Engels (1970: 46–7)

We might focus on the reiteration of the notions of the real and reality in this in Marx and Engels' thought. Individuals are 'conditioned' but, in turn, their real existence, their daily activities and expressions within social structures are as much responsible for the mediation of social form as they are products of that formation. From this, it can be seen that

a core thesis of historical materialism . . . is that the different socio-economic organizations of production which have characterized human history arise or fall as they enable or impede the expansion of society's productive capacity. The growth of the productive forces thus explains the general course of human history. The productive forces, however, include not just the means of production . . . but labour power – the skills, knowledge, experience, and other human faculties used in work. The productive forces represent the powers society has at its command in material production.
. . .

   Historical materialism contends that class conflict and the basic trajectory of human history is accounted for by the advance of the productive forces. Their advance, however, must be understood in terms of a theoretical model that reveals the character of the specific modes of production involved.

Tom Bottomore et al. (1983: 207, 209)

Here, we have another cogent summarization of materialist thinking.

In *Capital*, Marx breaks with [the] idealism of labour by thinking the concept of the material conditions of every labour process and by providing the concept of the *economic forms of existence* of these material conditions: in the capitalist mode of production, the decisive distinctions between constant capital and variable capital . . . Once Marx thought the reality of the material conditions of production as belonging to the concept of production, economically 'operational' concepts emerged in the field of economic analysis . . . which revolutionized its arrangement and nature.

Louis Althusser and Étienne Balibar (1970: 172)

It might not be clear to some how one might move from a supposedly purely economic, sociological, historical, or political critique to one which addresses aesthetic or literary relations and modes of production, especially as Marx offered no coherent or systematic critical programme pertaining to aesthetic matters. However, as is shown here, the text of Marx does make available the possibility of such approaches, chiefly perhaps through a dismantling of the conceptual separation between *praxis* and *poiêsis*.

Marx removed one of philosophy's most ancient taboos: the radical distinction between *praxis* and *poiêsis*.
   Since the Greeks, *praxis* had been that 'free' action in which man realizes and transforms only himself, seeking to attain his own perfection. As for *poiêsis* (from the verb *poiein*: to make), which the Greeks considered

fundamentally servile, this was 'necessary' action, subject to all the constraints of the relationship with nature, with material conditions. The perfection it sought was not that of man, but of things, of products for use.

Here, then, is the basis of Marx's materialism . . . (which is, effectively, a *new* materialism): not a mere inversion of the hierarchy . . . i.e. a primacy accorded to *poiêsis* over *praxis* by virtue of its direct relationship with matter – but the identification of the two, the revolutionary thesis that *praxis* constantly passes over into *poiêsis* and vice versa. There is never any effective freedom which is not also a material transformation, which is not registered historically in *exteriority*. But nor is there any work which is not a transformation of self, as though human beings could change their conditions of existence while maintaining an invariant 'essence'.

Étienne Balibar (1995b: 40–1)

Specifically, literature makes us think the question of materialism in a manner that addresses the interrelation between materialist and ideal or, as the citation here has it, 'mental' forms, and this in turn allows for the understanding of human agency within material conditions:

literature is both material and abstract because it takes material forms (the book, the money which is exchanged . . .) and obviously mental forms too (the experiences of reading, watching, listening). This is to define 'material' as that which is tangible, embodied, or 'real'. 'Materialism' might thus be defined as a philosophy which is grounded in material reality, insofar as it does not explain concepts by ideal constructions. To define materialist in this way is to keep the sense of a binary opposition (between ideal and material or subjective and objective) firmly in place. But in Marxist terms, this is a mechanical definition of materialism which dooms the idea and the material to mutual exclusion, instead of seeing the ways in which they interact. Thus Marxist philosophical or historical materialism attempts to hold this opposition in tension, to ground its thinking in material reality but also to include human activity as a primary force . . . If people were always determined by their context alone, by the material circumstances in which they find themselves, then no change would be possible . . . People are formed and constructed by their environment, but they also in turn form and construct that environment by their own interaction with it. We might say that people are determined by structures, and that they in turn alter structures through their own activity, or 'agency'; or that literary texts are determined by the institutional contexts of economic modes of production, distribution and reception, but they also work upon and transform these 'contexts'.

Moyra Haslett (2000: 35–6)

Materialist critique is thus a form addressing the work of difference, for the specific purpose of demystifying the occluded conditions of repression.

> Historical materialist critique is that knowledge practice that historically situates the possibility of what exists under patriarchal capitalist relations of difference – particularly the division of labor – and points to what is suppressed by the empirically existing: not just what *is*, but what could be. This 'could be', however, is not a utopian dream: it is a possibility (owing to the development of the dominant relations of production) that is suppressed (because of the dominant relations of production – the existing relations of private property and class). Materialist critique foregrounds the contradictions between the forces of production and the relations of production, what is historically and materially possible but is repressed . . . materialist critique is a mode of knowing that inquires into what is not said . . . in order to uncover the concealed operations of power and the socio-economic relations connecting the myriad details and representations of our lives. It shows that apparently disconnected zones of culture are in fact materially linked through the highly differentiated, mediated, and dispersed operation of a systematic logic of exploitation. In sum, materialist critique disrupts 'what is' to *explain* how social differences – specifically gender, race, sexuality, and class – have been systematically produced and continue to operate within regimes of exploitation, so that we can change them. It is the means for producing transformative knowledges.
>
> Teresa L. Ebert (1996: 7)

In thinking the implications of materialism and materiality, it is important to acknowledge not only the materiality of history and social relations, but also the materiality of the word or signifier.

> If I choose to make 'materiality' or the materiality of language the touchstone from which to undertake a series of transvaluative readings . . . it is nonetheless with a particularly unromanticized notion of the material in mind. What I mean does not point to a material, historical narrative which situates a textual event, but rather the manner in which the facticity of the textual event itself is thematized on the level of inscription, sound, letters, signature, and other figures; not as 'formalist' elements of play divorced from the realm of experience and social change, but as active agents of transformation in the inner history of reading/writing itself.
>
> Tom Cohen (1994: 1)

It can be understood therefore that there is no one materialism, as is made clear in this distinction between historical and dialectical materialism.

Historical materialism (the science of history) has as its object the concept of history, through the study of the various modes of production and social formations, their structure, constitution and functioning, and the forms of transition from one social formation to another.

Dialectical Materialism (Marxist philosophy) has as its particular object the production of knowledge, that is the structure and functioning of the process of thought. Strictly speaking, the object of dialectical materialism is the theory of the history of scientific production. Indeed, historical materialism founded dialectical materialism as a distinct discipline in one single theoretical movement, in that the constitution of a science of history, i.e. historical materialism, which is a science whose object is defined as the constitution of the concept of history, led to the definition of a theory of science which includes history as a constituent part of its particular object.

Nicos Poulantzas (1973: 11)

If dialectical materialism addresses the production of knowledge it should not be assumed that such epistemological production takes place unproblematically or without instances of contest or rupture. The radical dialogue between feminism and materialism has addressed such crisis in productive ways:

material feminism intervenes in the crisis of knowledge . . . by offering a way to make use of postmodern notions of the subject in conjunction with a theory of the social which is congruent with feminism's political goals . . .

. . . materialist feminism locates its theoretical object and its frame of inquiry in history and understands its project as revolutionary praxis always subject to revision from the disruptive force of its own historicity . . . materialist feminism shares much of postmodern feminism's concern with difference, subjectivity, and textuality, but it emphasizes their materiality and historical specificity. At the same time, as a political movement that struggles against patriarchal oppression, materialist feminism affirms the existence of social hierarchies as well as the necessity of rationalities and limits for political action.

Rosemary Hennessy (1993: 3–4, 13, 35)

The final consideration of matter and materiality reflects on the temporal dimension of 'materialization' or material productivity in socially regulative ways.

What I would propose . . . is a return to the notion of matter, not as site or surface, but as *a process of materialization that stabilizes over time to produce the effect of boundary, fixity, and surface we call matter.* That matter is always materialized has, I think, to be thought in relation to the productive and, indeed, materializing effects of regulatory power in the Foucaultian sense. Thus, the question is no longer, How is gender constructed as and through a certain interpretation of sex? (A question that leaves the 'matter' of sex untheorized), but rather, Through what regulatory norms is sex itself materialized? And how is it that treating the materiality of sex as a given presupposes and consolidates the normative conditions of its own emergence?

Judith Butler (1993: 9–10)

Questions for further consideration

1. While the aim, in part, of a materialist critique is to make available a study of the material conditions of the past through textual analysis, to what extent can the past be recovered?
2. Is a novel, play or other work of art ever free from the material conditions of either the historical moment of its production or the historical instances of its reception?
3. In what ways do the commentaries by Tom Cohen and Judith Butler extend, radicalize, or depart from, more traditional definitions of materialism?

Explanatory notes

1. *Positivism*: branch of philosophy elaborated by Auguste Comte, which addresses only positive facts and observable phenomena, along with the objective relations of these and the laws determining them. Positivist thought has no interest in causes or origins, seeing such inquiry as relegated to supposedly earlier stages of thought, such as metaphysics and theology; *determinism*: philosophical comprehension of human action as determined by causes and motives external to individual will.
2. *Praxis*: doing, action; adopted by Marx in 1844 to signify the conscious action by which a theory is put to work, becoming social actuality.

Further reading

Bhaskar, Roy (1989), *Reclaiming Reality: A Critical Introduction to Contemporary Philosophy* (London: Verso).
Cohen, Tom, Barbara Cohen, J. Hillis Miller and Andrzej Warminski (eds) (2001), *Material Events: Paul de Man and the Afterlife of Theory* (Minneapolis, MN: University of Minnesota Press 2001).

Dollimore, Jonathan, and Alan Sinfield (eds) (1985), *Political Shakespeare: New Essays in Cultural Materialism* (Manchester: Manchester University Press).

Haslett, Moyra (2000), *Marxist Literary and Cultural Theories* (Basingstoke: Macmillan).

Hennessy, Rosemary (1993), *Materialist Feminism and the Politics of Discourse* (New York: Routledge).

Kamps, Ivo (ed.) (1995), *Materialist Shakespeare: A History*, Afterword by Fredric Jameson (London: Verso).

Larsen, Neil (1990), *Modernism and Hegemony: A Materialist Critique of Aesthetic Agencies*, Foreword by Jaime Concha (Minneapolis, MN: University of Minnesota Press).

MODERNISM

At first glance there might appear to be a general critical and scholarly consensus that *modernism* defines works of art, books, paintings, films and so on which situate themselves in various self-conscious ways both in relation to the cultures from which they emerge, and in reaction to earlier and more conventionally shaped contemporary aesthetic models. Such definition usually sees modernism's arrival as beginning at the end of the nineteenth century, and continuing to develop, in distinct, heterogeneous ways, through the first decades of the twentieth century until the Second World War (more or less). However, such a narrative is constantly contested, the historical boundaries of modernism undergoing debate and, occasionally, revision. Furthermore, it is now generally accepted that modernism can no longer be thought of as a movement. There are often more dissimilarities and non-correspondences between so-called modernist works of art and the reasons – personal, political, material – for which they are produced, than there are shared ideas or assumptions. Perhaps – and at the risk of sounding too tricksy – the most modernist statement that can be made about modernism is that examples of modernisms define or affirm themselves by resisting categorial determination.

So, with the caveat that modernism cannot be defined unproblematically, we should perhaps get underway with a cautionary definition that is also, at the same time, a dismissal of definition.

Modernism is not a movement. It is a term that masks conflict and upheaval and any number of contradictory positions.

Vassiliki Kolocotroni et al. (1998: xvii)

'Modernism' is at best a convenient critical label applied retrospectively:

> 'modernism' is not a concept that emanates directly from literary texts;
> it is a construct created by the critical inquiry into certain kinds of texts.
> Colleen Lamos (1998: 5)

Such labels have cogency because, for many readers,

> literary periods . . . are convenient fictions, retrospective narratives of
> shaping authority that serve the definer's purposes. They overlap: new
> ones begin before earlier ones end; trends continue even as they are
> superseded. Modernism's beginnings are located in the Renaissance (or
> 'early modern period'); in the eighteenth century (with the rise of the
> middle class and mass literacy and communication); between 1815 and
> 1830; in the Victorian period with the industrial revolution, Marx,
> Darwin,[1] and the death of God; in 1900 . . . with the outbreak of World
> War One, or with England's first conscript army in 1916.
> Alan Warren Friedman (1995: 3)

If a concept of modernism assumed in relation to periodization survives
with any critical force it is as a term

> that refers to novelty-engendering interruptions of received practices and
> traditions. According to this concept, to call a poem, a painting, or a
> philosophical treatise 'modern' is to advert to the advent of the new; it is
> to assert that there has been a creative break with the past that has
> produced a work, the essential character of which is unprecedented.
> Thus understood, the concept of modernism acquires period-specific
> connotations . . . precisely where it is used to describe a phase of nine-
> teenth- and twentieth-century art embodying the spirit of Ezra Pound's[2]
> dictum 'Make it new'.
> Robert Gooding-Williams (2001: 3)

One of the ways in which modernism made art new was by rejecting earlier
forms, themselves previously considered as radical departures.

> Literary modernism, conventionally dated 1890–1930, is commonly
> seen as beginning by rejecting the dead end of naturalism,[3] with its
> pseudo-scientific emphasis on reportage.
> Alan Warren Friedman (1995: 3)

In order to define modernism, however, one cannot simply address historical contexts or external forces.

the received narrative of the emergence and triumph of modernism relies upon the promotion of certain aesthetic values such as irony, self-reflexivity, formal experimentation, textual autonomy, and so forth . . .

Colleen Lamos (1998: 2)

A particular aspect of modernism stressed through attention to aesthetic and formal concerns within works of literary modernism concerns those

tendencies towards a form-seeking and contemplative self-control, toward separation of self from world and from other selves, and toward fragmenting hyperawareness and a kind of cerebral self-interrogation.

Louis Sass (1992: 37)

Thus, a certain reading of modernism seeks to stress its purely formal or aesthetic properties, as though these and related concerns are intrinsic to the texts of modernism, something to be found in such works rather than being a reading imposed on the texts in question. However, it has also been argued that one has to bear in mind that

conceptions of modernism . . . are shaped by factors that go well beyond narrowly aesthetic concerns. These may include, among a welter of other elements, particularities of nationality, ethnicity, gender, and sexuality; questions of political engagement; concrete experiences of wars and other important historical events; developments in technology; and religious beliefs. Moreover, insofar as terms like 'modernism' . . . are used historically to situate a selection of artists and works within a certain geography and time span, they are subject to the conceptual, narrative, and figural parameters that shape all historical writing . . . Modernism has generated a number of different stories . . . modernism is the liberation of formal innovation; the destruction of tradition; the renewal of decadent conventions or habit-encrusted perceptions; the depersonalisation of art; the radical subjectivization of art. And so on.

Tyrus Miller (1999: 4)

Such a reading of modernism as explicitly ideological is extended here.

My thesis . . . is that modernism, as an ideology dominated by but not specific to the realm of aesthetics, is the inversion . . . of a historically objective 'crisis in representation' affecting the construction of what are initially social and political identities. This crisis . . . is the result of the modernization of capital itself during the nineteenth century, especially in the period leading up to the transformation of 'classical' free market capitalism into monopoly/state capitalism and imperialism . . . the 'crisis in representation' also entails a 'crisis in agency': the sense that social and historical agency is exercised by subjects linked to society as a whole by representational bonds of identity . . . falters in the face of events that indicate that the traditional 'heroes' have been usurped by anonymous forces. Modernism stems from this crisis – which it in turn grasps as stemming from an intrinsic falsity residing in a purely conceptual operation, representation – and inverts it. The crisis *in* representation becomes a crisis *of* representation: representation no longer 'works', no longer appears to offer the subject any cognitive access to the object.

Neil Larsen (1990: xxiv)

Another aspect of the ideology of modernism is its emphasis on the separation of art from the culture of the everyday.

> Ever since the mid-19th century, the culture of modernity has been characterized by a volatile relationship between high art and mass culture . . . Modernism constituted itself through a conscious strategy of exclusion, an anxiety of contamination by its other: an increasingly consuming and engulfing mass culture. Both the strengths and the weaknesses of modernism as an adversary culture derive from that fact . . .
> . . . modernism's insistence on the autonomy of the art work, its obsessive hostility to mass culture, its radical separation from the culture of everyday life, and its programmatic distance from political, economic, and social concerns was always challenged as soon as it arose . . . the opposition between modernism and mass culture has remained amazingly resilient over the decades.

Andreas Huyssen (1986: vii)

One manifestation of the desire for artistic autonomy is expressed in the following way through the reshaping of narrative form:

> modernist intolerance with linear narrative structures emerged from a concern to render the contents of consciousness rather than the flow of external events.

Allyson Booth (1996: 119)

Another way in which literary modernism sought to assert its autonomy was through a denial of temporality:

> modernist fiction attempts to deny its own temporality and approach the condition of the poetic image . . . To achieve this sense of encompassing experiential stasis, writers use a number of devices to draw attention away from the inherent temporality of language (which by its very

nature can only present one word after another, in a temporal sequence) and the implicit temporality of human action itself, with its purposes and causes. These include: the overwhelming of plot by mythic structures used as organizing devices . . . the movement from perspective to perspective instead of from event to event . . . and the use of metaphoric images as recurring leitmotifs[4] to stitch together separate moments and thereby efface the time elapsed between them . . .

In the objectivist variants of literary modernism . . . stasis is sought in events or objects themselves rather than in their human meaning or aesthetic significance. Often, such works will have an almost antiliterary tone – a stylised stylelessness that carefully avoids aesthetic devices such as metaphor, simile, and all the techniques for building suspense.

Louis Sass (1992: 34)

However, arguments running counter to the search for the autonomy of art in modernist aesthetics have been presented.

Contrary to the claims of champions of the autonomy of art . . . the realities of modern life and the ominous expansion of mass culture throughout the social realm are always already inscribed into the articulation of aesthetic modernism. Mass culture has always been the hidden subtext of the modernist project.

Andreas Huyssen (1986: 47)

Those questions concerning temporality and its comprehension already raised in relation to literary modernism inform thought beyond the literary realm.

Many thinkers associated with twentieth-century Modernism – Husserl, Heidegger, Wittgenstein, Bergson . . . Einstein, Freud, Bakhtin[5] – came to see that time is not an object, something that can be described, reported and referred to in a constative utterance. They also came to see that it is not something that can be simply presented and performed. Rather, time, they discovered, must be figured and, more precisely, *articulated* by something other than itself . . . In this understanding, representation and temporality arise in the same movement, the movement of signification – situated in the juncture between language conceived as observation and language conceived as action.

Ronald Schleifer (2000: 69–70)

Indeed, if modernism is understood provisionally as a heterogeneous network of irreversible epistemological transformations then such changes have to be comprehended as covering a wide range of discourses and disciplines.

The major thinkers associated with the onset of European modernism –
Marx, Darwin, Nietzsche, and Kierkegaard in the latter part of the nineteenth century; Einstein, van Gennep, and Freud after the turn of the
century[6] – produced radical reformulations of earlier paradigms[7] of
humankind and the universe . . .

Alan Warren Friedman (1995: 7)

Such radical reformulations concerning the grounds of perception, comprehension, representation, and ontology speak to a matter of cultural crisis.

Since the turn of the century, the revelation of the inadequacy of standard meanings and habitual constructions of reality, including conventional language, and the looming up of previously suppressed aspects of
the world have become prominent themes. In . . . early modernism, the
realization is felt as something devastating, a sudden and shocking trans-
mogrification of the familiar . . .

Such revelations and anti-epiphanies seem to be symptomatic of a
culture in crisis, one no longer comfortable with the armature of its own
categories . . .

Louis Sass (1992: 55–7)

Questions for further consideration

1. To what extent does the problem of defining modernism highlight all attempts
   at literary or aesthetic periodization?
2. A number of the citations address matters of social and economic transformation as typical of modernity. In what ways might the various aesthetic transformations of art identified as modernist be related to social, economic and
   other material conditions?
3. Consider the challenge to the notion of time made by modernism. In what ways
   does the modernist artwork rethink or transform common conceptions of time?

Explanatory and bibliographical notes

1. Charles Darwin (b.1809–d.1892): *On the Origin of Species*, Introduction by
   Ernst Mayr (Cambridge, MA: Harvard University Press, 1964); *The Voyage of
   the Beagle*, ed. Michael Neve and Janet Brown (London: Penguin, 1989); *The
   Descent of Man and Selection in Relation to Sex*, Introduction by John Tyler
   Bonner and Robert M. May (Princeton, NJ: Princeton University Press, 1992).
2. Ezra Pound (b.1885–d.1972): *Literary Essays*, Introduction by T. S. Eliot (New
   York: New Directions, 1968); *The Cantos* (London: Faber and Faber, 1986);
   Personae (London: Faber and Faber, 2001).

3. *Naturalism*: the original use of this term, historically associated with certain writers whose work marks a transition between the realism of the Victorian period and modernism in the early twentieth century, is ascribed to Émile Zola (*b*.1840–*d*.1902): *Thérèse Raquin*, trans. Leonard William Tancock (Harmondsworth: Penguin, 1962); *L'Assommoir*, trans. Margaret Mauldon, ed. Robert Lethbridge (Oxford: Oxford University Press, 1998); *La Bête humaine*, trans. Roger Pearson (Oxford: Oxford University Press, 1999). Zola sought to employ a clinical, empirical and scientistic approach to the composition of the novel. Naturalist writers, giving a documentary-like quality to narrative, laid stress on the importance of heredity and societal influence, causality or determinism, and, along with this, an often grim sense of inevitability in the representation of characters' lives and actions, along with the often brutal, impersonal condition of their environment. English novelists associated with naturalism (at least in part) are, amongst others, Thomas Hardy (*b*.1840–*d*.1928): *The Mayor of Casterbridge*, ed. Keith Wilson (London: Penguin, 1997); *Jude the Obscure*, ed. Cedric Watts (Toronto: Broadview Press, 1999); *Far from the Madding Crowd*, eds Rosmarie Morgan and Shannon Russell (London: Penguin, 2000); George Gissing (*b*.1857–*d*.1903): *The Odd Women*, ed. Elaine Showalter (London: Penguin, 1994); *New Grub Street*, ed. John Goode (Oxford: Oxford University Press, 1998); *The Nether World*, ed. Stephen Gill (Oxford: Oxford University Press, 1999); and D. H. Lawrence (*b*.1885–*d*.1930): *Sons and Lovers*, ed. David Trotter (Oxford: Oxford University Press, 1998); *The Rainbow*, ed. Mark Kinkead-Weekes, Introduction by Anne Fernihough (London: Penguin, 2000); *Women in Love*, ed. Mark Kinkead-Weekes (London: Penguin, 2000).

4. *Leitmotif*: the *Grove Concise Dictionary of Music* defines a *leitmotif* as: 'a clearly defined theme or musical idea, representing or symbolizing a person, object, idea etc., which returns in its original or an altered form at appropriate points in a dramatic (mainly operatic) work'.

5. Henri Bergson, (*b*.1859–*d*.1941): *Creative Evolution*, trans. Arthur Mitchell, Foreword by Irwin Edman (New York: Modern Library, 1944); *The Two Sources of Morality and Religion*, trans. R. Ashley Audra and Cloudsley Brereton (Notre Dame, IN: University of Notre Dame Press, 1977); *Matter and Memory*, trans. W. S. Palmer and N. M. Paul (Cambridge, MA: Zone Books, 1991); Albert Einstein (*b*.1879–*d*.1955): *The Collected Papers of Albert Einstein*, ed. John Stachel (Princeton, NJ: Princeton University Press, 1987–).

6. Friedrich Nietzsche (*b*.1844–*d*.1900): *Thus Spoke Zarathustra*, trans. R. J. Hollingdale (London: Penguin, 1987); *Beyond Good and Evil*, trans. R. J. Hollingdale (London: Penguin, 1988); *Ecce Homo*, trans. R. J. Hollingdale (London: Penguin, 1988); Sóren Kierkegaard (*b*.1813–*d*.1955): *Fear and Trembling*, trans. Alastair Hannay (London: Penguin, 1985); *The Sickness unto Death*, trans. and Introduction by Alastair Hannay (London: Penguin, 1989); *Either/Or*, abridged, trans. and Introduction by Alastair Hannay (London: Penguin, 1992); Arnold van Gennep (*b*.1873–*d*.1957): *The Rites of Passage*, trans. Monika B. Vizedom and Gabrielle L. Caffe, Introduction by Solon T. Kimball (Chicago, IL: University of Chicago Press, 1961).

7. *Paradigms*: examples or patterns.

Further reading

Gooding-Williams, Robert (2001), *Zarathustra's Dionysian Modernism* (Stanford, CA: Stanford University Press).

Huyssen, Andreas (1986), *After the Great Divide: Modernism, Mass Culture, Postmodernism* (Bloomington, IN: Indiana University Press).

Kolocotroni, Vassiliki, Jane Goldman and Olga Taxidou (eds) (1998), *Modernism: An Anthology of Sources and Documents* (Edinburgh: Edinburgh University Press).

Lamos, Colleen (1998), *Deviant Modernism: Sexual and Textual Errancy in T. S. Eliot, James Joyce, and Marcel Proust* (Cambridge: Cambridge University Press).

Larsen, Neil (1990), *Modernism and Hegemony: A Materialist Critique of Aesthetic Agencies*. Foreword by Jaime Concha (Minneapolis, MN: University of Minnesota Press).

Miller, Tyrus (1999), *Late Modernism: Politics, Fiction, and the Arts Between the World Wars* (Berkeley, CA: University of California Press).

Sass, Louis A. (1992), *Madness and Modernism: Insanity in the Light of Modern Art, Literature and Thought* (Cambridge, MA: Harvard University Press).

Schliefer, Ronald (2000), *Modernism and Time: The Logic of Abundance in Literature, Science, and Culture, 1880–1930* (Cambridge: Cambridge University Press).

MYTH/OLOGY

The *Oxford English Dictionary* describes a *myth* as 'a purely fictitious narrative usually involving supernatural persons, actions, or events, and embodying some popular idea concerning natural or historical phenomena [which is] properly distinguished from *allegory* and from *legend* (which implies a nucleus of fact)'. *Mythology* means, variously, a body of mythic narratives; the study and exposition of myth; fabulous tales or works of fancy and imagination, the purpose of which is to provide symbolic meaning for events such as the creation of the universe or the world, and other originary or founding moments. What emerges from a consideration of the various citations concerning myth and mythology is the pervasive insistence of the mythical and its power to inform, from micro-levels in what we might term *mythemes* – fundamentally irreducible signifying or meaningful units – within semantic structures, to macro-levels of grand narratives that serve to determine entire cultures. Such determining narratives can be understood in terms of religion and its cultural significance.

> Because it gives figuration a free reign . . . religion . . . is an expression of the pleasure principle or, like art, at least of its reconciliation with the

reality principle. It must be classed as one of the products of phantasy, of the avoidance of reality . . . myth is the initial form of phantasy; the real is precipitated into it, and is caught up in the matrix of meaning precisely because that matrix is not a discourse but a form, an initial compromise between a syntax and a scene . . . phantasy is bound up with the question of origins, with the question of fathers and mothers, and is simply repressed, exhibited in the façade of the myth which resolves the question . . . it is resolved by the social organization itself. . . . The West is the place where this form finally expires.

Jean-François Lyotard (1989a: 72–3)

Myth can also be seen as the vehicle for the promotion and maintenance of bourgeois ideology through secular narrative models.

If one hypothesizes (as Marxists do) that all the ideology of bourgeois political economy is summed up in the myth of Robinson Crusoe, then it must be admitted that everything in the novel itself agrees with . . . bourgeois thought. . . . Robinson Crusoe is the outcome of a total mutation that has been in progress since the dawn of bourgeois society. . . . Man was transformed simultaneously into a productive force and a 'man with needs.' . . . The myth of Robinson Crusoe is the bourgeois avatar[1] of the myth of terrestrial paradise. Every great social order of production (bourgeois or feudal) maintains an ideal myth, at once a myth of culmination and a myth of origin. Theology supported itself on the myth of the fulfillment of man in the divine law; political economy is sustained on the great myth of human fulfillment according to the natural law of needs. Both deal in the same finality: an ideal relation of man to the world through his needs and the rule of Nature, and an ideal relationship with God through faith and the divine rule of Providence . . . The logic and ideology are the same. . . . The Crusoe myth describes . . . the ideality of bourgeois relations . . .

Jean Baudrillard (1981: 140–1)

Whether religious or secular, mythical narrative components are so similar across time and diverse cultures that it is both possible and plausible to posit what is here described as a 'monomyth', an archetypal narrative structure.

The striking resemblance among all the myths of the male hero figure in diverse cultures has given rise . . . to a number of attempts to unearth a 'monomyth,' a prototypical plot common to all such myths. Whatever variants may arise as the prototype legend is established . . . the existence of a series of identical motifs subtending each of the individual heroic myths seems beyond question. The resemblances among the principal motifs of these stories and the similarities in their general articulation, from the condition of the hero's birth to his conquest of power, his marriage, and his death, allow us to posit the existence of the monomyth of the male hero, a prototype myth of royal investiture.

Jean-Joseph Goux (1993: 5)

The mythic structure operates across cultures because of the persistence of its symbolic units, which have universal appeal.

Mythical thought operates within the sphere of the symbol (as in the epic, folk tales . . .), through symbolic units that are *units of restriction* in relation to the symbolized universals ('heroism', 'courage', 'nobility', 'virtue', 'fear', 'treason', etc.).

Julia Kristeva (1986: 64–5)

While the majority of quotations given here are taken from texts addressing myth in the most commonly understood form of classical narratives, Roland Barthes offers a more radical rethinking, while remaining in essence true to fundamental structures and forms of mythical articulation. Barthes reads the power of myth in its rhetorical transformation or, more properly, translation.

Myth hides nothing and flaunts nothing: it distorts; myth is neither a lie nor a confession: it is an inflexion.

Roland Barthes (1972: 129)

In its ability to inflect and translate, to distort the material or historical as universal and symbolic, myth

is a system of communication . . . it is a message . . . myth cannot possibly be an object, a concept or an idea; it is a mode of signification, a form . . . we must . . . first describe it as a form . . . Myth is not defined by the object of its message, but by the way it utters this message: there are formal limits to myth, but no 'substantial' ones. Everything, then, can be a myth? Yes . . . Every object in the world can pass from a closed, silent existence to an oral state, open to appropriation by society, for there is no law, whether natural or not, which forbids talking about things . . . Myth can be defined neither by its object nor by its material, for any material can arbitrarily be endowed with meaning . . . we are no longer dealing here with a theoretical mode of representation: we are dealing with *this* particular image, which is given for *this* particular signification. Mythical speech is made of a material which has *already* been worked on so as to make it suitable for communication.

Roland Barthes (1972: 109–10)

The transformative efficacy assures myth's narrative power. For Barthes,

myth is depoliticized speech. One must naturally understand *political . . .* as describing the whole of human relations in their real, social structure, in their power of making the world . . . Myth does not deny things, on the contrary its function is to talk about them; simply, it purifies them, it makes them innocent, it gives them a natural and eternal justification, it gives them a clarity which is not that of an explanation but that of a statement of fact . . . In passing from history to nature, myth acts economically: it abolishes the complexity of human acts, it gives them the simplicity of essences . . . it organizes a world which is without contradictions because it is without depth, a world wide open and wallowing in the evident, it establishes a blissful clarity: things appear to mean something in themselves.

Roland Barthes (1972: 143)

Perhaps the most obvious, but simultaneously, the strangest aspect of myth is that it represents – or, more accurately, narrates – that which has never existed in a form that is comprehensible *as if* what is presented has or could have existed. Furthermore, to extend this logic, the strangeness of myth resides in the fact that its images do not signify directly any reality. Myth is thus not simply fantastic, it is phantasmic. It projects imaginary figures, human and superhuman, in their interrelations, in what is, strictly speaking, 'non-time'.

Only myth can name [an] idyllic non-time . . . Myth is thus both more and less than pre- or post-history: it is the name for the negation of history.

Thomas Pepper (1997: 38)

The time of myth is not that of history, nor even pre-history, yet its strange significance, its power and appeal is that it is a medium through which societies are interpellated, and by which they interpellate themselves:

the vocation of art can still be to recover an ancient destination and establish the type; or, if one prefers, the mythological figure, where humanity (a people, for example), could recognize itself.

Philippe Lacoue-Labarthe (1994: 59)

Hence, the significance of myth is its mutability, its ability to signify in different ways so as to appear to indicate – to be interpretable as – destiny and destination for specific social and historical groups beyond, or, more strictly speaking, outside, the struggles of past, present, and future historical instances.

> Myth, with its always circular structure, is indeed the story of a foundation. It permits the construction of a model according to which . . . different pretenders can be judged.
>
> Gilles Deleuze (1990: 255)

Questions for further consideration

1. Following Roland Barthes' definition, how does myth 'distort', and to what ends?
2. In what ways, if at all, do mythical elements inform or become mediated contemporary or secular narrative forms?
3. Does myth tend toward political or ideological repression or is it available to be read as articulating conditions and structures of human relations which otherwise remain silent?

Explanatory note

1. *Avatar*: an incarnation or embodiment, the manifestation of a ruling power or object of worship.

Further reading

Barthes, Roland (1972), *Mythologies*, trans. Annette Lavers (New York: Hill and Wang).
Goux, Jean-Joseph (1993), *Oedipus, Philosopher*, trans. Catherine Porter (Stanford, CA: Stanford University Press).
Vernant, Jean-Pierre (1980), *Myth and Society in Ancient Greece*, trans. Janet Lloyd (Brighton: Harvester Press).

NARRATIVE/NARRATION

Most fundamentally, to *narrate* is to tell a story, to give a sequence of events a particular form so as to produce a significance produced as, or greater than, the sum of the parts. Narration takes time, but the movement of time in any narrative is never simply linear or progressive; time in narratives often moves in different directions, and, moreover, never moves at one speed. Often, narrative temporality operates through acts of remembering on the part of particular characters. Narrative, it might also be said, is that which produces a particular identity or meaning through the singular arrangement of a temporal and spatial series of incidents, figures, motifs and characters. Such a network will function and generate meaning according to repetition, emphasis, amplification and other rhetorical devices. While the act of narration is therefore the telling of a tale, every narration will necessarily differ from every other. Because of this, every narrative is singular. Moreover, narrative is irreducible to a single type or genre of discourse, because, in its production and construction, narration has occasion to be constituted through the intermixing of multiple and heterogeneous discourses. Therefore, while aspects of narrative can be suggested, narrative cannot be reduced or generalized through an act of definition. It is for such reasons, whether explored implicitly or explicitly, that narrative comes to be defined, below, as an 'envelope', a 'mechanism', a 'genre', a 'medium'. While this might, quite correctly, make one hesitant to speak of narrative in any abstract or generalizing manner, what can be suggested is that narrative is a process, relying on an untotalizable range of effects. What can also be proposed is that narrative is fundamental to most, if not all societies and cultures throughout history, whether the act of narration is carried out orally, through pictures or pictograms, through staging or ritual, in film, or in writing. Narration offers patterns and images which acts of reading seek to comprehend in ways that see in narrative a mediation of individual or social beliefs, habits, or ideologies.

The complexity of narrative and narration is explored here, beginning first with its etymological and familial relations.

Narration both as a word and as an act . . . involves lines and repetition. The word 'narration' is from Latin 'narrare', to narrate, from 'gnarus,' knowing, expert, from the root 'gno-' . . . The word 'narration,' meaning 'to give an oral or written account of something, to tell (a story),' is a member of a family of words that includes 'can,' 'con,' 'cunning,' 'ken' . . . 'notion,' 'cognition,' 'gnosis,' 'diagnosis,' 'gnomon' (meaning pointer on a sundial, judge, indicator, a geometrical diagram made by removing from the corner of a parallelogram another smaller parallelogram similar in shape), physiognomy . . . 'norm,' 'normal'. . . Within the concept of narration are obscurely inscribed the ideas of judging and interpretation, of temporality in its complexity, and of repetition. To narrate is to retrace a line of events that has already occurred, or that is spoken fictively as having already occurred. At the same time this sequence is interpreted, as a gnomon on a sundial tells the time, reads the sun, or rather reads the moving shadow cast by its own interruption of sunlight. A (g)narration is a gnosis, a retelling by one who knows. It is also a diagnosis, an act of identifying or interpreting by a discriminating reading of signs. A narrator . . . often speaks or writes in riddles . . . that must be unriddled in their turn by the reader even when they seem most perspicuously to point to what they tell of and name. This unriddling is another narration, that story all readers tell themselves as they read, for example, my own narration here of the aporias of narration.

J. Hillis Miller (1998: 47)

As narration is involved in an act of reading (as has just been explored), which in turn produces, as its response, a counternarrative, so there is the matter of narrative time to be taken into account, involving consideration of duration, rhythm, and temporal order:

the internal temporality of a narrative [can be defined through] the order and frequency of its events . . .

Mark Currie (1998: 77)

Understanding temporal order also means gaining a comprehension of the relation between narrative events.

To study the temporal order of a narrative is to compare the order in which events or temporal sections are arranged in the narrative discourse with the order of succession these same events or temporal segments have in the story, to the extent that story order is explicitly indicated by the narrative itself or inferable from one or another indirect clue . . . in the classical narrative . . . narrative discourse never inverts the order of events without saying so . . .

Gérard Genette (1980: 35)

However, the time of a narrative is never simply that of its events (as is already implied in the consideration of the relation between acts of narrative and those of reading).

Narrative is a . . . double temporal sequence . . . There is the time of the thing told and the time of the narrative . . . This duality not only renders possible all the temporal distortions that are commonplace in narratives (three years of the hero's life summed up in two sentences of a novel or in a few shots . . . in film, etc.). More basically, it invites us to consider that one of the functions of narrative is to invent one time scheme in terms of another time scheme.

Christian Metz (1974: 18)

Such play with temporal order, with time schemes, and the distortion of the duration of temporal moments, implies the possibility of repetition.

> Symmetrically, a narrative statement is not only produced, it can be produced again, can be repeated one or more times in the same text: nothing prevents me from saying or writing, 'Pierre came yesterday evening, Pierre came yesterday evening, Pierre came yesterday evening.' Here . . . the identity and therefore the repetition of facts of abstraction; materially . . . or even ideally . . . none of the occurrences is completely identical to the others, solely by virtue of their co-presence and their succession . . . A system of relationships is established between these capacities for 'repetition' on the part of both the narrated events (of the story) and the narrative statements (of the text) . . . Schematically, we can say that a narrative, whatever it is, may tell once what happened once, n times what happened n times, n times what happened once, once what happened n times.
>
> Gérard Genette (1980: 114)

The structural relation between the various aspects of temporality and repetition suggests a constant negotiation between 'getting on' with the act of telling a story and holding up that story's progress so as to sustain interest, to create tension, or to frustrate – hopefully in a positive fashion – a reader's expectations or desires.

> Narrative is definable interchangeably as a closed form that is nothing if it does not digress and as a digression constrained by its dependence on structural closure. A story must have a beginning and an end, and some form of structural cohesion linking them. But a story that began with its beginning and proceeded directly to its end, without mediation . . . would not be a story so much as a case of digression . . . For the bookends of beginning and end to become a true story, the mediation of a middle must be supplied . . . A story coheres grammatically, then, only under the constraint of being dilatory, of not taking the shortest path (a straight line) between its opening and its conclusion . . . Plotting responds to a double necessity, that of the story's holding *interest* for a narrative (though having a discernible 'point'), and that of *holding* that narratee's interest, which . . . is a matter of simulating, but then of maintaining, a certain kind of desire, the desire for narration. Once aroused, though, desire is insatiable, and the narrator's temptation tends always to be to spin out the story. At the cost of extenuating the narrative's grammatical cohesion, the end to which the story tends . . . is delayed by means of dilatory practices that both satisfy and sustain the desire for narration but also produce a form of divided attention, the narratee

becoming split between one form of desire (the desire to know, corresponding to the question: How will it all turn out in the end?) and its
other (the desire to prolong the pleasure, corresponding to a[nother]
question . . . Will I ever want to stop reading [or listening]?). This split
is another form of the relation of difference and mutual alterity that links
(the desire for) comprehension, as an understanding dependent on
contextual closure, and (that for) comprehensiveness, predicated on the
permeability of contexts and the untotalizable globality it implies. A
felicitous narrative, of course, is held to take evenly between end-direct-
ness and the potentially endless exploration of dilating context(s), satis-
fying each desire only at the cost of frustrating its other.

Ross Chambers (1999: 19–21)

As all the questions concerning narrative temporality and ordering imply,
therefore, the notion of a simple narrative strand or line is endlessly complicated, and always open, of course, to further complexification.

In whatever way one uses the image of the line to think about narrative sequence in a given novel, the image itself . . . contains latent
contradictions that lead to a specific kind of impasse . . . This impasse
in thinking may be variously encountered: in problems of closure; in
problems of beginning; in problems setting curved, knotted, or broken
line against straight; in problems involving the doubling of the narrative line, not only the doublings of multiple plot, but also doublings
within a single story line, doublings of narrative voice by means of
multiple narrators, citations, letters, diaries, and so on; in problems
involving the means of producing the line and its relation to what it
copies, its referent.

J. Hillis Miller (1998: 50)

Time and temporality are not the only aspects of narrative with which
we should be concerned, however. Identity is also a product of narration.

Though identity is a permanent process of construction and reconstruc-
tion, this fluid or mutable nature does not mean that it never enjoys any
stability. Clearly, a person's identity does not vary significantly from day
to day, so that there must be a slowly varying envelope containing (and
constraining) the vicissitudes of self-enactment. This envelope is narrative . . . narrative plays a central role in the constitution and preservation
of identity. It is a carrier of meaning, the channel through which an individual tells him/herself and others the tale of his/her place in the world.
It provides the self with inertia, endowing it with some measure of
temporal continuity.

Human beings are social creatures, and from early childhood onward, narratives are an intrinsic part of their communal existence.

Irvin Cemil Schick (1999: 20–1)

First-person narration in particular creates the illusion of control and authority, over both the details of the narrative and the identity of the narrator.

In first-person fictional narrative, we . . . accept the convention that the narrator has a much more complete and detailed knowledge of her past life than is usually the case in reality. The rediscovery of the past and its re-creation in full detail is a popular narrative trope.

Nicola King (2000: 64)

A first-person narration also authorizes a degree of temporal control.

The 'first-person' narrative lends itself better than any other to anticipation, by the very fact of its avowedly retrospective character, which authorizes the narrator to allude to the future and in particular to his present situation, for these to some extent form part of his role.

Gérard Genette (1980: 67)

Such authority, coupled with the effects of mimesis, is afforded by narrative cinematic techniques.

Filmic narration tends to imply the complete reliability and authority of the camera on questions of identity, on the basis that seeing is believing.

Mark Currie (1998: 126)

All such dissemination of information in narrative form is often misunderstood simply as representation or point of view.

Narrative 'representation,' or, more exactly, narrative information, has its degrees: the narrative can furnish the reader with more or fewer details, and in a more or less direct way, and can thus seem . . . to keep at a greater or lesser *distance* from what it tells. The narrative can also choose to regulate the information it delivers, not with a sort of even screening, but according to the capacities of knowledge of one or another participant in the story (a character or group of characters), with the narrative adopting or seeming to adopt what we ordinarily call the participant's 'vision' or 'point of view;' the narrative seems in that case . . . to take on, with regard to the story, one or another *perspective*. 'Distance' and 'perspective,' thus provisionally designated and defined, are the two chief modalities of that *regulation of narrative information* that is mood.

Gérard Genette (1980: 162)

However, it is not only in technologically advanced societies, with wide-spread availability of print or film media, that narrative has such authority.

> [In so-called 'primitive' societies] . . . the power of the narrative mechanism confers legitimacy . . . Narrative is authority itself. It authorizes an unbreakable *we*, outside of which there can only be *they*.
>
> Such an organization is in every respect the complete opposite of that of the great narratives of legitimation that characterize Western modernity. The latter . . . are concerned of course with the 'transcendence' of particular cultural identities in favour if a universal civic identity.
>
> Jean-François Lyotard (1989b, 321)

In many of the comments concerning narrative, there has been an anthropomorphic tendency, binding all narrative elements together as so many elements subordinate to a central human figure. The final citation opens to our consideration the question of whether narrative analysis is possible that would eschew or escape the anthropomorphic interest.

> It . . . remains to be seen whether a narrative system is conceivable from which the anthropomorphic . . . [has] been completely eliminated . . . the ultimate blind spot . . . [of] *narrative analysis* is . . . to be found in the problem of the character . . . the concept of the narrative function is shackled to some ultimately irreducible nucleus of anthropomorphic representation . . . which then fatally retransforms narrative function into so many acts or deeds of a human figure.
>
> Fredric Jameson (1981: 123)

Questions for further consideration

1. Is there such a thing as a standard narrative form or is every narrative a 'deviation' without an original model?
2. Given the manipulations of time and repetition by which narrative proceeds, to what extent is it legitimate to speak of beginnings and endings?
3. What is the reader's role in producing narrative?

Further reading

Chambers, Ross (1999), *Loiterature* (Lincoln, NE: University of Nebraska Press).
Currie, Mark (1998), *Postmodern Narrative Theory* (Basingstoke: Macmillan).
Jameson, Fredric (1981), *The Political Unconscious: Narrative as Socially Symbolic Act* (Ithaca, NY: Cornell University Press).

King, Nicola (2000), *Memory, Narrative, Identity: Remembering the Self* (Edinburgh: Edinburgh University Press).

Miller, J. Hillis (1998), *Reading Narrative* (Norman, OK: University of Oklahoma Press).

OTHER

Notions of the *other* and otherness are employed throughout critical discourse in different and differing ways, which ways thereby attest to the impossibility of assigning a general or stable meaning which is anything other than nebulous at best. Broadly speaking, critical thinking concerning the other is encountered in politicized critical discourse, in psychoanalytic, specifically Lacanian-influenced criticism, and in philosophical thought, though of course none of these categories are anything more than arbitrary, and nor are they exclusive. Otherness might be said to name provisionally the quality or state of existence of being other or different from established norms and social groups, or otherwise, existentially and ontologically, the condition of that which is not-the-self; one might also suggest that otherness indicates the distinction that one makes between one's self and others in terms of sexual, ethnic, and relational senses of difference. In Lacanian psychoanalysis, there is the other and the Other: the former signifies that which is not really other but is a reflection and projection of the ego; the latter signifies a radical alterity irreducible to any imaginary or subjective identification. In the texts of Luce Irigaray,[1] the other indicates the position always occupied by woman within patriarchal culture and other masculinist cultures, which privileges masculinity as self-sameness, or otherwise a signifier of presence, origin or centrality. Levinas distinguishes between others, other beings who are so many singular instances of the not-self, and the Other, the figure of an absolute otherness or, as both Levinas and Althusser name it, alterity.

The first citation addresses Lacan's understanding of the Other.

Subjects in language persist in their belief that somewhere there is a point of certainty, of knowledge and of truth. When the subject addresses its demand outside itself to another, this other becomes the fantasized place of just such a knowledge or certainty. Lacan calls this the Other – the site of language to which the speaking subject necessarily refers. The Other appears to hold the 'truth' of the subject and the power to make good its loss. This is the ultimate fantasy. Language is the place where meaning circulates – the meaning of each linguistic unit can only be established by reference to another, and it is arbitrarily fixed. Lacan, therefore, draws

from Saussure's concept of the arbitrary nature of the linguistic sign . . .
the implication that there can be no final guarantee or securing of
language.

Jacqueline Rose (1986: 55–6)

The implication of Lacan's comprehension is that 'Without the Other, there
can be no subject' (Gilbert D. Chaitin, 1996: 7). Self and Other are not
simple, discrete, autonomous categories, two wholly separable ontological
locations in a binary opposition. Instead of understanding them as such, it
is important that we comprehend the extent to which the self is always
informed by the Other.

But just as opening oneself up [sichoffenbaren²] or closing oneself off is
grounded in one's having Being-with-one-another as one's kind of Being
at the time, and indeed is nothing else but this, even the explicit disclosure
of the Other in solicitude grows only out of one's primarily Being with
him in each case. Such a disclosure of the Other (which is indeed
thematic, but not in the manner of theoretical psychology) easily becomes
the phenomenon which proximally comes to view when one considers the
theoretical problematic of understanding the 'psychical life of Others'
[*fremden Seelenlebens³*]. In this phenomenally 'proximal' manner it thus
presents a way of Being with one another understandingly; but at the
same time it gets taken as that which, primordially and 'in the beginning',
constitutes Being towards Others and makes it possible at all.

Martin Heidegger (1962: 161)

In that being is a being-with-others, there is no absolute selfhood separable
from the trace of some alterity. Indeed,

In a dialectical relation, the I-subject, either dividing itself or dividing the
Other, affirms the *Other* as an intermediary and realizes itself in it (in
such a way that I is able to reduce the Other to the truth of the Subject).
In this . . . relation the absolutely Other and Self immediately unite . . .
The Self and the Other lose themselves in one another . . . But here the
'I' ceases to be sovereign; sovereignty is in the Other who is the sole
absolute.

Maurice Blanchot (1993: 66)

Certain aspects of critical thinking have tended towards attempts to limit
and thereby control the other.

The very activity of thinking, which lies at the basis of epistemological,
ontological, and veridical comprehension, is the reduction of plurality to

unity, alterity to sameness. The very task of philosophy, the very task of thinking is the reduction of otherness. In seeking to think the other, its otherness is reduced or appropriated to our understanding. To think philosophically is to comprehend ... and master the other, thereby reducing its alterity.

Simon Critchley (1999: 29)

This principle is observed once more.

> Western philosophy is in essence the attempt to domesticate Otherness, since what we understand by thought is nothing but such a project.
>
> Rodolphe Gasché (1986: 101)

Yet it has to be admitted that all thought is, in some sense, a response to some differential trace; no thought arrives from nowhere but, even in the most minimal examples, it is always as a response to some other:

> the Heideggerian, and even more the Derridean, notion of 'difference' implies a structure of language and a process of articulation that includes a practical, performative moment which, I am convinced, is where one has to start – and probably end – if one is to respond to the trace of the other, to that dimension of alterity to which thinking is so profoundly indebted.
>
> Samuel Weber (1996: 171)

Given that identity is the result of difference and alterity, there is no absolutely justifiable location or position in which one can situate oneself which is not an other for others:

> the subject is a subject to, and of, others; in fact, it is often an 'Other' to others, which also affects its sense of its own subjectivity. This construction of self in opposition to others ... is as characteristic of groups, communities, classes, and nations, as it is of individuals ...
>
> Regenia Gagnier (1991: 8)

The location of the other is irreducible to a single or individual determination.

> The dialectic between 'self' and 'other', or 'I' and 'not-I' has a long history in European thought, going back at least to the eighteenth century ... Though 'othering' and colonialism often go hand in hand ... the discourse of the 'other' in Western Europe during the modern period was not merely the intellectual arm of imperialism; equally ... it played

a central role in the process of self-definition . . . the notions of identity and alterity, of 'us' and 'them', are closely linked to the sense of place, that is, to notions of 'here' and 'there' . . . But there is no single 'here', nor even a simple 'here/there' dichotomy, that defines identity; rather, it is an entire archipelago of places, with which one engages in discursive relationships of inclusion and exclusion, attraction and repulsion, acceptance and rejection.

Irvin Cermil Shick (1999: 22–4)

Moreover, while European identity defines itself according to its relation to its non-European others, gender has also to be taken into account, as is remarked both here:

while western cultural discourses construct the self as masculine, they ascribe femininity a position of Otherness. As Other, Woman serves to define the self, and the lack or excess that is located in the Other functions as an exteriorisation of the self, in respect to both gender and death. Woman comes to represent the margins or extremes of the norm . . . The construction of Woman-as-Other serves rhetorically to dynamise a social order.

Elisabeth Bronfen (1992: 181)

and here, where Gayatri Spivak draws out the analogical relationship through the specific institutional model of feminist thought, presenting this real relationship as both a politics and a poetics, that is to say both real *and* textual, through the figure of the trope.

In the case of academic feminism the discovery is that to take the privileged male of the white race as a norm for universal humanity is no more than a politically interested figuration. It is a trope that passes itself off as truth and claims that woman or the racial other is merely a kind of troping of that truth of man – in the sense that they must be understood *as* unlike (non-identical with) it and yet *with* reference to it.

Gayatri Chakravorty Spivak (1999: 147)

Given such politicized accounts of the relation between Self and Other, it is easy to understand, though not to condone, the Self's attempted mastery over the Other. But such mastery is problematized by the estranging nature of the Other, its condition of being sufficiently like, but not the same as, the subject.

To be sure, the other . . . that is announced does not possess this existing as the subject possesses it; its hold over my existing is mysterious. It is not unknown but unknowable . . . But this precisely indicates that the other is in no way another myself, participating with me in a common existence. The relationship with the other is not an idyllic and harmonious relationship of communion, or a sympathy through which we put ourselves in the other's place; we recognize the other as resembling us, but exterior to us; the relationship with the other is a relationship with a Mystery.

Emmanuel Levinas (1987: 75)

That which is similar is not the same as the Self, and that which is visible as such poses a threat in a number of ways.

Signifying that which eludes the order of the self, because it is lacking or excessive, the stereotype of the Other is used to control the ambivalent and to create boundaries . . . Even as it is constructed to exteriorise anxiety outside the self or the community, the Other functions as the body at which the anxiety produced out of this tension between control and loss of power or distinction takes shape and continues to be preserved . . . The power of stereotypes of Otherness is enhanced by duplication and often embodies an interrelationship of images of difference . . .

Elisabeth Bronfen (1992: 182)

These comments find a further echo, here.

It is through this notion of splitting and multiple belief that, I believe, it becomes easier to see the bind of knowledge and fantasy, power and pleasure, that informs the particular regime of visibility deployed in colonial discourse. The visibility of the racial/colonial Other is at once a point of identity ('Look, a Negro') and at the same time a problem for the attempted closure within the discourse. For the recognition of difference as 'imaginary' points of identity and origin such as black and white is disturbed by the representation of splitting in the discourse . . . In the objectification of the scopic[4] drive there is always a threatened return of the look; in the identification of the Imaginary relation there is always the alienating other (or mirror) which crucially returns its image to the subject; and in that form of substitution and fixation that is fetishism there is always the trace of loss, absence.

Homi K. Bhabha (1994: 81)

The racial discourse of Self and Other clearly has a political history, where the maintenance of power is invested in representation:

social constructs of Self and Other provided the fundamental building blocks for the hierarchies of power which produced empires and the uneven relations among their citizenry. Under colonialism, negative constructions of the colonized Other established certain structures of domination through which the colonizer triumphed . . . The processes by which notions of the Self and Other are defined, articulated and negotiated are a crucial part of what might be thought of as the cultural dimension of colonialism and postcolonialism . . . The nineteenth-century imperial project most clearly, but not exclusively, depended upon racialised notions of Self and Other. Imperialism operated within an ideal of the Manichean[5] binary, which constructed a demonized Other against which flattering, and legitimating images of the metropolitan Self were defined. Such racialised constructs were never stable and were always threatened not only by the unpredictability of the Other but also the uncertain homogeneity and boundedness of the Self.

Jane M. Jacobs (1996: 2–3)

Perhaps the greatest fear concerning recognition of the Other has to do not merely with the comprehension of a localizable other – in the forms of difference of gender or race, for example – but in the abyssal implication that behind every instance of relative alterity lies an absolutely Other.

The phenomenon of the other (his face) must . . . attest to a radical alterity which he nevertheless does not contain by himself. The Other, as he appears to me in the order of the finite, must be the epiphany of a properly infinite distance to the other, the traversal of which is the originary ethical experience.

This means that in order to be intelligible, ethics requires that the Other be in some sense *carried by a principle of alterity* which transcends mere finite experience. Lévinas calls this principle the 'Altogether-Other' . . . There can be no Other if he is not the immediate phenomenon of the Altogether-Other. There can be no finite devotion to the non-identical if it is not sustained by the infinite devotion of the principle to that which subsists outside it.

Alain Badiou (2001: 22)

Questions for further consideration

1. Is it possible, or even appropriate, to think Bhabha's articulation of the colonizing self and the colonial Other in terms such as those proposed by Levinas, where one's relationship to the other is *both* proximal *and* enigmatic? Or, to put this another way, might Levinas's comprehension of the irreducible mystery of the other in general terms account in some manner for the 'threat' of otherness described by Bhabha?

2. Consider the ramifications of Derrida's suggestion that the other invents us.
3. Is it ever possible to conceive the self/other binarism in ways which are not informed by matters of power, mastery, or hierarchy?

Explanatory and bibliographical notes

1. Luce Irigaray (*b*.1930–): *Speculum of the Other Woman*, trans. Gillian C. Gill (Ithaca, NY: Cornell University Press, 1985); *This Sex Which is Not One*, trans. Catherine Porter and Carolyn Burke (Ithaca, NY: Cornell University Press, 1985); *The Irigaray Reader*, ed. Margaret Whitford (Oxford: Blackwell, 1991).
2. *Offenbaren*: to show or reveal oneself; *Sich*: oneself or to oneself; Heidegger's compound therefore doubles the self reflection already present, so that, at its most literal, *sichoffenbaren* might be translated, albeit awkwardly, as 'to reveal or open to oneself, one's self'.
3. *Seelenleben*: inner life; *fremden*, depending on context and use, can mean, variously: foreign, strange, alien, different, unknown, and other.
4. *Scopic*: referring to sight or observation; the scopic drive would be that by which the subject derives pleasure, often sexual, from looking.
5. *Manichean*: derived from a religious sect which flourished from the third to the fifth centuries. Manichean theology was dualist in nature, stressing that Satan was co-eternal with God.

Further reading

Bhabha, Homi K. (1994), *The Location of Culture* (London: Routledge)
Derrida, Jacques (1984), 'Deconstruction and the Other', trans. Richard Kearney. In Richard Kearney (ed.), *Dialogues with Contemporary Thinkers: The Phenomenological Heritage* (Manchester: Manchester University Press), pp. 107–26.
Derrida, Jacques (1988), *The Ear of the Other: Otobiography, Transference, Translation* (1985), ed. Christie McDonald, trans. Peggy Kamuf (Lincoln, NE: University of Nebraska Press).
Derrida, Jacques (1989), 'Psyche: Inventions of the Other', trans. Catherine Porter. In Lindsay Waters and Wlad Godzich (eds), *Reading de Man Reading* (Minneapolis, MN: University of Minnesota Press), pp. 25–65.
Irigaray, Luce (1985), *Speculum of the Other Woman* (1974), trans. Gillian C. Gill (Ithaca, NY: Cornell University, pp. 353–64.
Lacan, Jacques (1981), *Speech and Language in Psychoanalysis* (1968), trans. Anthony Wilden (Baltimore, MD: Johns Hopkins University Press).
Levinas, Emmanuel (1987), *Time and the Other* (1947), trans. Richard A. Cohen (Pittsburgh, PA: Duquesne University Press).
Wilden, Anthony (1981), 'Lacan and the Discourse of the Other'. In Jacques Lacan, *Speech and Language in Psychoanalysis* (1968), trans. Anthony Wilden (Baltimore, MD: Johns Hopkins University Press), pp. 159–311.

OVERDETERMINATION

Overdetermination has its most specific theoretical uses in the psychoanalytical and Marxist praxes of, respectively, Sigmund Freud and Louis Althusser. For Freud, the psyche produces representations, significations and meanings in situating the subject in relation to his or her world. However, how we produce meaning is not entirely (if at all) within our conscious control because the unconscious determines meaning through its generation and juxtaposition of images and symbols. Thus, the human mind generates overdetermined meaning where images and representations signify in more than a single manner, as Freud's example of the dream of Irma demonstrates:

> it will perhaps be worth while to consider a dream . . . so as to show how its content is overdetermined. For this purpose I will take the dream of Irma's injection . . .
>
> The principal figure in the dream-content was . . . Irma. She appeared with the feature which were hers in real life, and thus, in the first instance, represented herself. But the position in which I examined her by the window was derived from someone else, the lady for whom . . . I wanted to exchange my patient. In so far as Irma appeared to have a diphtheritic membrane, which recalled my anxiety about my eldest daughter, she stood for that child, and, behind her, through her possession of the same name as my daughter was hidden the figure of my patient who succumbed to poisoning. In the further course of the dream the figure of Irma acquired still other meanings, without any alteration occurring in the visual picture of her in the dream. She turned into one of the children whom we had examined in the . . . children's hospital, where my two friends revealed their contrasting characters. The figure of my own child was evidently the stepping-stone towards this transition. The same 'Irma's' recalcitrance over opening her mouth brought an allusion to another lady whom I had once examined, and, through the same connection, to my wife. Moreover, the pathological changes which I discovered in her throat involved allusions to a whole series of other figures.
>
> None of these figures whom I lighted upon by following up 'Irma' appeared in the dream in bodily shape. They were concealed behind the dream figure of 'Irma', which was thus turned into a collective image with, it must be admitted, a number of contradictory characteristics. Irma became the representative of all these other figures which had been sacrificed to the work of condensation . . .
>
> Sigmund Freud (1976: 398–400)

As Freud's commentary demonstrates, meanings are produced in excess of the psyche's capability to comprehend, control or organize at any one time. For example, any dream is the result of the symbolic construction which is produced by the unconscious, but every signifying element, every image, sign, or representation, verbal or visual, is overdetermined by the work of the unconscious, inasmuch as its meaning is always multiple and therefore available to different interpretations or analyses. An essential aspect of overdetermination is its polyvalent semantic nature, whereby a multiplicity of meanings compete within a complex network of signification. This leads Lacan to remark that 'overdetermination is strictly speaking only conceivable within the structure of language' (Jacques Lacan, 1977: 271). This comment is amplified here.

> As polysemic as an orchestral score is polyphonic, linguistic discourse resonates with a multitude of meanings, some momentarily more prominent than others, arranged along different levels of attention and relevance. This polysemy is an essential feature of discourse and is of interest to psychoanalysis, first, in grounding the possibility of multiple meaning that Freud called 'overdetermination'.
>
> Richard Boothby (1991: 126)

Within certain strands of Marxism, the notion of overdetermination, which Althusser imports specifically from Freud, operates at a social and cultural, rather than an individual, level, naming the totality of a social structure in all its relations.

> We are . . . obliged to renounce every teleology[1] of reason, and to conceive the historical relation between a result and its conditions of existence as a relation of production . . . and therefore as what . . . we can call the *necessity of its contingency*. To grasp this necessity we must grasp the very special and paradoxical logic that leads to this *production*, i.e., the logic of the conditions of the production of knowledges, whether they belong to the history of a branch of still ideological knowledge, or to a branch of knowledge attempting to constitute itself as a science or already established as a science. We can expect many surprises from this . . . like those we owe to Michel Foucault's studies of the disconcerting development of that complex cultural formation which in the seventeenth and eighteenth centuries grouped around the over-determined word 'Madness' a whole series of medical, legal, religious, ethical and political practices and ideologies in a combination whose internal dispositions and meaning varied as a function of the changing place and role of these terms in the more general context of the economic, political, legal and ideological structures of the time . . .
>
> Louis Althusser and Étienne Balibar (1970: 45)

The Althusserian understanding of overdetermination is closely related to, while extending in its complexity beyond the limits of, the idea of contradiction, originating in G. W. F. Hegel's writings, and first given an explicitly Marxist articulation in a 1937 essay by Mao Zedong.[2] Mao formulates the historical situation of China in the 1930s through an examination, as Arif Dirlik has put it, 'of the contradictoriness of its various moments [such as the contradiction between national and social needs], and the articulation of this contradictoriness as a contradiction between theory and practice'. The contradictory elements of society at a given historical moment produce an overdetermined identity for their society, Mao argues, and, as a result of this, social contradiction is, 'the basic law of materialist dialectics'. Social–historical moments are thus overdetermined inasmuch as various heterogeneous and contradictory beliefs, agendas, imperatives and systems or institutions coexist:

> the whole Marxist revolutionary experience shows that, if the general contradiction (. . . the contradiction between the forces of production and the relations of production, essentially embodied in the contradiction between two antagonistic classes) is sufficient to define the situation when revolution is the 'task of the day', it cannot of its own simple, direct power induce a 'revolutionary situation', nor *a fortiori* a situation of revolutionary rupture and the triumph of the revolution. If this contradiction is to become '*active*' in the strongest sense . . . there must be an accumulation of 'circumstances' and 'currents' so that whatever their origin and sense . . . they '*fuse*' into a *ruptural unity* . . . If . . . a vast accumulation of 'contradictions' comes into play . . . some of which are radically heterogeneous – of different origins, different sense, different *levels* and *points* of application – but which nevertheless 'merge' into a ruptural unity, we can no longer talk of the sole, unique power of the general 'contradiction'. Of course, the basic contradiction dominating the period . . . is active in all these 'contradictions' and even in their 'fusion' . . . The 'circumstances' and 'currents' [of the general contradiction] . . . derive from the relations of prŏduction, which are, of course, one of the *terms* of the contradiction, but at the same time its *conditions of existence* . . . the 'contradiction' is inseparable from the total structure of the social body in which it is found, inseparable from its formal *conditions* of existence, and even from the *instances* it governs; it is radically *affected by them*, determining, but also determined in one and the same movement, and determined by the various *levels* and *instances* of the social formation it animates; it might be called *overdetermined in its principle*.
>
> Louis Althusser (1977: 99–101)

The state of overdetermined social relations for Althusser (who draws on Lenin as well as Mao) is represented most starkly in the dialectical contradiction between labour and capital and is further articulated in his thinking on ideology. Moreover, Althusser's structural–materialist analysis and understanding of overdetermination demonstrates how it is specifically historical in that specific forms and circumstances are organized differently from period to period. The following citation describes the break made by Althusser from more traditional Marxist epistemologies through the incorporation of overdetermination.

> In opposition to the hierarchical and unilinear determinism implicit in the base/superstructure[3] metaphor, Althusser posits a more complex model of causality in which there is an interaction between one level of the structured whole which is dominant but which is not the sole or final cause, and other levels which are dominated but which are not merely secondary effects. 'Overdetermination' is the name Althusser gives to this process in which the general contradiction at the economic level is radically affected by the other levels which are both determined by and in turn determine the dominant level . . . the social formation is characterized by the uneven and nonteleological play of its elements, since the invariant structure of the complex whole exists only through the discrete variations for which it is the precondition. This is not a pluralism, but it allows an understanding of the effect of a plurality of determinations within a structure where one instance is dominant as a necessary condition of complexity . . . Althusser . . . conceives of the social whole as being constituted by distinct and relatively autonomous levels or instances which at any time are articulated in particular relations of domination and subordination and which are subject to structural causality. Each level is the site of specific practices (economic, political, ideological, technical, and theoretical).
>
> John Frow (1986: 22–3)

Another aspect of the Althusserian revision of Marxist discourse, in specific relation to the example of the Russian Revolution,[4] is given here.

> Taking the October Revolution of 1917 as his example, Althusser . . . [argues that the] basic contradiction between forces and relations of production, embodied in the struggle of antagonistic classes, is not in itself sufficient to provoke revolution . . . What is necessary is that it should 'fuse' . . . with other contradictions in a unity which provokes radical change. This unity of fused contradictions, he suggests, reveals its own nature, which is that contradiction is inseparable from its conditions of existence and from the moments, or instances, it governs.

Determining and determined by the various levels and moments of the social formation, contradiction is therefore 'overdetermined'.

Extending this analysis of a given revolutionary situation to explain the workings of societies in general, Althusser argues that all contradictions in a social formation are overdetermined . . . in this way. In other words, a society by itself and all the various levels of its activity are intimately affected by the state of relations within and between all those levels.

Michael Kelly (1982: 127)

A further helpful commentary notes not only the example of the Russian Revolution but also the influence of Gaston Bachelard[5] on Althusser's thinking on contradiction and overdetermination in historical-ideological terms.

Althusser . . . follows Bachelard in his pluralist conception . . . of contradiction. In his theory of over-determination, the notion of a fundamental, basic contradiction between the forces and relations of production, determining the whole of social development, has gone in favour of a complex scheme, in which each aspect of society is developing in its own time warp. The theory is applied most notably by Althusser to provide an explanation of the Russian Revolution, when all the different contradictions come together, are 'condensed' to create a revolutionary situation.

Thus, in Althusser, contradiction is not simple, but complex and uneven. It is not given the role of internal motor of all development and change. Rather it is used . . . to explain the particular external relations which exist between the different parts of a system, and how these relations are *reproduced* within a particular set of circumstances.

Margaret A. Majumdar (1995: 125)

Finally, Slavoj Žižek addresses the epistemological break in Marxist discourse, relating the notion of overdetermination to the Lacanian model of causality.

In *Reading Capital*, Louis Althusser sought to illuminate the epistemological break of Marxism by means of a new concept of causality, that of 'overdetermination'. Rather than posing an oppositional determination, he held that the very determining instance is overdetermined by the total network of relations within which it plays the determining role. Althusser contrasted this notion of causality to that of both mechanical transitive causality (the linear chain of causes and effects . . .) and expressive causality (the inner essence which expresses itself in the multitude of its forms-in-appearance) . . . This triad of expressive-transitive-overdetermined causality parallels the Lacanian triad Imaginary–Real–Symbolic. Expressive causality belongs to the level of the Imaginary; it designates the logic of an identical imago which leaves its imprint at different levels of material content. Overdetermination implies a symbolic totality, since such retroactive determination of the ground by the totality of the grounded is possible only within a symbolic universe. And, finally, transitive causality designates the senseless collisions of the real.

Slavoj Žižek (1994b: 52)

Questions for further consideration

1. How might the Althusserian notion of overdetermination be put to work so as to explain the various cultural or historical 'contradictions' which exist between different discourses within any given literary text?
2. In what ways does overdetermination enable the reader to perceive a form such as the novel as the articulation of different and differing social relations at a given historical or cultural moment?
3. In the light of Freud's model of psychic overdetermination, would it be possible to think Althusser's notion as a model of a socio-historical or collective unconscious?

Explanatory and bibliographical notes

1. *Teleology*: doctrine or study of final causes.
2. Mao Zedong (*b*.1893–*d*.1976): *Concerning Practice*, n.t. (London: Trinity Trust, 1951); *The Chinese Revolution and the Chinese Communist Party*, n.t. (Beijing: Foreign Languages Press, 1954); *Analysis of the Classes in Chinese Society*, n.t. (Beijing: Foreign Languages Press, 1956).
3. Marx conceived the base/superstructure model of society; in this model, the 'base' is the economic structure of society, its modes of production and the lived social relations that are in place according to the division of capital and labour; the 'superstructure' names those aspects of society such as politics, law, morality, religion, and art which are determined by the base and which, in turn, serve to maintain the economic base.
4. The Russian Revolution: dates are usually given as 1917–21, though, arguably, the seeds of the revolution were sown in 1905, when Tsarist troops opened fire on a peaceful workers' demonstration in St Petersburg.
5. Gaston Bachelard (*b*.1884–*d*.1962): *The Poetics of Space*, trans. Maria Jolas, Foreword by Étienne Gilson (Boston, MA: Beacon Press, 1964); *The New Scientific Spirit*, trans. Arthur Goldhammer, Foreword by Patrick A. Heelan (Boston, MA: Beacon Press, *c*.1984); *On Poetic Imagination and Reverie:*

Selections from Gaston Bachelard, trans., Preface and Introduction by Colette Gaudin (Dallas, TX: Spring Publications, 1987).

Further reading

Althusser, Louis, and Étienne Balibar (1970), *Reading Capital* (1968), trans. Ben Brewster (London: New Left Books).
Freud, Sigmund (1976), *The Interpretation of Dreams*, Penguin Freud Library, Volume 4, trans. James Strachey, ed. Angela Richards (Harmondsworth: Penguin).
Žižek, Slavoj (1994b), 'Identity and its Vicissitudes: Hegel's "Logic of Essence" as a Theory of Ideology'. In Ernesto Laclau (ed.), *The Making of Political Identities* (London: Verso), pp. 40–75.

PERFORMATIVITY

Performance is commonly understood as the act of public exhibition that results in a transaction between performer and audience; an utterance that, via its public display, causes a linguistic interaction with the exhibition's object. However, while there occurs on occasion an assumption on the part of some critics of equivalence between the idea of performance and that of *performativity*, the difference between the two is rather more pronounced. The condition of performative articulation is given particular consideration by Jacques Derrida in the context of the instability of speech acts. Derrida's analysis of the performative in 'Signature Event Context' comes as a response to the work of speech act theorist J. L Austin,[1] who distinguishes between constative and performative or illocutionary[2] utterances, the former being an 'assertion' or 'description', the latter being an 'utterance which allows us to do something by means of speech itself'. Here is Austin.

> [Of performative utterances such as 'I do', 'I name this ship', 'I give and bequeath'] In these examples it seems clear that to utter the sentence . . . is not to *describe* my doing . . . it is to do it. None of these utterances is either true or false . . . To name a ship *is* to say . . . the words 'I name, &c.'. When I say . . . 'I do', I am not reporting on a marriage: I am indulging in it.
>
> What are we to call a sentence or an utterance of this type? I propose to call it a *performative sentence* or a performative utterance, or, for short, 'a performative'. The term 'performative' . . . indicates that the

issuing of the utterance is the performing of an action – it is not normally thought of as just saying something.

J. L. Austin (1999: 6–7)

However, for Austin certain utterances that appear to be performative do not necessarily fulfil that function as a result of their context:

a performative utterance will, for example, be *in a peculiar way* hollow or void if said by an actor on the stage, or if introduced in a poem, or spoken in soliloquy . . . Language in such circumstances is in special ways . . . used not seriously, but in ways *parasitic* upon its normal use . . .

J. L. Austin (1999: 22)

Austin's sense of the 'proper' and, by implication, inflexible limits of the context of a speech act are both rigidly maintained and always implicit to any definition of such an act. To such postulations, Derrida responds,

is not what Austin excludes as anomalous, exceptional, 'non serious', that is *citation* (on the stage, in a poem, or in a soliloquy) the determined modification of a general citationality – or rather, a general iterability – without which there would not even be a 'successful' performative? Such that – a paradoxical, but inevitable consequence – a successful performative is necessarily an 'impure' performative . . .

Jacques Derrida (1982: 325)

Derrida's question undoes Austin's assumptions. Furthermore, the question unfolds for us the paradox inherent in Austin's model. Derrida also asks:

Could a performative statement succeed if its formulation did not repeat a 'coded' or iterable statement, in other words if the expressions I use to open a meeting, launch a ship or a marriage were not identifiable as *conforming* to an iterable model, and therefore if they were not identifiable in a way as 'citation'? . . . given this structure of iteration, the intention which animates utterance will never be completely present in itself and its content . . . One will no longer be able to exclude . . . the 'nonserious' . . . from 'ordinary' language.

Jacques Derrida (1982: 326–7)

Derrida's critique develops from his understanding that an utterance is never stable but always available for citation and iterability and, indeed, only aspires to communicability in being transmissible, repeatable, beyond its supposedly 'original' context (which itself is never self-sufficient). Thus the idea of a speech act as act is already troubled by the iterable condition of the sign. Of Derrida's critique, it is remarked that he

> recognizes that the possibility that *any* performance may fail . . . for Derrida [this possibility] is a structural element, indeed a condition of possibility of any utterance.
>
> Christina Howells (1999: 65)

The contradictory condition of the performative, its possibility of being both felicitous and infelicitous, is considered in detail here.

> On the one hand, the performative depends on the intentions or sincerity of the one who speaks . . . Austin's concept of the felicitous performative is closely tied to the presupposition of the self-conscious 'I' . . . The first-person pronoun as well as a present indicative verb uttered by a self-conscious ego or subject is a necessary condition of the paradigmatic performative . . . In order for a performative to be felicitous, I must mean what I say, and must know what I mean and that I mean what I say, with . . . no unconscious motives or reservations. A Freudian notion of the unconscious would pretty well blow Austin's theories out of the water . . .
>
> On the other hand, the performative must *not* depend on the intentions or sincerity of one who speaks . . . the words themselves must do the work, not the secret intentions of the speaker or writer. For civil order to be maintained, we must be able to hold speakers and writers responsible for their words, whatever their intentions at the time.
> . . .
> The smooth working of society, of 'law and order', depends, it can be argued, on ignoring whatever goes on secretly in people's hearts and holding them to the rule that says our word is our bond . . . This would seem to mean . . . that what I said or wrote when I was drunk, coerced, at the point of a gun, or insane would also be held to bind me. Austin . . . rules that out. I must be in my right mind and not coerced. That, however, is not the same thing as saying my word is my bond. It smuggles the concepts of seriousness and sincerity back in as necessary conditions of a felicitous performative. It must be uttered by a fully self-conscious ego in complete possession of its wits and its intentions.
>
> J. Hillis Miller (2001: 28–32)

Furthermore, the exclusion of rhetoric from the consideration of speech acts needs to be taken into account, as in this example.

> We have witnessed . . . a strong interest in certain elements in language whose function . . . excludes, or postpones, the consideration of tropes,

ideologies, etc., from a reading that would be primarily performative. In some cases, a link is reintroduced between performance, grammar, logic, and stable referential meaning . . . But the most astute practitioners of a speech act theory of reading avoid this relapse and rightly insist on the necessity to keep the actual performance of speech acts, which is conventional rather than cognitive, separate from its causes and effects – to keep, in their terminology, the illocutionary force separate from its perlocutionary function. Rhetoric, understood as persuasion, is forcefully banished . . . from the performative moment and exiled in the affective area of perlocution . . . What awakens one's suspicion about this conclusion is that it relegates persuasion, which is indeed inseparable from rhetoric, to a purely affective and intentional realm and makes no allowance for modes of persuasion which are no less rhetorical and no less at work in literary texts, but which are of the order of persuasion by *proof* rather than persuasion by seduction. Thus to empty rhetoric of its epistemological impact is possible only because its tropological, figural functions are being bypassed. It is as if . . . rhetoric could be isolated from the generality that grammar and logic have in common and considered as a mere correlative of illocutionary power . . . the characterization of the performative as sheer convention reduces it in effect to a grammatical code among others. The relationship between trope and performance is actually closer [and] more disruptive . . .

Paul de Man (1986: 18–19)

The disruptive intimacy spoken of at the close of the last citation is addressed here in exemplary detail.

Fable, Francis Ponge's fable[3] . . . is the tale of an invention, it recites and describes itself, it presents itself from the start as a beginning, the inauguration of a discourse or of a textual mechanism. It does what it says . . . *Fable*, owing to a turn of syntax, is a sort of poetic performative that simultaneously describes and carries out, on the same line, its own generation . . . its constative description is nothing other than the performative itself. '*Par le mot par commence donc ce texte.*'[4] Its beginning, its invention . . . does not come about before the sentence that recounts precisely this event. The narrative is nothing other than the coming of what it cites, recites, points out, or describes. It is hard to distinguish between the telling and the told faces of this sentence . . . By its very typography, the second occurrence of the word *par* reminds us that the first *par* . . . is being quoted. The quote institutes a repetition or an originary reflexivity that, even as it divides the inaugural act . . . we could say that the first *par* is used, the second quoted or mentioned. . . . The *used par* belongs to the mentioning sentence, but also to the mentioned

sentence . . . What the sentence cites integrally, from *par* to *par*, is nothing other than itself in the process of citing. . . . In the body of a single
line, on the same divided line, the event of an utterance mixes up two
absolutely heterogeneous functions, 'use' and 'mention' . . . The constative statement is the performative itself since it points out nothing that is
prior or foreign to itself. . . . An infinitely rapid circulation . . . *all at once*
shunts the performative into the constative, and vice versa . . .

The infinitely rapid oscillation between the performative and the
constative . . . does not just produce an essential instability. This instability constitutes that very event . . . whose invention disturbs . . . the
norms, the statutes, and the rules.

Jacques Derrida (1989: 33–5)

This analysis of Ponge's *Fable* and its performative dimension can be
summarized in the following manner, while at the same time offering a
broader comprehension beyond the immediate example:

differing from the classical assertion, from the constative utterance, the
performative's referent . . . is not outside it, or in any case or before it. It
does not describe something which exists outside and before language. It
produces or transforms a situation, it operates . . . The performative is a
'communication' which does not essentially limit itself to transporting
an already constituted semantic content guarded by its own aiming at
truth . . .

Jacques Derrida (1982: 321–2)

Another dimension of performativity is revealed here, through a description
of the act of naming.

What does it mean for a word not only to name, but also in some sense
to perform and, in particular, to perform what it names? On the one
hand, it may seen that the work – for the moment we do not know which
work or which kind of word – enacts what it names; where the 'what' of
'what it names' remains distinct form the name itself and the performance of that 'what' . . . But according to [Austin's] view . . . the name
performs itself, and in the course of that performing becomes a thing
done; the pronouncement is the act of speech at the same time that it is
the speaking of an act.

Judith Butler (1997a: 43–4)

While, initially, Derrida's formalization of the destabilizing processes of
the performative utterance and the undecidability attendant on this operated in the realm of linguistics, speech acts, and poetics, subsequently, the

issue of the performative has been engaged with regard to matters of the political, with questions of subjectivity and identity, as the remarks by Judith Butler just cited imply, and as her work repeatedly demonstrates.

> a theory of the performative is already at work in the exercise of political discourse (theory can work in implicit and fugitive ways). Understanding performativity as a renewable action without clear origin or end suggests that speech is finally constrained neither by its specific speaker nor its originating context. Not only defined by social context, such speech is also marked by its capacity to break with context. Thus, performativity has its own social temporality in which it remains enabled precisely by the contexts from which it breaks. This ambivalent structure at the heart of performativity implies that, within political discourse, the very terms of resistance and insurgency are spawned in part by the powers they oppose.
>
> Judith Butler (1997a: 40)

Apropos of the construction of subjectivity, Butler offers the following critique.

> Subjects who have been excluded from enfranchisement by existing conventions governing the exclusionary definition of the universal seize the language of enfranchisement and set into motion a 'performative contradiction', claiming to be covered by that universal, thereby exposing the contradictory character of previous conventional formulations of the universal. This kind of speech appears at first to be impossible or contradictory, but it constitutes one way to expose the limits of current notions of universality, and to constitute a challenge to those existing standards to become more expansive and inclusive. In this sense, being able to utter the performative contradiction is hardly a self-defeating enterprise; on the contrary, performative contradiction is crucial to the continuing revision and elaboration of historical standards of universality proper to the futural movement of democracy itself.
>
> Judith Butler (1997a: 89–90)

The notion of the subject is further explored by Butler in her account of performativity in the work of Pierre Bourdieu.

> In [Pierre] Bourdieu's account of performative speech acts, the subject who utters the performative is positioned on a map of social power in a fairly fixed way, and this performative will or will not work depending on whether the subject who performs the utterance is already authorized to make it work by the position of social power she or he occupies. In

other words, a speaker who declares a war or performs a wedding cere-
mony, and pronounces into being that which he declares to be true, will
be able to animate the 'social magic' of the performative *to the extent*
that the subject is already authorized or, in Bourdieu's terms, *delegated*
to perform such binding speech acts. Although Bourdieu is clearly right
that not all performative 'work' and that not all speakers can participate
in the apparently divine authorization by which the performative works
its social magic and compels collective recognition of its authority, he
fails to take account of the way in which social positions are themselves
constructed through a more tacit operation of performativity. Indeed,
not only is the act of 'delegation' a performative, that is, a naming which
is at once the action of entitlement, but authorization more generally is
to a strong degree a matter of being addressed or interpellated by prevailing forms of social power.

Judith Butler (1997a: 156)

Arguably, Butler's attention to the relationship between the performative
and social manifestations of power draws out implicit assumptions
concerning performativity in the network of power–knowledge–discourse
as traced by Michel Foucault. In this final citation the ideological import of
performatives is fully extrapolated.

Performatives do not merely reflect prior social conditions, but produce
a set of social effects, and though they are not always the effects of 'official' discourse, they nevertheless work their social power not only to
regulate bodies, but to form them as well. Indeed, the efforts of performative discourse exceed and confound the authorizing contexts from
which they emerge. Performatives cannot always be retethered to their
moment of utterance, but they carry the mnemic trace of the body in the
force that they exercise. One need only consider the way in which the
history of having been called an injurious name is embodied, how the
words enter the limbs, craft the gesture, bend the spine.
    When we say that an insult strikes like a blow, we imply that our
bodies are injured by such speech. And they surely are, but not in the
same way as a purely physical injury takes place. Just as physical injury
implicates the psyche, so psychic injury effects the bodily doxa, that lived
and corporeally registered set of beliefs that constitute social reality. The
'constructive' power of the tacit performative is precisely its ability to
establish a practical sense for the body, not only a sense of what the body
is, but how it can or cannot negotiate space, its 'location' in terms of
prevailing cultural conditions. The performative is not a singular act
used by an already established subject, but one of the powerful and insid-
ious ways in which subjects are called into social being from diffuse

social quarters, inaugurated into sociality by a variety of diffuse and powerful interpellations. In this sense the social performative is a crucial part not only of subject formation, but of the ongoing political contestation and reformulation of the subject as well.

Judith Butler (1997a, 159–60)

Questions for further consideration

1. In the light of Derrida's comments on *Fable* by Francis Ponge, consider the following sentence from James Joyce's *Ulysses*:

   Preparatory to anything else Mr Bloom brushed off the greater bulk of the shavings and handed Stephen the hat and ashplant and bucked him up generally in orthodox Samaritan fashion, which he very badly needed. (Joyce, 1993: 501)

   Is this, the first sentence of the 'Eumaeus' episode, a constative or performative statement? Is it both?
2. Consider the ways in which tropes and performances are closely related. Why should tropes as performative be disruptive, as Paul de Man claims?
3. Consider the possible relation between performatives and iteration.

Explanatory and bibliographical notes

1. J. L. Austin (*b*.1911 *d*.1960): *Sense and Sensibilia* (Oxford: Clarendon Press, 1962); *Philosophical Papers*, ed. J. O. Urmson and G. J. Warnock (Oxford: Clarendon Press, 1970); *How to Do Things with Words*, ed. J. O. Urmson and Marina Sbisà (Oxford: Clarendon Press, 1975).
2. *Illocution/Perlocution*: an illocutionary speech act or utterance is a performative; a perlocutionary act is one which attempts to persuade or convince.
3. Francis Ponge (*b*.1899–*d*.1988): *The Voice of Things*, ed., trans. and Introduction by Beth Archer (New York: McGraw-Hill, 1972); *The Making of the Pré/La fabrique du Pré*, trans. Lee Fahnestock (Columbia, MO: University of Missouri Press, 1979); *Selected Poems*, trans. C. K. Williams, John Montague and Margaret Guiton, ed. Margaret Guiton (Winston-Salem, NC: Wake Forest University Press, 1994).
4. *Par le mot par commence donc ce texte*: 'By the word *by* commences then this text'.

Further reading

Austin, J. L. (1999), *How to Do Things with Words* (1962) 2nd edn, ed. J. O. Urmson and Marina Sbisà (Cambridge, MA: Harvard University Press).

Butler, Judith (1997a), *Excitable Speech: A Politics of the Performative* (London: Routledge).

Derrida, Jacques (1982), *Margins of Philosophy* (1972) trans., with notes by Alan Bass (Chicago, IL: University of Chicago Press).

Derrida, Jacques (1988), *Limited Inc.*, trans. Samuel Weber and Jeffrey Mehlman (Evanston, IL: Northwestern University Press).

Derrida, Jacques (1989), 'Psyche: Inventions of the Other', trans. Catherine Porter. In Lindsay Waters and Wlad Godzich (eds), *Reading de Man Reading* (Minneapolis, MN: University of Minnesota Press), pp. 25–65.

Miller, J. Hillis (2001), *Speech Acts in Literature* (Stanford, CA: Stanford University Press).

POSTMODERNITY/POSTMODERNISM

There is little general consensus concerning the meaning of either *postmodernity* or *postmodernism*, and their use and history are chequered. The term has been used extensively in the field of architecture as the name for a school or movement. With reference to literature and culture, 'postmodernism' is often taken to refer to any work of art which knowingly refers to its own status as a work of art, or which otherwise, from the position as elite art form, jokingly addresses the status of the art object through construction from or reference to popular culture, thereby collapsing distinctions between high and low. The earliest appearances of postmodernism date back to the first decades of the twentieth century, as the first citation avers:

> the idea of a 'postmodernism' first surfaced in the Hispanic inter-world of the 1930s . . . to describe a conservative reflux within modernism itself . . .
>
> Perry Anderson (1998: 3–4)

While this historical commentary is useful, it does not get us very far. Although a number of definitions read the aesthetic and formal concerns with which the notions of postmodernism and postmodernity are associated, certain theorists of the postmodern, such as Fredric Jameson, Jean-François Lyotard and Teresa Ebert, find the problematic of defining postmodernism a question of its being a product of particular political overdeterminations, which serve to produce postmodernism's often apparently contradictory meanings, and whereby the postmodern condition is fundamentally misrecognized in aesthetic terms. The meaning or identity of the postmodern is understood, then, as a self-conscious aesthetic component of its constitution, rather than as a political effect of late twentieth-century global capitalism.

We might continue with a remark such as this:

> Postmodernism attempts a radical break with all of the major strands of post-Enlightenment thought.
>
> David West (1996: 189)

This is immediately problematic however, not least because the notion of 'post-enlightenment' thought (supposing thought to be so easily categorizable) immediately disturbs any historical dating, conventionally assumed, for the advent of postmodernism. Another form of determination might take the following causal tack.

> Modernism [is] the epoch of a metaphysical–historicist authorization of knowledge, and postmodernism is the explicit querying of this mode of legitimation. In other words, postmodernism is not simply what comes after modernism, or what arises from a completely different set of principles, for it emerges in a critical relationship with the preceding principles.
>
> Iain Chambers (1990: 96)

The historical 'progression' from modernism to postmodernism is again addressed here.

> In contrast to the modernist optimism relating to progress, postmodernism places a fundamental scepticism, and, in contrast to the pathos of a radical new beginning it places the inevitability of tradition . . . postmodernism no longer believes in the possibility of a last foundation in some one or other metanarrative,[1] and in contrast to modernism's claim to infinity, postmodernism stipulates the radical finiteness of the human existence . . . postmodernism contrasts the modern subjectivism, which has decisively determined philosophy since Descartes, with the 'death' of the subject.
>
> Jos de Mul (1999: 18)

Here is a further consideration of the shift historically from the modern to the postmodern.

> As substantive or adjective, postmodernity or postmodern indicates that it comes after and is not identical with modernity or the modern. Many areas of human activity in the western world, from architecture to the arts and philosophy and literature, indeed seem to function within the

context of a paradigm which is different from the earlier twentieth century. The paradigm of the later twentieth century indeed seems to produce a multiplicity of forms, a plurality of tastes, pastiches, it speaks of the unfoundationality of belief systems, of the incapacity of rationality to grasp the whole, of the contingency of scientific data on the position of the observer, of the positionality and indeterminacy of knowledge, and of the power inscribed in the arbitrariness of authority. Multiplicity, plurality, decentralization, unfoundationality, arbitrariness, non-accumulative structures of knowledge and so on are some of the supplemental terms which inform the discourse on and which describe the practices of postmodernity, thereby displacing more traditional descriptive ways, such as hierarchy, centralization, linearity, determinacy, causality and so on.

Renate Holub (1992: 171–2)

However, such arguments are somewhat insufficient, if not inaccurate, for the following reasons at least.

postmodernism as a distinct set of artistic practices – let alone a cultural dominant – [is] largely a figment. Virtually every aesthetic device or feature attributed to postmodernism – *bricolage*[2] of tradition, play with the popular, reflexivity, hybridity, pastiche, figurality, decentring of the subject – could be found in modernism.

Perry Anderson (1998: 80)

So, it is inadequate, to say the least, to think of postmodernism as either an aesthetic category or a set of aesthetic practices belonging to a moment in history that has emerged after the supposedly discernible and delimitable moment of modernism, and whose emergence is therefore definable as postmodernity. The inadequacy is to be found not only in the fact that aesthetic practices are irreducible to any one period but also in the fact that any homogenizing effort towards periodization is reductive and therefore inaccurate.

Ultimately, it is mistaken to conceive of postmodernism as a periodizing concept . . . The postmodern is not synonymous with the contemporary.

Thomas Docherty (1990: 15–16)

More than this though there are also the signs of profound historical and social contradictions, perhaps even the signs of overdetermination, to be discerned in notions of the postmodern.

[A]ny analysis of postmodernism is explicitly or implicitly a contribution to a theory of the mode of production and its place in social theory. Postmodernism . . . is the articulation on the level of the *super-structure* of changes in the social, cultural, political . . . which have come about as a result of new forms of deploying capital and extracting surplus labor around the world. As such, postmodernism is not simply a series of isolated, shifting aesthetic and architectural styles, proliferating commodifications, philosophical deconstructions, split subjectivities, or multiple identities and differences. Instead, postmodernism is a contradictory historical condition, and its contradictions are those of the material base: both postmodernism and the theories that try to explain it are divided by the social contradictions of capitalism itself.

Teresa Ebert (1996: 130)

Given this, any commentary which seeks to assign 'newness' or novelty to the idea of the postmodern, and with that a decisive break from previous epistemological or aesthetic modalities, still operates within classical or modern modes of determination with regard to its object, and is thus itself riven by the contradictions spoken of. The following citation exemplifies the problem.

Postmodernism can be understood as a new way of conceiving the relationship between intellectual disciplines, challenging conventional academic boundaries . . . Postmodernism has also become a topic of discussion within a number of different disciplines: in art, art theory and criticism, cultural studies, communication theory, philosophy, history, sociology, anthropology and geography among others.

David West (1996: 217)

The problem with which we are confronted would appear to be one of attempting to assert any dominant definition or narrative. This has led to the following statement.

Simplifying to the extreme, I define *postmodern* as incredulity toward metanarratives.

Jean-François Lyotard (1984: xxiv)

At the same time, the notion of postmodernism has also called into question the metanarrative we call History.

What postmodernism refuses is not history but History – the idea that there is an entity called History possessed of an immanent meaning and purpose which is stealthily unfolding around us even as we speak.

Terry Eagleton (1996: 30)

Thus postmodernism might be said to name a reaction against any universalizing, unifying, or homogenizing utterance or conceptualization.

> The postmodern critique of the 'unified subject' (or the interchangeability of discourses, or the autonomy of art), is a consequence of attributing to these concepts a *universal* status, of failing to historicize or to see them more broadly as moments within a particular cultural climate . . .
>
> Timothy Bewes (1997: 46)

From this, it should be stressed that one must not assume postmodernism as inherently nihilist, as suggesting that because there is no one meaning, it follows that there is no meaning or no more meaning. Rather, we might provisionally propose that so-called postmodernism, if any discursive act can be given this name, is a strategic and possibly ironic means of unveiling ideological embeddedness and cultural specificity. Such an argument leads to remarks such as this.

> Few words are more used and abused in discussions of contemporary culture than the word 'postmodernism'. As a result, any attempt to define the word will necessarily and simultaneously have both positive and negative dimensions . . . In general terms, it takes the form of self-conscious, self-contradictory, self-undermining statement. It is rather like saying something whilst at the same time putting inverted commas around what is being said . . . Postmodernism's distinctive character lies in this kind of wholesale 'nudging' commitment to doubleness, or duplicity . . . The postmodern's initial concern is to de-naturalize some of the dominant features of our way of life; to point out that those entities that we unthinkingly experience as 'natural' (they might even include capitalism, patriarchy, liberal humanism) are in fact 'cultural'.
>
> Linda Hutcheon (1989: 1–2)

The general political import of this comment is given specific focus here.

> As a form of ironic representation, parody is doubly coded in political terms: it both legitimizes and subverts that which it parodies. This kind of authorized transgression is what makes it a ready vehicle for the political contradictions of postmodernism at large. Parody can be used as a self-reflexive technique that points to art as art, but also to art as inescapably bound to its aesthetic and even social past. Its ironic reprise also offers an internalized sign of a certain self-consciousness about our culture's means of ideological legitimation . . . In her feminist pacifist work *Cassandra* . . . Christa Wolf[3] parodically rewrites Homer's[4] tale of men and war . . . Because we only know Cassandra through male representations of her,

Wolf adds her own feminist representation . . . In feminist art, written or visual, the politics of representation are inevitably the politics of gender . . . Postmodern parodic strategies are often used by feminist artists to point to the history and historical power of those cultural representations, while ironically recontextualizing both in such a way as to deconstruct them.

Linda Hutcheon (1989: 101–2)

Of course, whether such a gesture of rewriting is postmodern is ultimately not within the conscious control of the writer or artist, but is only ever received as such, if it is received at all, as something in excess of representation.

The postmodern would be that which in the modern invokes the unpresentable in presentation itself, that which refuses the consolation of correct forms, refuses the consensus of taste permitting a common experience of nostalgia for the impossible, and inquires into new presentations – not to take pleasure in them, but to better produce the feel that there is something unpresentable. The postmodern artist or writer is in the position of a philosopher: the text he writes or the work he creates is not in principle governed by preestablished rules and cannot be judged according to a determinant judgement, by the application of given categories to this text or work. Such rules and categories are what the work or text is investigating. The artist and the writer therefore work without rules and in order to establish the rules for what *will have been made*. This is why the work and the text can take on the properties of an event; it is also why they would arrive too late for their author, or, in what amounts to the same thing, why the work of making them would always begin too soon. *Postmodern* would be understanding according to the paradox of the future . . . anterior.

Jean-François Lyotard (1993a: 15)

Questions for further consideration

1. Despite its much vaunted 'break' with the past or its expression of suspicion towards grand narratives, if postmodernism assumes positions which are skeptical and cynical with regard to the possibility of transformation, does this suggest a political quietism on the part of postmodernism generally, if not in specific cases a conservatism complicit with reactionary cultural positions?
2. How 'post-' is postmodernism?
3. Is the fact that any statement concerning postmodernism inevitably takes on a self-conscious, self-contradictory, self-undermining form, as Linda Hutcheon suggests, itself a sign of postmodernity?

Explanatory and bibliographical notes

1. *Metanarrative*: narrative which defines the structural features of narratives in general; a narrative which speaks of other narratives. The history of Western civilization as a history of linear progress and successive technological advancements would be one such narrative.

2. *Bricolage*: colloquially, the act of throwing things together, or given in dictionaries as the French equivalent of 'D-I-Y'; here Anderson uses *bricolage* to suggest a tendency in postmodernism to throw together heterogeneous cultural elements, motifs, symbols, and so forth.

3. Christa Wolf (*b*.1929–): *Cassandra: A Novel and Four Essays*, trans. Jan van Heurck (New York: Farrar, Straus and Giroux, 1984); *The Quest for Christa T.*, trans. Christopher Middleton (New York, Farrar, Straus and Giroux, 1971); *The Author's Dimension: Selected Essays*, introduction by Grace Paley, ed. Alexander Stephan, trans. Jan van Heurck (New York: Farrar, Straus and Giroux, 1993).

4. Homer: little or nothing is known for certain about Homer, and it is a matter of critical contention whether he even wrote *The Iliad* and *The Odyssey* or whether these are the products of a group of poets.

Further reading

Anderson, Perry (1998), *The Origins of Postmodernism* (London: Verso).

Bewes, Timothy (1997), *Cynicism and Postmodernity* (London: Verso).

Chambers, Iain (1990), *Border Dialogues: Journeys in Postmodernism* (London: Routledge).

Docherty, Thomas (1993), *Postmodernism: A Reader* (New York: Columbia University Press).

Durham, Scott (1998), *Phantom Communities: The Simulacrum and the Limits of Postmodernism* (Stanford, CA: Stanford University Press).

Eagleton, Terry (1996), *The Illusions of Postmodernism* (Oxford: Blackwell).

Ebert, Teresa L. (1996), *Ludic Feminism and After: Postmodernism, Desire, and Labor in Late Capitalism* (Ann Arbor, MI: University of Michigan Press).

Elliot, Anthony (1996), *Subject to Ourselves: Social Theory, Psychoanalysis, and Postmodernity* (Cambridge: Polity Press).

Hutcheon, Linda (1989), *The Politics of Postmodernism* (London: Routledge).

Jameson, Fredric (1991), *Postmodernism or, the Cultural Logic of Late Capitalism* (London: Verso).

Lyotard, Jean-François (1984), *The Postmodern Condition: A Report on Knowledge* (1979), trans. Geoff Bennington and Brian Massumi, Foreword by Fredric Jameson (Minneapolis, MN: University of Minnesota Press)4.

Lyotard, Jean-François (1993a), *The Postmodern Explained: Correspondence, 1982–1985* (1988), trans. Don Barry et al., Afterword by Wlad Godzich (Minneapolis, MN: University of Minnesota Press).

Lyotard, Jean-François (1993b), *Toward the Postmodern* (1980), ed. Robert Harvey and Mark S. Roberts (Atlantic Highlands, NJ: Humanities Press).

Nash, Christopher (2001), *The Unravelling of the Postmodern Mind* (Edinburgh: Edinburgh University Press).
Vattimo, Gianni (1988), *The End of Modernity: Nihilism and Hermeneutics in Postmodern Culture*, trans. and Introduction by Jon R. Snyder (Baltimore, MD: Johns Hopkins University Press).

POWER

We all think we have an idea of the meaning of the term *power*, its meaning deceptively transparent. It is, we might say, an apparently simple, self-evident notion. Particular authorities, such as the police or the army, have particular forms of power over civilians. Education, the church, government, and other state institutions have, and exercise, power over their subjects. Power ensures and produces particular conditions, having material effects. While such effects undoubtedly take place it has to be stated that power is non-existent, if by this we mean to suggest that power is immaterial. What appears initially then is a paradox: in theory we know what we mean when we speak of power; however, in practice, power emerges as being difficult to define, given the many hidden, invisible ways in which it operates.

> Power is everywhere.
>   And nowhere.
>
> James R. Kincaid (1992: 17)

Modern critical thinking has thus defined the operation of power, its manifestations and effects, without assuming power to be locatable in any individual or source. Indeed,

> modern power functions not only as a tool of the state apparatus but also as a network of circulating forces, an economy of relations . . .
>
> Geoffrey Batchen (1997: 188)

Power is both part of material, social reality, and also available to comprehension as a profoundly complex textual structure, operating differentially and discursively. This being so, it has been remarked that

> individuals are the vehicles of power, not its points of application.
>
> Michel Foucault (1980: 98)

For reasons such as these, arguments as in the following example are presented.

We cannot *know* power. We cannot produce explanations of power that hope for anything more than being powerful, that somehow partake of the power they are not explaining but entering into. One negotiates with power for a share of the pot. One hopes, out of power, to produce accounts which succeed not in presenting but in coercing . . . It is not easy to determine what this power is, much less why it is so often used to form the center of investigations, the metaphoric base from which we construct our world.

James R. Kincaid (1992: 17)

Power is thus related to knowledge in a particular way.

Power needs knowledge, because knowledge can justify the idea that there is a thing (the 'subject') to be organized, categorized and measured, that human subjectivity is not an irreducible field of differences that continually counter and defy reduction to a single description.

Nick Mansfield (2000: 132)

Thus power can be employed to ensure subjection (though this is not its sole purpose, it being only one symptom of power), and to produce narratives of knowledge dividing an 'us' from a 'them'.

I suggest that power can deal with issues that evade its grasp or that threaten to expose its deficiencies only by saying no, telling stories of denial. In terms of pedophilia, one can locate these tales everywhere, in the gothic construction of the pedophile, for instance: the lurking stranger with the candy, the mentally retarded village hang-about, the homicidal wanderer. That people who in fact do engage in sexual relationships with children virtually never fit these images does not seem to matter. It appears to be a cultural necessity, a requirement of power discourse, to declare over and over again that these matters are marginal, controllable by power, and thus safely distanced from us, from me: whatever is going on in the heads of pedophiles, my head is clear of it. Power seems to promise me at least that protection.

James R. Kincaid (1992: 25)

The question concerning power should not be, therefore, of an ontological order.

We should not ask: 'What is power and where does it come from?', but 'How is it practised?' An exercise of power shows up as an affect, since force defines itself by its very power to affect other forces (to which it is related) and to be affected by other forces. To incite, provoke and produce (or any term drawn from analogous lists) constitute active affects, while to be incited or provoked, to be induced to produce, to have a 'useful' effect, constitute reactive affects. The latter are not simply the 'repercussion' or 'passive side' of the former but are rather 'the irreducible encounter' between the two, especially if we believe that the force affected has a certain capacity for resistance. At the same time, each force has the power to affect (others) and to be affected (by others again), such that each force implies power relations: and every field of forces distributes forces according to these relations and their variations.

Gilles Deleuze (1988: 71)

It is perhaps precisely because power is so nebulous, so dispersed and heterogeneous in its affects, that

the power that one man exercises over another is always perilous. I am not saying that power is evil by nature; I am saying that, owing to its mechanisms, power is infinite (which does not mean to say that it is all powerful; quite to the contrary). In order to limit power, the rules are never sufficiently rigorous. In order to displace it from all the opportunities which it fails upon, universal principles are never strict enough. Against power it is always necessary to oppose unbreakable law and unabridgeable rights.

Michel Foucault (1999b: 133)

In the work of Michel Foucault, power constitutes one of the three axes constitutive of subjectification, the other two being ethics and truth; for Foucault, the human subject is materially constituted 'through a multiplicity of organisms, forces, energies, materials, desires, thoughts, etc.'[1] For Foucault, power implies knowledge, and vice versa. Power is causal, it is constitutive of knowledge, even while knowledge is, concomitantly, constitutive of power: knowledge gives one power, but one has the power in given circumstances to constitute bodies of knowledge, discourses, and so on, as valid or invalid, truthful or untruthful. Power serves in making the world both knowable and controllable. It is frequently, if not always, the case that power asserts itself through epistemological rationalization.

The relationship between rationalization and the excesses of political power is evident. And we should not need to wait for bureaucracy or concentration camps to recognize the existence of such relations. But the problem is: what to do with such an evident fact?

. . .

First: it may be wise not to take as a whole the rationalization of society or of culture, but to analyse this process in several fields, each of them grounded in a fundamental experience: madness, illness, death, crime, sexuality, etc.

Michel Foucault (1999c: 135–6)

In order to begin such an analysis, Foucault's conception of power has to be understood as an endless process; it is not simply a question of analysing the ways the institutions named function, even though this is one possible, perhaps necessary inaugural gesture in any analysis of power.

> By power, I do not mean 'Power' as a group of institutions and mechanisms that ensure the subservience of the citizens of a given state. By power, I do not mean either, a mode of subjugation which, in contrast to violence, has the form of the rule. Finally, I do not have in mind a general system of domination exerted by one group over another . . . these are only the terminal forms power takes. It seems to me that power must be understood in the first instance as the multiplicity of force relations, immanent in the sphere in which they operate and which constitute their own organization; as the process which, through ceaseless struggles and confrontations transforms, strengthens, or reverses them; as the support which these force relations find in one another, thus forming a chain or a system, or on the contrary, the disfunctions and contradictions which isolate them from one another; and lastly, as the strategies in which they take effect, whose general design or institutional crystallization is embodied in the state apparatus, in the formulation of the law, in the various social hegemonies.

Michel Foucault (1990: 92–3)

Questions for further consideration

1. In what ways might we begin the analysis of rationalization as the manifestation of power, as suggested by Michel Foucault, in the specific example of the university?
2. Why are power and knowledge so closely linked?
3. Why and in what ways might the notion of the 'individual' and 'individual rights' limit an analysis of the various social articulations of power? Can this be considered in relation to matters of overdetermination and/or interpellation?

Explanatory and bibliographical note

1. Michel Foucault, *Power/Knowledge: Selected Interviews and Other Writings, 1972–1977*, ed. Colin Gordon (Brighton: Harvester Press, 1980), p. 97.

Further reading

Butler, Judith (1977), *The Psychic Life of Power* (Stanford, CA: Stanford University Press).

Fontana, Benedetto (1993), *Hegemony and Power: On the Relation between Gramsci and Machievelli* (Minneapolis, MN: University of Minnesota Press).

Deleuze, Gilles (1988), *Foucault*, trans. and ed. Séan Hand, Foreword by Paul Bové (Minneapolis, MN: University of Minnesota Press).

Foucault, Michel (1980), *Power/Knowledge: Selected Interviews and Other Writings, 1972–1977*, ed. Colin Gordon (Brighton: Harvester Press).

Foucault, Michel (1999), *Religion and Culture*, ed. Jeremy R. Carrette (London: Routledge), pp. 115–30.

Poulantzas, Nicos (1973), *Political Power and Social Classes* (1968), trans. Timothy O'Hagan, with David McLellan, Anna de Casparis and Brian Grogan (London: Sheed and Ward).

Simons, Jon (1995), *Foucault and the Political* (London: Routledge).

QUEER

A word which strategically resists any attempts at domestication or normative determination, *queer*, once undeniably a determination of hostility and opprobrium, and the signifier *par excellence* of homophobia, has been reclaimed in recent years, though not unproblematically (as the citation from Sally O'Driscoll makes plain), by gay and lesbian activists and scholars, precisely because of its radical, destabilizing potential with regard to the affirmation of difference and identity irreducible to matters of gender, sexuality or sexual preference. While, arguably, the signifier 'gay' may be said both to embrace and to elide 'lesbian', queer has, in its recent self-reflexive polemical usage in the context of identity politics, expanded and undone the stabilizing effects inadvertently operated in the name of 'gay studies'.

> Queer is a continuing moment, movement, motive – recurrent, eddying, *troublant*.[1] The word 'queer' itself means *across* – it comes from the Indo-European root *twerkw*, which also yields the German *quer* (transverse), Latin *torquere* (to twist), English *athwart* . . . queer . . . is . . . multiply transitive. The immemorial current that *queer* represents is antiseparatist as it is antiassimilationist. Keenly, it is relational, and strange.
> Eve Kosofsky Sedgwick (1993: xii)

Such significations imply a disruption from within of any stable constative or definitional function of the word. Thus it can be argued that queer is a performative signifier, in that it does not identify and represent a group 'prior' to its naming, but *enacts* a sodality[2] through its very enunciation, in that sense the dissonance of the groups it nominates is productive in the unforseeability of the political 'bodies' it produces.

Roger Luckhurst (1995: 333–4)

From any rhetorical or linguistic concern, one can move to the matter of identities.

queerness requires an understanding of individual identity that remains alert and responsive to the endless variety of positions in which the very notion of identity might be articulated.

Joseph Bristow (1995: 169)

The notion of queerness remarks 'a disturbing *mobility* or non-fixity between diverse sexualities' (Roger Luckhurst, 1995: 333). Which, to put it another way, points to the notion that

queerness is constantly refiguring itself, open to provisional and post-modern self-reconstruction . . .

Joseph Bristow (1995: 170)

Clearly, 'queer' troubles definition.

The minute you say 'queer' . . . you are necessarily calling into question exactly what you mean when you say it . . . Queer includes within it a necessarily expansive impulse that allows us to think about potential differences within that rubric.

Phillip Brian Harper et al. (1993: 30)

And, to go further still,

irreducible, undefinable, enigmatic, winking at us as it flouts convention . . . ['Queer' has become] the perfect postmodern trope, a term for the times, the epitome of knowing ambiguity.

Suzanne Walters (1996: 837)

The mobility of 'queer', its resistance to definition and its affirmation of that in identity which is irreducible to any heteronormative domestication calls into question the efficacy of any categorization.

[The] dissatisfaction with the categories of identification themselves and a questioning of their efficacy in political intervention . . . [brought with

it a] suspicion . . . strengthened by influential postmodern understandings of identity, gender, sexuality, power and resistance. These provide
the context in which queer becomes an intelligible – almost, one might
say, an inevitable – phenomenon.

Annamarie Jagose (1996: 71)

Moreover, such affirmation implies a critique of the limits of normative
concepts, if not the act of conceptualization itself.

Every person who comes to queer self-understanding knows in one way
or another that her stigmatisation is connected with gender, the family,
notions of individual freedom, the state, public speech, consumption and
desire, nature and culture, maturation, truth and trust, censorship, intimate life and social display, terror and violence, health care, and deep
cultural norms about the bearing of the body. Being queer means fight-
ing about these issues all the time, locally and piecemeal but always with
consequences.

Michael Warner (1993: xiii)

Finally, on the one hand it is important to recognize that the re-emergence
and re-invention of 'queer' has not been without a degree of political
ambivalence.

The existence of queer theory would be unimaginable without the
preceding decades of work in lesbian and gay studies and politics; yet the
goal of queer theory as defined by many critics is precisely to interrogate
the identity positions from which that work is produced. Using the same
word to refer to both fields has produced confusion and even some
bitterness on the part of those who fear that queer theory's critique of
the subject undermines their visibility and political ground.

Sally O'Driscoll (1996: 30)

On the other hand, it is impossible to overestimate the political and ethical
force of the return of the term, a force exceeding any merely institutional
concerns.

The aggression and ambition in the readoption of 'queer' are directly
proportionate to the degree to which its use proposes to overturn the
historic, hostile meaning. It plays for much higher stakes than if we tried
to reinstate, say, 'the third sex' . . . 'Queer' says, defiantly, that we don't
care what they call us. Also it keeps faith with generations of people,
before us, who lived their oppression and resistance in its initial terms.

Alan Sinfield (1994: 204)

Questions for further consideration

1. Consider the strategic political potential of a figure such as 'queer' in light of its semantic mobility. In what ways is it *both* affirmative *and* resistant?
2. In what ways do the citations distinguish between 'gay' and 'queer'?
3. In the light of Roger Luckhurst's suggestion that 'Queer is a performative signifier,' consider precisely the ways in which this might be the case, considering particularly Judith Butler's comments on performativity.

Explanatory notes

1. *Troublant*: disturbing; disconcerting.
2. *Sodality*: an association, fellowship, society, or companionship.

Further reading

Bristow, Joseph (1995), *Effeminate England: Homoerotic Writing after 1885* (New York: Columbia University Press).
Butler, Judith (1990), *Gender Trouble: Feminism and the Subversion of Identity* (London: Routledge).
Butler, Judith (1993), *Bodies that Matter: On the Discursive Limits of 'Sex'* (London: Routledge).
Jagose, Annamarie (1996), *Queer Theory: An Introduction* (New York: Routledge).
Sedgwick, Eve Kosofsky (1993), *Tendencies* (Durham, NC: Duke University Press).
Sinfield, Alan (1994), *The Wilde Century: Effeminacy, Oscar Wilde and The Queer Moment* (London: Cassell).
Smith, Anna Marie (1994), *New Right Discourse on Race and Sexuality: Britain, 1968–1990* (Cambridge: Cambridge University Press).
Warner, Michael (ed.) (1993), *Fear of a Queer Planet: Queer Politics and Social Theory* (Minneapolis, MN: University of Minnesota Press).

RACE

At its broadest, *race* may be said to refer to a family, tribe, people or nation sharing a set of common interests, beliefs, habits or characteristics. There are two principal approaches to racial categorization: genealogical and biological. The former concerns itself with notions of origin and heritage, while the latter interests itself in anatomical and corporeal differences. In genealogical narrations, Caucasian and Aryan groups are privileged as the apex of racial development, intrinsic to which narratives is the search for founding moments and the desire for racial purity.

However, the pre-eminent African-American literary and cultural critic Henry Louis Gates alerts the reader to a number of important details concerning the thinking and reading of race. To begin with, to speak of different 'races' such as 'black' or 'Jewish' is, says Gates, to 'speak in biological misnomers and, more generally, metaphors' (1990: 27). Thus, the very notion of race is highly contested. It has been argued, for example, that there are not different races and that any such assumption has only ever been, and continues to be, injurious.

> The truth is that there are no races: there is nothing in the world that can do all we ask race to do for us . . . [race] refers to nothing in the world at all. Talk of 'race' is particularly distressing for those of us who take culture seriously. For, where race works . . . it works as an attempt at metonym for culture, and it does so only at the price of biologizing what *is* culture, ideology.
>
> Kwame Anthony Appiah (1992: 45)

On the other hand though, it can be posited that the term does have social significance, as here:

> though biological and other sciences have shown that the complexes of characteristics thought to determine raciality do not constitute an unvarying *essence* that is determinable and constitutive of 'natural kinds', this does *not* mean that, thereby, there is no real referent for the term 'race', nor that the term is without positive social significance, even though it has been employed in rationalizations against racial 'others'.
>
> Lucius Outlaw (1996: 21)

What Gates's commentary, with which we began, does point out, through alerting us to the conflation of biology with the operations and effects of language, is that 'race', if it is a biological category at all (and this is in doubt), is not simply biological, but is rather an overdetermined term requiring careful unpacking. Any understanding of race owes much to the performative power of language to construct so-called racial identities, as is argued here:

> 'race' . . . is a constructed category . . . In the nineteenth century the word 'race' covered the terrain now also referred to by the term 'ethnicity' and was increasingly seen as a crucial dividing line between peoples
>
> Catherine Hall (1992: 25)

where the notion of race is acknowledged both as being constructed and as undergoing transformation; and, again, here:

there has been a recent call to view race as a construct, and a corresponding suspicion of any gesture that nods in the direction of acknowledging that even if the body does not ground race in an uncomplicated
or determining way, physical aspects of racial identity still have an overwhelming significance as markers of race. Race is inscribed in bodily
and visible ways, and bodies are made to symbolize race by bearing its
marks in complex and ambiguous ways that demand interpretation . . .
If we eliminate bodies in our analyses, in the interests of maintaining
that race . . . difference is, or should be, unimportant, and that therefore
its physical manifestations should be overlooked, then we deprive
ourselves of interrogating a privileged and organizing site for our
concepts of race . . .

Tina Chanter (2001: 11)

Despite the error of confusing biological fact with metaphor, such usage
persists both in everyday language and in literary texts and has, moreover,
a traceable history.

If gender hierarchy was inscribed at the heart of the missionary enterprise [in the nineteenth century], so was that of race. Missionaries
arrived in [Jamaica] with their heads full of images of 'poor Africans',
'savages', 'heathens'.
. . .
. . . in Jamaica . . . Negroes were thus constructed by the missionaries
and their friends, both for themselves and for an English audience,
through the filter of a set of assumptions as to what post-emancipation
society should be like – a set of assumptions which seesawed on the
ambivalence of racial difference: blacks were, and were not, equal.
    Black inferiority was further encoded in the language of the family.
Blacks were the 'sons of Africa', 'babes in Christ', children who must be
led to freedom, which meant adulthood.

Catherine Hall (1992: 234, 236–7)

Hall's insistence on the history of a concept is crucial to our comprehension. And here:

nationalism thinks in terms of historical destinies, while racism dreams
of eternal contaminations, transmitted from the origins of time through
an endless sequence of loathsome copulations . . . The dreams of racism
actually have their origin in ideologies of *class* rather than in those of
nation . . . Where racism developed outside Europe in the nineteenth
century, it was always associated with European domination . . .

Benedict Anderson (1991: 149–50)

One powerful literary mobilization from the nineteenth century of the rhetorical effects of racially determining language is witnessed through the example of *Jane Eyre*'s[1] Bertha Mason.

> The figure of Bertha Mason is significant, as she represents the failure of the . . . colonising enterprise . . . As a Creole, she is differentiated from the 'authentic' native, and represents multiple points of dislocation that the colonising venture had brought in its wake. The figure of the Creole had been brought into being solely by colonial/imperialist ventures. The Creole is sometimes a white person born in the colonies – of European origin, not born in their own country. Crucially, as a white European, the Creole is different from natives (Aboriginals), as also from Negroes, who had been brought to the islands as slaves. However, a person of mixed European and Indian . . . or Black descent would also be classified as a Creole. The racial classification is based not on colour alone but on displacement from the place of origin. The Creole is geographically displaced – s/he is born in the West Indies, and, because of the possibility of racial intermixture, cultural and racial displacement also become important. The category Creole is applicable only to European settlers and their descendants . . . It denotes access to colonial power and wealth. However, racial intermixture shakes the seat of this power. This meeting – of peoples, of cultures – was negotiated and guided by colonial and commercial interests, and . . . used class and racial differences to extend and strengthen colonial edifices. Bertha Mason, in *Jane Eyre*, is a Creole, constructed and formed under these conditions. Her racial origins remain vague. Her blackness, to which her madness is attributed, must be seen along with her possession of colonial wealth and fortunes . . . In this instance, the savage Other is represented by a Creole . . . the figure of the colonised double.
>
> Firdous Azim (1993: 182–3)

As the discussion of the Creole demonstrates, the rhetoric of race in colonial discourse emanates from a desire to fix identity in place, in particular the identity of the other.

> An important feature of colonial discourse is its dependence on the concept of 'fixity' in the ideological construction of otherness. Fixity, as the sign of cultural/historical/racial difference in the discourse of colonialism, is a paradoxical mode of representation: it connotes rigidity and an unchanging order as well as disorder, degeneracy and daemonic repetition. Likewise the stereotype, which is its major discursive strategy, is a form of knowledge and identification that vacillates between what is always 'in place', already known, and something that must be anxiously repeated . . . as if the essential duplicity of the Asiatic or the bestial

sexual license of the African that needs no proof, can never really, in discourse, be proved.

Homi K. Bhabha (1994: 66)

What emerges frequently in such discussions is the constant issue of distinctions between nature and nurture or nature and culture.

> Central to . . . debates [on gender and race] is a reworking of the classic nature/nurture distinction. Recent work in feminist theory and race theory has exposed the need for a thorough confrontation with the concept of history that is often invoked by those who argue against the view that gender or race is grounded in some unchanging, ahistorical, determinist category (such as innate characteristics, or a feminine or racial essence). The suggestion that race or gender is in some sense socially constructed, culturally mediated, or historically constituted, has served to combat racist or sexist assumptions that traditionally have been used to constrain the behavior and potential of certain groups of individuals. Presupposing some timeless or eternal essence has advanced and substantiated the privileges of other groups.
>
> Tina Chanter (2001: 11)

What the idea of race and its mobilization point to is the articulation of a sense of difference which is dynamic, to cite Henry Louis Gates once more, inasmuch as ' "race" has both described and inscribed differences of language, belief system, artistic tradition, and gene pool, as well as all sorts of supposedly natural attributes such as rhythm, athletic ability, cerebration, usury, fidelity, and so forth . . . Race has become a trope of ultimate, irreducible difference between cultures, linguistic groups, or adherents of specific belief systems' (1990). Thus, as a discursive, political and ideological signifier, race functions frequently as a means of definition based on binary oppositions between self and other, civilized and savage, and so on. One lasting, pernicious effect of the language of race has been that

> contemporary racist discourses . . . usually promote the differentiation of racial otherness: they include some aspects of blackness as the pseudo-assimilable, and they use this inclusion to legitimate the demonization and exclusion of other blacknesses as the unassimilable. The new racism defines the blackness which it wants to exclude not as that which is not white and therefore inferior, but as that which is inherently anti-British.
>
> Anna Marie Smith (1994: 95)

Modern definitions of race frequently emerge coterminously with national, colonial and ethnocentric discourses and practices. From the early

modern period onwards most notably, racial difference is determined in the
assumption of physical similarities and allegedly shared characteristics of
temperament, supposedly discernible as common to groups of people living
in a particular geographical domain. The language of racial difference slides
easily into racist discourse especially when associated with narratives of
national identity and nationalism.

> *Race* has become so closely linked with . . . nationalistic rhetoric that it
> does not need to be formally stated, having been transformed in Britain
> from being a 'sign' of physical difference to a 'symbol' with a large store
> of implicit connotations which can be commonly understood without
> being actually stated.
>
> Zig Layton-Henry and Paul Rich (1986: 10)

Such relations are so insistent that the relation becomes normalized, and
assumed to be inseparable:

> the fusion of race and nation in Britain has become so normalized that
> the differences between them have become almost imperceptible . . . If
> we were to investigate the relevance of 'race' in 1980s British politics, the
> Thatcherite deployment of nationalism would certainly be an important
> place to look, for post-colonial nationalist discourse has become one of
> the important sites for the re-coding of race. It makes sense that political
> scientists would tend to miss the re-codings of race, for we are trained to
> track explicit discourse rather than discursive reconstructions. In any
> event, I shall argue that race should not be excluded from our accounts
> of the legitimation of Thatcherism.
>
> Anna Marie Smith (1994: 14–15)

While Thatcherism serves to provide one relatively recent and acute example of the ideological concatenation between race and nation, the historical
development of Englishness as a rhetoric of race defined through racist
discourse concerning non-white immigration has long been institutionalized
in mainstream English politics:

> the Nationality Act [of 1981] codified the aspirations of a collection of
> conservative thinkers and parliamentarians explicitly committed to
> defending the distinctiveness of English culture . . . Primary among these
> individuals was Enoch Powell,[2] who . . . had repeatedly asserted the need
> to distinguish between English and British imperial culture . . .
> Englishness, he argued, did not emanate from British space but was,
> instead, an inheritance of race. All of these features of Powellite
> discourse are evident in the 'Rivers of Blood' speech, which he delivered

in Birmingham on April 20, 1968 . . . The centrepiece of the 'Rivers of Blood' address was a letter Powell claimed to have received from a constituent outlining the fate of an elderly woman who, finding her neighbourhood increasingly occupied by black immigrants, nevertheless refused to rent rooms in her home to 'negroes' and consequently became the 'victim' of abuse: 'She finds excreta pushed through her letterbox . . . she is followed by children, charming wide-grinning picaninnies. They cannot speak English, but one word they know. "Racialist", they chant . . . ' In these frequently cited sentences, the challenge that a collapsed empire puts to Powell's England is evident, as is, by negative definition, the essence of Powell's conception of Englishness. Threatened by racial pollution . . . the disappearance of the English language . . . and a territorial invasion . . . Englishness is here revealed, in the moment of its vanishing, as whiteness, a command of the English language, and a certain kind of domestic space. Most crucially, Powell represents Englishness as something that exists apart from . . . the lost empire – uncannily figured here as an invading black body.

Powell's strategy of disavowing blackness in order to negatively invoke a racially pure English identity draws on a long history of the reading of Englishness as primarily a racial category.

Ian Baucom (1999: 14–15)

Richard Dyer has argued that in many cultural and historical instances, racial imagery has relied on the assumption that non-white people are 'raced', as he puts it, while white people supposedly are not, or do not see themselves in racial terms, unless believing themselves to be threatened by racial difference.

There is no more powerful position than that of being 'just' human. The claim to power is the claim to speak for the commonality of humanity. Raced people can't do that – they can only speak for their race . . .

The sense of whites as non-raced is most evident in the absence of reference to whiteness in the habitual speech and writing of white people in the West. We (whites) will speak of, say the blackness or Chineseness of friends, neighbours, colleagues, customers or clients . . . but we don't mention the whiteness of the white people we know . . .

This assumption that white people are just people, which is not far off saying that whites are people whereas other colours are something else, is endemic to white culture.

. . .

The invisibility of whiteness as a racial position in white (which is to say dominant) discourse is of a piece with its ubiquity . . . in Western representation whites are overwhelmingly and disproportionately predominant . . . Yet precisely because of this and their placing as norm they seem not to be represented to themselves *as* whites but as people who are variously gendered, classed, sexualized and abled. At the level of racial representation, in other words, whites are not of a certain race, they're just the human race.

Richard Dyer (1997: 2–3)

Colour thus becomes a visible sign of apparent racial identity. Racial attitudes of this kind are, therefore, one particularly crude articulation of ethnocentrism.[3] Questions of race involve matters of identity and difference, the determination of humanity and (implicitly if not explicitly) what constitutes civilization and matters of representation, specifically corporeal representation allied to discourses on race. Non-white peoples are all too frequently reduced in cultural representations, in texts and films, to stereotypes where race signifies an overdetermined generation of meaning bringing together corporeality and behaviour or custom, as though there were some logical connection between these.

At its most neutral, according to Dyer, race 'is a means of categorizing different types of human body which reproduce themselves. It seeks to systematize differences and to relate them to differences of character and worth.' However, as Dyer goes on to argue, there are always implicit, if not explicit, connections made in the language of race between race, gender and heteronormativity, particularly in terms of reproduction. If race is about bodies,

it is also always about the reproduction of those bodies through heterosexuality. This is implicit in notions of genealogy (the chain of sexual reproduction leading back to the origins of race), degeneration (the bad chain of such reproduction) and genetics (the way we now understand the passing on of characteristics through reproduction), something the 'gene' root of all these terms indicates . . . If races are conceptualized as pure . . . then miscegenation threatens that purity . . .

Race and gender are ineluctably intertwined, through the primacy of heterosexuality in reproducing the former and defining the latter. It is a productively unstable alliance. The idea of race . . . locates historical, social and cultural differences in the body. In principle, this means all bodies, but in practice whites have accorded themselves a special relation to race and thus to their own and other bodies. They have more of that unquantifiable something, spirit, that puts them above race. This is a badge of superiority, yet it also creates an instability for whites at the hidden heart of the notion of race, namely heterosexual reproduction and its attendant sex roles. Whites must reproduce themselves, yet they must also control and transcend their bodies.

Richard Dyer (1997: 25, 30)

Questions for further consideration

1. Why are ideas of 'nature', 'human nature' and 'biology' so necessary to negative determinations of race? Why does racist discourse rely for its force on forms of representation, on physicality, and corporeality?
2. Why are the notions of race and national identity so frequently connected?
3. Consider the position put forward by Richard Dyer that 'whiteness' is 'invisible', a 'non-raced' position. Why is such a 'non-position' so powerful, and how does it maintain its power?

Explanatory and bibliographical notes

1. Charlotte Brontë (*b.*1816–*d.*1854): *Jane Eyre*, ed. Q. D. Leavis (London: Penguin, 1988).
2. Enoch Powell (*b.*1912–*d.*1998).
3. *Ethnocentrism*: the assumption that one's race or ethnic group is superior to others.

Further reading

Appiah, Kwame Anthony (1992), *In My Father's House: Africa in the Philosophy of Culture* (New York: Oxford University Press).
Azim, Firdous (1993), *The Colonial Rise of the Novel* (London: Routledge).
Dyer, Richard (1997), *White* (London: Routledge).
Layton-Henry, Zig, and Paul Rich (eds) (1986), *Race, Government and Politics in Britain* (Basingstoke: Macmillan).
Pellegrini, Ann (1997), *Performative Anxieties: Staging Psychoanalysis, Staging Race* (London: Routledge).
Smith, Anna Marie (1994), *New Right Discourse on Race and Sexuality: Britain, 1968–1990* (Cambridge: Cambridge University Press).
Olson, Gary A., and Lynn Worsham (eds) (1999), *Race, Rhetoric and the Postcolonial* (Albany, NY: State University of New York Press).

READER/READING

A *reader* may be defined provisionally as a person who evaluates intellectually a given manuscript or image in an effort to comprehend or interpret its contents or form for a range of reasons, whether these reasons are defined as 'entertainment', 'education', 'enlightenment', 'pleasure', or a combination of these and other purposes. What we call *reading* is an active participation with a piece of writing or an image for the purpose of producing meaning, or, more generally, to 'translate' the book or image (or, indeed, the world) from its condition as a perceived ensemble of potential signs to a text on which the process of interpretation is brought to bear.

It is important, if seemingly obvious, to note that reading takes time; the analysis of signs does not occur immediately, even if the object of reading is a poster or advertisement in a magazine. Reading is thus engaged in, and as, a temporal experience, an experience which is not limited to the time of holding the book open, standing in front of an image, or watching a film (whether in the cinema, on a video, or DVD). Moreover, reading is never simple or innocent, even when one reads 'for pleasure', as the phrase has it, because the reader, any reader, is always positioned through culture, history, education, ideology, and so on.

Thus the possibility of reading is constituted in various ways prior to any individual act of reading. We can never read simply as we choose. Indeed, it might be said with some justification that we never choose how we read. At the same time, every text has a singularity for which the act of reading should be responsible, and to which the act of reading should respond. One should therefore avoid producing a reading which is either, on the one hand, simply a passive consumption or, on the other, the proactive imposition of a particular meaning which suppresses or excludes other elements. Such a reading might be a 'politicized' reading which, in its address to matters of class representation, for example, ignores issues of gender or race. Or, there might be the formal reading which, in discussing the aesthetic aspects of the writing, ignores or downplays the roles of history or ideology, of the function of epistemological assumptions behind the value judgements which the text appears to advance or which we, as readers, bring to the text. How one reads is therefore irreducible to a prescription or formula because of singularity and the responsibility to that singularity which reading entails. In the light of the question of singularity, some critics have suggested that to impose a 'reading' along certain lines (the political, the purely formal) is to avoid the complex negotiation that reading involves; it is the imposition of a reading within limits and towards a limit or horizon (this being the 'political', 'philosophical' or 'historical' meaning which is sought), and is not, therefore, a reading at all, but the avoidance of reading.

At the same time, however, the responsibility of reading is such that one cannot simply read as one likes, as has been stated already; one has to be attentive to the ways in which the text is articulated, the ways in which it appears to articulate itself and the ways in which it appears to be silent on matters. There is, furthermore, in the act of reading, the experience of the undecidable. For these reasons, properly speaking the act of reading cannot come to an end. Reading always remains to come, not as a future moment or horizon in itself, at which textual explication will arrive eventually, so, therefore, that we can expect to have done with reading. Instead, reading-to-come remains – and names – the responsibility of the good reader's encounter with singularity, undecidability and otherness.

But what, exactly, might we imagine reading to be? What does it mean to be a reader and what might be the relation – supposing there to be any – between reading and writing?

> Reading is escaping in broad daylight, it's the rejection of the other; most of the time it's a solitary act, exactly like writing. We don't always think of this because we no longer read; we used to read when we were children and knew how violent reading can be. . . . Writing and reading are not separate, reading is a part of writing. A real reader is a writer, A real reader is already on the way to writing. . . . [Reading is] also a clandestine, furtive act. We don't acknowledge it. . . . Reading is not as insignificant as we claim. First we must steal the key to the library. Reading is a provocation, a rebellion: we open the book's door, pretending it is a simple paperback cover, and in broad daylight escape! We are no longer there: this is what real reading is. If we haven't left the room, if we haven't gone over the wall, we're not reading. If we're only making believe we're there, if we're pretending before the eyes of the family, then we're reading. We are eating. Reading is eating on the sly.
>
> Reading is eating the forbidden fruit, making forbidden love, changing eras, changing families, changing destinies, and changing day for night. Reading is doing everything exactly as we want and 'on the sly'.
> Hélène Cixous (1993: 19–22)

Reading brings about the chance – and it is no more than the merest chance – that an event might take place – in the otherwise unanticipatable affirmation of the other which no consciousness, whether a reading or a writing consciousness (assuming the two to be separable) can control.

> It is again a question of 'the other' . . . this term names the event in poetry, meaning and inscription which escapes human control, grounding or anticipation . . . The *other* is engaged in writing in terms of an ineluctable secondarity in written meaning – for even in being inscribed the written presents itself as simultaneously *read* through the resonance of significations unanticipated in the act of inscription . . . The other names the space 'of deferred reciprocity between reading and writing'.
> Timothy Clark (1992: 110–11)

Reading's chance therefore is in that, repeating the text, an other text, the other of the text and the text of the other, might arrive.

What takes place in deconstruction is double reading – that is, a form of double reading that obeys the double injunction for both repetition and the alterity that arises within that repetition. Deconstruction opens a reading by locating a moment of alterity within a text ... What takes place in deconstruction is a highly determinate form of double reading which pursues alterities within texts ...

Simon Critchley (1999: 28)

Such double reading takes place, if it takes place at all, not as a result of the 'external' contexts of a text – history, culture, the author's intention or psychology – but as a result of

> the rhetorical or tropological dimension of language, a dimension which is perhaps more explicitly in the foreground in literature (broadly conceived) than in other verbal manifestations or – to be somewhat less vague – which can be revealed in any verbal event when it is read textually. Since grammar as well as figuration is an integral part of reading, it follows that reading will be a negative process in which the grammatical cognition is undone, at all times, by its rhetorical displacement.

Paul de Man (1986: 17)

The rhetorical or tropological dimension is perhaps that which is feared because it can never be mastered by reading and because it is that which has the greatest potential to disrupt reading from the outset.

> If reading has historically been a tool of revolutions and of liberation, is it not rather because, constitutively, reading is a rather risky business whose outcome and full consequences can never be known in advance? Does not reading involve one risk that, precisely, cannot be resisted: that of finding in the text something one does not expect? The danger with becoming a 'resisting reader' is that we end up, in effect, *resisting reading*. But resisting reading for the sake of holding on to our ideologies and preconceptions (be they chauvinist or feminist) is what we tend to do in any case.

Shoshana Felman (1993: 5–6)

There is thus something strangely untimely in every act of reading, something which disjoints or undoes the comforts of taking as read a progressive linearity to the temporal.

> For even before the reading reproduces the sense of absolute knowing ... through its supplementary interpretive addition to the text, the reading in question has already entered the circle of the text, already become an

immanent moment of its movement. . . . And even before the reading becomes what it already is . . . this reading is still not yet what it already is, still halts before the threshold of its origin and falls short of its destination, arrives too early – and too late – for itself and its consciousness, and thereby opens out its hermeneutic–dialectical circle into a parabola. Although the reading does not approach its text in an external fashion, it is not yet the immanent movement of self-reproduction which it already is. The reading . . . must commence from the not yet in the unity of the not yet and the already present: at a remove from that unity of arché[1] and telos[2] which would constitute the finally successful reading itself as identical with the system of absolute self-consciousness. For the dialectical logos[3] the reading remains an endless foreword, one which transforms the logos into an anticipation of itself and without which that logos could not exist. . . . The reading introduces its 'self' into the circle of synthesis as a difference that cannot be synthesized.

This difference, which has both logical and phenomenological, structural and temporal determinants, is the condition for the reproduction of the text in its reading, and through those traits of delay, of remainder, of anticipation which it introduces into every act of interpretation, this difference presents the dialectical operation of reading with an insuperable obstacle at the very entrance to the dialectical circle: an incorrigible deviation from meaning's path and process of meaning towards itself . . .

Werner Hamacher (1998: 3–5)

The nature of reading is, then, to frustrate and incite desire, endlessly.

Why must we leave off reading only to return to it? What is its difficulty such that it does not simply frustrate us but instead incites us, regardless of our desire for simplicity, for the simplicity we associate with our selves, necessarily to return to what is impossible for us? What would reading be if we could do it, if we could finally succeed, stop this reading? This *sortie*,[4] and its retraction, is no accident but rather the very condition of reading, in its necessity and impossibility . . .

There is no road for reading, no path or method: simply the effort and the fatigue of the difficult chance. As chance, reading and its inability defy calculation in advance, refuse prediction.

Thomas Keenan (1997: 92, 102)

All of which is to say that

reading . . . is what happens when we cannot apply the rules. This means that reading is an experience of responsibility, but that responsibility is not a moment of security or of cognitive certainty. Quite the contrary:

the only responsibility worthy of the name comes with the removal of grounds, the withdrawal of the rules or the knowledge on which we might rely to make our decisions for us.

Thomas Keenan (1997: 1)

Responsibility without safeguards, without limits or conditions is perhaps terrifying to some. But it also means that

one must be able to stay nimble as one reflects, and stay on the 'surface' whilst reading between the lines. A task which requires one to elevate 'reading to the level of an art': there is no reading without interpretation, without commentary – in other words without a new writing which slightly displaces the meaning of the first, pushes the perspective of the aphorism in new directions and makes it come into its own. Every reading gives birth to a different text, to the creation of a new form: that is indeed an artistic effect. At the same time the text, the expression of a system of forces, acts on the reader and 'cultivates' him, in other words again it makes him come into his own. One must first of all be 'deeply wounded' and then 'secretly delighted' in order to be able to boast of having understood an aphorism: we can discover in a text only what we ourselves are but were unaware of. So reading transforms the reader and the text at the same time . . . A new reading/writing destroys the traditional categories of the book as a closed totality containing a definitive meaning, the author's; in such a way that it deconstructs the idea of the author as master of the meaning of the work . . . The aphorism, by its discontinuous character, disseminates meaning and appeals to the pluralism of interpretations and their renewal: only movement is immortal.

Sarah Kofman (1993: 116)

The endlessness of reading, the ineluctable vigilance and responsibility without programme or protocol, engages one in an ethics of reading, which has been defined in the following manner.

By 'the ethics of reading' . . . I mean that aspect of the act of reading in which there is a response to the text that is both necessitated, in the sense that it is a response to an irresistible demand, and free, in the sense that I must take responsibility for my responsibility and for the further effects . . . of my acts of reading.

J. Hillis Miller (1987: 43)

The full weight of the implications of reading is all the more daunting when one realizes that

the same goes for all commentary, on any author, on any text whatsoever. In a writer's text, and in a commentator's text (which every text in
turn is, more or less), what counts, what thinks (at the very limit of
thought, if necessary), is what does not completely lend itself to univo-
cality or, for that matter, to plurivocality, but strains against the burden
of meaning and throws it off balance . . .

This has nothing to do with nonsense or with the absurd . . . It is –
paradoxically – a manner of weighing, in the very sentence, in the very
words and syntax . . . a manner of weighing on meaning itself, on given
and recognizable meaning . . . And reading in turn must remain weighty,
hampered, and, without ceasing to decode, must stay just this side of
decoding. Such a reading remains caught in the odd materiality of
language. It attunes itself to the singular communication carried on not
just by meaning but by language itself, or, rather, to a communication
that is only the communication of language itself, without abstracting
any meaning, in a fragile, repeated suspension of meaning. True reading
advances unknowing, it is always an unjustifiable cut in the supposed
continuum of meaning that opens a book. It must lose its way in this
breach.

This reading – which is first of all *reading* itself, all reading, inevitably
given over to the sudden, flashing, slipping movement of a writing that
precedes it and that it will rejoin only by reinscribing it elsewhere and
otherwise, by ex–scribing it outside itself – this reading does not yet
comment. This is a *beginning* reading, an *incipit*[5] that is always begun
again.

                              Jean-Luc Nancy (1993a: 336–7)

That reading is always already a double reading, that it is also a writing, an
iterable displacement and doubling which disjoints time, we have already
seen. What we have yet to make explicit however, is that all such disrup-
tions *of* and *in* reading mean that every text is also unreadable, as well as
remaining to be read.

The unreadable is fixed only to the extent that it is apprehended as that
which remains to be read, even if that reading is theorised (as it is in
Derrida's work) as belonging as much to an immemorial past as to the
future. An example of this would be the piece of graffiti quoted by
Derrida in 'Border Lines': ' "do not read me" '.[6] This injunction must and
cannot be read . . . This piece of graffiti concisely illustrates the double-
bind of deconstruction, in other words the necessity and impossibility of
deconstructive reading. It demands and dissolves the strange time, which
is never proper, never *on* time, of reading. The reading of this injunction
not to read can never catch up with itself, can never coincide with itself,

not least because it can never have adequate authority to authorise its own reading . . . and because its very readability cannot be derived: what is readable is indissociable from what is iterable. The readable has no origin, it is immemorial, it precedes us and our reading. By the same token the readable would be necessarily still to come. It is still to come not as an act or event that might one day become present, but rather in the structural sense of a promise, a promise which is – in its affirmation and nonfulfilment – a double-bind.

Nicholas Royle (1995: 161–2)

And it is precisely this double bind in which reading entwines us, even as we gain an understanding of the fact that there is no present or presence to the time of reading, only the contrapuntal and rhythmic plays of a past which has never been present and a future which will never arrive.

Since the eventhood of an event of 'writing' is riven by iterability, there is never just one 'proper reading' of a 'text'; another reading is *always possible*. 'Writing' is such that it always offers itself to new readings, new responses – and, hence, new *responsibilities*. This rhythm of reading, and the ineluctable responsibility which it implies, is inescapable. It is a rhythm that does not end. Or barely, for example, ~~now~~.

Simon Glendinning (1998: 152)

Questions for further consideration

1. Examine, and question, the assumptions, the 'prejudgements or presuppositions' you bring to the act of reading. When you read for the purpose of study, how is this different from 'reading for pleasure'?
2. Why does reading resist the application of rules?
3. In the words of Rainer Nägele, what does it mean to read between texts? Why is any act of reading always this?

Explanatory and bibliographical notes

1. *Arché*: beginning.
2. *Telos*: end, ultimate object or aim.
3. *Logos*: word, speech, discourse, reason; more obscurely, God, Christ, or the Word of God.
4. *Sortie*: commonly 'exit', or occasionally sortie, as the word has passed into English, in the sense, usually military, of exploration for the purpose of gathering information.
5. *Incipit*: to begin, to commence.
6. Derrida (1987: 145).

Further reading

Felman, Shoshana (1993), *What Does a Woman Want? Reading and Sexual Difference* (Baltimore, MD: Johns Hopkins University Press).

Hamacher, Werner (1998), *Pleroma: Reading in Hegel* (1978), trans. Nicholas Walker and Simon Jarvis (Stanford, CA: Stanford University Press).

Miller, J. Hillis (1987), *The Ethics of Reading: Kant, de Man, Eliot, Trollope, James, and Benjamin* (New York: Columbia University Press).

Waters, Lindsay, and Wlad Godzich (eds) (1989), *Reading de Man Reading* (Minneapolis, MN: University of Minnesota Press).

Wolfreys, Julian (2000), *Readings: Acts of Close Reading in Literary Theory* (Edinburgh: Edinburgh University Press).

SEXUALITY/SEXUAL DIFFERENCE

A mobile notion, not easily contained through definition, *sexuality* presents considerable semantic, not to say political and philosophical difficulties with regard to any positive statements. In any enforced, socially normative sense (at least until very recently) sexuality has, for many, implied heterosexuality, any other expression of sexual identity having been deemed aberrant, deviant, or transgressive. Of course, one of the problems encountered in any definition of sexuality is the most basic: that of whether our sexuality is essential, 'the way we are', as though our sexual identity were imprinted on us at birth, or otherwise culturally constructed, whether due to influences in the home during our early formative years, or else through broader social interaction outside the family. To begin, therefore, it is necessary that we acknowledge the existence of at least four distinct definitions of sexuality:

> there are at least four different senses of this term [i.e., sexuality] which may be relevant to help specify the concerns . . . First, sexuality can be understood as a drive, an impulse or form of propulsion, directing a subject toward an object. Psychoanalysis is uncontestably the great science of sexuality as drive. Second, sexuality can also be understood in terms of an act, a series of practices and behaviours involving bodies, organs, and pleasures, usually but not always involving orgasm. Third, sexuality can also be understood in terms of an identity. The sex of bodies, now commonly described by the term *gender*, designates at least two different forms, usually understood by means of the binary oppositions of male and female. And fourth, sexuality commonly refers to a set of orientations, positions and desires, which implies that there are particular ways in

which the desires, differences, and bodies of subjects can seek their pleasure.

Elizabeth Grosz (1994: viii)

It would be a useful task to pause at these four determinations, looking at
the ways in which each may be said to overlap in certain ways with the
others. While the first example is purely internal, peculiar to, and a component of, the individual psyche, it may be suggested that it is the drive which
leads to particular acts, practices and behaviours, by the acknowledgement
of which we arrive at the second definition. We have thus travelled from the
subject's 'internal' identity, or one aspect of that, to an 'external', and
social, manifestation of that subjectivity; it is in this traversal – an artificial
figure because it posits cause and effect, priority and secondarity, which
organization cannot be shown conclusively – that one arrives at the third
definition, where sexuality is an aspect of identity, and where it comes to be
conflated with the signs of gender, and where constructedness becomes
occluded through the corporeal reading of gender. However, the signs of
gender, if I can put it like that, are not restricted to bodily form, and are
those traces which we read from others in relation to our own sexuality and
to the questions of orientation and desire – by which figure we find
ourselves back at the notion of the drive acknowledged in the first definition – implied in the sexuality we comprehend as our own.

Bearing in mind the circuitous route we have just taken, let us begin
again, therefore, by erasing any assumptions we may have, and by supposing that there is no essence to sexuality:

> let's say sexuality . . . but let us not assume that by doing so we can get
> back to some sort of basic experience, untrammeled by, well, love, well,
> culture. What if, after all, there is no stripped-down, basic sexuality, no
> simple animal or clinical experience outside our culturally induced
> expectations, hopes, anxieties, values? What if there is no sexuality, in
> other words, independent of the meanings it carries, and these meanings
> are culturally reproduced and learned?
>
> Catherine Belsey (1994: 33)

If sexuality is a construct, then there is no 'natural' or 'normal' position,
only those that are socially dominant or marginalized. From a psychoanalytic perspective,

> [b]ecause there is no continuity of psychic life, so there is no stability of
> sexual identity, no position for women (or for men) which is ever simply
> achieved.
>
> Jacqueline Rose (1986: 90)

Assuming this to be the case,

> [a]s a concept, sexuality is incapable of ready containment: it refuses to stay within its predesignated regions, for it seeps across boundaries into areas that are not apparently its own. As drive, it infests all sorts of other areas in the structures of desire. It renders even the desire not to desire, or the desire for celibacy, as sexual; it leaks into apparently nondrive-related activities through . . . sublimation, making an activity a mode of its own seeking of satisfaction. As a set of activities and practices, it refuses to accept the containment of the bedroom or to restrict itself to only those activities which prepare for orgasmic pleasure. It is excessive, redundant, and superfluous in its languid and fervent overachieving. It always seeks more than it needs, performs excessive actions, and can draw any object, any fantasy, any number of subjects and combinations of their organs, into its circuits of pleasure. As a determinate type of body, as sexually specific, it infects all the activities of the sexes, underlying our understandings of the world well beyond the domain of sexual relations or the concrete relations constituting sexual difference. Our conceptions of reality, knowledge, truth, politics, ethics, and aesthetics are all effects of sexually specific – and thus far in our history, usually male – bodies, and are all thus implicated in the power structures which feminists have described as patriarchal, the structures which govern relations between the sexes.
>
> Elizabeth Grosz (1994: viii–ix)

Sexual positions (if you'll pardon the phrase) are therefore unstable, while being at the same time locations of power and power relations:

> sexuality belongs in [an] area of instability played out in the register of demand and desire, each sex coming to stand, mythically and exclusively, for that which could satisfy and complete the other. It is when the categories 'male' and 'female' are seen to represent an absolute and complementary division that they fall prey to a mystification in which the difficulty of sexuality instantly disappears . . . There is a tendency, when arguing for the pre-given nature of sexual difference, for the specificity of male and female drives,[1] to lose sight of the more radical aspects of Freud's work on sexuality – his insistence on the disjunction between the sexual object and the sexual aim, his difficult challenge to the concept of perversion, and his demand that heterosexual object-choice be explained and not assumed.
>
> Jacqueline Rose (1986: 56)

Because of the fundamental instability of any sexual identity, the assertion of that identity has to be enacted repeatedly.

To the extent that the 'I' is secured by its sexed position, this 'I' and its 'position' can be secured only be being *repeatedly* assumed, whereby 'assumption' is not a singular act or event, but, rather, an iterable practice . . . This suggests that 'sexed positions' are not localities but, rather, citational practices instituted within a juridical domain – a domain of constitutive constraints. The embodying of sex would be a kind of citing the law, but neither sex nor law can be said to preexist their various embodyings or citings.

Judith Butler (1993: 108)

Because we have been proceeding in more or less tacit agreement with the idea that sexuality is constructed, other questions arise.

Is sexuality so highly constrained from the start that it ought to be conceived as fixed? If sexuality is so constrained from the start, does it not constitute a kind of essentialism at the level of identity? At stake is a way to describe this deeper and perhaps irrecoverable sense of *constitutedness and constraint* in the face of which the notions of 'choice' and 'free play' appear not only foreign, but unthinkable and sometimes even cruel. The constructed character of sexuality has been invoked to counter the claim that sexuality has a natural and normative shape and movement, that is, one which approximates the normative phantasm of a compulsory heterosexuality. The efforts to denaturalize sexuality and gender have taken as their main enemy those normative frameworks of compulsory heterosexuality that operate through the naturalization and reification of heterosexist norms.

Judith Butler (1993: 93)

The drive towards a de-essentialization of sexuality has emerged in large part from a dialogue between feminism and psychoanalysis.

Feminist theory which grounds itself in anti-essentialism frequently turns to psychoanalysis for its description of sexuality because psychoanalysis assumes a necessary gap between the body and the psyche, so that sexuality is not reducible to the physical. Sexuality is constructed within social and symbolic relations; it is most *un*natural and achieved only after an arduous struggle. One is not born with a sexual identity . . .

Mary Ann Doane (1991: 168)

However, even admitting that sexuality is constructed we still demonstrate discursive tendencies to slip into stable positions all too often maintained and serving to maintain what the following citation terms a 'heterosexual patriarchal power system'.

Heterosexuality depends upon the assumption that sex differences are binary opposites and the simultaneous equation of this binary sex difference with gender. The naturalizing function of this equation contributes to the expressive model of the individual in that the opposition of the sexes is taken to be substantive, preceding social and historical bodies as an essence which the core of the self manifests. In disguising itself as a law of nature, this 'fiction' regulates the sexual field it purports to describe . . . The fiction of heterosexual coherence is one of the most firmly entrenched and invisible anchors for the ideology of individualism . . . The heterosexual and patriarchal 'family cell' . . . provides sexuality with permanent support. It is the site where systems of sexuality, gender, and alliance are articulated . . . The four specific mechanisms of knowledge and power centering on sex which Foucault targets – the hysteriazation of women's bodies, the pedagogization of children's sex, the socialization of the couple as a reproductive unit, and the psychiatrization of 'perverse' pleasure – all reinforce a naturalized equation of sexuality and reproduction which assumes a heterosexual patriarchal gender system.

Rosemary Hennessy (1993: 88)

In any discussion of sexuality, Foucault argues, we must not comprehend sexuality as a psychic drive.

Sexuality must not be described as a stubborn drive, by nature alien and of necessity disobedient to a power which exhausts itself trying to subdue it and often fails to control it entirely. It appears rather as an especially dense transfer point for relations of power: between men and women, young people and old people, parents and offspring, teachers and students, priests and laity, an administration and a population. Sexuality is not the most intractable element in power relations, but rather one of those endowed with the greatest instrumentality: useful for the greatest number of maneuvers and capable of serving as a point of support, as a linchpin, for the most varied strategies.

Michel Foucault (1990: 103)

At the same time, we should neither equate sexuality with sex, nor subordinate the former to the latter:

we must not refer a history of sexuality to the agency of sex; but rather show how 'sex' is historically subordinate to sexuality. We must not place sex on the side of reality, and sexuality on that of confused ideas and illusions. Sexuality is a very real historical formation; it is what gives rise to the notion of sex, as a speculative element necessary to its operation.

Michel Foucault (1990: 157)

Making this necessary distinction, uncoupling sexuality from sex, it is arguable that the former functions socially and symbolically in endlessly complex and contradictory ways:

> to the extent that, as Freud argued and Foucault assumed, the distinctively sexual nature of human sexuality has to do precisely with its excess over or potential difference from the bare choreographies of procreation, 'sexuality' might be the very opposite of what we originally referred to as (chromosomal-based) sex: it could occupy, instead, even more than 'gender' the polar position of the relational, the social/symbolic, the constructed, the variable, the representational.
>
> Eve Kosofsky Sedgwick (1999: 251–2)

Questions for further consideration

1. In what exemplary ways might notions of sexuality be deployed strategically, in support of, or in resistance to, dominant social structures or discourses?
2. Does psychoanalysis obscure, occlude, or downplay particular aspects of sexuality's constructedness? Is there a sense in which psychoanalytic discourse on sexuality might be comprehended as being implicitly sexist in its assertions?
3. In what ways does sexuality call into question the opposition between nature and culture?

Explanatory and bibliographic note

1. Explaining how the drive is irreducible to any biological function or definition, thereby conflating and confusing psychoanalytic conceptualizations of sexuality with biological determination, Rose defines the concept of the drive in the following manner: '[t]he drive is not [an] instinct precisely because it cannot be reduced to the order of need (Freud defined it as an internal stimulus only to distinguish it from hunger and thirst). The drive is divisible into pressure, source, object and aim: and it challenges any straightforward concept of satisfaction – the drive can be sublimated and Freud described its object as "indifferent". What matters, therefore, is not what the drive *achieves*, but its process . . . the drive is something in the nature of an appeal, or searching out, which always goes beyond the actual relationships on which it turns . . . In Lacan's description of the transformation of the drive . . . the emphasis is always on the loss of the object around which it revolves, and hence on the drive itself as a representation' (Rose, 1986: 57).

Further reading

Butler, Judith (1993), *Bodies that Matter: On the Discursive Limits of 'Sex'* (London: Routledge).

Dollimore, Jonathan (1991), *Sexual Dissidence: Augustine to Wilde, Freud to Foucault* (Oxford: Oxford University Press).

Felman, Shoshana (1993), *What Does a Woman Want? Reading and Sexual Difference* (Baltimore, MD: Johns Hopkins University Press).

Foucault, Michel (1990), *The History of Sexuality. Volume I: An Introduction.* (1976), trans. Robert Hurley (London: Penguin).

Freud, Sigmund (1991), *On Sexuality: Three Essays on the Theory of Sexuality and Other Works*, Penguin Freud Library, Volume 7, trans. James Strachey, ed. Angela Richards (Harmondsworth: Penguin).

Irigaray, Luce (1993), *An Ethics of Sexual Difference* (1984), trans. Carolyn Burke and Gillian C. Gill (Ithaca, NY: Cornell University Press).

Lacan, Jacques (1998), *The Seminar: On Feminine Sexuality. The Limits of Love and Knowledge, Book XX: Encore 1972–73*, ed. Jacques-Alain Miller, trans. Bruce Fink (New York: W. W. Norton).

Rose, Jacqueline (1986), *Sexuality in the Field of Vision* (London: Verso).

Schick, Irvin Cemil (1999), *The Erotic Margin: Sexuality and Spatiality in Alteritist Discourse* (London: Verso).

Smith, Anna Marie (1994), *New Right Discourse on Race and Sexuality: Britain, 1968–1990* (Cambridge: Cambridge University Press).

SIMULACRUM/SIMULATION

Although the idea of the *simulacrum* originates in Plato at least, the notion and the related idea of simulation are often associated in current theoretical discourse with Jean Baudrillard's assertions concerning what he calls the reality effect, which relates to the ways in which reality is often established and becomes replaced for some individuals and cultures through hyperreal media such as photography or film; hence, 'simulacrum' refers to the image, representation, or reproduction in which the very idea of the real is no longer the concrete signified of which the simulacrum is the signifier. It only gestures to other signifiers and the work of a groundless signification in general. Simulation, the process whereby simulacra assume their function, similarly belongs to what Baudrillard terms the 'second order': there is no anterior 'real', the idea of the 'real' only comes into being through the cultural dissemination of images (such as those of advertising) or simulacra. Thus,

> [t]he distinctions between object and representation, thing and idea are no longer valid . . . simulacra . . . have no referent or ground in any 'reality' except their own. A simulation is different from a fiction or lie in that it not only presents an absence as a presence, the imaginary as the real, it also undermines any contrast to the real, absorbing the real within

itself. Instead of a 'real' economy of commodities that is somehow bypassed by an 'unreal' myriad of advertising images . . . [there is] only a hyperreality, a world of self-referential signs.

Mark Poster (1988: 5–6)

Our advent into a world of simulacra has been described in the following way by Baudrillard:

all of reality [is] absorbed by the hyperreality of the code and of simulation. It is now a principle of simulation, and not of reality, that regulates social life. The finalities have disappeared; we are now engendered by models.

Jean Baudrillard (1988: 120)

Furthermore,

[g]one are the referentials of production, signification, affect, substance, history, and the whole equation of 'real' contents that gave the sign weight by anchoring it with a kind of burden of utility . . . All this is surpassed by . . . total relativity, generalized commutative, combinatory simulation . . . simulation in the sense that from now on signs will exchange among themselves exclusively, without interacting with the real . . .

Jean Baudrillard (1988: 125)

Symbols, codes, models, all generate our world, neither offering us nor leaving us with any access to the real.

Simulation is no longer that of a territory, a referential being or a substance. It is the generation by models of a real without origin or reality: a hyperreal. The territory no longer precedes the map, nor survives it. Henceforth, it is the map that precedes the territory – *procession of simulacra* – it is the map that engenders the territory . . .

Jean Baudrillard (1988: 166)

Baudrillard maps out the irreversible process schematically.

Whereas representation tries to absorb simulation by interpreting it as false representation, simulation envelops the whole edifice of representation as itself a simulacrum.

These would be the successive phases of the image:

1 It is the reflection of a basic reality.
2 It masks and perverts a basic reality.

3   It masks the *absence* of a basic reality.
4   It bears no relation to any reality whatever: it is its own pure simu-
    lacrum.

. . .

The transition from signs which dissimulate something to signs
which dissimulate that there is nothing, marks the decisive turning
point.

Jean Baudrillard (1988: 170)

The result of this is that

[t]he era of simulation is thus everywhere initiated by the interchange-
ability of previously contradictory or dialectically opposed terms.
Everywhere the same 'genesis of simulacra' . . . All the great humanist
criteria of value, all the values of a civilization of moral, aesthetic, and
practical judgement, vanish in our system of images and signs.
Everything becomes undecidable. This is the characteristic effect of the
domination of the code . . .

Jean Baudrillard (1988: 128)

We are thus confronted with a paradox:

the referential orbit was permanently broken and we entered the age of
simulation, where it is as impossible to discover the real, as it is impossible to stage an illusion, because the real no longer exists . . . It is impossible to do more than simulate; and yet to simulate is precisely . . . to
substitute signs of the real for the real that is no longer there – so as to
leave the reality principle intact.

Dawne McCance (1996: 7)

Such an understanding provides the basis for a provisional definition of
postmodernism as an age of simulation and simulacra.

From one perspective, postmodernism has seemed the apotheosis of the
visual, the triumph of the simulacrum over what it purports to represent,
a veritable surrender to the phantasmagoric spectacle, rather than its
subversion. Images, it is claimed, are now set completely adrift from their
referents, whose putative reality has ceased to provide a standard of
truth or illusion.

Martin Jay (1994: 543–4)

Reference to the real is supplanted by constant processes of signification
which double and reiterate one another.

what constitutes the simulacrum as a form – its undecidable relation to its origins and to the various times and spaces it traverses through its repetitions – can neither be presented nor represented by the image as such, but only alluded to by its absences or excesses. Its effect is inseparable from a series that cannot be definitively rendered manifest in an individual image, nor exhausted by any preexisting code. It can only be recreated by the workings of memory and imagination, which retrospectively and prospectively weave between its various avatars relations of identity or difference, priority or secondariness, regularity or variation, being or becoming. The simulacrum . . . is at once removed from and infinitely proximate to its point of origin; as such, it is essentially displaced, elsewhere than itself. But, as the ambiguous 'return' of a model that it at once renders visible and withholds, it is also fundamentally untimely: nonsynchronous with and becoming other than itself.

The encounter with the simulacrum is thus more akin to memory and fantasy than it is to perception or communication. Through the simulacrum, one recalls, awaits, or imagines what is virtual or actualized in the very object that one sees. The simulacrum . . . is closer to the typologies of biblical exegesis, with their infinitely displaced figures and their layered and embedded narratives, than to the diacritical space of the Saussurean sign, whose meaning may in principle be derived from its differential relations with other elements sychronic with and on the same level as itself . . . The appearance of the simulacrum is in this sense not so much a phenomenal as an interpretive event. In its movement of doubling, it neither offers its evidence to our gaze nor communicates its significance to our understanding: it veils itself in a series of enigmas – is it the same or different? before or after? present or absent? real or imaginary? – which force the viewer and interpreter to come to terms with what, beyond the field of visibility, is nonetheless repeated in the image.

Scott Durham (1998: 17–18)

In coming to terms with the nature of simulacra it is necessary to distinguish between the simulacrum and the copy, a distinction reliant on the difference between simple repetition and iterability:

we started with an initial determination of the Platonic motivation: to distinguish essence from appearance, intelligible from sensible, Idea from image, original from copy, and model from simulacrum. But we already see that these expressions are not equivalent . . . *Copies* are secondary possessors . . . guaranteed by resemblance; *simulacra* are like false pretenders, built upon a dissimilarity, implying an essential perversion or deviation.

. . .

If we say of the simulacrum that it is a copy of a copy, an infinitely degraded icon, an infinitely loose resemblance, we then miss the essential, that is, the difference in nature between simulacrum and copy . . . The copy is an image endowed with resemblance, the simulacrum is an image without resemblance . . . God made man in his image and resemblance. Through sin, however, man lost the resemblance while maintaining the image. We have become simulacra . . . Without doubt, it [the simulacrum] still produces an *effect* of resemblance; but this is an effect of the whole, completely external and produced by totally different means than those at work within the model. The simulacrum is built upon a disparity or upon a difference. It internalizes a dissimilarity. This is why we can no longer define it in relation to a model imposed on the copies, a model of the Same, from which the copies' resemblance derives. If the simulacrum has a model, it is another model, a model of the Other . . . from which there flows an internalized dissemblance.

Gilles Deleuze (1990: 256–8)

The disruption manifest in iterability involves a form of ironic referentiality, which itself effects a powerful distortion.

Here we could glance at Deleuze's use of the term 'simulacrum' (he invokes this as an alternative to the Platonic Idea and its reincarnations) . . . It's not itself exactly a copy, but it queries that whole concept of the model plus its copy. It doesn't resemble; instead . . . it ironises. Then it follows that what 'ironises' must be something within or about the very repetition [of the simulacrum] that it enacts. Somehow it ironises by doing it again, over and over . . . The raw stuff of verbal irony, this iterability, possesses the odd power to make strange that which it familiarly reflects . . . Say it, read it, echo it often enough and at short enough intervals . . . It begins to look somewhat comical or grotesque in its isolation . . .

Denise Riley (2000: 158)

The distortions here alluded to involve, in our final citation, acts amounting to a cannibalization of the past:

the producers of culture have nowhere to turn but to the past: the imitation of dead styles through all the masks and voices stored up in the imaginary museum of a now global culture.

This situation evidently determines . . . the random cannibalization of all the styles of the past . . . The omnipresence of pastiche . . . is at least with addiction – with a whole historically original consumers' appetite for a world transformed into sheer images of itself and for . . . spectacles

... It is for such objects that we may reserve Plato's conception of the 'simulacrum', the identical copy for which no original has ever existed. Appropriately enough, the culture of the simulacrum comes to life in a society where exchange value has been generalized to the point at which the very memory of use value is effaced . . .

The new spatial logic of the simulacrum can now be expected to have a momentous effect on what used to be historical time. The past is thereby itself modified: what was once, in the historical novel as Lukács[1] defines it, the organic genealogy of the bourgeois collective project . . . has meanwhile itself become a vast collection of images, a multitudinous photographic simulacrum . . . the past as 'referent' finds itself gradually bracketed, and then effaced altogether, leaving us with nothing but texts.

Fredric Jameson (1991: 17–18)

Questions for further consideration

1. How has the simulacrum become productive rather than simply representative?
2. Why is the efficacity of the sign which dissimulates that there is nothing, in Baudrillard's words, more powerful than that of the sign which indicates, however indirectly, 'a basic reality'?
3. Do national flags bear any relation to reality or do they assume the function of simulacra?

Explanatory and bibliographic note

1. György Lukács (b.1885–d.1971): *The Historical Novel*, trans. Hannah and Stanley Mitchell (London: Merlin Press, 1962); *The Theory of the Novel: A Historico-Philosophical Essay on the Forms of Great Epic Literature*, trans. Anna Bostock (Cambridge, MA: MIT Press, 1971); *Realism in Our Time: Literature and the Class Struggle*, Preface by George Steiner, trans. John and Necke Mander (New York: Harper & Row, 1971).

Further reading

Baudrillard, Jean (1988), *Selected Writings*, ed. and Introduction by Mark Poster (Stanford, CA: Stanford University Press).
Durham, Scott (1998), *Phantom Communities: The Simulacrum and the Limits of Postmodernism* (Stanford, CA: Stanford University Press).
Jameson, Fredric (1991), *Postmodernism or, the Cultural Logic of Late Capitalism* (London: Verso).

SUBJECT/IVITY

Regardless of its function within particular discourses, it has to be admitted that the idea of the *subject* is immediately complicated, irreconcilably doubled in any initial utterance, if one acknowledges that by this word one indicates either oneself or another (singly or collectively) or whether, by the use of the signifier, one indicates one's focus or interest, one's research topic, in phrases, for example, such as the subject of study, the subject of a book, essay, or film. That there is more than one subject, and more than one history of the subject, will become clear from even the most cursory glance at the quotations below. It is possible, for example, to speak of the psychoanalytic subject, the individual subject, the subject before the law (and by which laws one becomes subjected), or the national, supposedly collective subject. While none of these categories of subjectivity are absolutely different from one another it is the case none the less that neither are they completely commensurate or coterminous,[1] within a range of possible determinations. This may be complicated further if one considers how, within the parameters of a particular discourse – say, psychoanalysis – there is no absolute agreement on the question of the subject. Thus, we might say, while the subject is the subject or, perhaps more specifically, subjectivity, this subject is far from being exhausted, at least inasmuch as the very ideas of subjectivity and the subject are subject to constitution through the analysis of multiple, provisional languages which cross and intersect the locus that is named subjectivity.

As a provisional starting point, some useful definitions and distinctions would appear to be in order.

First the subject is subject to itself, an 'I', however difficult or even impossible it may be for others to understand this 'I' from its own viewpoint, within its own experience. Simultaneously, the subject is a subject to, and of, others; in fact, it is often an 'Other' to others, which also affects its sense of its own subjectivity. This construction of self in opposition to others . . . is as characteristic of groups, communities, classes, and nations, as it is of individuals, as in the self-conception of Chartists,[2] or 'the working classes', or schoolboys, or ladies, or, today 'Women', or 'the Third World'. Third, the subject is also a subject of knowledge, most familiarly perhaps of the discourse of social institutions that circumscribe its terms of being. Fourth, the subject is a body that is separate . . . from other human bodies; and the body, and therefore the subject, is closely dependent upon its physical environment. Finally, subjectivity in its common Cartesian sense . . . is opposed to objectivity: the particular or partial view (the view in and for itself) is opposed to some other (if only hypothetical) universal view . . . Furthermore, in writing or self-representation . . . the *I* is the self-present subject of the sentence as well as the subject 'subjected' to the symbolic order of the language in which one is writing – the subject is subject to language, or intersubjectivity (i.e., culture).

Regenia Gagnier (1991: 8–9)

Clearly, the question of defining the subject is primarily articulated as the instituting question of ontology: 'What is?'

The different philosophies of the subject (since it is clearly impossible to speak of *the* philosophy of the subject) always attribute to the subject the faculty of questioning *itself*, or asking *itself* questions, in such a way as to appropriate the alterity or obscurity that troubles it, either from 'without' or from 'within'. In a sense, the status of the subject is inseparable from the status of the question, as well as the origin of the question. The subject puts the question *to itself*. The claim of subjective consciousness consists in believing that, essentially, it can question itself and answer for itself.

Sylviane Agacinski (1991: 9)

The history of this question is as old as thought itself. While we receive largely modern senses of the subject via psychoanalysis, its history is far older, being still grounded in ontological inquiry but irreducible to the human subject:

the 'subject' comes down to us, not from Freud himself, but from Lacan and his 'return to Freud', begun in the early 1950s . . .

Now, this word, as Lacan was well aware, is taken over from philosophy. We might even designate it as the key term of Western metaphysics. For the subject is not, first, the individual, and it is even less the psychological ego to which we nowadays so often find it reduced. Above all, it designates the *hypokeimenon*,[3] the 'underlying' or 'subadjacent' goal of basic, founding philosophical inquiry, the quest for which is posed . . . [in] Aristotle's *Metaphysics* . . . And . . . it is only to the extent that it is the heir, in the form of the Cartesian *Cogito*, to this ultimate basic position . . . that the *ego* becomes a 'subject' in the word's properly modern sense . . . in the sense that being *qua* being is henceforth conceived of according to the initially Cartesian notion of the auto-foundation or auto-positioning of a subject presenting itself to itself as consciousness, in the representation of the will, in labor or in desire, in the State, or in the work of art.

Thus it is this modern . . . concept of subject that Lacan has imported into psychoanalysis . . .

Mikkel Borch-Jacobsen (1991: 62–3)

As has been made clear, a decisive and irreversible shift in the determination of the subject occurs with the articulation of the Cartesian cogito, which is at the heart of human self-representation:

> the core of the representation of Man as the 'foundation' of his own thoughts, actions and history, has, for three centuries at least, not been simply a valorization of human individuality and the human species as the bearer of the universal, it has been the representation of *Man as* (a, the) subject. The essence of humanity, of being (a) human, which should be present both in the universality of the species and in the singularity of the individual, both as a reality and as a norm or a possibility, is sub-jec*tivity*. Metaphysics . . . relies on a fundamental equation – we might read it as the equation of foundation as such:
> Man = (equals) Subject
Or
The Subject is (equal to) the Essence of Man
> Étienne Balibar (1994: 3–4)

The idea of the subject allows for a thinking of both individuality and universality simultaneously, itself inscribed within the mainstream of the European philosophical tradition.

> The concept of the subject . . . has for a long time fulfilled two functions, first, a function of universalization in a field where the universal is no longer represented by objective essentials, but by acts, noetic[4] or linguistic . . . Second, the subject fulfills a function of individuation in a field where the individual can no longer be a thing or a soul, but is instead a person, alive and sentient, speaking and spoken to (I – You). Are these two aspects of the subject, the universal 'I' and the individual 'me', necessarily linked? Even if they are, isn't there a conflict between them, and how might it be solved? All these questions actuate what has been called the philosophy of the subject, already with Hume,[5] and also with Kant, who confronts an 'I' as the determination of time and a 'me' as determinable in time.
> Gilles Deleuze (1991: 94)

That the subject is comprehended as individual, that a subject comprehends him- or herself as individual, autonomous and free, suggests paradoxically that subjectivity is a position to which we are accorded access through ideological determinations concerning the limits of the subject under the law.

> [T]he subject is an accomplishment regulated and produced in advance. And is as such fully political; indeed, perhaps *most* political at the point in which it is claimed to be prior to politics itself.
> Judith Butler (1992: 13)

Subjectivity or selfhood is therefore a location constituted by the state and through ideological state apparatuses involving processes of domination, coercion, identification and regulation.

> I think that if one wants to analyse the genealogy of the subject in Western civilization, one has to take into account not only the techniques of domination but also techniques of the self. Let's say: one has to take into account the interaction between those two types of techniques – techniques of domination and techniques of the self. One has to take into account the points where the technologies of domination of individuals over one another have recourse to processes by which the individual acts upon himself. And conversely, one has to take into account the points where the techniques of the self are integrated into structures of coercion or domination. The contact point, where the individuals are driven by others is tied to the way they conduct themselves, is what we can call, I think, government. Governing people, in the broad meaning of the word, governing people is not a way to force people to do what the governor wants; it is always a versatile equilibrium, with complementarity and conflicts between techniques which assure coercion and processes through which the self is constructed or modified by oneself.
>
> Michel Foucault (1999d: 162)

Analysing the subject subjected to the coercive processes of the law, government, the state, and so on, it can be seen that the subject is produced not only at the individual level, but also at the collective level as what might be termed a political production.

> The State as political entity names the incarnation of a national people into a subject. Accordingly, political meta-narratives offer to work out the destiny of the subject. Thus, for instance, 'we the people' become Americans, call ourselves Americans . . . In this sense, political forms are the means to an end, and that end is the realization of a fully autonomous political subject. The instance of individual citizens subject to the State determines the nature of what it means to be an American. So rather than doing away with the subject in favor of the citizen, 'the subject' plays such a dominant role that modern politics could accurately be renamed 'the politics of the subject' . . . the subject is necessarily always a political subject, produced by and within the *polis*.[6] The subject does not enter into the realm of the political; rather, the subject is produced by the political itself as a way to regulate and control individuals.
>
> Diane Elam (1994: 70)

The act of collective subjectification offers an example of interpellation, in this case through the specific example of the call of religious ideology.

> the interpellation of individuals as subjects presupposes the 'existence' of a Unique and central Other Subject, in whose Name the religious ideology interpellates all individuals as subjects. All this is clearly written in . . . the Scriptures. 'And it came to pass . . . that God the Lord . . . spoke to Moses . . . And the Lord cried to Moses, "Moses!" And Moses replied "It is (really) I! I am Moses thy servant, speak and I shall listen!" And the Lord spoke to Moses and said to him, "*I am that I am*" '.
>
> God thus defines himself as the Subject *par excellence*, he who is through himself and for himself ('I am that I am'), and he who interpellates his subject, the individual subjected to him by his very interpellation . . . And Moses, interpellated–called by his Name, having recognized that it 'really' was he who was called by God, recognizes that he is a subject, a subject *of* God, a subject subjected to God, *a* subject *through the* Subject *and* subjected *to the* Subject.
>
> Louis Althusser (1971: 178–9)

However, because we are constituted as subjects, finding ourselves always already situated, this is not to imply that we have no agency.

> Granting the subject's social embeddedness, an embeddedness most pronounced when one begins to write, one must also grant . . . the subject's mediation (i.e., transformation) of structures and systems, including systems as large as language or the State.
>
> Regenia Gagnier (1991: 10)

Yet, there still remains the subject's illusion of self-presence: every time I speak I not only assume that I occupy a unique, stable position that goes by the name of 'I', I also assume my 'self' as undifferentiated, as fully self-present to myself. This is only possible however, through what is referred to here as the 'dialectic of the subject', of the difference by which any given subject is marked from any other subject.

> The dialectic of the subject – the dialectic, the subject – has two sides, however. It contains its death, it has it only as a *moment*, but it does have that moment, the moment of gaping difference. The subject contains its difference from itself. The subject not only has this difference, it *is* this difference. If the subject did not differ from itself, it would not be what it is: a subject *relating* itself to itself. A = A signifies that A *in itself* is its difference from itself, and that it derives its equality, its being-equal to itself, only from this difference. (It must be understood

what A means. It is not a logical symbol; it is the initial of every initial: it is a proper name, a face, a voice. Perhaps it is not, properly speaking, an individual, since it is divided by its equality and by difference from that equality, but it is a singularity. The A of speculative idealism is both the first notation of an algebra of ontological identity and the name of the singular in its singularity.)

Jean-Luc Nancy (1993a: 11)

Moreover, from a psychoanalytic perspective, which takes into account the social formation of the subjects, the subject is only ever constituted by a lack and is thus always divided from itself.

In its most audacious moments current (Lacanian) psychoanalytic theory proposes a theory of the subject as a divided unity which arises from and is determined by lack (void, nothingness, zero, according to the context) and engages in an unsatisfied quest for the impossible, represented by metonymic desire . . . Psychoanalysis teaches us this: that any subject, inasmuch as he or she is social, supposes this unitary and split instance, initially proposed by Freud with the Unconscious/Conscious schema, while it also points to the role of originary repression in the constitution of the subject. If originary repression institutes the subject at the same time as the symbolic function, it also institutes the distinction between signifier and signified in which Lacan sees the determination of 'any censorship of a social nature'. The unitary subject is the subject instituted by this social censoring.

Julia Kristeva (1998: 133)

To reiterate an earlier assertion, the problem inherent in addressing the question of the subject in whichever of its many senses is always one concerning full presence or identity.

If we still wish to speak of the subject – the juridical, ethical, political, psychological subject, etc. – and of what makes its semantics communicate with that of the subject of a proposition (distinct from qualities, attributes viewed as a substance, phenomena, etc.) or with the theme or the thesis (the subject of a discourse or of a book), it is first of all necessary to submit to the text of questioning the essential predicates of which all subjects are the subject. While these predicates are as numerous and diverse as the type or order of subjects dictates, they are all in fact ordered around being present . . . presence to self – which implies therefore a certain interpretation of temporality: identity to self, positionality, property, personality, ego, consciousness, will, intentionality, freedom, humanity, etc.

Jacques Derrida (1991: 109)

Lastly, Gilles Deleuze has proposed a notion of a radically different self-hood, termed here *nomadic*, in which the subject, in a constant state of becoming, sidesteps the static positions implicit in many, if not all, normative conceptions of subjectivity.

> [Of the Deleuzian concepts of becoming and nomadic subjectivity] A self, a conversation, a book . . . can be seen as a configuration of random and aleatory elements converging to form one location with its own peculiar topology, strata, and atmosphere. The contours of this self suggest a rich sense of connectedness, inevitable and mutually informing contact with surrounding terrain, and the arbitrariness of any one way of staking out one's boundaries. Mapping such terrain involves attentiveness to the intricate convergence of multiple singularities that defy any imposition of a preconceived grid.
>
> The writer who would map the terrain of [such a radically reconceived] subjectivity . . . must follow the lines of flight that run through herself and the multiplicities of which she is a part. This process entails betraying any recognizable positioning and ignoring conventional boundaries in order to follow the moving lines of this terrain. The image of a nomadic subject evokes a multiply overdetermined sense of a subject actively participating with rather than in or on the world. Nomadic subjectivity participates in a terrain that includes and engages processes other than itself as well rather than acting as a distinct entity upon objects. The interconnections of this subject and its world reach out in all directions and cannot be reduced to any one linear chain of cause and effect. Instead, this subject is a multiplicity among multiplicities, the various lines of which actualize movements of becoming. This model problematizes dichotomies of active/passive and agent/object and evokes an image of collaboration of embodied subject and world, a singular coming together of multiple lines in which the specific location and shape of the subject is impossible to pin down to any one point.
>
> Tamsin Lorraine (1999: 125–6)

Questions for further consideration

1. Is the subject an intertextual position or location?
2. In what ways can language be understood as revealing the subject's social embeddedness?
3. What role does the State or nation play in the production, and subjectification, of its subjects? What are some of the ways in which subjection is achieved, and in what ways, if any, are education or the media complicit in the process?

Explanatory and bibliographical notes

1. *Coterminous*: having a common boundary or being exactly co-extensive.
2. *Chartism*: Victorian labour movement, which achieved its greatest visibility between 1839 and 1842 and continued to make its voice heard throughout the 1840s. The Chartists drew up the *People's Charter*, in which six key demands for parliamentary reform were made, these being (i) voting by ballot; (ii) universal suffrage for men; (iii) annual parliaments; (iv) equal electoral districts; (v) payment for MPs; (vi) abolition of property qualification for parliamentary candidates.
3. *Hypokeimenon*: a key term in Aristotle's *Metaphysics*, *hypokeimenon* means 'that which lies under' or, to put it another way, 'that which is the basis of', and thus corresponds with the Latin *sub-ject*, meaning 'thrown under'. Thus the term has nothing to with human subjectivity as such. It is, however, understood in Aristotelian metaphysics to address things out there in the world which can be spoken of and attributed predicates.
4. *Noetic*: adjectival variant of *noesis*, signifying thought.
5. David Hume (*b*.1711–*d*.1776): *A Treatise of Human Nature*, ed. Ernest C. Mossner (London: Penguin, 1985); *An Enquiry Concerning Human Nature*, ed. Tom L. Beauchamp (Oxford: Oxford University Press, 1999); *An Enquiry Concerning the Principles of Morals*, ed. Tom L. Beauchamp (Oxford: Oxford University Press, 1998).
6. *Polis*: the word from which *politics* derives, *polis* signified the city-state or community in Ancient Greece.

Further reading

Cadava, Eduardo, Peter Connor and Jean-Luc Nancy (eds) (1991), *Who Comes After the Subject?* (London: Routledge).
Copjec, Joan (ed.) (1994), *Supposing the Subject* (London: Verso).
Elliot, Anthony (1996), *Subject to Ourselves: Social Theory, Psychoanalysis, and Postmodernity* (Cambridge: Polity Press).
King, Nicola (2000), *Memory, Narrative, Identity: Remembering the Self* (Edinburgh: Edinburgh University Press).
Mansfield, Nick (2000), *Subjectivity: Theories of the Self from Freud to Haraway* (St Leonards, NSW: Allen Unwin).
Williams, Linda Ruth (1995), *Critical Desire: Psychoanalysis and the Literary Subject* (London: Edward Arnold).

UNCANNY

Most often associated with the work of Freud, but also found in Heidegger's discussion of Being as a fundamental experience of one's being in the world, and one's relationship to existence, *uncanny* is the somewhat inaccurate translation for the German *unheimlich* (lit. 'unhomely'). Freud employs this in the essay of the same name (1919) to signify a feeling of discomfort and strangeness arising in the self without warning. As Freud suggests, the feeling of the uncanny is uncanny precisely to the extent that the sensation comes about in places where one should feel most secure, or with which one is most familiar. Freud's 'loosening' of the semantic oscillation in the German demonstrates how the experience of the uncanny is structural, that is to say the sense of being 'not-at-home' or 'unhomely' arises from within the very idea of the home and the familiar as its internal necessity of identity's other, rather than being that which is supposedly external, a binary opposition and, therefore, an identity in its own right.

Freud remarks first that

> [t]he subject of the 'uncanny' is . . . undoubtedly related to what is frightening – to what arouses dread and horror . . .
>
> Sigmund Freud (1997: 193)

But then alerts us to the essentially repressed aspect of any uncanny experience:

> the uncanny is that class of the frightening which leads back to what is known of old and long familiar.
>
> Sigmund Freud (1997: 195)

The Freudian uncanny, a mechanism of return, is therefore:

> a function of *enlightenment*: it is that which confronts us, paradoxically, after a certain *light* has been cast.
>
> Terry Castle (1995: 7)

Of the structural relationship in German, Freud observes that the uncanny (*unheimlich*) and the familiar or homely (*heimlich*) appear as opposites, and this assumed opposition is the cause of a certain misunderstanding of that which causes fear in the subject.

> The German word '*unheimlich*' is obviously the opposite of '*heimlich*' ['homely'], '*heimisch*' ['native'] – the opposite of what is familiar; and we are tempted to conclude that what is 'uncanny' is frightening precisely because it is *not* known and familiar . . .
>
> Sigmund Freud (1997: 195)

However, the opposition is not as absolute as it might appear initially, for there are sedimented, latent semantic layers to the *Heimlich*, which direct

Freud towards the sense of the uncanny as that which is familiar, but which has been forgotten.

> What interests us most . . . is to find that among its different shades of meaning the word '*heimlich*' exhibits one which is identical with its opposite, '*unheimlich*'. What is *Heimlich* thus comes to be *unheimlich* . . . In general we are reminded that the word '*heimlich*' is not unambiguous, but belongs to two sets of ideas, which, without being contradictory, are yet very different: on the one hand it means what is familiar and agreeable, and on the other, what is concealed and kept out of sight.
>
> Sigmund Freud (1997: 199)

So, the uncanny is precisely that which, having been repressed, subsequently comes to light in the most familiar places:

> everything is *unheimlich* that ought to have remained secret and hidden but has come to light.
>
> Sigmund Freud (1997: 200)

Importantly, the aspect of recurrence is involuntary, as that which surfaces from the unconscious can be neither predicted nor controlled:

> this factor of involuntary repetition . . . surrounds what would otherwise be innocent enough with an uncanny atmosphere, and forces upon us the idea of something fanciful and inescapable when otherwise we should have spoken only of 'chance'.
>
> Sigmund Freud (1997: 213)

Another aspect of the uncanny is the motif of doubling.

> Hoffmann['s] . . . novel *Die Elixire des Teufels* [*The Devil's Elixir*],[1] contains a whole mass of themes to which one is tempted to ascribe the uncanny effect of the narrative . . . These themes are all concerned with the phenomenon of the 'double' . . . there is a doubling, dividing and interchanging of the self. And . . . there is the constant recurrence of the same thing – the repetition of the same features or character-traits or vicissitudes . . .
>
> Sigmund Freud (1997: 209–10)

Freud summarizes the uncanny effect in this fashion.

> In the first place, if psycho-analytic theory is correct in maintaining that every affect belonging to an emotional impulse, whatever its kind, is

transformed, if it is repressed, into anxiety, then among instances of frightening things there must be one class in which the frightening element can be shown to be something repressed which *recurs*. This class of frightening things would then constitute the uncanny; and it must be a matter of indifference whether what is uncanny was itself originally frightening or whether it carried some *other* affect. In the second place, if this is indeed the secret nature of the uncanny we can understand why linguistic usage has extended *das Heimliche* ['homely'] into its opposite, *das Unheimliche* . . . for this uncanny is in reality nothing new or alien, but something which is familiar and old-established in the mind and which has become alienated from it only through the process of repression.

Sigmund Freud (1997: 217)

The double causes an especially uncanny feeling because it returns to us as a figure of death.

> The double is an ambivalent figure of death since it signifies an insurance that one will continue to live, that the soul is eternal even as the body decomposes and as such signifies a defence against death. The composition of representation serves as a triumph over and against material decomposition in the realm or system of the real. However, the double is by definition also a figure for a split or gap . . . The double, simultaneously denying and affirming mortality, is the metaphor of the uncanniness of the death drive, of '*Unheimlichkeit par excellence*', grounding all other versions of the uncanny because it points to what is most resistantly and universally repressed, namely the presence of death in life and at the origin of life.

Elizabeth Bronfen (1992: 114)

The ambiguity, not to say undecidability, which marks the problem of translation and definition, is read as central to Freud's articulation of the uncanny, its functions and effects.

> In his discussion of the concept *das Unheimliche*, Freud turns the lack of a clear definition into the crux of this concept's rhetorical strategy – namely a semantic subversion based on the blurring of stable concepts . . . As a situation of undecidability, where fixed frames or margins are set in motion, the uncanny also refers to moments where the question whether something is animate (alive) or inanimate (dead), whether something is real or imagined, unique, original or a repetition, a copy, can not be decided. . . . Because the uncanny in some sense always involves the question of visibility/invisibility, presence to/absence from sight . . . the

uncanny always entails anxieties about fragmentation, about the disruption or destruction of any narcissistically informed sense of personal stability, body integrity, immortal individuality.

Freud locates the main source for an experience of the uncanny in the compulsion to repeat, to re-present, double, supplement; in a return to the familiar that has been repressed. This doubling, dividing and exchanging can, furthermore, involve the subject in his relation to others as he either identifies with another, as he substitutes the alterior self for his own, or as he finds himself incapable of deciding which of the two his self is ... the most important boundary blurring inhabited by the uncanny is that between the real and fantasy ... This effacement of the boundary distinction between fantasy and reality occurs when something is experienced as real which up to that point was conceived as imagined.

Elisabeth Bronfen (1992: 113)

The suggestion of a mobility of the uncanny, between presence and absence, visibility and invisibility, just discussed, marks it both as being akin to a psychic trope and as having a spectral, ghostly quality.

Uncanny experiences are haunting experiences. There is something there and you 'feel' it strongly. It has a shape, an electric empiricity, but the evidence is barely visible, or highly symbolized. The investigation of these qualities of feelings is ... a more properly aesthetic than psychoanalytic topic of inquiry ... uncanny experiences are usually frightening ... all manner of phantom doubles conjure up ... desires for dead things to come alive, a haunting experience, if nonetheless increasingly common in the modern world.

Avery F. Gordon (1997: 50–1)

Continuing on from the comprehension of the uncanny as tropological, as spectral, and as a motion, it is important to stress it as process rather than object:

the return of the repressed ... is associated, not with any *thing* unconscious, but with the movement of signifiers ... the uncanny manifests the mobility of meaning and the operations of metaphorical substitution unanchored by any final ground or meaning ... the uncanny is more than an objectified wish returning from an unconscious identified as a seat of instincts ... the uncanny marks the decomposition of the fantasy underpinning imaginary subjective integrity and the assumption of symbolic consistency ...

Fred Botting (1999: 33–4)

Heidegger also understands the uncanny as process, but comprehends it not simply as a psychic effect, seeing it rather as constitutive of our sense of being. The uncanny manifests itself through a sensation of fear causing us to flee. But the fear is not grounded in any external thing, any object or event, so much as it is made evident through a 'reminder' if you will of the condition of what Heidegger calls our being-in-the-world.

> What is this fleeing of Dasein[2] from itself? . . . All fleeing is grounded in fearing . . . Fleeing from something is grounded in being afraid of something . . . fearing is precisely the mode of being in which something threatening is uniquely disclosed and can be encountered in concern in being approached by the world . . . Indeed, what threatens in this indefinite way . . . can be so near and yet not present as this or that, not something fearful, something to be feared by way of a definite reference of the environing world in its meaningfulness. Dread can 'befall' us right in the midst of the most familiar environment . . . We then say: one feels *uncanny* . . . One no longer feels at home in his most familiar environment . . . in dread, being-in-the-world is totally transformed into a 'not at home' purely and simply . . . *the of-which of dread is nothing*, that is to say, nothing that takes place in the world, nothing definite, nothing worldly . . . Because that of which dread is in dread is this nothing in the sense of 'nothing definite and worldly', the nothing amplifies its proximity . . . This absolute helplessness in the face of the threatening, because it is indeed indefinite, because it is nothing, offers no ways and means of overcoming it . . . The of-which of dread, which is nothing worldly, is the in-which which is constitutive of Dasein, of in-being itself. That *of which* dread is in dread is the *in-which of being-in-the-world*, and that *about which* one is in dread is this *very same being-in-the-world*, specifically in its primary discoveredness of 'not at home' . . . Dread is nothing but *the disposition to uncanniness* . . . in the flight from itself, Dasein is still constantly there for itself. . . . What is at stake in the flight from uncanniness [*Unheimlichkeit*, not-being-at-home] is precisely a cultivation of Dasein itself as being-in-the-world.
>
> Martin Heidegger (1992: 282–93 *passim*)

Heidegger adds a dimension to the experience of the uncanny missing from Freud's analysis, termed by Heidegger 'the law of historicality', which is given explication in this final citation.

> Heidegger thinks man's essential 'uncanniness' (*Unheimlichkeit*) on the basis of what he calls the law of history, or, better, 'the law of historicality' (*das Gesetz der Geschichtlichkeit*). This law is to be thought as 'the altercation of that which is foreign and that which is one's own'

which is 'the grounding truth of history'. If man is *unheimlich* – the most *unheimlich* of all that is *unheimlich* – it is because his essence consists in 'coming to be at home' (*Heimischwerden*); and if his essence is 'coming to be at home' (*Heimischwerden*), then this means that it is at the same time 'not *being* at home' (*Unheimischsein*). 'Coming to be at home' (*Heimischwerden*) and 'not *being* at home' (*Unheimischsein*) are mutually implicated, mutually determine the essence of man: if man has to *come to be* at home, then he *is* not at home; if man *is* not at home, then he has to *come to be* at home.

. . .

This 'law of historicality' – the mutual implication and intrication of not being at home (*Unheimischsein*) and coming to be at home (*Heimischwerden*) – is given an ontological interpretation by Heidegger . . . man's uncanniness (*Unheimlichkeit*) is grounded in his homelessness (*Unheimischkeit*) and this homelessness in turn has its hidden ground in man's relation (*Bezug*) to Being. In short: 'The uncanniness of man has its essence in homelessness, but this homelessness is what it is only through this, that man is at home at all in Being'.

Andrzej Warminski (1999: 204–5)[3]

Questions for further consideration

1. Consider the differences and similarities between Freud's and Heidegger's suppositions concerning the uncanny.
2. Is there a relationship between uncanny experience and the sensation of *déjà vu*?
3. What might theories of the uncanny reveal about the constitution of the subject in Gothic fiction?

Explanatory and bibliographical notes

1. E. T. A. Hoffmann (*b.*1776–*d.*1824): *Tales of Hoffmann*, trans. R. J. Hollingdale (London: Penguin, 1982); '*The Golden Pot' and Other Stories*, ed. Ritchie Robertson (Oxford: Oxford University Press, 1999).
2. *Dasein*, sometimes written as *Da-sein* (lit. 'there-being'), is Heidegger's term for 'being'. For humans there is no sense of being before the experience of being-in-the-world, thus, existentially, the experience of being is always an experience of 'being-there', rather than a 'sense of being' in the abstract.
3. Warminski is citing Heidegger's *Hölderlin's Hymne "Der Ister"*, Gesamtausgabe (Frankfurt am Main: Klostermann, 1984), pp. 61, 113–14. English edition, Martin Heidegger, *Hölderlin's Hymn 'The Ister'*, trans. William McNeill and Julia Davis (Bloomington, IN: Indiana University Press, 1996), pp. 69, 128.

Further reading

Bronfen, Elisabeth (1992), *Over Her Dead Body: Death, Femininity, and the Aesthetic* (Manchester: Manchester University Press).

Castle, Terry (1995), *The Female Thermometer: Eighteenth-Century Culture and the Invention of the Uncanny* (New York: Oxford University Press).

Freud, Sigmund (1997), 'The "Uncanny" ' (1919), trans. James Strachey. In Sigmund Freud, *Writings on Literature and Art*, Foreword by Neil Hertz (Stanford, CA: Stanford University Press), pp. 193–233.

Heidegger, Martin (1992), *History of the Concept of Time: Prolegomena* (1979), trans. Theodore Kisiel (Bloomington, IN: Indiana University Press).

UNCONSCIOUS

In psychoanalytic discourse, the *unconscious* is the mental realm or, perhaps more precisely, process (Lacan names it a 'field') wherein those aspects of mental life that are related to forbidden desires and instincts are consigned through another process, that of repression. The unconscious is absolutely unknown and unlocatable, as well as being inaccessible directly to the subject except where it exerts pressures on conscious life, as when repressed objects refuse to remain repressed. The instincts and desires the unconscious contains are usually disguised through a repressive censorship that turns forbidden ideas into different images by the processes of condensation and displacement (Freud's terms), where they operate in a manner akin to metonymies and metaphors, analogies employed by Lacan; hence his now-famous remark that '*the unconscious is structured like a language*' (Jacques Lacan, 1994: 20). These censored images, which are, themselves, not stable bearers or guarantors of meaning, seek to re-enter consciousness through the structures of dreams, symptoms, verbal and physical tics. The subject is unable to interpret the new images him/herself and must submit to analysis to 'read' the pulsions of his or her own unconscious. However, it has to be stressed, following Lacan, that there is no access, or possibility thereof, to the unconscious as such. Rather, any analytical process will lead in the 'reading' of images, tropes, and other signifiers to yet more signifiers in an endless signifying chain of substitutions.

Freud defines the specificity of the unconscious in the following manner:

'unconscious' is no longer the name of what is latent at the moment; the unconscious is a particular realm of the mind with its own wishful impulses, its own mode of expression and its peculiar mental mechanisms which are not in force elsewhere.

Sigmund Freud (1982: 249)

The inaccessibility of the unconscious, its radical alterity, and its manner of interruption and eruption in conscious life, are described here:

> we call a psychical process unconscious whose existence we are obliged to assume ... but of which we know nothing ... we call a process unconscious if we are obliged to assume that it is being activated *at the moment*, though *at the moment* we know nothing about it ... In order to explain a slip of the tongue ... we find ourselves obliged to assume that the intention to make a particular remark was present in the subject. We infer it with certainty from the interference with his remark which has occurred; but the intention did not put itself through and was thus unconscious. If, when we subsequently put it before the speaker, he recognizes it as one familiar to him, then it was only temporarily unconscious to him; but if he repudiates it as something foreign to him, then it was permanently unconscious. From this experience we retrospectively obtain the right also to pronounce as something unconscious what had been described as latent. A consideration of these dynamic relations permits us now to distinguish two kinds of unconscious – one which is easily ... transformed into something conscious, and another with which this transformation is difficult and takes place only subject to a considerable expenditure of effort or possibly never at all ... We call the unconscious which is only latent, and thus easily becomes conscious, 'preconscious' and retain the term 'unconscious' for the other.
>
> Sigmund Freud (1973: 102–3)

Lacan identifies as discontinuities in the psychic life of the subject those instances investigated by Freud in the analysis of the operations of the unconscious.

> Impediment, failure, split. In a spoken or written sentence something stumbles. Freud is attracted by these phenomena, and it is there that he seeks the unconscious ... Discontinuity ... is the essential form in which the unconscious first appears to us as a phenomenon – discontinuity, in which something is manifested as a vacillation.
>
> Jacques Lacan (1994: 25)

The unconscious appears as that which disrupts identity:

> the unconscious is always manifested as that which vacillates in a split in the subject ...
>
> Jacques Lacan (1994: 28)

Not only does the unconscious disorder or interrupt the subject's ontology, it is itself not available to ontological inquiry or definition.

The gap of the unconscious may be said to be *pre-ontological.* I have stressed that all too often forgotten characteristic . . . of the first emergence of the unconscious, namely, that it does not lend itself to ontology. Indeed, what became apparent to Freud . . . [is that] what truly belongs to the order of the unconscious . . . is neither being, nor non-being, but the unrealized.

Jacques Lacan (1994: 29–30)

Given the difficulties of definition with which we are confronted by the radically groundless nature of the unconscious, how might it be possible to discuss it? Here are three interrelated statements premised on the notion that the unconscious is neither a place nor an object, but rather, a strange form of discourse.

The unconscious is a discourse. Freud is not the first to have discovered the unconscious, but the first to have discovered the essential fact that *the unconscious speaks*: in slips of the tongue, in dreams, in the symbolic language of the symptoms. The unconscious is not simply a forgotten or rejected bag of instincts, but an indestructible infantile desire whose repression means that it has become symbolically unrecognizable, since it is differentially articulated through rhetorical displacements (object substitutions). Repression is, in other words, the rejection not of instincts but of symbols or of signifiers: their rejection through their replacement, the displacement or the transference of their original libidinal meaning onto other signifiers.

The unconscious is a discourse that is other, or ex-centric, to the discourse of a self. It is in effect a discourse that is other to itself, not in possession of itself; a discourse that no consciousness can master and that no speaking subject can assume or own.

The unconscious is a discourse that is radically intersubjective. Since it is a discourse that no consciousness can own, the only way a consciousness can hear it is as coming from the Other. In this way, the formula describes the analytic situation as coincident with the radical structure of the unconscious, that is, the analytic (dialogic) situation as the condition of possibility for the production of psychoanalytic truth (an audible speech of the unconscious). 'The Other' thus stands in the psychoanalytic dialogue both for the position of the analyst, through whom the subject hears his own unconscious discourse, and for the position of the subject's own unconscious as other to his self (to his self-image and self-consciousness).

Shoshana Felman (1987: 123–4)

We have said that the unconscious is not determinable ontologically; yet, in relation to the consciousness, a provisional ontological definition is made here.

In any case, beyond consciousness and as its explicative principle, psychoanalysis posits what is not conscious, the unconscious. Just like the concept of consciousness, the concept of the unconscious is equivocal, simultaneously ontic[1] and ontological. In the ontic sense, the unconscious consists of drives and their representatives, unconscious representations with their adjuncts, the primary processes to which they are submitted (i.e., the mechanism of displacement, condensation, and symbolization as at the origin of dreams, parapraxes,[2] and symptoms), repressed or phylogenetic contents, a great part of childhood experiences, and so on. But such contents are subsumed under the concept of the unconscious only because they are deprived of being-conscious as such . . . What is unconscious is what is situated outside the field opened by appearance and circumscribed by its phenomenality. Since the concept of the unconscious, even if first understood in the ontic sense, cannot take form and be defined outside its relation to ontological consciousness, it is itself ontological.

What does 'the unconscious' mean in the ontological sense? Is it more than a purely negative determination, a simple barring of the determination 'being-conscious' or 'pure appearances' as such? Because the simple fact of not being conscious, of not appearing, is a purely negative determination, because it does not appear 'rich in perspectives,' we can understand why Freud excluded it from his research, substituting the processes that effectively account for mental content, just as that content is substituted for the simple quality of being conscious . . . which is also formal and empty. In this way, psychoanalysis creates a cleavage that definitively separates it from philosophy while simultaneously establishing its own concept of the unconscious: no longer the empty negation of the formal quality . . . but the whole of the processes to be discovered, whose coherent totality determines the human psyche and makes it what it is – the unconscious as a system.

Michel Henry (1993: 283–4)

Understood as a system, however inaccessible it may be to any direct comprehension, the unconscious comprehended ontologically is a 'strange kind of being':

the unconscious . . . is both a modality of nothingness and a modality of being. It is a strange kind of being that appears when it ought not to: precisely when a strange intention is being realized. Lacan chose to stress the unconscious as subject, a subject which has no substance . . . the unconscious also appears as repetition . . . The unconscious is also an articulation of signifiers . . . It is important to stress the unconscious as repetition, because it is completely different from stressing the unconscious as resistance, which is so fundamental in ego-psychology.

Jacques-Alain Miller (1995: 10)

Thus we only apprehend the workings of the unconscious indirectly, by analogy rather than through any means of direct representation, in everyday speech through the manifestation of symbolization inappropriate to the context of a given utterance:

> there is a certain unconscious component in ordinary discourse as in all mental productions, which carries the ineradicable expression of the subject's voice . . . Free association can accomplish the task of liberating the unconscious constituent contained in an utterance, because it isolates the signifiers which constitute the discourse by setting them free from the context of conscious meaning . . . The chain of signifiers which constitutes the unconscious consists . . . of the results of the subject's repeated attempts to symbolize her experience. And the most visible sign of these only partially successful efforts are the analysand's[3] symptoms . . . If there were no repression, if symbolization were perfect, then there would be no unconscious, for everything would be contained within conscious meaning. If repression were perfect, however, the unconscious would be totally inaccessible, for the repressed would leave no traces whatsoever behind to mark its disappearance.

Gilbert D. Chaitin (1996: 197–8)

Literature is one privileged form which allows us insight into the rhetorical and grammatical functions of the unconscious.

> Literature is . . . a privileged use of language in such a way as to evoke the Other of the unconscious. This is not to say that literature gives us direct access to the unconscious. Rather its rhetorical effects take us past grammar to structuring dynamics that are parallel to those of the unconscious: metaphor and metonymy are cognate with condensation and displacement; repetition echoes the process by which a *moi* is constituted . . . A literary text does not reveal to us a specific truth dug up from our unconscious. Rather it evokes the truth *of* the unconscious, of the modes that have made us without our knowing it. Nor can we know them now, except in an allusive dynamics like that of dreams.

Peter Schwenger (1999: 36)

The truth of the unconscious is that it operates at a level of signification that is always beyond, and in excess of, direct subjective access or control.

The unconscious exists, not because there is unconscious desire, in the sense of something impenetrable . . . which emerges from the depths of all its primitiveness, in order then to raise itself to the higher level of consciousness. Quite the contrary, if there is desire, it is only because there is the unconscious, i.e., a language, whose structure and effects escape the subject: because at the level of language, there is always something that is beyond consciousness, which allows the function of desire to be situated.

Jacques Lacan (1967: 45)

Questions for further consideration

1. If the unconscious is most appropriately thought as structure and process akin to the workings of language, and if there is no direct access to the unconscious, what are some of the implications for literary study?
2. Given the insistence on inaccessibility, on failure, frustration, slippage, and discontinuity, in addressing the unconscious, what are the implications for theories of subjectivity?
3. Consider the relationship between the uncanny and the unconscious.

Explanatory and bibliographical notes

1. *Ontic*: relating to knowledge concerning the facts that can be known about entities.
2. *Parapraxes*: more commonly referred to as 'Freudian slips'. Freud termed parapraxes inadvertent, i.e. unconscious, errors in speech or writing, slips of the tongue or pen or, otherwise, a misreading of some phrase or word: we say, write or read something erroneously and fail to notice that we have done this, at least until after the fact or until we have this pointed out by someone else. Freud suggests that such slips are significant, symptoms released from the unconscious of what we have repressed but which return to trouble us none the less. See the *Introductory Lectures on Psychoanalysis* (Freud, 1982: 39–110).
3. *Analysand*: generally, the patient in the psychoanalytic encounter; however, Lacan employs the term in order to signify that it is not the analyst who does the analysing so much as the patient who analyses him- or herself, while the analyst is there to guide the self-analysis.

Further reading

Abraham, Nicolas (1995), *Rhythms: On the Work, Translation, and Psychoanalysis*, collected and presented by Nicholas T. Rand and Maria Torok, trans. Benjamin Thigpen and Nicholas T. Rand (Stanford, CA: Stanford University Press).

Abraham, Nicolas, and Maria Torok (1994), *The Shell and the Kernel*, vol. I, ed., trans., and with an Introduction by Nicholas T. Rand (Chicago: University of Chicago Press).

Botting, Fred (1999), 'The Gothic Production of the Unconscious'. In Glennis Byron and David Punter (eds), *Spectral Readings: Towards a Gothic Geography* (Basingstoke: Macmillan), pp. 11–36.

Forrester, John (1990), *The Seductions of Psychoanalysis: Freud, Lacan and Derrida* (Cambridge: Cambridge University Press).

Freud, Sigmund (1976), *The Interpretation of Dreams*, Penguin Freud Library, vol. 4, trans. James Strachey, ed. Angela Richards (Harmondsworth: Penguin).

Freud, Sigmund (1982), *Introductory Lectures on Psychoanalysis*, Penguin Freud Library, vol. 1, trans. James Strachey, ed. Angela Richards (Harmondsworth: Penguin).

Henry, Michel (1993), *The Genealogy of Psychoanalysis* (1985), trans. Douglas Brick (Stanford, CA: Stanford University Press).

Lacan, Jacques (1977), *Écrits: A Selection* (1966), trans. Alan Sheridan (New York: W. W. Norton).

Leclaire, Serge (1998a), *Psychoanalyzing: On the Order of the Unconscious and the Practice of the Letter*, trans. Peggy Kamuf (Stanford, CA: Stanford University Press).

Nasio, Juan-David (1998), *Five Lessons on the Psychoanalytic Theory of Jacques Lacan* (1992), trans. David Pettigrew and François Raffoul (Albany, NY: State University of New York Press).

WRITING

Let us conclude the present volume with the subject of *writing*, that medium through which the book is made to appear, by which it is, in principle, transmissible, and by which, again, there is made possible the assumption of communication. By the word 'writing' it will have been assumed on the part of many readers of this volume that there is signified the graphic representation of speech. In such an assumption there is the cognate supposition that the marks on the page serve to give access to a voice, belonging to someone presumably, and therefore, to both a human presence and to thought. Writing is therefore understood as being supplementary, secondary, a necessary adjunct to thought, speech and presence, when access to these is not immediately possible. However, though writing in this sense is apparently a familiar enough concept referring to 'the model of phonetic writing, which we privilege only by ethnocentrism' (Jacques Derrida, 1981a: 26), it has to be admitted that there is no purely phonetic writing (by reason of the necessary spacing of signs, punctuation, intervals, the differences indispensable for the functioning of graphemes,[1] etc.) . . .

Jacques Derrida (1981a: 26)

Thus, when one acknowledges those aspects of writing which, properly speaking, escape, exceed, or are irreducible to any reproductive or representational process connected to phonetic articulation, the traditional concept of writing is seen to be both narrow and superficial. Beginning, then, from the traditional definition only to expose its limits, it is possible to understand writing in the following way:

according to its traditional determination . . . writing has no direct signified or referent . . . but refers to the phonic signifier of which it is supposed to be no more than a transcription . . . We write when we cannot speak, when contingent obstacles, which can be reduced to so many forms of distance, prevent the voice from carrying. Writing is a form of telecommunication.

Geoffrey Bennington (1993: 42–3)

As a form of telecommunication, writing must be transmissible and iterable.

My 'written communication' must . . . remain legible despite the absolute disappearance of every determined addressee for it to function as writing, that is, for it to be legible. It must be repeatable – iterable – in the absolute absence of the addressee or of the empirically determinable set of addressees. This iterability . . . structures the mark of writing itself, and does so moreover no matter what type of writing . . . A writing that was not structurally legible – iterable – beyond the death of the addressee would not be writing . . . Let us imagine a writing . . . idiomatic enough to have been founded and known . . . only by two 'subjects'. Can it still be said that upon the death . . . of the two partners, the mark left by one of them is still a writing? Yes, to the extent to which, governed by a code . . . it is constituted, in its identity as a mark, by its iterability in the absence of whoever, and therefore ultimately in the absence of every empirically determinable 'subject'. This implies that there is no code . . . that is structurally secret. The possibility of repeating, and therefore of identifying, marks is implied in every code, making of it a communicable, transmittable, decipherable grid that is iterable for a third party, and thus for any possible user in general. All writing, therefore, in order to be what it is, must be able to function in the radical absence of every empirically determined addressee in general.

Jacques Derrida (1982: 315–16)

Iterability, spacing, absence: all pertain to the condition of writing beyond the superficial, conventional understanding. Even as I write, a spacing, and thus a displacement from full presence, takes place.

> As author, I am *already* addressee at the moment I write . . . in order to write I must read myself, if only in the minimal sense, in the moment that I write. The act of writing is from the first divided by this complicity between writing and reading, which immediately prevents one from considering this act so easily as an act, and blurs at the same time the activity/passivity (or production/consumption) distinction that underlies the usual understanding of writing.
>
> Geoffrey Bennington (1993: 53–4)

Writing therefore does not imply presence or meaning but, instead, disseminates:

> as a disseminating operation *separated* from presence (of Being) according to all its modifications, writing, if there is any, perhaps communicates, but does not exist, surely.
>
> Jacques Derrida (1982: 330)

Such dissemination opens up a potentially endless play of writing:

> to write is to enter into the affirmation of the solitude in which fascination threatens. It is to surrender to the risk of time's absence, where eternal starting over reigns. It is to pass from the first to the third person, so that what happens to me happens to no one, is anonymous insofar as it concerns me, repeats itself in an infinite dispersal. To write is to let fascination rule language. It is to stay in touch, through language, in language, with the absolute milieu where the thing becomes image again, where the image, instead of alluding to some particular feature, becomes an allusion to the featureless, and instead of a form drawn upon absence, becomes the formless presence of this absence, the opaque, empty opening onto that which is when there is no more world, when there is no world yet.
>
> Maurice Blanchot (1982: 33)

Or, to put it more succinctly: ' "writing" implies repetition, absence, risk of loss, death' (Geoffrey Bennington, 1993: 49). The radical absence, the abyssal dispersal that writing opens, finds its exemplary figure in Robert Browning's *Pippa Passes*.[2]

> One of the most startling paradoxes inherent in writing is its close association with death. This association is suggested in Plato's charge that writing

is inhuman, thing-like, and that it destroys memory . . . In *Pippa Passes*, Robert Browning calls attention to the still widespread practice of pressing living flowers to death between the pages of printed books, 'faded yellow blossoms / twixt page and page'. The dead flower, once alive, is the psychic equivalent of the verbal text. The paradox lies in the fact that the deadness of the text, its removal from the living human lifeworld, its rigid visual fixity, assures its endurance and its potential for being resurrected into limitless living contexts by a potentially infinite number of living readers.

Walter Ong (1982: 81)

Understood in this extended fashion, writing addresses and comprehends the operation of all language.

if 'writing' has always meant a signifier referring to other signifiers, and if . . . *every* signifier refers only to other signifiers, then 'writing' will name properly the functioning of language in general.

Geoffrey Bennington (1993: 49–50)

Moreover, and in conclusion, the radical extension of the notion of writing bears upon our comprehension of the impossible time of reading.

Since the eventhood of an event of 'writing' is riven by iterability, there is never just one 'proper reading' of a 'text'; another reading is *always possible*. 'Writing' is such that it always offers itself to new readings, new responses – and, hence, new *responsibilities*. This rhythm of reading, and the ineluctable responsibility which it implies, is inescapable. It is a rhythm that does not end. Or barely, for example, ~~now~~.

Simon Glendinning (1998: 152)

Questions for further consideration

1. Consider the relationship between writing and death. Why is it that writing is always haunted by absence and deferral?
2. Is an act of writing possible which would not be, in principle, transmissible?
3. Consider the reasons for the erasure of the final word in the extract by Simon Glendinning.

Explanatory and bibliographical notes

1. *Grapheme*: literally, a written (*graph*) or inscribed unit (*-eme*), the suffix being common in linguistic determinations of the components of a particular

language; a grapheme is a group of letters, single letter or visual symbol signifying a phoneme; the grapheme is that inscription which is the smallest meaningful unit.
2.   Robert Browning (*b.*1812–*d.*1889): *Pippa Passes: A Drama* (1841). Robert
Browning, *The Poems*, ed. John Pettigrew and Thomas J. Collins
(Harmondsworth: Penguin, 1981), pp. 297–344.

Further reading

Barthes, Roland (1977), *Roland Barthes by Roland Barthes*, trans. Richard Howard
(Berkeley and Los Angeles, CA: University of California Press).
Bennington, Geoffrey (1993), 'Derridabase'. In Geoffrey Bennington and Jacques
Derrida, *Jacques Derrida*, trans. Geoffrey Bennington (Chicago, IL: University of
Chicago Press), pp. 3–316.
Cixous, Hélène (1993), *Three Steps on the Ladder of Writing*, trans. Sarah Cornell
and Susan Sellers (New York: Columbia University Press).
Derrida, Jacques (1974), *Of Grammatology*, trans. Gayatri Chakravorty Spivak
(Baltimore, MD: The Johns Hopkins University Press).
Derrida, Jacques (1982), *Margins of Philosophy*, trans., with notes Alan Bass
(Chicago, IL: University of Chicago Press).

AFTERWORD

LITERARY AND CULTURAL THEORY: THE CONTESTED GROUND OF CRITICAL LANGUAGE OR, TERMS, CONCEPTS AND MOTIFS

> Language dresses up a thought which could receive another, more appropriate set of clothing ... understanding would like a fixity and exactitude that is not found in existing language.
>
> Jean Hyppolite (1997: 46)

Consider, for a moment, the title of this essay: *Literary and Cultural Theory: The Contested Ground of Critical Language or, Terms, Concepts and Motifs*. The first part appears straightforward enough, and I have no wish to complicate this here. 'Literary and cultural theory' names – if it names at all[1] – one particular, and particularly overdetermined,[2] field or area of study, albeit a field which is internally heterogeneous, not to say fraught,[3] in what are called the humanities. More specifically, and to cite the words of Tom Cohen, I understand 'theory' to indicate 'a philosophically inflected amalgam of programs interfacing linguistic concerns with the redefinition of "history" ... human agency, meaning, impositions of power[4] ... [also displaying] a certain auto-reflexivity associated with its linguistic preoccupations' (Cohen, 1998: 5). The language of this citation might be read by some as typical in a certain way of what is perceived as literary theory. It might be read by some – neither you nor me – as opaque, dense, resistant, obscurantist. A particularly antagonistic and negative response might suggest that its language is 'cumbersome and verbose', while even a more positive reading might call this 'oblique and difficult'. It is a truism, if not exactly true, that literary theory is often characterized, if not caricatured, in such terms. The debates concerning the language of theory have always been carried on so, they have always been contested. It might be asked, somewhat disingenuously: What is not contested, in the humanities, in literary studies, today? But, if you pause for a moment to consider what Tom Cohen's words do say, you might perhaps comprehend why the issue of so-called theory has been the site of such contest. Cohen is claiming nothing more nor less for 'theory' than that it may be comprehended as a complex and interdisciplinarily informed number of approaches to reading and writing that is constituted not by one model of critical thinking but by several, and not all of these either in equal measure or without internal antagonisms and struggles. What goes by the name of theory is, in truth, the effort to make explicit what takes place every time one reads, whether reading is an act carried on 'at home' or 'for pleasure', or whether one is expected to read within given institutional situations. Reading and writing, in relation to terms such as 'literature' and 'culture', have undergone significant sea changes according to the overt or explicit engagement on the part of critics with the languages of other disciplines, such as philosophy, history, psychoanalysis, political science, and linguistics. Such engagement will necessarily have produced a different, perhaps more visible form of critical language than that traditionally associated with literary studies, a language which imposes itself on the reader, causing the reader to reflect upon the very act of reading and writing. So: literary and cultural theory,[5] momentarily defined, and yet available for further consideration; halted, and yet moving elsewhere.

What remains of the title seems somewhat less certainly placed, it has to be said, and could be read,[6] perhaps, as a little nervous in its refusal to settle on just the right word or phrase. After all, there is not that much difference[7] between what is expressed by 'terms', 'concepts', or 'motifs', is there? It would appear, to borrow Jean Hyppolite's metaphor, that I cannot find the appropriate clothing. I cannot quite settle on the appropriate figure which would then serve to acknowledge in an Afterword the subject[8] or contents of this volume. Titles are supposed to dress up, and thus cover (in at least two senses of this word) in a more or less coordinated fashion, the range of thoughts dispersed throughout a text. There is, nevertheless, something slightly troublesome, some apparent irresolution or hesitancy here.

Perhaps there are other ways to read what is taking place in the subtitle, other approaches to considering the vacillation at work. What can be taken as vacillation on my part might equally be an oscillation, a wavering or trembling, some form of disturbance within the words themselves, conventionally assumed to be the location – the place and identification – of meaning. Perhaps this uncertainty is not mine at all or, at least, not mine alone. What may have been read as 'my' indecision may be a strategic indecision, the announcement, or more radically, the enactment or performance of a displacement emerging from within the very possibility of the semantic guarantee known as a title.[9] What may be readable may well be some expression of contest at work in the title (as the title of this Afterword announces).

In announcing struggle, disturbance, and other unsettling phenomena within language, and in addressing critical language as contested (supposing, for the moment, that what we will call 'critical language' is artificially separable from language in general), it should be stressed from the outset that I am not attempting to create drama or hyperbole where none exists. Nor do my comments concerning my subtitle pertain only to that. What I have said about the subtitle applies from the microtextual to the macrotextual level. It is applicable to each of the words considered through the citations and fragments that are gathered in this book, to the book as a whole, and to a whole genre of books, to which the present volume may be identified as belonging. (There will be more to say on this, with regard to the choice of words in *Critical Keywords in Literary and Cultural Theory*.) Furthermore, the contest or strife to which I have alluded has little, if anything, to do with any institutional or journalistic debate over the merits or evils of something named 'literary theory'. Yes, these have taken place, and continue to take place. My interest, however, and, accordingly, the focus of and reason for the present volume, is in the contested ground, the contest – in the sense of calling to witness – for any grounding, which comes to take place in critical language generally, and in this specific instance, in writing[10] and editing a 'foundational' project such as a glossary, a dictionary, or a lexicon. The question of the contest is articulated not merely in the very idea and assumptions made about the identity of any such reference work or pedagogical project, but also, more significantly I feel, in the effort made to define every word, every term, concept, or motif. Before considering the question of the choice of particular words that the subtitle has raised, let us turn to the identity of volumes such as the one you are presently holding.

Such volumes are seen as necessary and the necessity resides in the assumption that foundations have to be laid – in this case in the provision of definition and identification – on which to build knowledge. Nevertheless, the desire[11] to build foundations is always predicated on not recognizing that we are on doubtful ground,[12] or that there is no ground as such. The problem of non- or misrecognition is therefore central to carrying out such a project. A certain blindness must be maintained. Now, it has to be admitted at this juncture that to describe this as a problem appears to complicate things unnecessarily, especially in an Afterword to a volume bearing more than a passing resemblance, a family likeness if you will, to such works. The definition of the glossary/dictionary genre and the principal difficulty which also constitutes its identity therefore needs to be addressed.

If there is a single problem with glossaries, dictionaries, and other such forms, it is that they *define*. Indeed, this will be the only definition which can be put forward in the present volume with any assurance: the work of the genre (if such it is) with which we are concerned can be defined in, by, its efforts at, or will to, definition. This is the function of all such examples of the type, their purpose. Not simply their *raison d'être*, it is a self- or auto-determination of the 'being' of such publications. Justification and definition produce a mutually and reciprocally supporting, generative structure. Glossaries and all the other family members of this kind are somewhat positivist[13] in nature, as has already been implied. To reiterate: their definitions assume that what is being defined is, or, in principle, can be, discernibly, fixably knowable, whether one is speaking of an object or an abstraction, an entity or the specific form taken by thought and called a concept. Somehow, there is a 'reality' or ideal form of sorts, a self-sufficient meaning or identity with specific contours, features, and parameters. The purpose of the glossary or dictionary entry is to represent and re-present these formal, conceptual, and structural elements without complication or equivocation, as fully and as homogeneously as possible, and yet, at the same time, in other words. The underlying paradox, one I would suggest which is irresolvable and intrinsic to the form with which we are concerned here, is expressed by Jean Hyppolite in the comment I have taken as my epigraph. While the language which clothes a thought can always be changed, the search for understanding is predicated on a belief that the 'style' of clothing is either irrelevant (merely, it might be and indeed has been suggested, a question of form or aesthetics[14]) or, ideally, completely unnecessary because, in principle, one ought to be able to achieve a fixity.

However, despite the fact that glossaries operate in this way, much, if not all language in its operation does not function so simply, but relies upon equivocation, paradox, contradictoriness, and so on. The very possibility of making words mean, as many literary critics have been telling us for quite some time, relies upon the operative, productive machinery and effects of the constantly fraying web of language, despite that quasi- or pseudo-positivist, representational impulse. Indeed, one can say, and again this is articulated without any hint of hyperbole at all, that it is *because* of the persistence of the mistaken assumption that written or spoken language can produce unequivocal definition, that efforts at definition not only persist but proliferate and are productive themselves, generating not some final image, identity or truth of an object or concept, but instead – paradox of language itself – more language requiring further definition.

One of the problems then – if, in fact, it really is a problem at all, and not merely the state of language – with the critical language associated with 'literary and cultural theory' is that such language is often resistant and irreducible to simple semantic determination. Language has limits, and there is a limit to how far language, especially language concerned with the workings of language, can go. Such limits are not those, however, supposedly reachable in any attempt at producing a stabilizing or normalizing definition, thereby terminating the process of inquiry. Instead, the limits of which I am speaking have to do with an exhaustion of resources in the face of that which is excessive, and which cannot be accounted for by a project such as a glossary, the very principle of which, in the light of simultaneous excess and irreducibility, can be comprehended no longer as either foundational or final. Thus, to cite Hyppolite once more, the desire to fix exactly a particular meaning is to ignore both the 'perpetual equivocation and ambiguity of words' and the 'variations of signification arising from context' (1997: 46). Critical language often self-reflexively disturbs the assumption of the work of definition, thereby announcing the impossibility of all kinds of determining projects at every level. (Parenthetically, it should be noted that the contest and disturbance within critical language, that which I have had recourse to describe as its haunting, is not peculiar to that language. Rather, the difficulties that critical language presents, especially in those aspects of the oscillation or ambiguity, if not undecidability,[15] of critical discourse,[16] only serve to highlight the very condition of all language.) Hence, the subtitle's multiple choices: terms, concepts, motifs.

To explore the definitions of these words briefly, as a way to address the volume as a whole: of *concept*, the *Oxford English Dictionary* remarks that it is the 'product of the faculty of conception; an idea of a class of objects, a general notion or idea'; it is also 'a thing conceived', not merely in any fashion but 'formal, in set form'. The idea of formality is what is most suggestive here, and it is also that which most gives me occasion to question whether the words in this book are, properly considered, concepts. What the *OED* implies is that for a notion to be elevated to the level of *concept*, thought has to be both disciplined and generalized if it is to assume an auto-coterminous form, an identity or unity enclosed within a common boundary or having structural elements that dovetail into one another in a general production of that which is selfsame, undifferentiated in any aspect of its conceptual framework. All aspects of a concept must be, ideally, of the same order of meaning or otherwise sufficiently similar, so that whatever difference there is, it makes no difference, allegedly.

The difficulty here is that it is impossible, strictly speaking, to articulate a *concept*, as such, which is neither articulated nor transmissible without difference, non-identity, heterogeneity. Therefore, while it is conventionally accepted that we employ concepts in thought and speech, and while, moreover, we refer to concepts every day, for example in making moral or aesthetic judgements concerning what is 'good' or 'bad' (or, for that matter, what is 'good' or 'evil'), it is doubtful that we consider the fact that concepts are not undifferentiated wholes but constructs; what I wish to suggest is that, at the very least, the idea of the concept should be regarded warily, especially when it comes to the question of critical language because many of the keywords of critical language implicitly call into question the possibility of conceptualization conventionally thought. However, on the one hand the fact that *concept* is retained in the title of this essay indicates an assumption that, in critical practice relating to literary and cultural theory, particular words have been read as determined by conceptual transcendence, while, on the other, there is the recognition that, however problematic a word *concept* is apropos of critical language, it cannot simply be done away with or dismissed easily.

Term names a limit; whether spatial or temporal, it signifies a boundary of sorts. The idea of a critical term, and of critical terminology in general, operates on the assumption therefore that the use of a specific word, such as postmodernism[17] for example, *terminates* the analysis or, more importantly, reading of the so-called term in question. Employing a word, any word but, specifically, those words taken to have a 'discourse-specific' or otherwise what is, in some manner, a 'specialized' function, assumes we know what we are referring to, what is being announced, and that the work of reading this term has reached an end, a limit or a boundary. As will have been seen from not a few of the headnotes and various citations throughout *Critical Keywords in Literary and Cultural Theory*, the very idea of the limit or boundary is called into doubt because, on the one hand, the word in question is used in ways suggestive of multiple, occasionally contradictory meanings, or on the other hand, there is disagreement as to either meaning, definition or usage. No amount of effort to 'come to terms' resolves or can resolve the contest that such a word engenders. That the word transforms itself, resisting de*term*ination in the process of reiteration,[18] suggests that the limit, the boundary of the very idea of *termination* is constantly being crossed and, equally, erased. If this for no other reason, one should be cautious about the promotion of any so-called term to the realm of the conceptual.

Specific 'terms', therefore, can hardly be said to be terms at all, unless we admit another meaning for the ~~term~~[19] 'term', a meaning that is, itself, contradictory and therefore disruptive of semantic or conceptual unity. (Another brief parenthesis: to employ certain of the words considered in this volume, within the supposed identity of *term* there is difference, or possibly a non-identity or alterity, which is disjunctive and yet is that which makes possible the articulation of meaning. Arguably, in the very possibility of a motion beyond the limit, and, with that, the interminable signification of *term*, there is traced or re-marked the passage of différance as that which makes possible and yet is irreducible to the notion of *term*.) In contest with the idea that *term* names termination either as such or finally, is the definition of *term* as an item or number in a series, or an element of a complex whole. This sense both puts in place a provisionality to the location of a limit while also being indicative of a momentary coming to rest before motion elsewhere within a greater series or structures. Signification is thus admitted as not terminal at all but the marking of a strategic hiatus.

In light of this connotation, *term* acquires a sense of motivation, as that which both calls to a halt *and* motivates or propels, thereby enacting the possibility for transition or transposition, transformation or translation: in short, all manner of transport. In this, it displays the qualities of another of the subtitle's words, *motif*,[20] that is, a type of incident, situation or figure which incites, induces or causes movement, which instigates or prompts: arriving at what appears to be a terminus, we find ourselves moved elsewhere by that on which we had supposedly come to rest. It is precisely a condition of the problematic nature of the *term* which tends to influence volition, that uncanny[21] impulse driving the act of reading further in response to a recognition that reading has not come to an end. This is the motive propelling the ways in which this book has been conceived; it is this motivation, to give consideration to processes that contest the very idea of definition and determination, thereby articulating that which informs much critical language; it is this motivation that impels the motion in the subtitle (which oscillation should in turn prompt or incite), as well as informing the choice of words collected here for consideration. These are not so much final, authoritative *terms*, as they are – or might be comprehended as – so many *motifs* in critical language, figures or marks indicative of a certain gathering of critical energy, moments of punctuation in a field of forces, temporary locations along intersecting lines of flight in an open, untotalizable series.

Critical Keywords in Literary and Cultural Theory represents in its fragmented, citational fashion one imagined variation of such an untotalizable series, then. The multiplicity and seriality of the subtitle of the present essay extends this work, offering to counter the certainty and authority of subject and form apparently promised in the principal part of the chapter's title. This particular aspect of contestation is not simply dialectical, however. At the risk of repeating myself, the contest emerges from within language and as a result of either a conscious resistance to the interrogation of form or an unconscious[22] blindness to the intrinsic problems of the assumption of form, as I hope to have shown thus far. Form is central to any consideration of the practice and theory of literary and cultural criticism.

Yet, as Paul de Man reminds us, it is the question of form that presents us with the greatest of difficulties:

> The main theoretical difficulty inherent in the teaching of literature is the delimitation of borderlines that circumscribe the literary field by setting it apart from other modes of discourse . . . In a manner that is more acute for theoreticians of literature than for theoreticians of the natural or the social world, it can be said that they do not quite know what it is they are talking about, not only in the . . . sense that the

whatness . . . of literature is hard to fathom, but also in the more elusive sense that, whenever one is supposed to speak of literature, one speaks of anything under the sun (including, of course, oneself) except literature. The need for determination thus becomes all the stronger as a way to safeguard a discipline which constantly threatens to degenerate into gossip, trivia or self-obsession. The most traditional term to designate these borderlines is 'form'; in literature, the concept of form is, before anything else, a definitional necessity. No literary metadiscourse would ever be conceivable in its absence. Before berating a critic or a theoretician for his formalism, one should realize that it is the necessary precondition of any theory. This does not mean, however, that the concept of form is itself susceptible to definition. (Paul de Man, 1986: 29–30)

Here, in drawing our attention to what is perhaps best described as the 'unformalizable' condition of form (and, hence, the radically formal or material[23] condition of literature), de Man foregrounds what is undoubtedly an irreconcilable tension at work in literary and cultural studies generally, and that which becomes particularly heightened in the question and name of 'theory'. I have given space and attention to what might seem relatively insignificant, the subtitle, as a means of drawing attention precisely to this irreducible concern. At the same time as providing a focus on the double question of form and definition, the work of the subtitle in some measure anticipates and announces the mode of consideration given the different and differing types of words that are chosen for inclusion in the present volume. Moreover, in as much as the title neither settles into a nominative 'exactitude' nor decides on a definitive formal nomenclature, it partakes of the recognition that critical language cannot be made unequivocally to conform to any one category. The very force of many critical words circulating in literary and cultural theory, that energy on which I have just remarked, comes from their formal material ability to dislocate consensus.

Having what can be described therefore, albeit provisionally, as a 'lawless efficacy',[24] such words function within and yet simultaneously resist accommodation according to the laws, protocols or programmes of normative, or what might be called hegemonic,[25] manifestations of critical practice. Through such resistance, the words in question, no longer simply terms or even concepts, can, in the words of Peggy Kamuf, 'no longer be heard as merely descriptive . . . in other words, they do not only describe . . . Without drama, but with indisputable emphasis', these words 'do something'. Each word appears through a number of different citations under each heading and, to pick up Kamuf's words again, '[e]ach repetition differs in force, but with each quotation or repetition, the affirmative declaration remains, as it were, in excess over the descriptive value' that they might be read as having (Kamuf, 2000: 154).

What does happen, it might be asked. What do these words 'do'? What is affirmed? What takes place when a glossary of what, for want of a better word, can be described as keywords, presents the possibility of comprehension of those words through a series of citations, so many postcard-like extracts? What takes place when the proliferation of passages calls into question any single act of determination?

Perhaps nothing very much would happen, or will have happened. For all talk of the possibility of something taking place, such an event cannot be predicted or programmed. Perhaps nothing other than a certain condition of language is affirmed. On the other hand however, it might be the case that, in adopting this fragmentary, citational procedure in this instance (and without proposing it as a programme for any possible future method of definition), it becomes possible to rethink definition in a more faithful and open-ended, self-opening, exploratory and explanatory manner, one that generates rather than closes off with the pretence or assumption of authority. The work of citational reiteration in conjunction with multiplication suggests the performative and, therefore, transformative, excessive possibility as that trembling or disturbance of which I spoke earlier. It is that which, in returning again and again, in the various manifestations and guises of projects such as glossaries, dictionaries and other reference works, haunts all desire for determination, and which cannot be laid to rest.

There are the signs here of the very haunting of language. Yet what arrives to haunt is not outside of language or something other than language so much as it is that which is within the possibility of any linguistic communication, the other of language.[26] Understanding language as a haunted structure is to recognize the phantom-effects both *of* and *in* language and the spectral condition of that strangest of determinations, literature. As Derek Attridge has suggested, '[t]he peculiar institution we know as "literature" is haunted by many ghosts . . . But not only is it possible to talk about ghosts in literature; we can say that the ghost *is* literature' (Attridge, 2000b: 176). Literature merely amplifies the spectral oscillation; accordingly, it is the responsibility of critical language to attend and respond to such resonance. It is as a response to the hauntedness of language that the contest, the struggle over meaning, between meanings, and the desire for identification inevitably takes place. And thus, equally inevitably, we find ourselves, through the act of reading, again on shaky ground whenever we seek to reach agreement or settlement. Perhaps, though, what takes place in recognizing the ghostly demand is that the affirmative waywardness inscribed in and as the possibility of every repetition translates even as it transgresses.

Citations are ghosts (Attridge, 2000b: 176). They are fragmentary repetitions, terminal and yet interminable interruptions returning the other's voice, demanding a response. In returning and thereby disturbing the effort to have the final word, the ghost redefines the work of definition, through the intimation of that which is other than authoritative designation, which is never available to explanation as such and yet which arrives with, and in, every instance of determination. It might be the case that each definition, in being re-presented in ruins, as so many citational ruins, neither being complete nor assuming an apparent or assumed totality of representation as such, might open for the reader a process of definition in other words, in order that the reader might pursue a more responsible relation to the understanding of so many so-called concepts and terms, rather than assuming passively that all is already either fully, finally represented or representable.

Notes

1. The problem, and I believe it is one, is that this nominal, this definitional gesture might well have come to occlude more than it names.
2. See the entry on 'Overdetermination'.
3. Contestation is already announced here. This is not the place to go into some, by now, formulaic recapitulation of the recent history and fortunes of so-called literary theory, the very idea of which is itself misleading inasmuch as it assumes that (a) there is some identifiable and coherent, if not homogeneous, body of work, separable from matters of rhetoric, poetics and other manifestations of criticism, to which the label 'theory' can be appended; and (b) that there are procedures, protocols, programmes and methods which, separable from the act of reading, can be learnt in a utilitarian fashion – the 'thinking-as-tool-box' approach – and then applied wholesale to whichever cultural artefact happens to engage the reader's interest. However, as one of the more succinct and salient polemical accounts of 'theory' and reactions to this institutionally generated phenomenon, I would recommend to the reader the rest of Tom Cohen's cogent account, which follows immediately from the passage I have cited. It should be noted briefly, for now, that the question of contestation is both historical and of particular moment, taking place either between different interests, for example, feminism and Marxism, or internally within particular fields of inquiry.
4. See the entry for 'Power'.
5. See the entries for 'Literature' and 'Culture'.
6. See the entry for 'Reader/Reading'.
7. See the entry for 'Difference/Différance'.
8. See the entry for 'Subject/ivity'.
9. See the entry for 'Performativity'.
10. See the entry for 'Writing'.

11. See the entry for 'Desire'.

12. As a sign of disturbance, it should be acknowledged that the figure of the ground problematizes the architectural metaphor on which I am playing, in being a double-figure, signifying also, albeit more obscurely today, though dating back at least to the sixteenth century, the initial figure, tune or motif in a piece of music, from which the rest of the piece extends and develops, or otherwise, the melody or plain-song from which the descant is raised. Here and elsewhere in this introduction, wherever etymology of words is discussed I have referred to the *Oxford English Dictionary* (*OED*).

13. As the *OED* puts it, 'the belief that every intelligible proposition can be scientifically verified or falsified, and that philosophy can only be concerned with the analysis of language used to express such propositions' or, more generally, 'definiteness, certainty, assurance'.

14. See the entry for 'Aesthetics'.

15. See the entry for 'Aporia'.

16. See the entry for 'Discourse'.

17. See the entry for 'Postmodernity/Postmodernism'.

18. See the entry for 'Iterability/Iteration'.

19. Borrowing the practice of striking through particular words the function of which is exhausted, from Martin Heidegger, Jacques Derrida and others, I have crossed through the word and retained both the word and the partial crossing-out, in order to indicate that, while the meaning-limit of the word has been exceeded, its signification is still partially operable, and therefore must be retained. Having exceeded its semantic term, the final word (to borrow a phrase employed by Jacques Derrida on the subject of 'afterwords') on the notion of the term is that there can be no final word, no appropriate term by which to bring to an end the reading of the notion of the term (no longer a term, it is even less appropriate to determine term a concept, for reasons I will explain shortly in the body of this introduction).

20. Related etymologically to notions of motive, motivation, and motion, the *motif* of *motif*, if I can put it this way, marks a passage or motion from internal, psychological, imaginary states to 'external' physical conditions, and across the limits or boundaries of either in both the play of its meanings and its linguistic family relations. *Motif* names and acts the possibility of impossibility in an articulation locatable as neither simply internal nor external, and yet of both.

21. See the entry for 'Uncanny'.

22. See the entry for 'Unconscious'.

23. See the entry for 'Materialsm/Materiality'.

24. I am taking this phrase from the work of Arkady Plotnitsky, particularly his essay 'Algebra and Allegory: Nonclassical Epistemology, Quantum Theory, and the Work of Paul de Man' (2001a: 49–89). In this work, Plotnitsky proposes that while 'certain collectivities' such as practices, programmes, methodologies and forms of knowledge acquire and maintain regulatory rules and laws as part of a process of formalization, within any system radically singular, lawless effects or efficacities take place. Within a classical model of any lawful system, it is impossible even to predict the lawless and the singular

'event' (see entry for 'Event'). Plotnitsky considers such questions in relation to the question of what constitutes postmodernism and postmodernity in another essay: 'Postmodernism and Postmodernity: Literature, Criticism, Philosophy, Culture' (2001b: 261–92).

25.   See the entry for 'Hegemony'.
26.   See the entries for 'Other' and 'Alterity'.

WORKS CITED

Abraham, Nicolas (1995) *Rhythms: On the Work, Translation, and Psychoanalysis*, collected and presented by Nicholas T. Rand and Maria Torok, trans. Benjamin Thigpen and Nicholas T. Rand (Stanford, CA: Stanford University Press).

Adorno, Theodor W. (1997) *Aesthetic Theory*, trans. R. Hullot-Kentor (London: Athlone).

Adorno, Theodor W. and Max Horkheimer (1999) 'The Culture Industry: Enlightenment as Mass Deception', in Simon During (ed.), *The Cultural Studies Reader* (1993), expanded edn (London: Routledge, 1999).

Agacinski, Sylviane (1991) 'Another Experience of the Question, or Experiencing the Question Other-Wise', trans. Michael Syrotinski and Christine Laennec, in Eduardo Cadava, Peter Connor and Jean-Luc Nancy (eds), *Who Comes After the Subject?* (London: Routledge), pp. 9–23.

Alarcón, Norma (1990) 'The Theoretical Subject(s) of *This Bridge Called My Back* and Anglo-American Feminism', in Gloria Anzaldúa (ed.), *Making Face Making Soul/Haciendo Caras: Creative and Critical Perspectives by Women of Color* (San Francisco, CA: Aunt Lute), pp. 356–69.

Althusser, Louis (1971) *Lenin and Philosophy and Other Essays*, trans. Ben Brewster (New York: Monthly Review Press).

Althusser, Louis (1977) *For Marx* (1965), trans. Ben Brewster (London: NLB).

Althusser, Louis (1994), 'Ideology and Ideological State Apparatuses (Notes towards an Investigation)' (1970), trans. Ben Brewster, in Slavoj Žižek (ed.), *Mapping Ideology* (London: Verso), pp. 100–40.

Althusser, Louis (1996) *Writings on Psychoanalysis: Freud and Lacan*, trans. Jeffrey Mehlman (New York: Columbia University Press).

Althusser, Louis, and Étienne Balibar (1970) *Reading Capital*, trans. Ben Brewster (London: NLB).

Anderson, Benedict (1991) *Imagined Communities* (London: Verso).

Anderson, Perry (1998) *The Origins of Postmodernism* (London: Verso).

Appiah, Kwame Anthony (1992) *In My Father's House: Africa in the Philosophy of Culture* (New York: Oxford University Press).

Arac, Jonathan (1979) *Commissioned Spirits: The Shaping of Social Motion in Dickens, Carlyle, Melville, and Hawthorne* (New Brunswick, NJ: Rutgers University Press).

Armour, Ellen T. (1999) *Deconstruction, Feminist Theology, and the Problem of Difference: Subverting the Race/Gender Divide* (Chicago, IL: University of Chicago Press).

Attridge, Derek (1988) *Peculiar Language: Literature as Difference, from the Renaissance to James Joyce* (Ithaca, NY: Cornell University Press).

Attridge, Derek (1995) 'Singularities, Responsibilities: Derrida, Deconstruction, and Literary Criticism', in Cathy Caruth and Deborah Esch (eds), *Critical Encounters: Reference and Responsibility in Deconstructive Writing* (New Brunswick, NJ: Rutgers University Press), pp. 106–26.

Attridge, Derek (2000a) 'Deconstruction and Fiction', in Nicholas Royle (ed.), *Deconstructions: A User's Guide* (London: Palgrave), pp. 105–18.

Attridge, Derek (2000b) 'Ghost Writing', in Martin McQuillan (ed.), *Deconstruction: A Reader* (Edinbrugh: Edinbrugh University Press), pp. 175–7.

Austin, J. L. (1999) *How to Do Things with Words*, 2nd edn, ed. J. O. Urmson and Marina Sbisà (Cambridge, MA: Harvard University Press).

Azim, Firdous (1993) *The Colonial Rise of the Novel* (London: Routledge).

Badiou, Alain (2001) *Ethics: An Essay on the Understanding of Evil*, trans. Peter Hallward (London: Verso).

Bakhtin, Mikhail, and P. N. Medvedev (1978). *The Formal Method in Literary Scholarship: A Critical Introduction to Sociological Poetics* (1928), trans. Albert J. Wehrle (Baltimore, MD: the Johns Hopkins University Press).

Bakhtin, Mikhail (1984) *Rabelais and His World*, trans. Hélène Iswolsky (Bloomington, IN: Indiana University Press).

Balibar, Étienne (1988) 'The Vacillation of Ideology', in. Cary Nelson and Lawrence Grossberg (eds), *Marxism and the Interpretation of Culture* (Urbana, IL: University of Illinois Press), pp. 159–210.

Balibar, Étienne (1994) 'Subjection and Subjectivation', in Joan Copjec, (ed.), *Supposing the Subject* (London: Verso), pp. 1–15.

Balibar, Étienne (1995a) 'Culture and Identity (Working Notes)', in John Rajchman (ed.), *The Identity in Question* (New York: Routledge).

Balibar, Étienne (1995b) *The Philosophy of Marx*, trans. Chris Turner (London: Verso).

Barilli, Renato (1993) *A Course in Aesthetics*, trans. Karen E. Pinkus (Minneapolis, MN: University of Minnesota Press).

Barrett, Michèle (1991), *The Politics of Truth: From Marx to Foucault* (Stanford, CA: Stanford University Press).

Barrett, Michèle (1992) 'Max Raphael and the Question of Aesthetics', in Stephen Regan (ed.), *The Politics of Pleasure: Aesthetics and Cultural Theory* (Buckingham: Open University Press), pp. 33–58.

Barrett, Michèle (1999) *Imagination in Theory: Culture, Writing, Words, and Things* (New York: New York University Press).

Barthes, Roland (1972) *Mythologies*, trans. Annette Lavers (New York: Hill and Wang).

Barthes, Roland (1972) *Roland Barthes by Roland Barthes*, trans. Richard Howard (Berkeley and Los Angeles, CA: University of California Press).

Barthes, Roland (1983) *On Racine*, trans. Richard Howard (New York: Octagon Books).

Batchen, Geoffrey (1997) *Burning with Desire: The Conception of Photography* (Cambridge, MA: MIT Press).

Baucom, Ian (1999) *Out of Place: Englishness, Empire, and the Locations of Identity* (Princeton, NJ: Princeton University Press).

Baudrillard, Jean (1981) *For a Critique of the Political Economy of the Sign*, trans. and Introduction by Charles Levin (St Louis, MO: Telos Press).

Baudrillard, Jean (1981) *Simulations* (New York: Semiotext(e)).

Baudrillard, Jean (1988) *Selected Writings*, ed. and Introduction by Mark Poster (Stanford, CA: Stanford University Press).

Beardsworth, Richard (1996) *Derrida and the Political* (London: Routledge).

Belsey, Catherine (1994) *Desire: Love Stories in Western Culture* (Oxford: Blackwell).

Benjamin, Andrew (1997) *Present Hope: Philosophy, Architecture, Judaism* (London: Routledge).

Bennington, Geoffrey (1993) 'Derridabase', in Geoffrey Bennington and Jacques Derrida, *Jacques Derrida*, trans. Geoffrey Bennington (Chicago, IL: University of Chicago Press), pp. 3–316.

Bennington, Geoffrey (1996) 'X', in John Brannigan, Ruth Robbins and, Julian Wolfreys (eds), *Applying: to Derrida* (Basingstoke: Macmillan), pp. 1–21.

Berger, Karol (2000) *A Theory of Art* (Oxford: Oxford University Press).

Bewes, Timothy (1997) *Cynicism and Postmodernity* (London: Verso).

Bhabha, Homi K. (1994) *The Location of Culture* (London: Routledge).

Bhaskar, Roy (1989) *Reclaiming Reality: A Critical Introduction to Contemporary Philosophy* (London: Verso).

Blanchot, Maurice (1982) *The Space of Literature*, trans. and Introduction by Ann Smock (Lincoln, NE: University of Nebraska Press).

Blanchot, Maurice (1993) *The Infinite Conversation*, trans. and Foreword by Susan Hanson (Minneapolis, MN: University of Minnesota Press).

Blanchot, Maurice (2001) *Faux Pas*, trans. Charlotte Mendell (Stanford, CA: Stanford University Press).

Booker, M. Keith (1991) *Techniques of Subversion in Modern Literature: Transgression, Abjection and the Carnivalesque* (Gainesville, FL: University Press of Florida).

Booth, Allyson (1996) *Postcards from the Trenches: Negotiating the Space between Modernism and the First World War* (Oxford: Oxford University Press).

Boothby, Richard (1991) *Death and Desire: Psychoanalytic Theory in Lacan's Return to Freud* (New York: Routledge).

Borch-Jacobsen, Mikkel (1991a) *Lacan: The Absolute Master*, trans Douglas Brick (Stanford, CA: Stanford University Press).

Borch-Jacobsen, Mikkel (1991b) 'The Freudian Subject, from Politics to Ethics', trans. Richard Miller, in Eduardo Cadava, Peter Connor and Jean-Luc Nancy (eds), *Who Comes After the Subject?* (London: Routledge), pp. 61–78.

Botting, Fred (1999) 'The Gothic Production of the Unconscious', in Glennis Byron and David Punter (eds), *Spectral Readings: Towards a Gothic Geography* (Basingstoke: Macmillan), pp. 11–36.

Bottomore, Tom, Laurence Harris, V. G. Kiernan and Ralph Miliband (eds) (1983) *A Dictionary of Marxist Thought* (Cambridge, MA: Harvard University Press).

Bourdieu, Pierre (1984) *Distinction: A Social Critique of the Judgement of Taste* (1979), trans. Richard Nice (Cambridge, MA: Harvard University Press).

Bourdieu, Pierre, and Terry Eagleton (1994) 'Doxa and Common Life: An Interview', in Slavoj Žižek (ed.), *Mapping Ideology* (London: Verso), pp. 265–77.

Bourdieu, Pierre (1996) *The Rules of Art: Genesis and Structure of the Literary Field*, trans. Susan Emanuel (Stanford, CA: Stanford University Press).

Braidotti, Rosi (1991) *Patterns of Dissonance: A Study of Women in Contemporary Philosophy*, trans. Elizabeth Guild (Oxford: Polity Press).

Brandt, Joan (1997) *Geopoetics: The Politics of Mimesis in Poststructuralist French Poetry and Theory* (Stanford, CA: Stanford University Press).

Brault, Pascale-Anne, and Michael Naas (2001) 'To Reckon with the Dead: Jacques Derrida's Politics of Mourning', in Jacques Derrida, *The Work of Mourning*, ed. Pascale-Anne Brault and Michael Naas (Chicago, IL: University of Chicago Press), pp. 1–30.

Bristow, Joseph (1995) *Effeminate England: Homoerotic Writing after 1885* (New York: Columbia University Press).

Brodsky Lacour, Claudia (1996) *Lines of Thought: Discourse, Architectonics, and the Origin of Modern Philosophy* (Durham, NC: Duke University Press).

Bronfen, Elisabeth (1992) *Over Her Dead Body: Death, Femininity, and the Aesthetic* (Manchester: Manchester University Press).

Burgin, Victor (1984) 'Man-Image-Desire', in Lisa Appignanesi (ed.), *ICA Documents 1: Desire* (London: ICA), pp. 32–34.

Butler, Judith (1990) *Gender Trouble: Feminism and the Subversion of Identity* (London: Routledge).

Butler, Judith (1992) 'Contingent Foundations: Feminism and the "Question of Postmodernism" ', in Judith Butler and Joan W. Scott (eds), *Feminists Theorize the Political* (New York: Routledge).

Butler, Judith (1993) *Bodies that Matter: On the Discursive Limits of 'Sex'* (London: Routledge).

Butler, Judith (1997a) *Excitable Speech: A Politics of the Performative* (London: Routledge).

Butler, Judith (1997b) *The Psychic Life of Power* (Stanford, CA: Stanford University Press).

Caputo, John (1997) 'Deconstruction in a Nutshell', in John Caputo (ed.), *Deconstruction in a Nutshell: A Conversation with Jacques Derrida* (New York: Fordham University Press), pp. 31–202.

Castle, Terry (1995) *The Female Thermometer: Eighteenth-Century Culture and the Invention of the Uncanny* (New York: Oxford University Press).

Chaitin, Gilbert D. (1996) *Rhetoric and Culture in Lacan* (Cambridge: Cambridge University Press).

Chambers, Iain (1990) *Border Dialogues: Journeys in Postmodernism* (London: Routledge).

Chambers, Ross (1999) *Loiterature* (Lincoln, NE: University of Nebraska Press).

Chanter, Tina (2001) *Time, Death, and the Feminine: Levinas with Heidegger* (Stanford, CA: Stanford University Press).

Cixous, Hélène (1993) *Three Steps on the Ladder of Writing*, trans. Sarah Cornell and Susan Sellers (New York: Columbia University Press).

Clark, Timothy (1992) *Derrida, Heidegger, Blanchot: Sources of Derrida's Notion and Practice of Literature* (Cambridge: Cambridge University Press).

Cohen, Tom (1985) *Ideology and Inscription: 'Cultural Studies' after Benjamin, De Man and Bakhtin* (Cambridge: Cambridge University Press).

Cohen, Tom (1994) *Anti-Mimesis: From Plato to Hitchcock* (Cambridge: Cambridge University Press).

Copjec, Joan (1994) *Read My Desire: Lacan against the Historicists* (Cambridge, MA: MIT Press).

Cornell, Drucilla (1992) *The Philosophy of the Limit* (New York: Routledge).

Creed, Barbara (1993) *The Monstrous–Feminine: Film, Feminism, Psychoanalysis* (London: Routledge).

Critchley, Simon (1999) *The Ethics of Deconstruction: Derrida and Levinas* (1992), 2nd edn (Edinburgh: Edinburgh University Press).

Currie, Mark (1998) *Postmodern Narrative Theory* (Basingstoke: Macmillan).

Curtius, Ernst (1953) *European Literature and the Latin Middle Ages* (New York: Pantheon Books).

Deleuze, Gilles (1988) *Foucault*, trans. and ed. Séan Hand, Foreword by Paul Bové (Minneapolis, MN: University of Minnesota Press).

Deleuze, Gilles (1990) *The Logic of Sense*, trans. Mark Lester, with Charles Stivale, ed. Constantin V. Boundas. (New York: Columbia University Press).

Deleuze, Gilles (1991) 'A Philosophical Concept . . .', in Eduardo Cadava, Peter Connor and Jean-Luc Nancy (eds), *Who Comes After the Subject?* (London: Routledge), pp. 94–5.

Deleuze, Gilles (1994) *Difference and Repetition*, trans. Paul Patton (London: Athlone Press).

Deleuze, Gilles, and Félix Guattari (1983) *Anti-Oedipus: Capitalism and Schizophrenia*, Preface by Michel Foucault, trans. Robert Hurley, Mark Seem and Helen R. Lane (Minneapolis, MN: University of Minnesota Press).

Deleuze, Gilles, and Félix Guattari (1994) *What is Philosophy?* trans. Graham Burchell and Hugh Tomlinson (London: Verso).

De Man, Paul (1986) *The Resistance to Theory*, Foreword by Wlad Godzich (Minneapolis, MN: University of Minnesota Press).

De Man, Paul (1996) *Aesthetic Ideology*, ed. and Introduction by Andrzej Warminski (Minneapolis, MN: University of Minnesota Press).

De Mul, Jos (1999) *Romantic Desire in (Post)modern Art and Philosophy*. (Albany, NY: State University of New York Press).

Derrida, Jacques (1973) *Speech and Phenomena: And Other Essays on Husserl's Theory of Signs*, trans. and Introduction by David B. Allison, Preface by Newton Garver (Evanston, IL: Northwestern University Press).

Derrida, Jacques (1981a) *Positions*, trans. Alan Bass (Chicago, IL: University of Chicago Press).

Derrida, Jacques (1981b) *Dissemination*, trans. Barbara Johnson (Chicago, IL: University of Chicago Press).

Derrida, Jacques (1982) *Margins of Philosophy*, trans., with notes by Alan Bass (Chicago, IL: University of Chicago Press).

Derrida, Jacques (1984) 'Deconstruction and the Other', trans. Richard Kearney, in Richard Kearney (ed.), *Dialogues with Contemporary*

Thinkers: The Phenomenological Heritage (Manchester: Manchester University Press), pp. 107–26.

Derrida, Jacques (1985) 'Letter to a Japanese Friend', trans. David Wood and Andrew Benjamin, in David Wood and Robert Bernasconi, (eds), *Derrida and Différance* (Coventry: Parousia Press), pp. 1–6.

Derrida, Jacques (1986) 'Point de folie – maintenant l'architecture', trans. Kate Linker, in Bernard Tschumi, *La Case Vide: La Villette 1985*, inc. essays by Jacques Derrida and Anthony Vidler, Interview by Alvin Boyarsky (London: Architectural Association), pp. 4–19.

Derrida, Jacques (1987) *Living on • Borderlines*, trans. James Hulbert. In Harold Bloom et al., *Deconstruction and Criticism* (New York: Continuum Books), pp. 75–176.

Derrida, Jacques (1988a) 'Limited Inc a b c . . .', trans. Samuel Weber, *Glyph* 2 (1977), rpt. in *Limited Inc.*, trans. Samuel Weber and Jeffrey Mehlman (Evanston, IL: Northwestern University Press), pp. 29–110.

Derrida, Jacques (1988b) 'Roundtable on Translation', in Jacques Derrida, *The Ear of the Other: Otobiography, Transference, Translation*, ed. Christie McDonald, trans. Peggy Kamuf (Lincoln, NE: University of Nebraska Press), pp. 93–162.

Derrida, Jacques (1989) 'Psyche: Inventions of the Other', trans. Catherine Porter, in Lindsay Waters and Wlad Godzich (eds), *Reading de Man Reading* (Minneapolis, MN: University of Minnesota Press), pp. 25–65.

Derrida, Jacques (1991) ' "Eating Well", or the Calculation of the Subject: An Interview with Jacques Derrida', trans. Peter Connor and Avital Ronell, in Eduardo Cadava, Peter Connor and Jean-Luc Nancy (eds), *Who Comes After the Subject?* (London: Routledge).

Derrida, Jacques (1992a) ' "This Strange Institution Called Literature": An Interview with Jacques Derrida', trans. Geoffrey Bennington and Rachel Bowlby, in Jacques Derrida, *Acts of Literature*, ed. Derek Attridge (London: Routledge), pp. 33–75.

Derrida, Jacques (1992b) 'Passions: "An Oblique Offering" ', trans. David Wood, in David Wood (ed.), *Derrida: A Critical Reader* (Oxford: Blackwell), pp. 5–35.

Derrida, Jacques (1993) *Aporias*, trans. Thomas Dutoit (Stanford, CA: Stanford University Press).

Derrida, Jacques (1995) *Khōra*, in Jacques Derrida, *On the Name*, ed. Thomas Dutoit, trans. David Wood, John P. Leavey, Jr and Ian McLeod (Stanford, CA: Stanford University Press), pp. 89–130.

Derrida, Jacques (1996) ' "As if I were dead": An Interview with Jacques Derrida', in John Brannigan, Ruth Robbins and Julian Wolfreys (eds), *Applying: to Derrida* (Basingstoke: Macmillan), pp. 212–27.

Derrida, Jacques (1997) *Politics of Friendship*, trans. George Collins (London: Verso).

Derrida, Jacques (2000a) 'Demeure: Fiction and Testimony', in Maurice Blanchot, *The Instant of My Death*, and Jacques Derrida, *Demeure*, trans. Elizabeth Rottenberg (Stanford, CA: Stanford University Press), pp. 33–104.

Derrida, Jacques (2000b) 'Et Cetera', trans. Geoffrey Bennington, in Nicholas Royle (ed.), *Deconstructions: A User's Guide* (Basingstoke: Palgrave), pp. 282–305.

Derrida, Jacques (2001) 'Deconstructions: The Im-possible', trans. Michael Taormina, in Sylvère Lotringer and Sande Cohen (eds), *French Theory in America* (London: Routledge), pp. 13–32.

Deutscher, Penelope (1997) *Yielding Gender: Feminism, Deconstruction, and the History of Philosophy* (London: Routledge).

Doane, Mary Ann (1991) *Femmes Fatales: Feminism, Film Theory, Psychoanalysis* (London: Routledge).

Docherty, Thomas (1990) *After Theory: Post Modernism/Post Marxism* (London: Routledge).

Docherty, Thomas (1993) *Postmodernism: A Reader* (New York: Columbia University Press).

Dollimore, Jonathan, and Alan Sinfield (1985) 'Foreword: Cultural Materialism', in Jonathan Dollimore and Alan Sinfield (eds), *Political Shakespeare: New Essays in Cultural Materialism* (Manchester: Manchester University Press), pp. vii–viii.

Dollimore, Jonathan (1991) *Sexual Dissidence: Augustine to Wilde, Freud to Foucault* (Oxford: Oxford University Press).

Durham, Scott (1998) *Phantom Communities: The Simulacrum and the Limits of Postmodernism* (Stanford, CA: Stanford University Press.

Düttman, Alexander García (2000) *Between Cultures: Tensions in the Struggle for Recognition*, trans. Kenneth B. Woodgate (London: Verso).

Dyer, Richard (1997) *White* (London: Routledge).

Eagleton, Terry (1976) *Marxism and Literary Criticism* (Berkeley and Los Angeles, CA: University of California Press).

Eagleton, Terry (1981) *Walter Benjamin, or Towards a Revolutionary Criticism* (London: Verso).

Eagleton, Terry (1990) *The Ideology of the Aesthetic* (Oxford: Blackwell).

Eagleton, Terry (1991) *Ideology: an Introduction* (London: Verso).

Eagleton, Terry (1996) *The Illusions of Postmodernism* (Oxford: Blackwell).

Ebert, Teresa L. (1996) *Ludic Feminism and After: Postmodernism, Desire, and Labor in Late Capitalism* (Ann Arbor, MI: The University of Michigan Press).

Elam, Diane (1994) *Feminism and Deconstruction: Ms. en Abyme* (London: Routledge).

Elliot, Anthony (1996) *Subject to Ourselves: Social Theory, Psychoanalysis, and Postmodernity* (Cambridge: Polity Press).

Evans, Dylan (1996) *An Introductory Dictionary of Lacanian Psychoanalysis* (London: Routledge).

Fanon, Frantz (1986) *Black Skin, White Masks*, Introduction by Homi K. Bhabha (London: Pluto Press).

Felman, Shoshana (1987) *Jacques Lacan and the Adventure of Insight: Psychoanalysis in Contemporary Culture* (Cambridge, MA: Harvard University Press).

Felman, Shoshana (1993) *What Does a Woman Want? Reading and Sexual Difference* (Baltimore, MD: Johns Hopkins University Press).

Fontana, Benedetto (1993) *Hegemony and Power: On the Relation between Gramsci and Machiavelli* (Minneapolis, MN: University of Minnesota Press).

Forgacs, David, and Geoffrey Nowell-Smith (1985) 'Introduction', in Antonio Gramsci, *Selections from Cultural Writings*, ed. David Forgacs and Geoffrey Nowell-Smith, trans. William Boelhower (London: Lawrence and Wishart), pp. 1–15.

Forrester, John (1990) *The Seductions of Psychoanalysis: Freud, Lacan and Derrida* (Cambridge: Cambridge University Press).

Foucault, Michel (1972) *The Archaeology of Knowledge and the Discourse on Language*, trans. A. M. Sheridan Smith (New York: Pantheon Books).

Foucault, Michel (1973) *The Order of Things: An Archaeology of the Human Sciences* (New York: Vintage Books).

Foucault, Michel (1980) *Power/Knowledge: Selected Interviews and Other Writings, 1972–1977*, ed. Colin Gordon (Brighton: Harvester Press).

Foucault, Michel (1990) *The History of Sexuality, Volume I: An Introduction*, trans. Robert Hurley (London: Penguin).

Foucault, Michel (1997) 'Self Writing', trans. Paul Rabinow, in *Ethics: The Essential Works, Volume 1*, ed. Paul Rabinow (London: Penguin), pp. 207–22.

Foucault, Michel (1998) 'On the Archaeology of the Sciences: Response to the Epistemology Circle', in *Aesthetics, Method, and Epistemology. Essential Works of Foucault, 1954–1984, Volume 2*, ed. James D. Faubion (New York: The New Press), pp. 297–334.

Foucault, Michel (1999a) 'Sexuality and Power', trans. Richard A. Lynch, in Michel Foucault, *Religion and Culture*, ed. Jeremy R. Carrette (London: Routledge), pp. 115–30.

Foucault, Michel (1999b) 'Is it Useless to Revolt?' trans. James Bernauer, in Michel Foucault, *Religion and Culture*, ed. Jeremy R. Carrette (London: Routledge), pp. 131–33.

Foucault, Michel (1999c) 'Pastoral Power and Political Reason', in Michel Foucault, *Religion and Culture*, ed. Jeremy R. Carrette (London: Routledge), pp. 135–52.

Foucault, Michel (1999d) 'About the Beginning of the Hermeneutics of the Self', transcription Thomas Keenan and Mark Blasius, in Michel Foucault, *Religion and Culture*, ed. Jeremy R. Carrette (London: Routledge) pp. 158–81.

Freud, Sigmund (1973) *New Introductory Lectures on Psychoanalysis*, Penguin Freud Library, Volume 2, trans. James Strachey, ed. Angela Richards (Harmondsworth: Penguin).

Freud, Sigmund (1976) *The Interpretation of Dreams*, Penguin Freud Library, Volume 4. trans. James Strachey, ed. Angela Richards (Harmondsworth: Penguin).

Freud, Sigmund (1982) *Introductory Lectures on Psychoanalysis*, Penguin Freud Library, Volume 1, trans. James Strachey, ed. Angela Richards (Harmondsworth: Penguin).

Freud, Sigmund (1991) 'Fetishism', in Sigmund Freud, *On Sexuality: Three Essays on the Theory of Sexuality and Other Works*, Penguin Freud Library, Volume 7, trans. James Strachey, ed. Angela Richards (Harmondsworth: Penguin).

Freud, Sigmund (1997) 'The "Uncanny" ', trans. James Strachey, in Sigmund Freud, *Writings on Literature and Art*, Foreword by Neil Hertz (Stanford, CA: Stanford University Press), pp. 193–233.

Friedman, Alan Warren (1995) *Fictional Death and the Modernist Enterprise* (Cambridge: Cambridge University Press).

Frow, John (1986) *Marxism and Literary History* (Cambridge, MA: Harvard University Press).

Frow, John (1990) 'Intertextuality and Ontology', in Michael Worton and Judith Still (eds), *Intertextuality: Theories and Practice* (Manchester: Manchester University Press).

Gagnier, Regenia (1991) *Subjectivities: A History of Self-Representation in Britain, 1832–1920* (New York: Oxford University Press).

Gallop, Jane (1984) *The Daughter's Seduction: Feminism and Psychoanalysis* (Ithaca, NY: Cornell University Press).

Gane, Mike (1991) *Baudrillard's Bestiary: Baudrillard and Culture* (London: Routledge).

Gasché, Rodolphe (1986) *The Tain of the Mirror: Derrida and the Philosophy of Reflection* (Cambridge, MA: Harvard University Press).

Gates, Henry Louis (1990) *The Signifying Monkey: A Theory of Afro-American Literary Criticism* (Oxford: Oxford University Press).

Genette, Gérard (1980) *Narrative Discourse: An Essay in Method*, trans. Jane. E. Lewin, Foreword by Jonathan Culler (Ithaca, NY: Cornell University Press).

Geyer-Ryan, Helga (1994) *Fables of Desire: Studies in the Ethics of Art and Gender* (Cambridge: Polity Press).

Gillis, Stacy (2002) 'Cybercriticism', in Julian Wolfreys (ed.), *Introducing Criticism at the 21st Century* (Edinburgh: Edinburgh University Press), pp. 202–16.

Glendinning, Simon (1998) *On Being with Others: Heidegger–Derrida–Wittgenstein* (London: Routledge).

Glover, David, and Cora Kaplan (eds) (2000) *Genders* (London: Routledge).

Gooding-Williams, Robert (2001) *Zarathustra's Dionysian Modernism* (Stanford, CA: Stanford University Press).

Gordon, Avery F. (1997) *Ghostly Matters: Haunting and the Sociological Imagination* (Minneapolis, MN: University of Minnesota Press).

Goux, Jean-Joseph (1993) *Oedipus, Philosopher*, trans. Catherine Porter (Stanford, CA Stanford University Press).

Gramsci, Antonio (1971) *Selections from the Prison Notebooks*, ed. and trans. Quintin Hoare and Geoffrey Nowell Smith (London: Lawrence and Wishart).

Gramsci, Antonio (1985) *Selections from Cultural Writings*, ed. David Forgacs and Geoffrey Nowell Smith, trans. William Boelhower (Cambridge, MA: Harvard University Press).

Gramsci, Antonio (1988) *An Antonio Gramsci Reader: Selected Writings, 1916–1935*, ed. David Forgacs (London: Lawrence and Wishart).

Gregson, Ian (1996) *Contemporary Poetry and Postmodernism: Dialogue and Estrangement* (Basingstoke: Macmillan).

Grosz, Elizabeth (1994) *Volatile Bodies: Toward a Corporeal Feminism* (Bloomington, IN: Indiana University Press).

Hall, Catherine (1992) *White, Male and Middle Class: Explorations in Feminism and History* (Cambridge: Polity).

Hall, Stuart (1988) *The Hard Road to Renewal: Thatcherism and the Crisis of the Left* (London: Verso).

Hamacher, Werner (1998) *Pleroma: Reading in Hegel*, trans. Nicholas Walker and Simon Jarvis (Stanford, CA: Stanford University Press).

Hardt, Michael, and Antonio Negri (2000) *Empire* (Cambridge, MA: Harvard University Press).

Harper, Phillip Brian, E. Francis White and Margaret Cerullo (1993) 'Multi/Queer/Culture', *Radical America*, 24:4.

Hartman, Geoffrey H. (1979) 'Preface', in Harold Bloom, Paul de Man, Jacques Derrida, Geoffrey H. Hartman and J. Hillis Miller, *Deconstruction and Criticism* (New York: Continuum Books).

Hartman, Geoffrey H. (1997) *The Fateful Question of Culture* (New York: Columbia University Press).

Haslett, Moyra (2000) *Marxist Literary and Cultural Theories* (Basingstoke: Macmillan).

Hayles, N. Katherine (1997) 'The Condition of Virtuality', in Jeffrey Masten, Peter Stallybrass and Nancy J. Vickers (eds), *Language Machines: Technologies of Literary and Cultural Production* (New York: Routledge), pp. 183–208.

Heidegger, Martin (1962) *Being and Time*, trans. John Macquarrie and Edward Robinson (New York: Harper and Row).

Heidegger, Martin (1992) *History of the Concept of Time: Prolegomena*, trans. Theodore Kisiel (Bloomington, IN: Indiana University Press).

Hennessy, Rosemary (1993) *Materialist Feminism and the Politics of Discourse* (New York: Routledge).

Henry, Michel (1993) *The Genealogy of Psychoanalysis*, trans. Douglas Brick (Stanford, CA: Stanford University Press).

Hutcheon, Linda (1989) *The Politics of Postmodernism* (London: Routledge).

Holub, Renate (1992) *Antonio Gramsci: Beyond Marxism and Postmodernism* (London: Routledge).

Howells, Christina (1999) *Derrida: Deconstruction from Phenomenology to Ethics.* (Cambridge: Polity Press).

Huyssen, Andreas (1986) *After the Great Divide: Modernism, Mass Culture, Postmodernism.* (Bloomington, IN: Indiana University Press).

Hyppolite, Jean (1997) *Logic and Existence*, trans. Leonard Lawlor and Amit Sen (Albany, NY: State University of New York Press).

Irigaray, Luce (1985) ' "Woman's" *Jouissance*', in *Speculum of the Other Woman*, trans. Gillian C. Gill (Ithaca, NY: Cornell University Press), pp. 353–64.

Irigaray, Luce (1991a) 'The Bodily Encounter with the Mother'. In Margaret Whitford (ed.), *The Irigaray Reader* (Oxford: Blackwell), pp. 34–46.

Irigaray, Luce (1991b) 'Women-mothers, the Silent Substratum of the Social Order', in Margaret Whitford (ed.), *The Irigaray Reader* (Oxford: Blackwell), pp. 47–52

Irigaray, Luce (1991c) 'Women-Amongst-Themselves: Creating a Woman-to-Woman Sociality', in Margaret Whitford (ed.), *The Irigaray Reader* (Oxford: Blackwell), pp. 190–7.

Irigaray, Luce (1993) *An Ethics of Sexual Difference*, trans. Carolyn Burke and Gillian C. Gill (Ithaca, NY: Cornell University Press).

Jacobs, Jane M. (1996) *Edge of Empire: Postcolonialism and the City* (London: Routledge).

Jagose, Annamarie (1996) *Queer Theory: An Introduction* (New York: Routledge).

Jay, Martin (1994) *Downcast Eyes: The Denigration of Vision in Twentieth-Century French Thought* (Berkeley and Los Angeles, CA: University of California Press).

Jameson, Fredric (1981) *The Political Unconscious: Narrative as Socially Symbolic Act* (Ithaca, NY: Cornell University Press).

Jameson, Fredric (1991) *Postmodernism or, the Cultural Logic of Late Capitalism* (London: Verso).

Joyce, James (1993) *Ulysses* (1922, 1984), ed. Hans Walter Gabler (London: Bodley Head).

Kamps, Ivo (1995) 'Materialist Shakespeare: An Introduction', in Ivo Kamps (ed.), *Materialist Shakespeare: A History*, Afterword by Fredric Jameson (London: Verso), pp. 1–19.

Kamuf, Peggy (1991) 'Introduction: Reading Between the Blinds', in Jacques Derrida, *A Derrida Reader: Between the Blinds*, ed. Peggy Kamuf (New York: Columbia University Press), pp. xii–xlii.

Kamuf, Peggy (1997) *The Division | of Literature or the University in Deconstruction* (Chicago, IL: University of Chicago Press).

Kamuf, Peggy (2000) 'Deconstruction and Love', in Nicholas Royle (ed.), *Deconstructions: A User's Guide* (London: Palgrave), pp. 151–70.

Kant, Immanuel (1952) *The Critique of Judgement*, trans. James Creed Meredith (Oxford: Oxford University Press).

Kant, Immanuel (1997) *Prolegomena to Any Future Metaphysics That Will Be Able to Come Forward as Science, with Selections from the* Critique of Pure Reason, trans. and ed. Gary Hatfield (Cambridge: Cambridge University Press).

Kelly, Michael (1982) *Modern French Marxism* (Baltimore, MD: Johns Hopkins University Press).

Keenan, Thomas (1997) *Fables of Responsibility: Aberrations and Predicaments in Ethics and Politics* (Stanford, CA: Stanford University Press).

Kincaid, James R. (1992) *Child-Loving: The Erotic Child and Victorian Culture* (London: Routledge).

King, Nicola (2000) *Memory, Narrative, Identity: Remembering the Self* (Edinburgh: Edinburgh University Press).

Kofman, Sarah (1993) *Nietzsche and Metaphor*, trans. Duncan Large (London: Athlone Press).

Kolocotroni, Vassiliki, Jane Goldman and Olga Taxidou (1998) 'Introduction', in *Modernism: An Anthology of Sources and Documents* (Edinburgh: Edinburgh University Press), pp. xvii–xx.

Kristeva, Julia (1980) *Desire in Language: A Semiotic Approach to Literature and Art*, ed. Leon S. Roudiez, trans. Thomas Gora, Alice Jardine and Leon S. Roudiez (New York: Columbia University Press).

Kristeva, Julia (1982) *Powers of Horror: An Essay on Abjection*, trans. Leon S. Roudiez (New York: Columbia University Press).

Kristeva, Julia (1984) *Revolution in Poetic Language*, trans. Margaret

Waller, Introduction by Leon S. Roudiez (New York: Columbia University Press).

Kristeva, Julia (1986) 'From Symbol to Sign', trans. Seán Hand, in Toril Moi (ed.), *The Kristeva Reader* (Oxford: Blackwell), pp. 62–73.

Kristeva, Julia (1998) 'The Subject in Process', trans. Patrick ffrench, in Patrick ffrench and Roland-François Lack (eds), *The Tel Quel Reader* (London: Routledge, 1998. 133–78.

Kronick, Joseph G. (1997) *Derrida and the Future of Literature* (Albany, NY: State University of New York Press).

Lacan, Jacques (1967) 'Psychanalyse et médicine', *Lettres de l'École freudienne* 1.

Lacan, Jacques (1977) *Écrits: A Selection*, trans. Alan Sheridan (New York: W. W. Norton).

Lacan, Jacques (1988) *The Seminar of Jacques Lacan, Book II: The Ego in Freud's Theory and in the Technique of Psychoanalysis, 1954–1955*, ed. Jacques-Alain Miller, trans. Sylvana Tomaselli, notes by John Forrester (New York: Norton).

Lacan, Jacques (1991) *The Seminar of Jacques Lacan, Book I: Freud's Papers on Technique, 1953–1954*, ed. Jacques-Alain Miller, trans. John Forrester (New York: Norton).

Lacan, Jacques (1992) 'The *Jouissance* of Transgression', in *The Ethics of Psychoanalysis, 1959–60: The Seminar of Jacques Lacan, Book VII*, ed. Jacques-Alain Miller, trans. Dennis Porter (London: Routledge), pp. 191–204.

Lacan, Jacques (1993) *The Psychoses: The Seminar of Jacques Lacan, Book III: 1955–1956*, trans. and annotated by Russell Grigg (London: Routledge).

Lacan, Jacques (1994) *The Four Fundamental Concepts of Psycho-Analysis* (1973), ed. Jacques-Alain Miller, trans. Alan Sheridan, Introduction by David Macey (London: Penguin).

Lacan, Jacques (1998) *The Seminar: On Feminine Sexuality*, in *The Limits of Love and Knowledge, Book XX: Encore, 1972–73*, ed. Jacques-Alain Miller, trans. Bruce Fink (New York: W.W. Norton).

Laclau, Ernesto (1977) *Politics and Ideology in Marxist Theory: Capitalism–Fascism–Populism* (London: Verso).

Laclau, Ernesto, and Chantal Mouffe (1985) *Hegemony and Socialist Strategy: Towards a Radical Democratic Politics* (London: Verso).

Laclau, Ernesto (2000) 'Identity and Hegemony: The Role of Universality in the Constitution of Political Logics', in Judith Butler, Ernesto Laclau and Slavoj Žizěk, *Contingency, Hegemony, Universality: Contemporary Dialogues on the Left* (London: Verso), pp. 44–89.

Lacoue-Labarthe, Philippe (1994) *Musica Ficta: Figures of Wagner*, trans. Felicia McCarren (Stanford, CA: Stanford University Press).

Lamos, Colleen (1998) *Deviant Modernism: Sexual and Textual Errancy in T. S. Eliot, James Joyce, and Marcel Proust* (Cambridge: Cambridge University Press).

Larrain, Jorge (1996) 'Stuart Hall and the Marxist Concept of Ideology', in David Morley and Kuan-Hsing Chen (eds), *Stuart Hall: Critical Dialogues in Cultural Studies* (London: Routledge), pp. 41–70.

Larsen, Neil (1990) *Modernism and Hegemony: A Materialist Critique of Aesthetic Agencies*, Foreword by Jaime Concha (Minneapolis, MN: University of Minnesota Press).

Lauretis, Teresa de (1987) *Technologies of Gender: Essays on Theory, Film, and Fiction* (Basingstoke: Macmillan).

Layton-Henry, Zig, and Paul Rich (1986) 'Introduction', in Zig Layton-Henry and Paul Rich (eds), *Race, Government and Politics in Britain* (Basingstoke: Macmillan), pp. 1–16

Leclaire, Serge (1998a) *Psychoanalyzing: On the Order of the Unconscious and the Practice of the Letter*, trans. Peggy Kamuf (Stanford, CA: Stanford University Press).

Leclaire, Serge (1998b) *A Child is Being Killed: On Primary Narcissism and the Death Drive*, trans. Maric Claudc Hays (Stanford, CA: Stanford University Press).

Levinas, Emmanuel (1987) *Time and the Other*, trans. Richard A. Cohen (Pittsburgh, PA: Duquesne University Press).

Lorraine, Tamsin (1999) *Irigaray and Deleuze: Experiments in Visceral Philosophy* (Ithaca, NY: Cornell University Press).

Luckhurst, Roger (1995) 'Queer Theory (And Oscar Wilde): Review Essay', *Journal of Gender Studies*, 4:3.

Lyotard, Jean-François (1984) *The Postmodern Condition: A Report on Knowledge*, trans. Geoff Bennington and Brian Massumi, Foreword by Fredric Jameson (Minneapolis, MN: University of Minnesota Press).

Lyotard, Jean-François (1989a) 'Figure Foreclosed', trans. David Macey, in Andrew Benjamin (ed.), *The Lyotard Reader* (Oxford: Basil Blackwell), pp. 69–110.

Lyotard, Jean-François (1989b) 'Universal History and Cultural Differences', trans. David Macey, in Andrew Benjamin (ed.), *The Lyotard Reader* (Oxford: Basil Blackwell) pp. 314–23.

Lyotard, Jean-François (1993a) *The Postmodern Explained: Correspondence, 1982–1985*, trans. Don Barry et al., Afterword by Wlad Godzich (Minneapolis, MN: University of Minnesota Press).

Lyotard, Jean-François (1993b) *Toward the Postmodern*, ed. Robert Harvey and Mark S. Roberts (Atlantic Highlands, NJ: Humanities Press).

Lyotard, Jean-François (1994) *Lessons on the Analytic of the Sublime*, trans. Elizabeth Rottenberg (Stanford, CA: Stanford University Press).

MacCabe, Colin (1985) *Tracking the Signifier: Theoretical Essays: Film, Linguistics, Literature* (Minneapolis, MN: University of Minnesota Press).

MacCannell, Juliet Flower (1994) 'Things to Come: A Hysteric's Guide to the Future Female Subject', in Joan Copjec (ed.), *Supposing the Subject* (London: Verso), pp. 106–33.

Majumdar, Margaret A. (1995) *Althusser and the End of Leninism?* (London: Pluto Press).

Mansfield, Nick (2000) *Subjectivity: Theories of the Self from Freud to Haraway* (St Leonards, NSW: Allen Unwin).

Martin, Bill (1995) *Humanism and its Aftermath: The Shared Fate of Deconstruction and Politics* (Atlantic Highlands, NJ: Humanities Press).

Marx, Karl, and Friedrich Engels (1970) *The German Ideology*, ed. and Introduction by C. J. Arthur (London: Lawrence and Wishart).

McCance, Dawne (1996) *Posts: Re-Addressing the Ethical* (Albany, NY: State University of New York Press).

McAfee, Noëlle (1993) 'Abject Strangers: Toward an Ethics of Respect', in Kelly Oliver (ed.), *Ethics, Politics, and Difference in Julia Kristeva's Writing* (New York: Routledge), pp. 116–34.

Metz, Christian (1974) *Film Language: A Semiotics of the Cinema*, trans. Michael Taylor (New York: Oxford University Press).

Miliband, Ralph (1986) *Marxism and Politics* (Oxford: Oxford University Press).

Miller, Jacques-Alain (1995) 'Context and Concepts', in Richard Feldstein, Bruce Fink and Maire Jaanus (eds), *Reading Seminar XI: Lacan's Four Fundamental Concepts of Psychoanalysis* (Albany, NY: State University of New York Press) pp. 3–15.

Miller, J. Hillis (1987) *The Ethics of Reading: Kant, de Man, Eliot, Trollope, James, and Benjamin* (New York: Columbia University Press).

Miller, J. Hillis (1991a) *Theory Now and Then* (Hemel Hempstead: Harvester).

Miller, J. Hillis (1991b) *Hawthorne and History: Defacing It* (Oxford: Basil Blackwell).

Miller, J. Hillis (1995) *Topographies* (Stanford, CA: Stanford University Press).

Miller, J. Hillis (1998) *Reading Narrative* (Norman, OK: University of Oklahoma Press).

Miller, J. Hillis (2001) *Speech Acts in Literature* (Stanford, CA: Stanford University Press).

Miller, Tyrus (1999) *Late Modernism: Politics, Fiction, and the Arts Between the World Wars* (Berkeley, CA: University of California Press).

Morris, Pam (1994) 'Introduction', in Pam Morris (ed.), *The Bakhtin Reader: Selected Readings of Bakhtin, Medvedev, Voloshinov* (London: Edward Arnold), pp. 1–24.

Morson, Gary Saul, and Caryl Emerson (1990) *Mikhail Bakhtin: Creation of a Prosaics* (Stanford, CA: Stanford University Press).

Moruzzi, Norma Claire (1993) 'National Abjects: Julia Kristeva on the Process of Political Self-Identification', in Kelly Oliver (ed.), *Ethics, Politics, and Difference in Julia Kristeva's Writing* (New York: Routledge), pp. 135–49.

Mulvey, Laura (1984) 'The Image and Desire', in Lisa Appignanesi (ed.), *ICA Documents, 1: Desire* (London: ICA), pp. 28–30.

Nägele, Rainer (1997) *Echoes of Translation: Reading Between Texts* (Baltimore, MD: Johns Hopkins University Press).

Nancy, Jean-Luc (1993a) *The Birth to Presence*, trans. Brian Holmes et al. (Stanford, CA: Stanford University Press).

Nancy, Jean-Luc (1993b) *The Experience of Freedom*, trans Bridget McDonald, Foreword by Peter Fenves (Stanford, CA: Stanford University Press).

Nash, Christopher (2001) *The Unravelling of the Postmodern Mind* (Edinburgh: Edinburgh University Press).

Nasio, Juan-David (1998) *Five Lessons on the Psychoanalytic Theory of Jacques Lacan*, trans. David Pettigrew and François Raffoul (Albany NY: State University of New York Press).

Norris, Christopher (1990) *What's Wrong with Postmodernism: Critical Theory and the Ends of Philosophy* (Baltimore, MD: Johns Hopkins University Press).

O'Driscoll, Sally (1996) 'Outlaw Readings: Beyond Queer Theory', *Signs: Journal of Women, Culture, and Society*, 22:1.

Ong, Walter J. (1982) *Orality and Literacy: The Technologizing of the Word* (London: Methuen).

Outlaw, Lucius (1996) ' "Conserve" Races? In Defense of W. E. B. Dubois', in Bernard W. Bell, Emily Grosholz and James B. Stewart (eds), *W. E. B. Dubois on Race and Culture: Philosophy, Politics, and Poetics* (New York: Routledge), pp. 15–37.

Patton, Paul (2000) *Deleuze and the Political* (London: Routledge).

Pellegrini, Ann (1997) *Performative Anxieties: Staging Psychoanalysis, Staging Race* (London: Routledge).

Pepper, Thomas (1997) *Singularities: Extremes of Theory in the Twentieth Century* (Cambridge: Cambridge University Press).

Plotnitsky, Arkady (2001a) 'Algebra and Allegory: Nonclassical Epistemology, Quantum Theory, and the Work of Paul de Man', in Tom Cohen, Barbara Cohen, J. Hillis Miller and Andrzej Warminski (eds), *Material Events: Paul de Man and the Afterlife of Theory* (Minneapolis, MN: University of Minnesota Press), pp. 49–89.

Plotnitsky, Arkady (2001b) 'Postmodernism and Postmodernity: Literature, Criticism, Philosophy, Culture', in Julian Wolfreys (ed.), *Introducing*

Literary Theories: A Guide and Glossary (Edinburgh: Edinburgh University Press), pp. 261–92.

Poovey, Mary (1989) *Uneven Developments: The Ideological Work of Gender in Mid-Victorian England* (Chicago, IL: University of Chicago Press).

Poster, Mark (1988) 'Introduction', in Jean Baudrillard, *Selected Writings*, ed. and Introduction by Mark Poster (Stanford, CA: Stanford University Press), pp. 1–9.

Poulantzas, Nicos (1973) *Political Power and Social Classes*, trans. Timothy O'Hagan, with David McLellan, Anna de Casparis and Brian Grogan (London: Sheed and Ward).

Rajan, Tilottama (1991) 'Intertextuality and the Subject of Reading/Writing', in Jay Clayton and Eric Rothstein (eds), *Influence and Intertextuality in Literary History* (Madison, WI: University of Wisconsin Press).

Rancière, Jacques (1999) *Disagreement: Politics and Philosophy*, trans. Julie Rose (Minneapolis, MN: University of Minnesota Press).

Redfield, Marc (1996) *Phantom Formations: Aesthetic Ideology and the Bildungsroman* (Ithaca, NY: Cornell University Press).

Riley, Denise (2000) *The Words of Selves: Identification, Solidarity, Irony* (Stanford, CA: Stanford University Press).

Rose, Jacqueline (1986) *Sexuality in the Field of Vision* (London: Verso).

Royle, Nicholas (1995) *After Derrida* (Manchester: Manchester University Press).

Russo, Mary (1994) *The Female Grotesque: Risk, Excess and Modernity* (New York: Routledge).

Said, Edward W. (1983) *The World, the Text, and the Critic* (Cambridge, MA: Harvard University Press).

Sass, Louis A. (1992) *Madness and Modernism: Insanity in the Light of Modern Art, Literature and Thought* (Cambridge, MA: Harvard University Press).

Schick, Irvin Cemil (1999) *The Erotic Margin: Sexuality and Spatiality in Alteritist Discourse* (London: Verso).

Schleifer, Ronald (2000) *Modernism and Time: The Logic of Abundance in Literature, Science, and Culture, 1880–1930* (Cambridge: Cambridge University Press).

Schulte-Sasse, Jochen (1984) 'Foreword: Theory of Modernism versus Theory of the Avant-Garde', in Peter Bürger, *Theory of the Avant-Garde*, trans. Michael Shaw (Minneapolis, MN: University of Minnesota Press).

Schwenger, Peter (1999) *Fantasm and Fiction: On Textual Envisioning* (Stanford, CA: Stanford University Press).

Sedgwick, Eve Kosofsky (1993) *Tendencies* (Durham, NC: Duke University Press).

Sedgwick, Eve Kosofsky (1999) 'Axiomatic', in Simon During (ed.), *The Cultural Studies Reader* (1993), expanded edn (London: Routledge).

Sheridan, Alan (1977) 'Translator's Note', in Jacques Lacan, *Écrits: A Selection* (New York: W. W. Norton), pp. vii–xii.

Simmonds, Felly Nkweto (1990) 'SHE'S GOTTA HAVE IT: The Representation of Black Female Sexuality on Film', in Terry Lovell (ed.), *British Feminist Thought: A Reader* (Oxford: Blackwell), pp. 314–24.

Simons, Jon (1995) *Foucault and the Political* (London: Routledge).

Sinfield, Alan (1989) *Literature, Politics, and Culture in Postwar Britain* (Berkeley, CA: University of California Press).

Sinfield, Alan (1994) *The Wilde Century: Effeminacy, Oscar Wilde and The Queer Moment* (London: Cassell).

Smith, Anna Marie (1994) *New Right Discourse on Race and Sexuality: Britain, 1968–1990* (Cambridge: Cambridge University Press).

Spivak, Gayatri Chakravorty (1996) 'Revolutions that As Yet Have No Model: Derrida's "Limited Inc." ', in Donna Landry and Gerald MacLean (eds), *The Spivak Reader: Selected Works of Gayatri Chakravorty Spivak* (London: Routledge), pp. 75–106.

Spivak, Gayatri Chakravorty (1999) *A Critique of Colonial Reason* (Cambridge, MA: Harvard University Press).

Spivak, Gayatri Chakravorty (2001) 'A Moral Dilemma', in Howard Marchitello (ed.), *What Happens to History: The Renewal of Ethics in Contemporary Thought* (New York: Routledge), pp. 215–36.

Stallybrass, Peter, and Allon White (1986) *The Politics and Poetics of Transgression* (Ithaca, NY: Cornell University Press).

Staten, Henry (1995) *Eros in Mourning: Homer to Lacan* (Baltimore, MD: Johns Hopkins University Press).

Stoller, Robert J. (1968) *Sex and Gender: On the Development of Masculinity and Femininity* (London: Hogarth Press).

Tagg, John (1988) *The Burden of Representation: Essays on Photographies and Histories* (London: Macmillan).

Taussig, Michael (1993) *Mimesis and Alterity: A Particular History of the Senses* (London: Routledge).

Thompson, E. P. (1968) *The Making of the English Working Class* (London: Penguin).

Tschumi, Bernard (1994a) *Architecture and Disjunction* (Cambridge, MA: MIT Press).

Tschumi, Bernard (1994b) *Event-Cities: Praxis* (Cambridge, MA: MIT Press).

Varadharajan, Asha (1995) *Exotic Parodies: Subjectivity in Adorno, Said, and Spivak* (Minneapolis, MN: University of Minnesota Press).

Vattimo, Gianni (1988) *The End of Modernity: Nihilism and Hermeneutics in Postmodern Culture*, trans. and introduction by Jon R. Snyder (Baltimore, MD: Johns Hopkins University Press).

Vernant, Jean-Pierre (1980) *Myth and Society in Ancient Greece*, trans. Janet Lloyd (Brighton: Harvester Press).

Walters, Suzanne Danuta (1996) 'From Here to Queer: Radical Feminism, Postmodernism, and the Lesbian Menace (Or, Why Can't a Woman Be More Like a Fag?)', *Signs: Journal of Women, Culture, and Society*, 21:4.

Warminski, Andrzej (1996) 'Introduction: Allegories of Reference', in Paul de Man, *Aesthetic Ideology* (Minneapolis, MN: University of Minnesota Press), pp. 1–33.

Warminski, Andrzej (1999) 'Monstrous History: Heidegger Reading Hölderlin', in Aris Fioretos (ed.), *The Solid Letter: Readings of Friedrich Hölderlin* (Stanford, CA: Stanford University Press), pp. 201–14.

Warner, Michael (ed.) (1993) *Fear of a Queer Planet: Queer Politics and Social Theory* (Minneapolis, MN: University of Minnesota Press).

Weber, Samuel (1991) *Return to Freud: Jacques Lacan's Dislocation of Psychoanalysis* (1990) (Cambridge: Cambridge University Press).

Weber, Samuel (1996) *Mass Mediauras: Form Technics Media* (Stanford, CA: Stanford University Press).

Welsch, Wolfgang (1997) *Undoing Aesthetics*, trans. Andrew Inkpin (London: Sage).

West, Cornel (1999) 'The New Cultural Politics of Difference', in Simon During (ed.), *The Cultural Studies Reader* (1993), expanded edn. (London: Routledge).

West, David (1996) *An Introduction to Continental Philosophy* (Cambridge: Polity Press).

Wilden, Anthony (1981) 'Lacan and the Discourse of the Other', in Jacques Lacan, *Speech and Language in Psychoanalysis,* trans. Anthony Wilden (Baltimore, MD: Johns Hopkins University Press), pp. 159–311.

Williams, Linda Ruth (1995) *Critical Desire: Psychoanalysis and the Literary Subject* (London: Edward Arnold).

Williams, Raymond (1961) *Culture and Society, 1780–1950* (Harmondsworth: Penguin).

Williams, Raymond (1968) 'Culture and Revolution: A Comment', in Terry Eagleton and B. Wicker (eds), *From Culture to Revolution* (London: Sheed and Ward), pp. 22–34.

Williams, Raymond (1977) *Marxism and Literature* (Oxford: Oxford University Press).

Winter, Sarah (1999) *Freud and the Institution of Psychoanalytic Knowledge* (Stanford, CA: Stanford University Press).

Wood, Ellen Meiksins (1986) *The Retreat from Class: A New 'True' Socialism* (London: Verso).

Worsham, Lynn, and Gary A. Olson (1999) 'Hegemony and the Future of Democracy: Ernesto Laclau's Political Philosophy', in Gary A. Olson and

Lynn Worsham (eds), *Race, Rhetoric and the Postcolonial* (Albany, NY: State University of New York Press).

Worton, Michael, and Judith Still (1990) 'Introduction', in Michael Worton and Judith Still (eds), *Intertextuality: Theories and Practice* (Manchester: Manchester University Press).

Žižek, Slavoj (1989) *The Sublime Object of Ideology* (London: Verso).

Žižek, Slavoj (1991) *For They Know Not What They Do: Enjoyment as a Political Factor* (London: Verso).

Žižek, Slavoj (1993) *Tarrying with the Negative: Kant, Hegel, and the Critique of Ideology* (Durham, NC: Duke University Press).

Žižek, Slavoj (1994a) 'The Spectre of Ideology', in Slavoj Žižek (ed.), *Mapping Ideology* (London: Verso), pp. 1–33.

Žižek, Slavoj (1994b) 'Identity and its Vicissitudes: Hegel's "Logic of Essence" as a Theory of Ideology', in Ernesto Laclau (ed.), *The Making of Political Identities* (London: Verso), pp. 40–75.

INDEX OF TERMS

INDEX OF AUTHORS